D1233403

THE NORTH LAND

A History of Roseau County

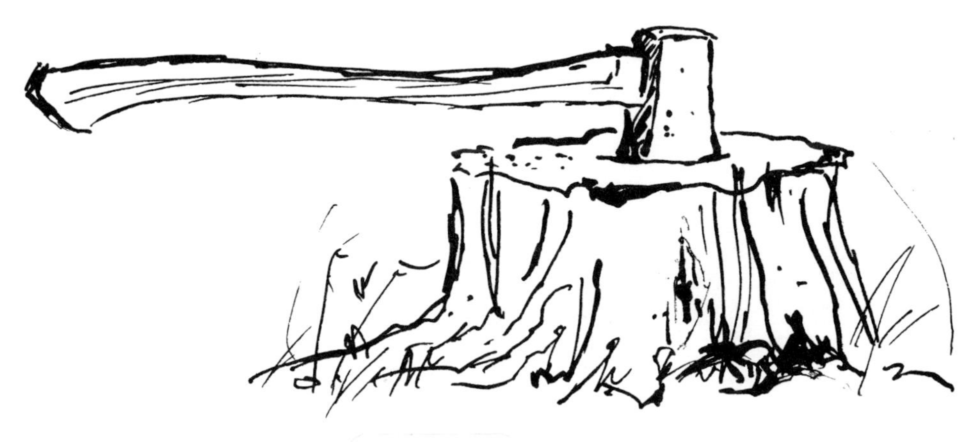

Hazel H. Wahlberg

By Hazel H. Wahlberg

1975

The Roseau County Historical Society Museum

Dedicated 1975

Commemorating
THE AMERICAN REVOLUTION BI-CENTENNIAL

Library of Congress Catalog Card No. 75-11310

There was a tree . . .

a sapling, the same as many others;
growing, reaching, each spring,
whispering in the summer wind,
leaning in winter's blast.

Seasons, years, decades, then a century
passed.

Enduring fire, drouth, flood . . . and man,
It grew on a northern Minnesota ridge.

This tree . . .

guided wandering tribes,
marked the path of trappers,
sheltered the hardy pioneers,
grew straight and tall . . .
as true as the dreams of the homesteaders.

It marked a point between village and
farm.
It turned the highway builders aside.
Grandfathers remembered, children
wondered.

This tree . . .

remembered by strangers, travellers,
whoever passed . . .
we called it "the Lone Pine."

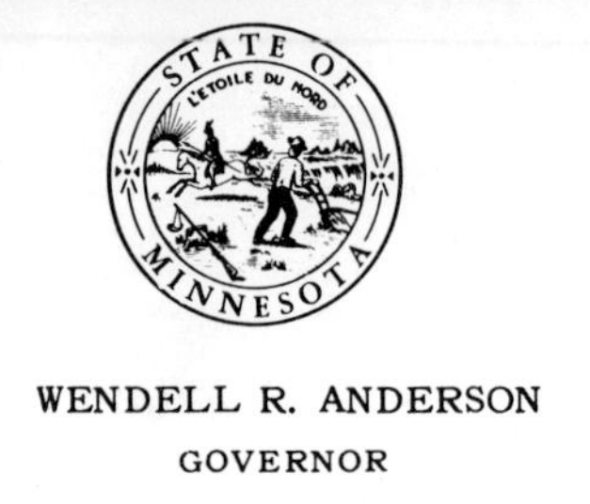

WENDELL R. ANDERSON
GOVERNOR

STATE OF MINNESOTA
OFFICE OF THE GOVERNOR
ST. PAUL 55155

FOREWARD

I am pleased to add my commendation to the publication of The North Land: A History of Roseau County by Mrs. Carl Wahlberg.

This new history of Roseau County -- enjoyably augmented by numerous photographs -- will provide enjoyment and enlightenment for its readers over a long future. Mrs. Wahlberg's history fortunately makes its appearance during 1976 -- our nation's Bicentennial year. It also coincides with a highly significant achievement in Roseau County -- the completion of a new museum and library.

As we face an uncertain future, our best preparation is to foster a sense of our roots and a knowledge of our past. The North Land: A History of Roseau County makes an enduring contribution to that end.

To all people of Roseau County, congratulations on all you have done and are doing to preserve your noteworthy past.

Sincerely,

Wendell R. Anderson

Wendell R. Anderson
Governor

WRA:ske

BOB BERGLAND
7TH DISTRICT, MINNESOTA

WASHINGTON OFFICE:
1008 LONGWORTH HOB
WASHINGTON, D.C. 20515
TELEPHONE: (202) 225-2165

COMMITTEES:
AGRICULTURE
SELECT COMMITTEE ON SMALL BUSINESS
SCIENCE AND ASTRONAUTICS

Congress of the United States
House of Representatives
Washington, D.C. 20515

DISTRICT OFFICE:
IRENE MARING
SECRETARY
920 28TH AVENUE SOUTH
MOORHEAD, MINNESOTA 56560
TELEPHONE: (218) 236-5050

BOB KINSMAN
DISTRICT REPRESENTATIVE
BOX 390
THIEF RIVER FALLS, MINNESOTA 56701
TELEPHONE: HOME (218) 681-4509
OFFICE (218) 681-2127

JACK DRESSEN
DISTRICT REPRESENTATIVE
BROWERVILLE, MINNESOTA 56438
TELEPHONE: (612) 594-2738

December 9, 1974

Dear Friends:

Those of us who claim Roseau County as our home are rightfully proud.

In many ways, our history reflects the history of the mid-west and indeed, our nation.

Our parents, grandparents and even our great grandparents demonstrated the courage and determination that have made the United States the kind of country that the entire world respects.

Fighting the exploitation of early monopolies, the cruelties of weather, disease, insects and the rest, we somehow hung on. We established a permanent settlement. We made our contribution to the national economy. We sacrificed our sons, in all corners of the earth, to maintain freedom.

As you read this history, a history of many diverse peoples from many counties, I hope it will help you understand our pride and our contributions.

Sincerely,

BOB BERGLAND
Member of Congress
Seventh District, Minnesota

PREFACE

Compiling the data, and writing the history of Roseau County has indeed been a satisfying experience for the author. It is intended that the history be as complete as possible with the information available, from prehistory of the area through the present day.

A history book is an impassive recitation of experience until we relate it to ourselves with sensitive awareness. It answers the question in part at least of why we are here, and what conditions we find ourselves in, and what has created the situation. To the young this book may be considered "a book about the olden days and my ancestors"; for all parents it will hopefully evoke appreciation for the ideals and dreams, the heartaches and labors, as well as the joys and satisfactions of those who have gone before us courageously to settle our county. But for the older folks it is a book of remembrance, summoning back to life the early years in which many who read it have played their gallant part and made their enduring contributions. However, it is to the very young in the county that I lay the charge to perpetuate the history of our county so that the records may bear out the physical, spiritual, and patriotic zeal in their day and so forward, as it began with our pioneers. I dedicate the book then to all the youth, and especially to my grandchildren, Anthony, Melanie, and April Fichter, and to Susan, Sally, and Sarah Wahlberg, and in this spirit:

Hope

Look to this day!
For it is life
the very life of life.
In its brief course
Lie all the varieties and
realities of your existence:
The bliss of growth;
The Splendor of beauty;
For yesterday
is already a dream,
and tomorrow
is only a vision;
But today, well lived,
makes every yesterday
a dream of happiness
and every tomorrow
a vision of hope.

From the Sanskrit

CONTENTS

CHAPTER SIX
INFANCY – (1908-1918)

Automobiles – Road building – Drainage and waterways – Agricultural development – Commercial clubs – Roseau County Develompment Organization – State fair – Cow-testing – Red River Valley Shows – Newspapers – Doctos and hospitals – Dr. J. L. Delmore, Sr. – Education – Mail – Timbering – Baudette-Spooner and other forest fires of 1910 – Inventions – Politics – Civic Improvements – Music – Sports – Fourth of July – World War I.

CHAPTER SEVEN
ADOLESCENCE – Era Between Wars (1919-1945)

Agricultural development – Flood control – Weather – William Crooks train – Road building – Radio – White way – Banks – Depression of '30's – Businesses – Oil – Mink Ranching – Commercial Fishing – Beltrami Resettlement – Timbering – Hockey – Lakers – Fires – Sports – Health – P. O. Fryklund and museum – Consolidation of schools – Cultural pursuits – Pow-wows – Chautauqua and Lyceum courses – Princess Theater – Boy Scouts – Girl Scouts – 4-H clubs – Inventions – World War II – Living Civil War Veterans – Elkwood School House – Lobdell murder – Indian graves – C. A. Malmskog – Warroad Liquor Store – Rural Electrification Administration.

CHAPTER EIGHT
MATURITY – The State of Things – The Present (1946-1974)

Bluegrass and timothy – Agriculture – Roseau County Extension – SCS – ASCA – AAA – PMA – NFO – Roseau River floods – Blizzard of 1966 – Wind storm of 1973 – Highways established – Voyageurs National Park – Telegraph – TV – Telephone developments – Radio – KRWB – Airplane – Newspaper – Polaris – Marvins – Vocational education – Library – Community developments – Bob Bergland – Civil Defense – Sheltering Oaks – Dr. "Jack" Delmore – Crippled Children's Clinic – Children's Home – Roseau River Wildlife Project – Sports activities – Ice Revues – Rural-Play Days – Walk For Development – Springsteele Island – Cal's Resort – Warroad tourism – Hayes State Park – Cultural activities – Archeological finds – UFO's Vernon Pick – Lone Pine Tree – "Toy" – Fay Young – Northern Upholstery – Amco – Progressive Tool and Die – North Star Transport – Litterbugs.

CHAPTER NINE
TOWNS – Capsule History of the Beginnings

Badger – Fox – Greenbush – Lake of the Woods – Malung – Northwest Angle – Pinecreek – Roosevelt – Roseau – Ross – Salol – Strathcona – Swift – Wannaska – Warroad – Pelan (not in Roseau County, but contains stage coach history)

CHAPTER TEN
FUTURE

Conjectures

ACKNOWLEDGEMENTS

One of the joys of writing this book has been the enthusiastic cooperation of people to provide data and interviews so essential in a work of this kind. Gratefully I acknowledge the help following specificially and all others for answers in a general way:

William Adams, Editor of the *Roseau Times Region* for access to papers starting with the 1897 edition, and for pictures.

Sigfus Olafson for the complete data on the prehistory of the area
Obert Wammer for the history of the postal development
Ingvard Sunset for an informational tour of the museum and interviews

The rural teachers of Roseau County for compiling the book *Footsteps in Education*, Chester Dahlquist, Mrs. Maurine Flagstad, Hube Dieter (now deceased), Fay Young (now deceased) Irvin Parker (son of Dr. Laurence Parker), Maggi Lightning Aas, John Lightning, Tom Thunder, Robert Ka-Ka-Geesick, Jim Thunder, Mrs. Sam Evans (*Greenbush Tribune*), Les Lockhart (*Badger Enterprise*) Hilbert Pheifer, Richard Bergan, Mathilda and Willie Strandberg, Mrs. Alvin Johnston, Sr., Lillie and Burt Roberts, Julius Anderson, Mrs. Jack Starren, George Marvin Sr., Cal Marvin, William Christian, Duane Fausher, John Heinen, Mrs. Albin Erickson, Mrs. Ineborg Dahlgren, Sigurd Nelson, Marie Olson, Mrs. Hector Reese, Mrs. Harry Prosser, Mrs. Helen Klefstad, Mrs. Bertina Setran, Rudy and Gladys Rice, Nels Braaten, Gordon Sillerud, Gustav Kveen, Carl Listug, Paul Buran, Carl Peterson, Elmer "Cap" Nelson, Jack Jensen, Estelle Brenden, Meredith Haslerud, John Lawson, Mrs. Emil Olson, Mrs. Sylvia Lissell, Albert Johnson, David Johnson, John Billberg, Lloyd Nelson, John Miller, Leland Lee, Esther Feick, Clara Smith, Gladys AuBuchon, Raymond Sauve, Henry Herbert (White Bear Lake) Elden Johnson, auditor of Kittson County, Alice Boucha, Mrs. Frolander (*Warroad Pioneer*), Franklin Rykken.
Ray Young for picture layouts.

The art work was graciously provided by Frances Karlsson, for which I am deeply grateful.

Also thank you to all who collected church and organization information, the files of the Warroad Historical Society lent by Huldah Wahlberg with additional pictures, the files of the Roseau County Museum collected chiefly by Jacob Snustad and Amos Fikkan (both deceased)

My deep appreciation is also extended to Mrs. Valborg Tweet for editing the book.
Peggy Magnusson for typing the history.

Note: It seemed an impossible task to incorporate all the data from each town into the history. Therefore an additional essay concerning the very beginnings of the communities is included in Chapter Nine. The history of the town of Roseau was woven more consistently into the first eight chapters because there was more material available, and also because it is the county seat. Therefore, there is no separate account of the town of Roseau.

This book was published for the American Revolution Bicentennial Commission with assistance of a grant in aid from the State of Minnesota.

Chapter 1

ICE

"The Creator made the world – And we have come to see it" – Puma Prayer

Chapter 1

ICE

The North Star has beamed its light on the earth for billions of years. So much of the very beginnings of all times is shrouded in mystery that man's scientific knowledge can only be speculative. A series of glaciers named after the states they most profoundly affected are the Nebraskan, Kansan, Illinoisan, and the last ice age, the Wisconsan. It is this last sheet of ice that created the glacial Lake Agassiz, and its outlets, the Hudson Bay and the glacial river Warren (now the Minnesota). The rigors of the climate, the forests, the soil, the wildlife, and the moraines left in the wake of the mighty sheet of ice have been forces that have molded the character of the red man first, and the white pioneer after him to their places in destiny.

The geology of Roseau County is relatively simple as all of its rocks and soils were desposited during the short Quaternary Period which includes the Pleistocene, or ice age, and the time that has elapsed since its close, and all of its physical features were formed by the ice, the water, the waves, and the winds of Pleistocene time. However, what caused great ice sheets to form in the North during Pleistocene time and to flow over most of Canada and much of the northern United States is not simply explained and is not yet well known. About all that can be said now is that from causes as yet unknown the earth did not receive its normal quota of heat from the sun. This caused a high rate of precipitation and the snow in the north fell the year around and in time accumulated to a great thickness, and from its own weight was compacted into ice.

Ice is not a structurally strong material and when subjected to great pressure its crystals slip on one another and it begins to flow in the manner of a liquid, though much more slowly. The ice sheets that formed far north in Canada flowed outward, eventually covering millions of square miles and extending as far south as Nebraska and Kansas, and even Missouri. How often they flowed over Roseau County can only be conjectured but it must have been very many times. It is definitely known that there were at least four mentioned major periods of glaciation during the Pleistocene, each lasting for many thousand years, and each may have had many ice oscillations when the ice front advanced or melted back in response to changing climatic conditions. In between these periods of ice flow were periods of what might be called normal climate, when the ice disappeared or retreated far to the north, and these too lasted many thousand years.

The watersheds of Minnesota are separated by a major divide, a height of land extending from a point in the Ontario Boundary line in Cook County southwesterly to a point in the South Dakota boundary between Lake Traverse and Big Stone Lake. North of this divide all the streams eventually drain into Hudson Bay. South of it most Minnesota streams drain into the Gulf of Mexico via the Mississippi River and the rest into the Atlantic via the Great Lakes and St. Lawrence River. When the glacial ice fronts melted back over the height of land the natural northward drainage of streams north of it was still blocked by ice, so a lake was formed. This happened each time an ice sheet retreated over the divide, which must have been many times, and the waters of all of these lakes escaped over the low point in it, which is at the Minnesota-South Dakota boundary, and there they have channeled a gorge more than 30 miles long, up to 3 miles wide, and as much as 300 feet deep, and much of it through granite. Lake Traverse and Big Stone Lake lie in this gorge. Little is known about the earlier lakes in this area as later ice sheets destroyed the surface evidence relating to them, but a lot is known about the last two, which geologists call Lakes Agassiz I and II.

The Wisconsin glacier helped hew out the basin of the Great Lakes and created a lake larger than the combined area of the five Great Lakes. It was named Agassiz after the scientist, Louis Agassiz, who has contributed substantially to man's knowledge of the why and wherefore of glaciers. This huge body of water covered most of Manitoba, some of Saskatchewan, a good piece of North Dakota, and a large triangular area of northern and western Minnesota. The land in the north central part of the state was left higher to form the central core of the continent, and has been named The Great Laurentian Highland Divide where theoretically a raindrop falling on the peak of the ridge would be split into three parts, one part flowing north into Canada and the Arctic Ocean via Hudson Bay, another part would flow eastward into Lake Superior and the Atlantic Ocean, and the third part would flow into the Mississippi and finally the Gulf of Mexico. The apex of this majestic tri-watershed system is a spot 2 miles north of Hibbing, Minnesota.

It is believed that the ice of the fourth major glaciation began to melt back with a warming climatic trend about 15,000 years ago, and after crossing the height of land the usual lake came into being, and like its predecessors drained through the Lake Traverse-Big Stone Lake gorge. It grew to an enormous size, extending far north into Canada. Its highest beach is called the Herman Beach which is not visible in Roseau County as it passes south of Red Lake. This was Lake Agassiz I.

In time some of the debris left in the outlet gorge was swept out, providing a lower outlet, and the lake level fell to what is called the Norcross Beach. It is probable that Beltrami Island first appeared from the waters of Lake Agassiz I at this time. The most prominent of these beaches in Roseau County is on the northerly side of Beltrami Island where it is locally called Bemis Hill, and is more than 60 feet high. It is also called Blueberry Hill farther east. This is the Norcross Beach, or a phase of it. Perhaps also during the Norcross phase an island appeared in the south central part of the county, the area once called Klondike Ridge and adjacent regions, where there is a maze of low sandy beaches. Another factor also was important in the formation of minor beaches in Roseau County and elsewhere in northern Minnesota. The weight of glacial ice had pushed the crust of the earth into the underlying magma and now, with the weight of the ice removed, it was springing back into its original position.

Further lowering of the Lake Traverse-Big Stone Lake outlet brought the level of Lake Agassiz I to what is called the Tintah Beach. Its position can be clearly seen farther south in Minnesota but is rather obscure in Roseau County. From Highway 89, south of Roseau, the rising slope that can be seen to the west, is part of the Tintah Beach. During the time of the Tintah Beach much of the southern and southeastern part of the county had emerged as dry land and the Roseau River had come into existence and drained into Lake Agassiz I near Wannaska. It appears that during this time an island emerged in the southeast corner of Manitoba, which is now the high land around Sprague and which in places touches the northern edge of Roseau County. Not long after this the continued northward melting of the ice front opened new drainage outlets to the north, whereupon the level of Lake Agassiz I fell below the elevation of the Traverse-Big Stone outlet and it was abandoned. With the opening of new northern outlets the lake level continued to drop until it was largely drained. The extent of this lowering is not known but it seems certain that all of Roseau County became dry land during this period and that Lake Agassiz I ceased to exist as a geological and geographic feature.

The Red River Valley, flat and fertile, was at one time the bed of the mighty Lake Agassiz, and the glacial river Warren carved out the Minnesota Valley. The rivers of Minnesota which provided a glorified highway for its people are even today changing their winding courses as the swamps are draining and the creeks are being pushed back to establish new plains and valleys. Major Powell, archeologist, put it succintly when he said, "America is a land of constant change".

This state of affairs was not to last long as a climatic reversal brought on another intensely cold period. The preceding ice sheet, perhaps not yet entirely melted, began to grow and surge forward again. The center from which it emanated seems to have been in and immediately east of Hudson Bay and the ice spread outward from there, closing the St. Lawrence River, getting into Lakes Huron and Michigan, filling up Lake Superior, and overrunning northern Wisconsin. This ice movement is called the Valders ice advance from a little village of that name in Wisconsin, where its nature and effects were first studied.

Valders ice did not reach Roseau County as its front during its maximum stage lay well to the northeast of Lake of the Woods. However, it blocked all the drainage to the north, including all streams running into Hudson Bay, impounding all the water that accumulated north of the height of land mentioned above, and thus Lake Agassiz II was born, and it rose until its waters could escape through the old Traverse-Big Stone outlet. The beach that formed at this level is called the Campbell Beach and from Lake Traverse it runs almost due north for 200 miles to Karlstad, then northeast and easterly through Greenbush, Badger and Fox (our old "sand ridge") to a point about 4 miles west of Roseau. There it turns south and its sand bars can be seen on the slope of the earlier Tintah Beach. It swings east around Wannaska and then turns north to a point about 4 miles southeast of Roseau, this section being indistinct and broken by the Roseau River and some of its tributaries cutting through it. At the point 4 miles southeast of Roseau, the Campbell Beach turns almost due east and in reduced size runs to Warroad River. In pioneer times the Summer Road to Warroad ran along the little ridge formed by this beach as the marshes on other routes were very difficult except in winter when they were frozen. East of Warroad River the Campbell Beach turns southeast and gradually fades out against Rainy River near the Koochiching County line.

Valders ice reached its maximum extent about 11,600 years ago but with the advent of a new warm climatic cycle appears to have begun a hasty retreat. Lake Agassiz II maintained its level at the elevation of the Traverse-Big Stone outlet for some time, but eventually the ice thinned and its front melted north to a point where outlets in that direction were again provided, and the Traverse-Big Stone outlet to the south was permanently abandoned. Continued northward ice melting opened successively lower outlets, but between these episodes the lake level stood still at times, long enough to form minor beaches or features of this kind. Among those that may be readily seen are the sandy ridge west of Warroad which is crossed by Rte. 11, Juneberry Ridge, Moose Point, both at the Kittson County line, and several others.

Lake Agassiz II was eventually fully drained, but remnants of it still exist. Lake of the Woods was once a part of it, as were the large lakes in Manitoba, Lakes Winnipeg, Winnipegosis, Manitoba, and several lesser ones. The last part of Roseau County to become dry land was a broad strip south of the Manitoba boundary extending from Lake of the Woods to northeast Kittson County, much of which is or was covered by thick beds of peat. This band narrows down between Ross and Pinecreek but is quite wide in the western part of the county. Roseau Lake lay within this band and was originally much larger than at the time the first settlers arrived, and has its own system of fossil beaches which show that it was originally all of 5 miles in diameter. The Indian village at Ross stood on this beach where Roseau River cuts through it and from that point it can be easily traced for a considerable distance, both north and south of the river.

The streams of Roseau County have an interesting history. During the Herman Beach stage of Lake Agassiz I all of Roseau County was under water. During Norcross Beach time the lowered lake level permitted Beltrami Island to emerge, perhaps also a small island in Huss Township. These islands grew larger as the lake level fell and by Tintah Beach time they had joined and a large portion of the southern and southeastern part of the county was dry land. This is when the first streams came into being, the Roseau River and several of its tributaries, most of which discharged separately into an embayment in the Tintah Beach which extended as far south as Wannaska. When Lake Agassiz I was drained these tributaries joined Roseau River as the rest of it came into being. The Channel that formed at this time probably followed much the same course as the present channel, all the way to Kittson County, but we can't be certain as Lake Agassiz II, which came into being later, again put the area through which the river runs under water, practically up to the old Tintah Beach, including the Wannaska embayment. It is quite possible that wave action had filled this earlier channel with sediment while the lake was rising, or when it was falling during its final drainage, but the present channel from Wannaska to Kittson County is likely to be following the same course as the channel that existed between Lakes Agassiz I and II. The streams below the Campbell Beach, in Roseau County and elsewhere, are the youngest streams in the United States and have not yet had enough time to create meander valleys. In part this is due to the extreme flatness of the land. For instance, from Roseau Lake to Kittson County, a distance of 24 miles, Roseau River falls only 13 feet. Above Campbell Beach the streams have had time to erode shallow meander valleys, but this is partly due to their steeper gradients.

Roseau River enters the county near its southeasterly corner and runs northwesterly to former Roseau Lake, an airline distance of 36 miles, and then westerly to where it enters Kittson County near the Canadian border. It drains more than half of the county. Warroad River and Willow Creek, both of which empty into Lake of the Woods, drain the eastern part of the county. Drainage from the southwestern part of the county finds its way into Two Rivers, now largely by ditches. A small area in Huss Township, the south of the island that emerged there in Norcross Beach time, is drained by Tamarac River. Since the county was settled stream beds have been dredged and innumerable ditches have been dug, all of which has affected drainage greatly. Early settlers could remember occasions when Indians would use their canoes in traveling from Lake of the Woods to Roseau Lake, going through Algoma and Norland Townships to Mud Creek, dragging them over a few dry spots, but on ponds and intermittent streams most of the way.

The soils of Roseau County are nearly all water deposited but beds of peat once covered large areas. Peat is formed from decayed vegetation, the plants that grew in wet or poorly drained places. Much of the peat has now been burned off down to mineral soil, but a lot still remains. The large peat areas are in the portion of the county that was covered by Lake Agassiz II, but the sandy areas in the southeastern part of it have large peat areas where the drainage is poor. There is considerable difference between the soil patterns of the area covered by Lake Agassiz II, all of which lies below the Campbell Beach, and what lies above it, the former bed of Lake Agassiz I. In the former, aside from peat areas, the black lakebed clay predominates, often locally called gumbo, which is composed of fine particles carried into the lake by streams or blown into it by the wind. The old bed of Lake Agassiz I, all above the Campbell Beach, has similar clay soils too, but less of them and the deposits are small and interspersed with sandy beaches and areas of gravel and sand.

In many places in Roseau County the ground is very stony with large boulders on or near its surface. Glacial ice picked up soil and rocks in its advance and often transported them long distances. When the ice melted this debris settled on the ground but was often covered by silt and soil washed in by glacial meltwater. In the glacial lakes the story differs somewhat. Their northern shores were composed of glacial ice and icebergs often broke loose from them, which the wind carried southward to lodge against their beaches or in shallow offshore spots, where they dumped their loads of debris when they melted. There are several places along the lakeward side of the Campbell Beach where accumulations of iceberg transported boulders may be seen, one immediately north and west of Fox and others westward to Greenbush.

And what lies under the surface of the ground? No deep drilling has been done that will reveal this and one can only make conjectures based on what is known of the surroundings of Roseau County. The numerous artesian wells are practically all in the deposits left by the glaciers. Within these deposits are occasional layers of hardpan, lakebed clays of earlier lakes now compacted to nearly the hardness of stone, or perhaps glacial till similarly compacted by the first glacier that rode over it. Under the glacial deposits may be deposits of Cretaceous age, which was the age of the dinosaurs, when an ocean extended from the Arctic to the Gulf of Mexico. Elsewhere Cretaceous deposits are thick and within them are valuable oil pools and coal seams, but if any underlie Roseau County they are too thin to offer hope of finding more than traces of these materials.

Eastward in Canada lies what is called the Canadian Shield, composed of some of the oldest rocks on the earth, the roots of old mountains long gone. These rocks are mostly igneous (volcanic) in origin with occasional sedimentary rocks greatly altered by heat and pressure. Such rocks cannot contain oil but in spots they do contain valuable minerals. The rocks of the Canadian shield extend westward to the east edge of Lake of the Woods, where they dip below the surface. In the oilfields at Williston in western North Dakota they are found at a depth of 13,000 feet. Such rocks certainly underlie Roseau County and if the dip from Lake of the Woods to Williston is gradual they should lie at no great depth in the county. The highest part of Beltrami Island at the southeast corner of Roseau County has an elevation of 1270 feet, 230 feet higher than the village of Roseau. Does an upthrust of igneous rocks underlie it? Again, one can only make conjectures.

Sigfus Olafson, a native of Pohlitz township, and now a resident of Madison, West Virginia, supplied the data for the most part, for Chapter One. As a youth his intellectual curiosity was aroused by the existence of Minnesota Hill and Bemis Hill in a land where flat country was the predominating characteristic. This curiosity has led Mr. Olafson into many channels of study of geology and archeology, with the result that he has turned his interest into a life-long scientific study. His interest in a published account of the history of Roseau County has prompted him to graciously offer to provide the above information.

Chapter 2

HERITAGES

There was a child went forth every day;
And the first object he looked upon, that object he became!
And that object became a part of him for the day, or a
certain part of the day, or for many years, or stretching
cycle of years.

— *Walt Whitman*

Chapter 2

HERITAGES

The concept of time, put as it must be against our immediate present tends to dim our view of the geological past. Scientists call the Present the last 7000 to 8000 years, so geographical changes are often so minute as to be almost imperceptible to each generation. A human life span, biblically speaking is three score and a possible ten, and this period of time geologically speaking is a wink of the eye. The presence of man on earth has been conjectured to be a possible 35,000 years. If we were to compute a life span at an exaggerated 100 years, then computed against the geological clock of 12 hours, a man's life would be something like two minutes long — a sliver of time out of a clouded past. Our country then is indeed old — or young, depending on where the hands of time are set.

What kind of prehistoric people warred and loved, sang and wept, hungered and feasted, lived and died on the land we now call our own? Our conjectures can only be made from the artifacts which have been found, many of them by accident. We attempt to piece together from bits and pieces the kind of culture, the kind of physique, and the kind of spiritual beings these forbears of ours have been.

The Pleistocene glacier receded 10,000 years ago so the Indian either existed before that time or made his way through the glacial ice to our area. The Indian is the first race of people known to exist. His blood types, pure A, O, and B, and some entirely lacking in the A type substantiate his aboriginal claims. These people, if they existed as we assume they did, during the last Pleistocene glaciation period, lived when the wooly mammoths, primitive horses, and giant sloths roamed the earth.

In Minnesota there was a skeletal find of great consequence. In Pelican Rapids construction workers found a white object as their heavy machinery cut into the earth. When they recognized a skeleton beneath the sediments of the old glacial lake called Pelican Lake, they carefully disengaged it and sent it to A. E. Jenks of the University of Minnesota for study. Whether the skeleton dates back to the Pleistocene age or was the result of a later burial is not firmly established, and the carbon-dating tests are inconclusive because the bones had been treated with shellac at a laboratory. With the skeleton were two artifacts, an antler ornament and a shell ornament which is found only in the Gulf of Mexico region. Actually the skeleton is believed to be that of a young girl who may have fallen out of a boat. The shape of the head bears out the belief that she was of Mongolian descent, further substantiating the now accepted theory that the Bering Sea was once a grassy plain over which the Asiatics could easily have crossed to this continent. This skeletal find is known as "The Minnesota Man."

In 1933 The Brown's Valley Man was found by William H. Jenson of Browns Valley. It is believed that this skeleton was in an intruded burial after a channel drained the glacial lake in the Tintah stage. This skeleton which more closely resembles the Eskimo Indian in skull structure, is estimated to have been buried around 6000 B. C.

Before 1600 when European explorers invaded the North American shore there were four archaeological eras which were:

Mississippi	1000 A.D. to 1700 A.D.
Woodland	1000 B.C. to 1700 A.D.
Eastern Archaic	5000 B.C. to 1000 B.C.
Big Game or Paleo-Indian	Before 5000 B.C.

The archaeologists have arrived at these divisions chiefly by a study of various projectile points (arrow heads). The Clovis points are long and fish-shaped, the Folsom points are smaller and stubby with a gashed out surface, while the Plano points have fluted surfaces and a sharper point. These artifacts have been found at different depths in the earth and have been the greatest single factor in dividing history into these classifications.[1]

Of momentous interest to our locality has been the "find" near the Pauli Church which is located west of Greenbush. During the summer of 1971, David Nystuen, working with the Minnesota Department of Highways and the Federal Department of Transportation, unearthed many artifacts at this location which revealed that a community of Indians made this site at least a temporary home. The flaked points which were found pin-pointed the culture to have existed some time before 5000 B. C. At two places the bones of animals, bison and bear, were buried about a foot below the surface. The forms of the extinct large Bison Occidentalis and the Bison Antiquus have been found in the county with carbon datings that go back to 7200 years of age. Some 55 tools and 4,300 chips or parts of the flaked points were included in the discovery. This seems to indicate that arrow heads were being made in an assembly line operation. The tools that were found were stone hammers and stone knives. This discovery at Pauli Church is listed as the fourth great discovery of archeological finds in Minnesota.

When the road between Greenbush and Pelan was under construction, the iron and brass works of an old flint lock gun were unearthed a short distance east of Pelan. It was believed to have belonged to one of the warriors of the Chippewa-Sioux engagements. The Indians travelled along the ridge to the edge of the prairie each fall to secure their winter supply of buffalo for food and robes. The Sioux considered this an encroachment on their territory and were angry. The Chippewa hunters reportedly had completed their work and were to start on their return journey the next day but stayed for an evening of revelry. One hunter kept coming and going all night and was dubbed "Squaw man." About three in the morning he was said to have rushed in and told them that the Sioux were sneaking up on their camp. The Chippewa rushed out and did battle with the Sioux until daylight when the Sioux retreated. In the process of roadbuilding many artifacts have been unearthed.

In Elden Johnson's essay entitled "The Prehistory of the Red River Valley" he says about another site of historical importance in our area:

> An Archaic site of importance, not yet fully studied, was found a few miles south of Roseau on the banks of the Roseau River. Excavations begun in August 1960, revealed that though apparently lacking in copper, it is characterized by a series of concave-based projectile points. It seems to have been a camping area for hunters, as considerable broken and charred animal bone is found through the site.
>
> The Archaic stage is of particular importance, for it is very poorly defined in Minnesota, and the Agassiz basin offers a good opportunity to understand it in greater detail. The region is important also, for it seems probable that the postglacial valley itself has always been a prairie. In addition, large areas east of the lake margins which are now wooded may have been prairie for much of the time period in which the Archaic culture developed. Understanding the relationship of these cultures to such ecological factors is one of the major goals in the study of the region's archaeology.[2]

However, these are not the only important "finds" in our region. Sigfus Olafson, early resident of Roseau County whose interest in archaeology has led him to some fascinating studies wrote to *the Times Region* in the fall of 1971:

> That was a very interesting article in the Times-Region about the archaeological finds near Greenbush, but it is not the first thing of this kind found in Roseau County. Several years ago I saw a collection made by Lawrence Johnson, consisting of artifacts found around his home near Malung, and in it were some projectile points of types known to be 8,000 to 9,000 years old in Wyoming and elsewhere on the High Plains.
>
> I brought this to the attention of Dr. Lloyd Wilford who was then the head of the Department of Anthropology at the University of Minnesota, but he found it difficult to believe that artifacts of this age would be found under the Campbell Beach. This is our old "sand ridge" that enters the county near Karlstad, passes through Greenbush and Badger, turns southeast of Fox and runs nearly to Wannaska, then comes back east of the river to a point about 3 miles southeast of Roseau, and from there the Summer Road of pioneer days followed it to the Warroad River. It is the high water mark of the last glacial lake in the region.
>
> Dr. Wilford later sent two men from his department to examine Mr. Johnson's collection and they did find

1Elden Johnson, "The Prehistoric Peoples of Minnesota" (Minn. Prehistoric Archeology Series. 1969)

2Elden Johnson, "The Prehistory of the Red River Valley," 162-3.

that there were very early types of projectile points in it.

My brother-in-law, the late Alvin Magnuson of Ross, had a collection of more than a hundred artifacts found on his farm northwest of what was once Roseau Lake. An old beach of Roseau Lake, when it was much larger than in pioneer days, was west of his house and these artifacts were found on a high spot adjacent to this beach. Among them were also projectile point types known to be very early. My sister, Mrs. Alice Magnuson of Roseau, donated this collection to the University of Minnesota.

Tollef Tollefson lived just north of Roseau Lake and had a collection of artifacts found on a high spot on his farm. In it was a beautiful specimen of one of the early types found on the High Plains. And among the artifacts found at the southern base of Minnesota Hill I saw a fluted point made from the distinctive Knife River Flint found in the Bad Lands of North Dakota. I suspect that it had been found by later Indians somewhere else and carried to this point because it had been converted into a chisel-like implement.

In the Roseau Museum is a fluted point from the Fryklund collection marked as having been found at Roseau Lake. These distinctive spear points are all more than 10,500 years old and the type that is found with the bones of mammoths and other long extinct animals.

The discoveries by these archaeologists, made near Greenbush, show once again the interesting things one may find in Roseau County (and elsewhere) if one looks for them.

The cultural stages of prehistoric people can be determined by archaeological methods but only under unusual circumstances do they reveal anything about tribal identities. Most of the information concerning the peculiarities of each tribe must be derived from the reports of the early travelers and explorers, or from Indian tradition. Perhaps the simplest way to explain the situation in Minnesota is to say that when the Europeans first became acquainted with the northeastern United States they found it occupied by the people of three distinct linguistic stocks, each consisting of numerous tribes speaking related languages or dialects. Around them along the Atlantic Coast, in south Canada, the Ohio Valley, and much of the Great Lakes region were a large number of tribes speaking Algonkian languages. In Virginia and North Carolina were several tribes speaking Siouxan, while in Minnesota, Iowa, Missouri, and the Dakotas and the adjacent regions were a larger group of tribes also speaking Siouxan languages.

This wide grouping of the Sioux is not explained but linguistic similarities prove beyond doubt that they had a common origin, which is also true of other linguistic stocks. The Iroquois do not enter into the Minnesota picture except that perhaps in the early or middle 1500's the Huron tribe drove north into Ontario, splitting apart an Algonkian speaking tribe, perhaps the Ottawas, and forced part of them westward to become the Ojibway, more commonly called Chippewa. They established themselves around Sault Ste. Marie, but also proceeded westward on both sides of Lake Superior. On reaching present Minnesota they collided with a Sioux tribe then occupying the Minnesota woodlands.

From the French who reached the area in the early 1700's we learn that this particular group of Sioux were recent arrivals in the area and that some time previously they had driven from the area another Sioux tribe, the Assiniboines, whom the Ojibway called Poulaks. The French in the 1730's found Assiniboines in eastern Saskatchewan, still at war with other Sioux tribes.

The presence of the Assiniboines in northeastern Minnesota is well confirmed by Indian report and tradition, as well as by archaeological finds. They did occupy the area around Rainy Lake and on up to Lake of the Woods as well as elsewhere. Their presence in Roseau County is uncertain, but it seems likely that they were here for awhile.

The Sioux were great fighters but the Chippewa were equally tough, and eventually, with the advantage of the Frenchman's firearms, drove the Sioux from most of the Minnesota woodlands and established themselves in northeastern North Dakota. The war between the Chippewa and the Sioux that had begun before 1600 was to continue for 250 years. The Father Aulneau-La Verendrye massacre was an incident of that war. Giacomo Beltrami, the Italian traveler (also the inspiration for the name of the Beltrami forest area) became involved in it in 1823 just east of Red Lake Falls. Ka-Ka Geesick related that Mickinock's father was killed by the Sioux while on a raid "far west of the prairie."

The Mandans were another Sioux tribe living in the region of Mandan and Bismarck, North Dakota, but at one time they too appear to have been in Roseau County. Their pottery was very distinctive and easily recognized. Much of the pottery shards found in the Indian Village site at Ross is Mandan. Dr. Elden Johnson has found several Mandan sites farther south in Minnesota, particularly in Clearwater County. He is not certain if the Mandans were actually permanent residents or if they came seasonally to gather wild rice.

The Sioux changed their way of life from woodsmen to plains Indians after being driven out of the forest area by the Chippewa. At first they had to be mobile people for their existence depended on the mighty buffalo. Thus the era of buffalo exploitation began. After the Spaniards imported horses to Mexico and some found their way north, the Sioux readily adapted their lives to the pursuit of the animal on horseback and they were able to better establish home grounds. The annals of history concerning the periodic buffalo hunts makes for fascinating study.

But it is with the Chippewa that this account must be concerned, for this tribe established itself in our northern area, became our worthy neighbors and taught us invaluable lessons.

What manner of man directly preceded our early pioneers in the settlement of Roseau County? What did they eat and wear, what were their religious and social behaviors, and what have we learned from them?

The Chippewa home was called a wigwam and was most often made of birchbark. It could be tripod shaped for a one family dwelling or dome shaped to accommodate the communal type of life of the tribe. The beds or pallets were arranged around the edge of the structure. The larger wigwams had two fires, and two entrances, and each person was assigned to a place in the home. Sometimes the Chippewa decorated his home with paintings of bright colored flowers, while the Sioux used geometrical designs. The Indians discovered how to make dyes from berries and plants.

That the Indians had plenty to eat we cannot doubt, for the land provided well the larder. Without the advantage of buffalo, except in small numbers, the Chippewa used deer for food and clothing and the antlers for tools or ornaments. There were all manner of wild berries even as they can be found in lesser numbers today. The blueberries, cranberries, raspberries, Juneberries and strawberries were succulent desserts. Besides deer and moose there was plenty of fish and smaller animals for food. Sometimes a wary bear would lead them to honey caches. And there were young plants that provided their salad dishes.

Mickinock's camp at Ross showing the two types of teepees.

Although it was mostly the Sioux who perfected the making of pemmican, the Chippewa knew the art as well, and it is of importance to our account because this food figured so strongly in the success of the fur trade and transportation via ox-cart. The white man tried to imitate the red man in the preparation of this food, but could never quite equal his skill. This food, a counterpart of the cowboy's jerky, keeps indefinitely, was easy to transport, and was nourishing and tasty. Here is how it was made: after boiling the buffalo meat (later deer or moose meat was used) it was shredded and put into a large sack made of buffalo or deer hide which held 80-100 pounds. This sack was placed into the ground, and packed solidly, and the lard of the animal was boiled hard and poured into the casing. It was then sewed up tightly in its sack and was ready to be sliced off.[3]

One food so native to our territory that we have almost taken it for granted is wild rice, which grows abundantly in Lake of the Woods. The Indian learned early that the birds enjoy a feast of wild rice as much as man, so he tied up the stalks to save some of the kernels. Even now, as in the days before the white man, the Indians paddle along the rice reeds and beat the ripe grain into the canoe with sticks. It was dried out with the sun or

3 During the Napoleonic wars the British army issued pemmican to its troops in the same manner as our soldiers were given C- rations.

The Hudson's Bay Company set up organizations in the Red River Valley to hunt buffalo and make pemmican. Enclosures called "parks" were built, into which the animals were driven and slaughtered. Park River, North Dakota is such a place and so named.

by warming it in huge pans. The hulls were removed by stomping on the kernels as it was contained in a deep vessel or hole, and the chaff was allowed to blow away in the wind when it was spread out. Then it was stored — sometimes in vessels, or in holes in the ground that were lined with moss. Lake of the Woods rice plants are still harvested annually by the local Indians.

It is interesting to know that Indians from all parts of the country have contributed over half of the farm crops of today. Our corn which they called maize was developed over a long period of years. Potatoes and peanuts, as well as tomatoes, squash, many varieties of beans, and peppers were among their common foods. The Chippewa did not grow all of these, but did raise some of them.

The social life of the Chippewa arose mostly from the necessity of daily living. Hunting, skinning out the animals, tanning the hides, and their communal type of life created all the sociability they needed. Feasting (on white dog in some parts of the country) on their natural foods gave them savory meals and the sociability of their neighbors.

The making of an Indian canoe was truly a work of art. The birch bark was peeled in large patches, sewed together with wattape which was the fiber of the root, and caulked with the gum of the pine tree. It had to be strong to stand the pounding rapids, as well as light enough for portages. Lake of the Woods would prove the mettle of any small craft with its moods of tranquility, as well as its turbulent ravishing wild waves. The canoe was useful too as a shelter against the weather when men camped. Sometimes the artistic Chippewa took time to paint some beautiful trees or flowers on their canoes, for the Chippewa have an inherent aesthetic sense of beauty.

Religion to the Chippewa was not a Sunday garment to be put on or taken off as the occasion demanded. The Great Spirit was to the Indian a spiritual being that entered into every phase of his life. It was the Great Spirit, or Manito, who created all the wonderful aspects of nature that the Indian needed and enjoyed. It was this Spirit who created the trees and all the living things. The Great Manito did allow illness and death, however. The red man tried hard to please the Spirit, and when at times the sun shone too little or too much, the rain fell too heavily or too sparsely, the Indian expressed his pleadings in his songs and dances. Also they honored this spirit when things were well with man and his earth.

There were rain dances, snowshoe dances, and game dances. Probably the dance most dramatic for its very essence of horror was the sun dance. It was a dual ritual — honoring the source of energy, the sun and finding those braves who by reason of endurance would best be suited as leaders. A cross bar was erected. The crowds of Indians arrived, laying their gifts and offering at the base of the cross where an effigy of a man and an animal were suspended. Two gashes were made in the chest of the dancer, and through the slits a stick was pierced with leather strips tautly fastened to the top of the pole. Then to the dourful chanting, the dirge-like beat of the drum the gruesome event took place. The dancers must keep their eyes upon the top of the pole at all times. One by one the weaker of the braves fell to the ground in a faint, but the one enduring for the longest period of time was the newly selected leader or chief.

Chanting was an Indian musical art. They sang:

Sacred I stand
Within the four winds.
Behold me
At the center of the earth,
At the wind center,
At the place of the four winds
May you be reverenced —
The tribes sit,
They wish to live.[4]

Red Bird said:

There is a great deal in what a man believes and if a man's religion is changed for the better or worse he will know it. The Sun Dance was our first and only religion. We believe there is a mysterious power, greater than all other, which is represented by nature, one form being the sun. This we made sacrifices to and our petitions were granted. I believe we had the true faith at that time. But there came a year when the sun died. There was a period of darkness and from that day a new religion came to the Indian. It was the white man's religion. We are timid about it. In the old days our faith was strong and our lives were cared for. Now our faith is weaker and we die.[5]

Something like 55 years ago, well within the memory of many local residents, the Sun Dance was carried on at Buffalo Point. Since the government forbade this practice it was

4 Le Seur, North Star Country
5 Ibid

often done in secret. Bill Rader often took passengers on his boats, the **Defiance** and the **Nina** to watch the colorful, but gruesome ceremony. More often pow-wows were held, and some of the white people entered into the spirit and fun of these dances. The Indian pow-wows would go on for two or three days with a monotonous chant and a shuffling footwork to the beat of a drum. Some would take time out to cook, nap, or eat, but the continuity was not broken. Warroad residents recall the sound of the tom-toms wafting across Lake of the Woods and the Warroad River initiating the Fourth of July to herald the coming of the celebration.

There were times for fun and games too for the Indian. A grand feast was held when a boy shot his first game. The game of La Crosse was enjoyed by old and young alike. In this game the player had a stick with a leather bag on the end. The point of the game was to catch the leather ball in the leather pouch. Miniature toys were made by devoted parents even as they are given to our children today. In the evening when the work was done and the group gathered in the wigwam there would be story telling time – often the grandmother was the narrator. Sometimes the events would be acted out. To get the children to sleep they often used the strategy of awarding a prize to the child who could be quiet the longest.

The illness and death and burial customs of the Chippewa were interesting. The Indian felt that illness came from evil spirits, so all manner of devices were used to ward off their offensive tricks. Sometimes it was an herb ground up and worn around their necks, or it may have been a charm that was worn which was thought to be powerful enough to keep them well. Once the evil spirit got the upper hand the medicine man was sent for, and he used dances, contortions, potions, and sometimes torture to rid the poor patient of the ailment.

An archaeologist's paradise has been the mounds that have been found in the upper Midwest. Minnesota is said to have had over 10,000 of these mounds, many but by no means all of which have been excavated for science. Most of these mounds were the burial sites of their people, and beside yielding the skeletons, important artifacts have been unearthed which have been invaluable for scientific study. The Indians loving their departed brothers gave gifts to the Great Spirit so that their path to the happy hunting grounds would be assured.

There were two kinds of mounds – the dome shaped ones and the effigy mounds, which were in the shape of an animal. In Jake Nelson's account he tells about an important effigy mound in Marshall county. It reads:

> On the following day some of those northern people crossed over to the west ridge which was no easy task since the west ridge still remained quite a body of water. Arriving on the ridge they found signs which convinced them that those southern people had been using that ridge as a camping ground for quite some time. Knowing that the invasion of both plant and animal came from the south, they reasoned that the invasion of men would come from the same direction. They concluded that there must be people farther south where those people came from, so they began to plan ways and means to prevent invasion of the sand ridges. They struck upon a happy plan of which the evidence still remained intact the last time I visited that neighborhood in July, 1900.
>
> This plan was to build a great serpent mound. On the highest part of the ridge on the northwest fourth of section fifteen in the Town of Nelson Park in Marshall County these people built a great snake seventy feet. The head was several feet across and the body three feet or more in diameter, larger in the center and gracefully tapering to the end of the snake. The snake was not stretched full length along the ridge, but lay in graceful curves as if ready to move and grasp whatever blocked its way. It was made of a kind of black sand found in that vicinity which packs hard and resists the action of the wind and glistens in the sunlight.
>
> The people would not permit a weed or blade of grass to grow on any part of this mighty serpent. They groomed it faithfully and kept it black and shining. We can imagine the surprise and fear of these people when they came back up the ridge and saw the great shining monster lying there on the site of their old camp ground apparently waiting for them, and ready to glide down the ridge to devour them.
>
> When the people for whom it was intended saw it, they hastened back to tell their friends. Some would not believe it, and so went to see for themselves. Then they fled away to return no more. This snake guarded the sand ridges faithfully for many years and its fame spread abroad among the Indians to the south until it reached the Cherokee tribes in eastern Tennessee. Finally the waters subsided and the country became dry; people came into this region from other sources and the truth about the snake became generally known. By that time the northern people were sufficiently numerous to take care of themselves, so they no longer needed the assistance of the snake.
>
> I first heard of this serpent mound more than fifty years ago from Jack Guthridge and John McKenzie, two old time cart drivers on the St. Paul-Pembina, and Old Garry trail, which passed near this serpent mound. The short bend of the Tamarack River just south of the serpent mound was formerly a favorite camping ground of those old time cart drivers.

When James and I first saw this serpent mound we found it was just as described by Gutheridge and McKenzie. That was in 1883. If that part of the sand ridge had not been plowed and cultivated the serpent mound would no doubt be plainly visible.

A mound at Laurel, Minnesota is called the Grand Mound because it is one hundred feet wide and 45 feet high. It has not been excavated. From the mounds which have been searched it has been found that the Indians used two means of caring for the dead. One called primary burial was the type where the body remained intact and was placed in a crouching position. The secondary type of burial had the body wrapped in a blanket or fur, put on a scaffold until decomposed, and then buried in parts. Usually the skull, arms and legs were buried together.

From J. W. Durham's book *Minnesota's Last Frontier*, he has this to say about the mounds in Roseau County near Two River Crossing (west of Greenbush near the former site of Pelan).

Some distance this side of Two River, or Pelan, several mounds have held awake conjecture and speculations as to their coming into existence. Imagination has created a story that this spot marks a desperate struggle between the Sioux and the Chippewa in the past. This, however, cannot be possible according to Mr. Semat's story. (Semat was an old furtrader of the Northwest Fur Co., who later did his fur trading in Roseau County.) His claim was that Indians never intrenched, nor had it ever come to his knowledge that the two tribes ever met in a battle at this point. Personally, I am inclined to have the same theory as Mr. Semat, who scoffed at such a possibility. He was speaking with personal knowledge of this territory covering a period of forty-eight years from the time I first met him. This was not even a tradition handed down by the Indians from time previous to this.

Contributions to our way of life by the Indian would make an almost inexhaustible list. From our friend, the red man we learned much of what we know of animal lore – the methods of trapping, the characteristics of the animals, how to skin out the meat and preserve the valuable hides. The aesthetic heritage of the Indian is a delight to the white man – his craft of bead work, basket weaving, canoe construction to name only a few. History records over and over again the valuable aid of the Indian to the white man in guiding and advising him in a rugged resisting land. There was Schoolcraft finding the source of the Mississippi with an Indian guide, the romantic story of Sacagawea guiding the Lewis and Clark explorers, and the aid the red men gave to La Verendrye. The Indian has aided progress, and enriched the lives of all who have lived after him.

Man is constantly tampering with his environment, sometimes through necessity, sometimes through ignorance and sometimes through neglect. From his path the buffalo had to flee to become almost extinct, the animal called the coyote changed its ways to gain the name of brush wolf, and the deer has had to find a home in retreat from the ravishes of the lumbering industry. Once we had lynx, otter, fisher, and caribou in abundance in our area, but now these are mostly names in nature books.

The key words to our survival are ecology, environment, and pollution, and our response will spell the outcome. The Indian would make us a worthy teacher. He loved all creation and revered it. He did not lay waste

The Indian scene before 1900. The first four men were visiting Red Lake Indians. The man with the dress coat was Na-May-Puck, then Jim Cobenas, Charley Cobenas, first lady is unidentified, Mike Holm, Mrs. Mike Holm, boy drummer one of Holm boys, girl unidentified, sitting Indian unidentified, and A. O. Houkom.

Ka-Ka-Geesick "Everlasting Sky" in full headdress. This venerable Indian who attained the age of 124 years was a medicine man of the Chippewa Indians in the Warroad vicinity.

the land and its resources, but regarded creation as under his stewardship.

A Russian Proverb says: "The landscape makes the people."

Roseau County is proud of its Indian heritage, and of the Indians who have helped mold the character of its people. Mickinock, who is referred to in several incidents through this account was from the Pembina band of Indians. His Indian name is written Ba-Ba-Gush Ki Bung, which interpreted means "mud turtle." His mother's name was Cordila Feathers. There was one son and three daughters born to Mickinock. Julia was married to John Jones who was a mixed blood Indian. It was their son Max, who lived for most of his young life in Warroad, and acted as chief for a time. A headdress belonging to Max Jones has been given to the Warroad museum. The Jones' daughter was named Sally.

There are other worthy Indian families in the Warroad and Buffalo Point areas, among them the Lightnings, Accobees, Thunders, Ka-Ka-Geesicks, Angus's, Bouchas, Sandys, Gibbons, Pawassons, and Cobenas. All have made an invaluable contribution to the county.

The Indians of the Warroad area have been a definite asset in the field of high school and college sports. There were the Accobees boys, Oliver and James who starred in baseball and basketball, John Lightning who played outstanding basketball in high school and college and there were several hockey players. Perhaps the most outstanding Indian athlete is Henry Boucha who got his start in hockey playing for the Warroad High School Hockey team, under the coaching of Richard Roberts. Henry Boucha played for the Detroit Red Wings in the NHL, and now for the Minnesota North Stars. It was Henry who helped the U. S. win the silver medal in the Olympics. In an interview in 1973 between periods on a national broadcasting TV station, Henry explained that the current fad of wearing beaded head bands was his idea and that Margaret Lightning Aas made his beautiful band.

A brief biography or interview follows about some of the Indian friends in the area.

From the files of the Warroad Museum: John Ka-Ka-Geesick – Medicine Man of the Chippewa

John Ka-Ka-Geesick, Medicine Man of the Warroad Chippewa was born, according to authenticated records, in the spring of 1844. He lived and died in Warroad, Minnesota. At his death on December 8, 1968, it was accepted that he was 124 years old. Of course no official records were made at the time of Ka-Ka-Geesick's birth. There seems to be proof that he may have been born 2 years earlier, 1842 instead of 1844. The month and the date, naturally, are not known. His memory has it that his birth took place "some time after the ice had gone out of the Lake of the Woods and at the time the geese were beginning to return from spending their winter in a warmer climate." The city fathers of Warroad believed that everyone should have a birthday to celebrate and in the last years of his life Ka-Ka-Geesick did celebrate his birthday according to town proclamation on May 14th. Those who attended to him were surprised at the amount of chocolates that he could enjoy without ill effects.

Tommy Lightning, when he was near eighty, in an interview with Ka-Ka-Geesick said, "He was an old man when I was a little boy in the village. He is my uncle." Tommy, who knew the ancient Indian ways, says, "He no use butcher knife like today; he pour medicine and cure you." He turned to the dignified old man and spoke softly for a time. "He say if anyone use knife on him he die right away. He no believe in it . . . cost too much . . . Indian Medicine better."

A park is now named after him – It is where he was born in the teepee of Chief Ay-Ash-A-Wash. It is fitting that he was given the name of Everlasting Sky (Ka-Ka-Geesick) as it is known how the sky seems to become more significant to those who live close to a large lake as is Lake of the Woods.

He outlived all of his own family except his daughter Mary (Mrs. John Angus).

Na-May-Puck, son of Ay-Ash-A-Wash (Oshwash) and brother of Ka-Ka-Geesick and Little Thunder.

In the original family growing to adulthood were three brothers – Ka-Ka-Geesick, NayMayPuck and Little Thunder, and three sisters – Mrs. Major, Mrs. Bambi, and Mrs. Blackburde. Mrs. Bambi lived to a vigorous 108. Shortly before her death she paddled a canoe 22 miles up Reed River, got lost in a storm, but still reached her goal.

Ka-Ka-Geesick's father was a medicine man and passed on the magic bag to his son, who still clings to it. The medicine has indeed been strong for he has retained the Indian powers. In his last years he consented to come to the strange home of the white man – the Warroad Rest Home. It is said that for a time he was not too spry and his spirits were not so bright as they had been. When his room was changed so he could see the little house across the river where he had lived so many years, he improved immediately.

It was this land that had been granted to him personally by President Theodore "Teddy" Roosevelt before the turn of the century. It was from this place his tall, erect figure could be seen each morning, walking with an easy, swinging stride, or paddling his canoe across the river to visit his Indian and white friends in Warroad. Old timers such as Erick Starren and George Marvin will tell you that Ka-Ka-Geesick is well deserving of every respect. . . .

Mr. John Wahlberg can remember well how the old medicine man would come to the store, slap two fingers and say "book" – pulling out two dollars to be paid on his account. Others remember how he "borrowed" a sack of potatoes from a merchant in the winter – and paid them back from his own fresh garden in the spring. Warroad residents unanimously agree "He was as honest as the day is long – you could bet your life on his word."

Erick Starren, now deceased, venerable lake captain, could look back 62 years when Ka-Ka-Geesick came to his father's house to visit. "He looked as old then as he does today – can't see any difference." The steam boat the **Na-Ma-Puck** was named after the medicine man's older brother who was a chief. "He too was much respected," old timers remember. . . .

Winter weather can be cold in northern Minnesota, but even in the bitterest winter weather when white man may stay indoors, the moccasin tracks of Ka-Ka-Geesick (who never wore the white man's shoes) marked the streets and his muskrat hat and buckskin mittens came off only when indoors.

Until about 12 years before he died, the old Indian tended his own trap line – rising early to stride along the trails where his expertly set traps yielded the furs long tradition told him were his.

The bow and arrow had only started giving way to the rifle when he was a little boy. The white man was a rarity and he still remembered the cold and hunger which were sometimes the Indians' lot.

Like the blue tatoo marks on his face which were made to keep away headaches, he was many generations past the changes in his beloved home. In his last years, as honor guest of Warroad, he was happy with his memories, and with his pipe made of catlinite from the quarries of Pipestone, Minnesota. The "tobacco" that he liked best was prepared by his great nephew, Tom Thunder, of the bark of the Ka-mick-ka-nich bush, but should he have none, he filled his pipe with tobacco from the can "with the man in a black hat". . . .

Ka-Ka-Geesick is buried in a special cemetery with his brother NaMayPuck in Warroad. Some how – some one has erected his little Indian rest house . . . Some one takes care of him . . . and many will know of him. . . .

The Robert Ka-Ka-Geesick Story

Robert Ka-Ka-Geesick, 24 year old great grandson of John Ka-Ka-Geesick, the medicine man, is a young man with a dream. He lives with his wife and daughter in Warroad. He tells his story:

"In the past we were the Buffalo Point Band of Indians, but now we are American Indians with our own treaty. I am not a medicine man like my great grandfather because I have not studied to become one. I am more interested in art. My godfather Jack Blackhead from Red Lake is the medicine man of our tribe.

"I graduated from Warroad High School and then I went to Milwaukee to MIT for 6 months before I could get under the BIA program. My dad had taught me to draw an airplane and from that time on, I was interested in drawing and all forms of art. Now I work at Marvins, and although I like my job, I often dream of other things that I would like to do, and all of it is centered around art.

"I love animal art. The animals were, and still are, killed for their fur and just for sport, and that hurts me. It was the animals that kept the Indians alive in former days, and I have great respect for them. I do not want to paint the animals just as they appear, but I want to paint them as if they are creatures with a spirit. I was named after the bear because my parents thought there was great strength in the bear. There is power in the thunderbird, and there is playfulness in the otter. I want to paint that.

"The Chippewa have been known to be artistic people from historic times and they painted symbols wherever they could – on their teepees, on their canoes, and they made designs on their clothes and any place they could.

"We still have some of the old Indian traditions. I go to Red Lake every once in awhile and we dance in the pow-wows and I like that. I feel close to my people when I dance. At our pow-wows the Tribal Council meets and we talk about the problems of our people. After the business we dance the dances that are religious and those that we do just for fun. We have contests too in dancing and singing. We chant about the creation of the world. Our religion is great reverence for the land, its beauty, and great respect for nature and the animals. I couldn't live in a city for these things are a part of my life.

"There are somethings that I worry about. I do not like how TV has taught the children that the Indians are usually the "bad guys." This is not fair, because the Indian was made to feel angry when his land was taken over. TV should show more pictures of how the Indian suffered, and how he would like to be a partner to the white man.

"Also I would like to have the Indian traditions taught in school, and the history of the Indians. We learn the history of America, but we do not learn about the Indians from former times in history. Also we do not learn about the Indians arts and crafts. This headband with all the beads that I wear is one craft that all the Indians learned and almost all the Indian women can make them. Also they can make beautiful baskets.

"My dream is very close to me. I would like my art – the spirit of the animals – to become the Indian national art. I would like to have it recognized by all as true Indian American art that is more than a picture, but is really the soul of the Indian people."

The Lightning Story:

Tom Lightning, a congenial friend of all, whose Indian name was Bee-Boway-Way-Bense, meaning "thundering sky," was married to Ethel Gardner. There were three children, Margaret, whose Indian name was "As-She-Day-Ashiek" which interpreted means "lady of the flying beautiful cross," and John, whose Indian name Ash-shaquee-Gee-Shiek means "the end of the sky," and also a son Hans.

Tom Lightning was a familiar figure about town, and everyone had a friendly exchange of greetings with him. More can be learned of the family through the account of Margaret Lightning Aas, affectionately call "Maggi" who tells her story thus:

"I must have been around seven or eight years old when I started to go to boarding school up at Shoal Lake, Ontario, with my oldest brother Hans. We were put to work there, and not on the books, and we didn't even learn to read or write. The girls did the housework and the boys did the outside work.

Tom, my father, saw that it was useless to go to school there, so he took us home to Warroad where we went to school.

"The children at school said that I was dirty because I have dark skin, so I was never very happy in school. My brother John really loved school, but he went sometime after Hans and I did. I went as far as the sixth grade.

"Besides our parents, there was our grandmother, and Louie Goodin, whose mother was Na-May-Puck's daughter, and who died when Louie was a baby. My grandmother treated Louie just like a son. We had to get along most of the time without my parents around for they had to make a living for us by fishing and cutting wood. Our first home was a birchbark teepee. I remember how good John Gould was to us for when we would cut wood for our stove, he would let us use his team of horses to haul it to our home. We would all go to the woods then. I would drive the team. The boys came along too and even grandmother came along to help. It was quite a job to haul the big logs out of the woods in the deep snow, but we would all pull together, even grandmother who was quite a strong woman.

"My mother would go with my father to tend the trap lines, and would fish with him to feed the children. We had quite a struggle in those days, but we did not get aid of any kind and somehow we managed.

"We would help harvest wild rice in Lake of the Woods. Although we don't remember our father making birchbark canoes we know that the Indians around us did make them and we used them when we riced. They rice the same now as they did then by holding the stalks over the canoe and beating the kernels into the canoe, and on a blanket.

"I learned the art of making baskets from my parents. We use the willows that we find around our home here in Warroad, and I use the red ones for decorations. It is quite a lot of work to make the baskets as you have to make a strong frame, and boil the willows and then weave them. But the baskets last a long time.

"Also I learned the bead work from my parents, and I have trimmed hundreds of moccasins and wampums, and jackets and even wedding dresses. Also I have made pretty deer skin baby clothes with bead designs on them.

Margaret Lightning Aas demonstrates her skill with the artistic works of the Chippewa Indians. Here she displays her basket made from reeds taken near Lake of the Woods, and her bead work.

"It was sad in our family when my dad lost his leg. His skinning knife slipped when he was preparing a moose hide and he got a sore on his knee which would not heel. He was in the cold a long time and he got an infection in the sore and blood poison set in and he had to have the leg amputated. But dad did not sit around and brood, but got a peg leg and worked as hard as ever to try to make a living.

"It hurts me when some white people think we have no religion. My grandmother always preached to me about God, and the good things God has given us and that I must not destroy anything good that He gave us. She told us stories when we were young, and later on in life I read the same stories in the Bible. She couldn't read or write so she must have learned the stories from her mother.

"There is much conflict now between the whites and the Indians and I wish it were not so. We do not want bad feelings, and I like to live in peace with all my friends and neighbors, Indians and whites."

John Lightning Story:

"I graduated from high school in 1934 and because I really wanted an education I went to Carleton College for two and a half years, and then joined the navy in 1942 and retired in 1970 with the rank of Senior Chief

Boatswain. I had the honor to be the first Indian to graduate from Warroad, the first Indian to go to college from this area, and the first Indian to be in the military service from Roseau County and the first to retire from the military service.

"I feel that there must be a united feeling, the whites and the Indians, and that this is our strength for the future of America. The treaties made between the whites and the Indians were supposed "to stand as long as the river flows, the grass grows, and the sun rises and sets." It has not been so. I feel that movements like AIM have gone to extremes to get their point across, but at least it has brought the needs and feelings of the Indians to the white man. In all my travels in many foreign countries I see that the people from the U. S. are hated by most foreigners. This is true in spite of the tax dollars we donate to them to make their lives better. So I feel that this money were better spent at home helping our own people.

"I love this country very much and was glad to serve it in the armed forces and I hope that the day may come when we do know each other better and so come to live better with each other."

John spoke fondly of his father, and said that old Tom really thought well before he spoke and expressed it this way, "When my mind speaks to me — I speak to you."

John's name in Indian is A-shaque-gee-shiek which means "the last of the bright skies."

The Tom Lightning Story
Mrs. Levi Ganyo
From the Grand Forks Herald — October 14, 1964

Tom Lightning, the son of John Lightning, was born on the edge of the Warroad River near the mouth of the big Lake of the Woods. Each morning Tom would look out the door of the teepee in the summertime to see what mood the lake might have for the day, for the family spent long days fishing for a living. Not that they waited only for the calm, peaceful waters, for to the Lightnings, the wild waves meant only a little more challenge. In the winter when they lived in a log house they would look over the expanse of whiteness on the lake and wonder about what they might have in their traps when they took their long treks around the shore.

Tom married the daughter of a white father and an Indian mother, Ethel Gardner, who made him a good help mate for she too loved the hunting and fishing and accompanied him on most of his trips while the grandmother cared for the family at home.

One day Tom made up his mind to have a barber cut off his long hair, a kindly source of joking he carried on with his white friends. He walked into the barber shop and announced, "You can have hair for $15.00." The barber seated Tom in the barber chair, braided his long hair into 12 braids and cut them off. He handed Tom his money, and gave him a bonus of a fur cap "to keep his head warm." One citizen remarked, "Where was Tom when the Indians sold Manhattan?"

During the harvest, Tom and his father walked to Stephen to work, and would return with their money in silver and gold. They were paid $3.00 a day. Tom's father once traded with a man at Devils Lake so that Tom could have a pony.

The tragedy in Tom's life came when he suffered a severe wound in his leg while skinning an animal. After the accident he walked home the five miles, and found in two weeks that he had blood poison. The leg had to be amputated and Tom had to spend several months in the hospital. However, the accident did not deter Tom after he was released from the hospital, for he and Ethel continued to make a living in their peaceful Indian fashion.

It bothered Tom to have small children be frightened of him, for he was frightened when he first saw a white trader. He would tell the children that he wouldn't hurt them and that he had a heart somewhere. Everyone who knew Tom loved him for he was friendly and kindly and only wanted to help people.

After Tom was 80 years old, he and his wife took a trip in their boat up the Reed River. He recalled that when he was younger, it was nothing for him to go all the way to Kenora, which was about a hundred miles by boat. He felt as at home on Lake of the Woods as most folks did around the county.

Tom and Ethel's children are Maggi Lightning Aas who resides in Warroad and still carries on the art of basket weaving and bead work. John Lightning is in Minneapolis, working as a coordinator for the Chippewa people, and a son, Hans is dead.

Early Indian Village at Warroad.

Tom lived to the ripe old age of 94 years, and Ethel was also in her 90's at the time of her death. The genial Indians were greatly missed, not only by their own people, but by all the people who knew them in the territory.

Tom Thunder Story:

"Long before the white man came to this country, my great grandfather Ay-Ash-A-Wash lived on the Warroad River, a little south of Warroad, in a wigwam made of birchbark. My great grandfather was the chief who had fought off the Sioux when they raided the homes of the Chippewa. The Sioux were beaten off, but Ay-Ash-A-Wash got half of his scalp taken off. He came back to his people holding his head, all bloody. The Sioux did not come back.

"The land around Warroad had much woods, and many animals. Buffalo Point was named after all the buffalo there were around here when great grandfather lived. There were also elk, moose, ducks, and geese and many deer. Lake of the Woods looks different now, too, than it did in those days, because it was sandy beach and little islands all the way from Warroad to Buffalo Point. The Indians got Buffalo Point because of Treaty 3 that gave the land to them on Buffalo Point. Some of the land got lost under the big water though.

"We have had many chiefs in our family. My great grandfather became chief in 1867. My son Jim is the chief now. First it was great grandfather Ay-Ash-A-Wash, then his son (my grandfather) Little Thunder was chief until 1905, and then Warren Thunder who we called "Shorty" was chief until 1940, and then I could have been chief, but I turned it over to my son Jim because he has ambition to do more things for the Indians.

"We lived happy in those days. We hunted and fished and had plenty to eat. We made pemmican out of fish and deer meat. We had gardens, especially on Garden Island. This is changed now too.

"With low water that we had we could walk from Warroad to Driftwood Point. We used birchbark canoes to go the islands, and work the gardens. Fred Sandy could make birchbark canoes. We never lived only in one place, but lived in many places wherever we could find ducks and deer. If the food got too scarce we would eat dog meat, but that was later on. We ate a lot of wild rice too, and we riced to sell too.

"We trapped all the time, and sold furs. My grandmother traded with the Hudson's Bay people. She said she bought a gun once but had to give a stack of pelts as high as the gun was long for it. And I have some experience too in selling my furs. Once I brought 3000 muskrat skins in to Segal (he had a store in Warroad where the Standard Oil filling station is now). He said he would give me 10c or 15c and maybe 35c for the best ones. I sold them to him. Then while I was in

Tom Lawson, and Chief Jim Thunder and family in 1900.

the store a buyer from the east came in and looked at my furs. He said to Segal, 'I'll give you $3.50 for each skin.' Segal looked to see if I heard it and then he said to me, 'Tom, have you got a warm sweater?' 'No', I said. He said, 'Pick one out – anyone you want.' I did, but I guess I paid plenty for that sweater. All the Indians trapped in those days, but we got very little for our work. Sometimes we walked 20 to 30 miles on the trap line.

"The Indians know the story about Massacre Island and Gull Rock, and they do not want to go there. We know that a priest went to Massacre Island with a medicine man, and they never came back. We stay away from there. My father had many secrets of how to get the best animals in the traps and some he showed me, but I forgot some too. My dad was a medicine man, but he did not give me the secrets of healing that he carried in his bag.

"We believe in God too and call him the Great Spirit. We always want to give something back to the Great Spirit to thank him for giving us so much. So we give him some of our rice harvest, and we put some gifts at the graves of our dead. We do not waste anything that is given us by the Great Spirit.

"Now my son is Chief. He is a good Chief. When Jim was little we lived at Reed River and did our hunting and fishing there, and we had cows, and pigs and sheep and a big garden. When Jim was seven we moved to Middleboro, and took our stuff on a travois (a blanket stretched across two poles and pulled by a horse). In 1946 we went to Warroad and Jim went to the first year of high school there. Then he quit and worked in the woods and then enlisted in the U. S. Air Force. He has six children, Jim Jr., Diana, Timothy, John, Kenny, and Wendy, and they live in Warroad. My other boys Frank and Oliver were in the army too, and Oliver was killed in World War II. Glenn was the youngest. Now Jim has the dream to develop Buffalo Point into a resort area. There is not any place more beautiful. He is working with the Canadian government, and hopes that someday it will be a beautiful park and resort. Jim is proud of the meaning of his name which is "go like the wind across the big water."

July 11, 1970, was a day the Thunders will never forget. Jim got a nickel medal inscribed to the Chief at the Pas by Her Majesty, Queen Elizabeth, to commemorate the

Manitoba Centennial. The inscription reads: "Presented to the Chiefs of the Manitoba Indian Brotherhood for the Bands." On one side is a picture of an Indian and a white man shaking hands, and there is an image of the Queen on the other.

The story of "Laughing Mary" (Mrs. Mary Pawasson) as told by Mrs. George Boucha (Alice), her granddaughter

My grandmother's name was Mash-Kaee-Ga-Bawick which means "standing firmly." She got the name of "Laughing Mary" because she was always so friendly and smiled all the time.

Grandmother had many tales to relate. Although I do not know the date of her birth or death, I do know that she lived at the time the white people first came up to the Warroad area. She told about the night her grandfather took them out in a canoe to the mouth of the Warroad River where they could watch some Sioux warriors. Hidden among the weeds they watched the enemy Sioux tribe as they took their horses out of the corral, and stole away before daylight.

The fur traders came to our house when we (the Pawassons) were living on the shore of Lake of the Woods where the liquor store used to be. The children were very afraid of the big white traders, but very curious about their wares. However, when they became aware that the traders would not hurt them, they came out from their hiding place to see for the first time what sugar, flour and tea were like. The white men showed us how to use these foods, and grandmother really loved the tea and sugar. The family never used salt in any of their cooking.

Grandmother married a man from Buckaday (now spelled Bucketye) Island. Bucketye means "hungry". She lived on the island with her husband and two children, a boy Joe and myself until her husband died and then she moved back to Warroad.

My own mother died when I was two years old so I was raised by my grandmother. How true it was that we needed each other, my grandmother and I, and how interesting my life has been with this wonderful woman. Even though grandmother could not read or write, she was a wise woman, and she taught us to love, be humble, respectful and to care for our neighbors."

One of Laughing Mary's dearest white friends was the author's mother-in-law. Every week the Indian lady would come to visit Grandma Wahlberg as we all so affectionately called her, but she wouldn't come in the house. However, on baking day at the Wahlberg home, the two women would sit on the back porch and enjoy the fresh home baked bread and rolls, with Laughing Mary taking a loaf home for the family. One Saturday when the timid tap came on the door, there stood Laughing Mary with a large beautifully made clothes basket, made so strong and sturdy that the Wahlbergs could use the basket for many years. The Wahlberg children always waited for the dear old Indian lady, and learned an object lesson in loving and sharing.

Laughing Mary is Henry and Eddie Boucha's great grandmother.

Our great state of Minnesota and Roseau County have haunting echoes of the Indians of the past and those of today that remind us of our heritage. Hopefully we have learned to respect and appreciate the contributions of these, our brothers. Indian legends, Indian true accounts, the artifacts and history of these people are as fascinating as they are colorful. The cliche, "With understanding comes tolerance" was never more applicable than today.

Baptiste, the Voyageur

(Written for the Minnesota Territorial Centennial, 1948 entitled "Minnesota's Birthday Parade" by Harold Searls)

Baptiste, the Voyageur speaks: "I am what you call Ba'tees, the Voyageur. Weeth me is my frien' Meeshel. We understan' the canoe, the waterfall, the portage, and the fur. All day long we paddle the canoe an' carry the fur. Many tam we carry all on back 'cross the portage. The sun, she eez hot; the insec bite the face and han'; the load, she eez heavy, but Ba'tees, and Meeshel don't mind' – they seeng the voyeur song and laugh weeth the waterfall.

"We sleep under canoe; somtan eet eez col', but not too col' for voyageur – he eez tough feller. We eat the corn and lar' and the pea soup, wheech eez bes' food in worl; for mak voyageur beeg and strong.

"Up and down reevair an' lak, 'cross portage, y'rough brush an' beeg tree the voyageur carry the fur. The fur she go to Montreal, Paree, London for mak' the fine hat and coat. Theez teeng would not be eef voyageur did not breeng fur out of wilderness country.

"Come weentertine, we trap the fur, drive the dog sled, and veezit Indian Friend'.

"Sometan we stop at settlement in Minnesota. Theez is moche fun. The fiddle she eez play, the voyageur seeng and dance for day an' night. Oh, eet eez great life for voyageur. He would not like to change for life on farm, or settlement. To be happy, he mus' be all day on trail weeth laugh and song, and all tam carry the fur. Now we go, but firs' we seeng for you, "Allouette," the voyageur song."

Chapter 3

FUR

Alouette, gentille Aluette,
Alouette, Jete plumerai . . .

From an old French Voyageur song

Chapter 3

FUR

Billions of years ago what we know now as Minnesota was an area of great mountain ranges and wildly active volcanoes. There were vast lava streams flowing in every direction.

A particularly hard and dense type of rock, since labelled, "Ely-Greenstone" was quite prevalent in northeastern Minnesota. This rock was so hard that the great inland sea that subsequently covered the area, the four great glaciers that gouged and wore their way across Minnesota over the past million years, the winds and rains that followed were unable to completely erode this rock. It is this hard rough rock that forms the "height of the land" that winds across Minnesota from Lake Traverse through Lake Itasca above Grand Rapids and Virginia and works up into Ontario, a short way above Grand Portage on Lake Superior. It forms part of the Continental Divide.

Waters falling on this Minnesota division flow into the Arctic Ocean, the Atlantic, and by the way of the Mississippi, the Gulf of Mexico.

It is because of this "height of the land" which caused the water to flow in all directions that this area was discovered and explored so much earlier than the central part of the United States.

Radisson and Groseilliers were generally believed to be the first white men to set foot in the country we now know as Minnesota. At least they were the first to leave an account of their travels. They were astonished by what they saw and the Indians were equally amazed at the Frenchmen. They established the facts about the Northwest heretofore unknown; that the Indian lived here with a culture vastly different from their own, that the Northwest was rich in furs which could start a whole new business enterprise, and the Indian people, in their opinion, needed the spiritual help of the Jesuits.

From their first journey west in 1648 they returned in triumph to Montreal with a vast quantity of prime furs which were promptly confiscated by the governor of New France. Heartbroken when they were unable to secure a license to return to the west they defected to the British with whom they helped form the great Hudson's Bay Company in 1690.

In 1680 Father Louis Hennepin, a Belgian priest, on an expedition to the Mississippi with the great explorer La Salle left the main party at the confluence of the Wisconsin and Mississippi Rivers and travelled north along the great river with two companions. He was promptly captured by a band of Sioux who took him to their main camp at Mille Lacs Lake.

Daniel Greysolon, Sieur du Luth, who had been trading in this area for some time, on hearing that a white priest was being held captive hastened to Mille Lacs Lake where he rescued Father Hennepin and saw to it that he was safely returned to Montreal.

A vast fur enterprise fired the imagination of the English and resulted in the formation of the Hudson's Bay Company. The Journals that had been written by the early explorer assured the entrepreneurs of the abundance of fur, so in 1680 Daniel Greysolon, Sieur du Luth added to the development of the Minnesota territory in the name of the furtrade. Until Radisson's account was published, du Luth was thought to be the first white man in Minnesota. That the fur business was as lucrative as expected was evidenced by the fact that du Luth headed a group of two hundred voyageurs, to bring the largest of all cargoes of beaver skins from the west going from Mackinac to Montreal.

There can be no business enterprise of any time that rivals the fur trade for intrigue, romance, danger, and courage with the stakes at such a high premium. It called for a special breed of men, and the voyageurs, lusting for adventure, had just the right temperament to be the all in all.

To develop and carry on this enterprise there had to be three divisions in the commercial framework. The owners, or managers, hard-headed, autocratic and often wily, were called the bourgeois, and were the big bosses of the forts. The voyageurs, hard, swashbuckling and cunning, with the help of the Indians brought in the pelts, and the Indians – the trappers and skinners were often paid in rum or whiskey, trinkets, or for a layer of pelts five feet high they might be able to buy a firearm.

There is an interesting hierarchy and a colorful vocabulary in the history of the fur trade. Besides the bourgeois (traders) there were the "commis" who were the clerks, and it is to them that we owe a debt of gratitude for their meticulous journals. Along with a list of engage' (employees) there was a day to day account of the "deal", the weather reports, information on the locale and other pertinent data. There were guides who acted also as interpreters, "pork eaters" as they were called. This term evolved from the communal pot of thick soup which contained much pork, and came to suggest that these men were the novices who went only from Montreal to Grand Portage and thus did not require the abundant provisions that the "hivernants" or winterers required. Mention must be made of the "coureur de bois", the wood runners who carried on an illegitimate trade, being unlicensed. Prestige was earned merit for those who crossed the land between Lake Superior and the Rainy River as far as Wheeler's Point and those who accomplished it were called the "winterers." There was an initiation rite. The promotion was observed with the sprinkling of water from a cedar bough on the head of "winterer elect" and a plume of feathers was put in his cap. Incidentally the oath at the ceremony was to insure that the noviate help to initiate other voyageurs into the new order, and not to kiss another winterer's wife – against her wishes.

The garb of the voyageur too was as colorful as it was practical. He wore a long sleeved shirt, and leggings that reached above his knees. If he wore loose pants he tied the colorful sash around each leg below the knee. He wore a beaded pouch tied around his waist in which he could tuck clay pipe and tobacco. A blanket made into a coat with a hood kept out the cold wind of the winter. He wore the Indian type mocassins. On his head was a bright red woolen stocking cap, but it was the elite among them that sported the coveted plume. A voyageur had to be short – 5 ft. 5 inches at the most, so that ten or twelve men could fit in one canoe.

The canoe was the Indian type made of birch bark sewed with wattape gummed with the sap of the pine tree. The largest of the canoes holding 14-20 men was called the Montreal, which was up to 40 feet long and in spite of its frailty this craft often carried as much as four tons in weight. There was the guide who was called the Bowsman or steersman who stood up alerting the men to the dashing rapids and calling for split second maneuvering. The North canoe was the easiest to steer, being only up to 24 feet long. Each canoe had its own emblem, an animal or star, on its bow, and was painted a bright color. Imagine a procession of canoes gliding swiftly across the waters of Lake of the Woods, the voyageurs in all their regalia dipping their paddles in perfect unison, singing one of their happy rhythmical songs.

Because of the ice in the lakes and rivers in the northern two-thirds of North America four to seven months each year it was impossible for the fur companies to transport their trade goods from Montreal to the trading posts in the far western and northern parts of the continent and return for the furs that were gathered in a single season. So for the forty different kinds of furs in Minnesota there had to be small branch trading posts. Grand Portage, established in 1768, near the extreme northwestern point where the Pigeon River flows into Lake Superior and separates Canada and the United States, became the largest of the fur trading posts in the northwest. In 1776 this thriving post run by the North West Fur Company, later a part of the Hudson's Bay Company, controlled all the fur business in Minnesota and all of northern and western North America. Grand Portage was aptly named for it means "great carry." In April as soon as the ice in the St. Lawrence broke up, great flotillas of Montreal canoes with eager voyageurs and their goods would leave Montreal for Lachine and head west. The route from Grand Portage on Lake Superior would take the voyageurs up the Pigeon River past Gunflint Lake, Saganaga and Lake Croix to Rainy Lake and Rainy River, then they paddled through Lake of the Woods, down the

Winnipeg River to Lake Winnipeg and west to Athabasca.

At the same time hundreds of smaller north canoes, loaded with furs left trading posts all over western and northern North America as soon as the ice went out and hastened to reach Grand Portage by July.

Thus there were each year as many as a thousand voyageurs, bourgeoise, traders and partners congregating at Grand Portage for the "Great Rendezvous," a meeting of all men engaged in the fur enterprises. At least a thousand Indians would come there too. For three weeks each summer Grand Portage became the busiest, the most exciting, the most populous place in all of the interior of North America.

During these three weeks the ninety pound bales of trade goods would be carried up the difficult nine miles of portage to Fort Charlotte over the "height of the land." Down this portage hundreds of bales of fur – actually the year's supply of the fur traders bounty would be carried to the Fort at Grand Portage and placed in Montreal canoes for shipment to London, Paris, and Montreal.

During the rendezvous great balls were held every night in the main hall with dancing, much feasting, and much drinking. Hivernants were paid their wages for the year. Letters were received from home and loved ones in the east, and old acquaintances were renewed.

But finally the festivities came to an end. All the trade goods had been carried up the portage and all the furs had been carried down the portage and good-byes were said. Then all the loaded canoes, both the Montreal and Northern types were paddled as fast as possible in order to reach their destinations before ice locked the lakes and rivers. And Grand Portage, the first town in Minnesota, again became the sleepy little trading post, resting as it were, for the next season's excitement.

Grace Lee Nute, noted writer and authority on the fur trade era records in her book *The Voyageur's Highway* that John Jacob Aster who owned and operated the American Fur Company and competed energetically with a company known as the X Y Company, had posts at Grand Portage, Grand Marais, Moose Lake, Vermillion Lake, Rainy Lake, Basswood Lake, Rainy River, War Road (as it was spelled at that time) and Roseau Lake.

The Warroad Post was located at the southeast end of what is now the Warroad Park. The stone marker erected by the Minnesota Historical Society states:

Site of
The American Fur Post
1820

Information about this post was first made in a report by Henry Schoolcraft who is credited with the discovery of the source of the Mississippi River, dated August 9, 1824:

"Pursuant to instructions, I have determined on the following places where trade may be carried on with the different bands within the limits of this agency . . . 18. At Rainy Lake. 19. At War Road."

A considerable amount of investigation has gone on to determine the location of the Roseau Trading Post. No conclusive site is agreed upon to date. The late Amos Fikkan from Roseau carried on correspondence with the Hudson's Bay Co. of Winnipeg. The late Andrew E. Lind, former Roseau County resident wrote to Mr. Fikkan on March 23, 1964 and said:

"I don't believe that there was a stockade or fortification. "Old Brule" (half-breed born on the Red River about 1805) who made the trip from Roseau River to Rainy River before 1825 and who died at the age of 100 in 1907, said the Hudson's Bay Co. had a post there and took furs to the Red River in the spring. This was probably one of the sites west of the lake. This post was burned down by rivals in the fur business."

Mr. Lind wrote further:

"In 1822 Pierre Corte' wrote a letter accusing the Hudson's Bay men of trading at Roseau Lake, in American territory."

This last suggestion of a controversy arose since the men or company with the most whiskey to sell or give away was the one who garnered the most furs, and unfortunately the Canadian government allowed the sale, while the Americans did not.

The search for the Roseau Trading Post has yielded no authoritative site. In a column of the Roseau Times Region of August 6, 1931, headed "35 Years Ago," this article appeared:

J. W. Durham and E. E. Billberg, Jim Cobenas, and a Canadian Indian last week located the Hudson Bay Trading Post in this county. It is located on the Roseau River on the Mickelson farm northwest of Roseau. The place is one mile northwest of Hans Erickson's place where the river makes a sharp bend north. The Indian named this place "Ka-Bo-Geo-Nay-Go-Dea-Og: which means "a good place where there is an opening." About all that was left to show there had been a post there were indentations in the bank."

On the Manfred Holm farm, which was originally the Emanuel Holm farm many evidences have been found of an Indian encampment, and there are some artifacts that suggest that the post may have been located on the SE quarter of the SW quarter of Section 14. This is the highest spot on the north side of the river near a ravine. Shards of pottery, a Hudson's Bay hatchet, an Indian corn hoe, numerous arrow heads, and a fleshing tool have been unearthed here.

However, there is insufficient evidence to lend authenticity to this site as the true location of the Roseau Trading Post.

From a manuscript belonging to Mr. John Billberg of Roseau there are a few interesting excerpts from letters concerning the post at Reed Lake (Roseau Lake). A kind of supervisory post was set up at Pembina "to watch the proceedings of the American traders settled near the boundary," and in "preventing illicit trade in spirituous liquors, or any other import from the United States." Chief Trader William Sinclair, who was in charge of the Lac La Pluie (Rainy Lake) District at Fort Frances, when writing to Sir George Simpson on the 3rd of Feb. 1849 refers to American opposition as follows:

> The rival traders are pressing hard on our Indians to abandon us, hitherto they have failed to gain any from the North side – in Lake of the Woods and its neighborhood on neutral ground the Indians are scattered over a large extent of the country and cannot be guarded by us, they of course are subject to frequent visits from the Americans of Reed Lake and those of Lake of the Woods. . . .

Again the 24th of September 1849, and the 31st of January, 1850, he writes:

> My arrangements for the winter are now almost complete. . . . At the different Posts the scarcity of rabbits will seriously affect the trade, particularly at Reed Lake, but we have met with less opposition than I expected. . . .

By the 13th of February he finds the Indians "are literally starving" and the trade very poor. Finally on the 25th of May, 1859 the order for the removal of the post came. It read:

> As it is intended that the Post of Reed Lake is to be attached to this District, it will be necessary as I have said before, it be removed to Shoal Lake and the charge of it given to Mr. Manson.

Miss S. A. Hewitson, librarian for the Hudson's Bay Company, in a letter to Amos Fikken, dated September 24, 1948, wrote in regard to the trading posts:

> The North West Company, X Y Company, John Jacob Astor's American Fur Company, and the Hudson's Bay Company, all had forts in what is now the State of Minnesota.

> According to Voorhis' "Historic Forts and Trading Posts" the Hudson's Bay Co. post was at the outline of lake Des Roseaux on the right bank of river Aux Roseaux, 96° West and just south of 49° north.

That there were three posts on the American side close to the boundary is substantiated by a letter to John Jacob Astor of November 31, 1821 written by Ramsay Crooks, a fur buyer, who wrote, "Since the British Government has legislated us out of Canada we shall next year occupy three posts within our lines from the vicinity of Rainy Lake to Lake of the Woods."

The problem of liquor to the Indian trappers was mentioned in a letter by Mr. Stuart to Mr. Stone, a business partner in Stone, Boswick Co., which merged with the American Fur Company who decried the use of whiskey for the furs. It says in part ". . . forbidden by our government. At each post (say three in number) . . . we found it impossible to oppose them successfully." This letter was written in 1823, which might indicate that the Warroad post was established in 1822 instead of 1820 as the marker suggests. There is no other information on the Warroad Post to the author's knowledge.

On a map received by request from the Public Archives of the National Library of Ottawa, Ontario, the post is indicated to be on the southwest bank of what was Roseau Lake, and this seems to be as conclusive as we can be. The farms of Alvin Magnusson and Tollef Tollefson have been suggested as the most likely possible sites.

The canoe routes of the Voyageurs, passing as they did through Roseau County, need mention. The difficulty in tracing these routes is expressed in a letter to Amos Fikkan dated March 23, 1963 and written by A. Lind:

> In looking for signs always remember that this country was one big lake. Before the ridge near Caribou was broken down about half of Roseau County was a bay of Lake of the Woods. Between Warroad and the International boundary there was a channel about a quarter of a mile wide. The water level was about 1065, more or less. Eventually freezing broke up the rocks at Rat Portage Kenora and the lake dropped to 1045. Wind and water erosion broke down the Caribou dam and the channel at Warroad filled up with peat and debris. The ice pushed sand up and made a new beach line. Roseau Lake eventually dropped to the level of the junction between Mud Creek and the Roseau River, so that each river

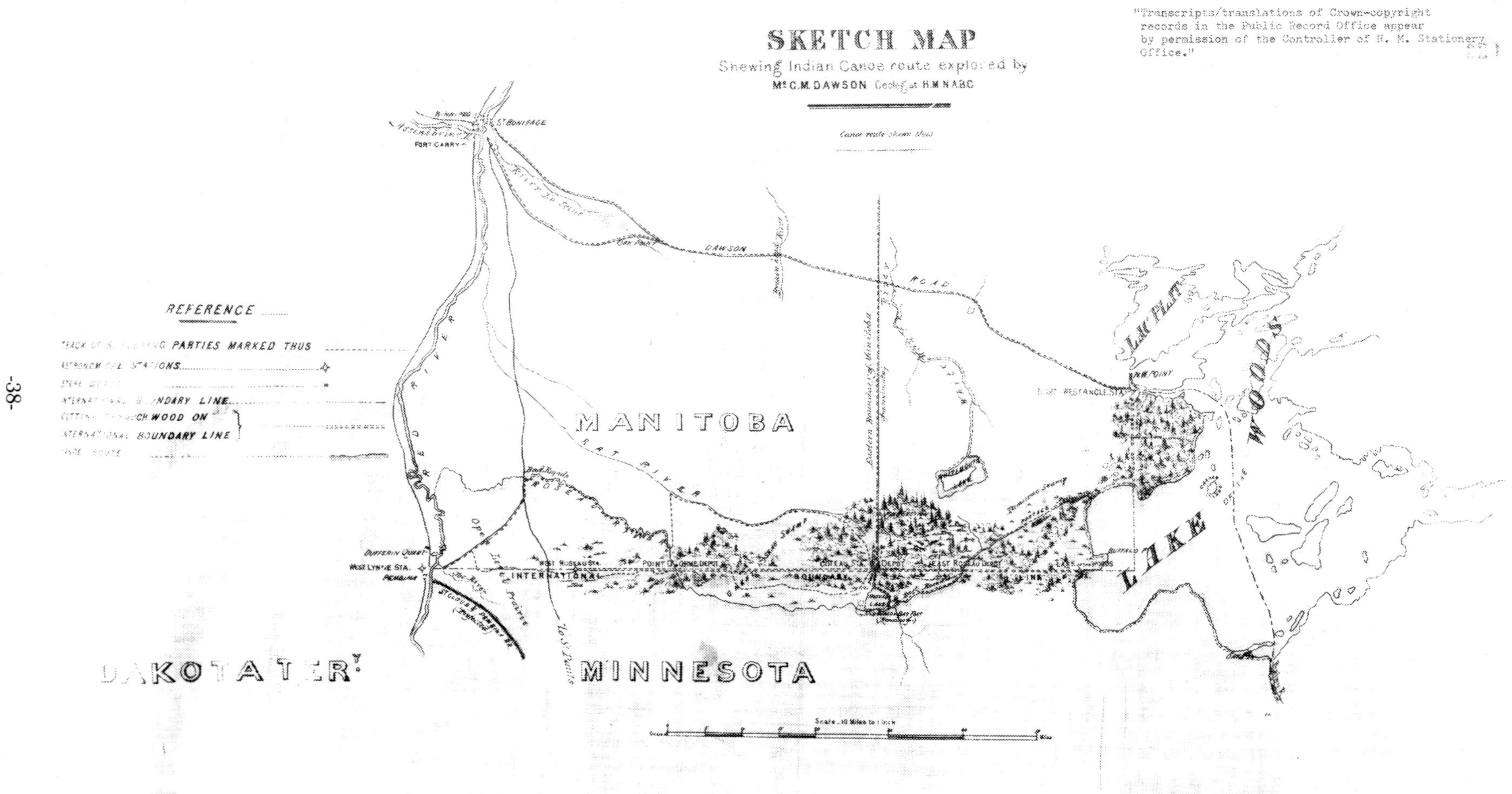
"Transcripts/translations of Crown-copyright records in the Public Record Office appear by permission of the Controller of H. M. Stationery Office."
SKETCH MAP
Shewing Indian Canoe route explored by
Mr. C. M. DAWSON
Canoe route shewn thus
REFERENCE
PARTIES MARKED THUS
STATIONS
BOUNDARY LINE
WOOD ON
INTERNATIONAL BOUNDARY LINE
ST. BONIFACE
FORT GARRY
DAWSON
ROAD
RED RIVER
RAT RIVER
MANITOBA
Eastern Boundary of Manitoba
LAC PLAT
NW POINT
LAKE OF THE WOODS
INTERNATIONAL
BOUNDARY
LINE
DUFFERIN
WEST LYNNE STA.
PEMBINA
Open Level Prairie
To St. Paul
DAKOTA TERY.
MINNESOTA

flowed into the lake at a different point. There it remained for a long time. Eventually a great spring flood washed out more of the Caribou dam, and the D. E. Sprague Lumber Co. blasted out the rocks to get their logs through.

However, A. E. Lind and others have made a thorough study of the routes and these are:

I. Portage Route. Lake of the Woods to Warroad River for six miles to old summer road. Carried canoes over sandridge to where Hay Creek cuts through it (about 4 miles S. E. of Salol.) From thence they paddled down the Roseau River.

II. Small creek from Lake of the Woods just south of the International boundary to pond called Lost Lake in Algoma Township. Crossing this and streamlets it reached Mud Creek and flowed to Roseau River.

III. Roseau River into far Southeast of Roseau County as well as down Red River. Hay Creek was navigable to where old summer road crossed it 4 miles southeast of Salol. From there a six mile portage along the sand ridge, the old War Road of the Chippewa and the Sioux and later the summer road of old settlers led to Warroad and Lake of the Woods.

There were, of course, overland routes to the Northwest territories also which the fur traders used extensively. The Dawson Trail starting at Harrison Creek in the Northwest Angle, wound its way to Winnipeg and the northwest carrying cargo from the eastern seaboard. Several thousand ox-carts traversed this route and it is said it is still discernable from the air.

Our area is haunted by the ghosts of the intrepid voyageurs, fur traders, Indian trappers, Indian runners and all manner and description of men who lived in one of the most dangerous, lucrative, and romantic eras in all of history.

One such intrepid voyageur-explorer was Sieur de La Verendrye in whose honor Warroad holds an annual memorial day. It was this stalwart adventurer who founded Fort St. Charles on Magnuson Island in Lake of the Woods. It was La Verendrye and some of his men who travelled on the Warroad and Roseau Rivers, where they went up the Warroad River for ten miles and portaged to Hay Creek and came down the Roseau River.

La Verendrye followed somewhat the route of De Noyons who is believed to have been the first white man to travel on Lake of the Woods. Like many other adventurers, La Verendrye was obsessed with the desire to find the Great Northwest Passage which would supposedly lead him to the golden land of spices and silks. An old Indian, Ochagach said there was a vast body of water that "tasted bad and that swayed back and forth." [6] LaVerendrye was convinced that he must find that sea, and he finally persuaded the old Indian to draw him a map. This was the first known indication that there were water routes to the west of Lake Superior. Then came the desperate efforts to get permission and financial backing from his government to make the trip. Although the Canadian government was wary of the adventure they did compromise to allow La Verendrye to use his gain from the fur trade.[7]

It is fortunate that accurate records and logs were kept of La Verendrye's expeditions, recounting the environs, the wild life of the regions, the types of gardens they grew, the forest fires they encountered, and the disposition of the men. In all they constructed seven posts and founded a fur trade far more lucrative than trade in the spices or silks could have provided had their endeavors to find the "passage" been successful.

Although Magnuson Island, the scene of the famous La Verendrye expedition is not in Roseau County, yet it is so much a part of the history of northern Minnesota that the bizarre episode of the Aulneau-LaVerendrye massacre is included in this history, using the account of Inga and Eddy Billberg which was published in the Minnesota Leader:

In the spring of 1734 Sieur de La Verendrye was making plans to return to Montreal. He had spent three strenuous years in the Lake of the Woods territory. His results had been far greater than he had dared expect. Upon leaving French-Canada he had been commissioned to build two forts but instead he had built four.

Fort St. Pierre – 1731
Ft. St. Charles – 1732
Ft. Roseaux in 1734 and Fort Maurapas also in 1734.

Besides this building program he had pressed his explorations far inland, made friends with the Indians, traded furs with them, taught them agriculture and acted as a pacifier between hostile tribes.

Now he was anxious to return to Canada with a report of his activities and to endeavor to secure financial aid for further discovery.

He left the middle of June and travelled until the 16th of August before he reached Montreal. His reception was not a pleasant one. Instead of being honored for his accomplishment of so stupendous a task he was harrassed by jealous enemies, and hounded by creditors and

6The map drawn by Ochagach remains intact in a London museum and many places familiar to Minnesotans can readily be located.

7The commission the Sieur de La Verendrye received from the King of France is photostated and a copy is in the Roseau Museum.

Fort St. Charles on Magnuson Island in Lake of the Woods. Headquarters for La Verendrye and voyageurs at the time of the massacre.

merchants. Although the fur trade had been greatly extended, the profits had not been sufficient to carry the burden of the terrific expenses incurred in building and providing for the needs of the men.

The only person to whom he could look for help was the governor. It was through his efforts that La Verendrye had been allowed to press on into Lake of the Woods in the first instance, and now upon hearing the extent of the work accomplished he felt that the King of France should undertake some of the expenses of the expedition in return for the land discovered. The governor accordingly wrote a letter to the French court giving a report of the discoveries and projects of La Verendrye, and asking financial aid of the King.

The Minister replied that the King could not be expected to share in the proposed expenses, and consequently the Court of France turned a deaf ear to all the entreaties of the governor. Le Verendrye was then left to his own resources entirely and in the end was forced to rent the forts to his creditors for three years, besides giving them the right to manage the posts.

On June 5, 1735 La Verendrye accompanied by his youngest son, Louis Joseph, and a French Missionary, Father Aulneau, who had been sent by a Jesuit order in compliance with La Verendrye's plea to send another priest to replace the one who was incapacitated because of illness, turned their canoes toward Fort St. Charles. The strenuous journey was completed in September, and upon their arrival they found the people at the fort starving. The crop of wild rice, upon which the bread depended, had not been harvested because of heavy rains, and the other provisions were at an end.

He immediately dispatched a group of men to procure provisions at Fort Maurepas and another group to the fishing grounds farther east.

Thus, with these resources and the help of the Indians, he was able to support his garrison in a meager way during the winter. However, spring found the supplies exhausted. They had neither food nor sufficient ammunition, and the canoes which were to bring them the necessary articles did not arrive. In desperation, he sent a man named Bourassa to meet the men from Michillimakinac, in an effort to hurry them.

Three days passed and Bourassa did not return. The situation at the fort was becoming desperate. A council was held and it was decided that another party of men should immediately be sent from the fort. Father Aulneau insisted upon accompanying the men as a precaution to safety, for rarely did the Indians dare kill a missionary. Much against his will, La Verendrye consented to let his son head the convoy. Jean Baptiste had just returned from an exhausting journey to the Red River and was much in need of rest. But the priest thought that the son's presence and leadership would be necessary on so dangerous a voyage.

The entreaties to employ every conceivable means of safety were urged upon the men chosen to go. La Verendrye says he picked twenty-one of his very finest men and after each had received a supply of gunpowder and shot, the journey began.

The next morning, on June 6, a band of Monsonis arrived at the fort with the information that the Sioux were on the war path and had plundered Bourassa. This report was confirmed, for on the 14th of June, La Verendrye received a letter from Bourassa in which he relates that he narrowly escaped death at the hands of the Sioux, and that the timely intervention of a Sioux squaw slave, whom the French had at one time befriended, saved his life.

The garrison was becoming uneasy. One canoe of supplies had at last reached them and relieved their hunger, but their anxiety knew no bounds when they were informed, by the men bringing the supplies, that the expedition sent out to meet them had not been seen. Both Indian and French runners were sent out for information, but not until June 22, did the report of the slaughter of the expedition come to them. The men had been found with their heads severed from the rest of the body. Most of the heads were wrapped in beaver robes, and were lying in a close circle as though they had been killed when holding a council.

There are numerous versions as to the incidents relating to the actual murder. Some very interesting details are found in the Aulneau collection. One reads:

> "A number of French Canadians saw the bodies of these 21 Frenchmen on Massacre Island a few days after the deed was done. They saw the heads of the Frenchmen placed on beaver skins, most of them scalped. The missionary had one knee on the ground, an arrow stuck in his head, his chest cut open, his left hand on the ground and his right raised. Lieutenant La Verendrye lay on his stomach, his back cut open in many places with knife slashes and a hoe stuck in his loins. His headless body was garnished with stripes and bands of porcupine."[8]

Father F. Marin states in his notes that the travellers had landed on an Island for breakfast and that a party of marauding Sioux discovered them by the smoke of their fire. They crept stealthily in and fell upon the French without having been seen. They killed them with tomahawks or pierced them with arrows. Some were able to make their way to the shore but perished in the waters of the lake. Father Aulneau fell upon one knee, wounded

8Bulletin St. Boniface Historical Society.

17
Lowther
Laolu
Keewatin
Devils Gap
Moth L.
Bare Hill L.
High L.
Granite L.
Clearwater Bay
Falcon Lake
Falcon
High Cr.
Rush Bay
Crowduck L.
Northern Pen
Labyrinth Bay
WESTERN PENINSULA
Shoal Lake
Portage Bay
Monument Bay
Hi - Neighbor
Northernmost P. O. in U.S.A.
Northwest Angle Inlet
Poplar
Falcon Island
Gabeskosing Bay
AULN
PENIN
Oak I.
Sugar Pt.
DOMINION OF CANADA
UNITED STATES OF AMERICA
Lumbering
Moose L.
Driftwood Pt.
Alexandria I.
Split Rock I.
Sandpoint Bay
Garden I.
Painted Rock
Big Island
Stoney Pt.
Sugar Pt.
Reed R.
Buffalo Bay
Basils Channel
Dawson I.
LAKE
Bigsby Island
between Sioux and Chippewa
MINNESOTA
ONTARIO
Hooper Pt.
Deep Bay
Long Pt.
Rocky Pt.
Old Fisheries
Windy Pt.
RROAD
Fur Traders
Missionaries
Swift
Sable Islands

with an arrow. Then a Sioux struck him on the head with a tomahawk from behind, and ended his sufferings. The Indians did not dare touch the body of the missionary but carried off his belongings.

A party of Indians from Sault Ste. Marie landing on that island a few days later buried the bodies under a pile of stones five or six feet high. They could not be buried in the ground because no grave could be dug in the rock.

No sooner had this crime been perpetrated than a clap of thunder struck fear into the hearts of the Sioux. A young warrior, seeking distinction, had killed the missionary against the advice and knowledge of the other warriors.

LeVerendrye was heart broken. Within a few months he had lost his oldest son and his nephew. The Indians, who had adopted Jean Baptiste as a chief into their tribe, were crazed with rage. The Indian code allowed no crime to go unavenged in blood, and they immediately offered to come to the fort in the autumn, chose Verendrye as commander of their party, to avenge the death of his son. La Verendrye, however, put them off by saying it was necessary to await word from the great father before embarking on this mission.

About this time new information had been found regarding the event at Massacre Island. La Verendrye says: "On August 18, two Monsonis, having gone the rounds of the Lake of the Woods found in the southern part our two French canoes, in which the bundles were rotted, also more than 20 Sioux canoes, tied two by two, in which were blood-stains, which means that they had some of their men wounded and perhaps killed, for they have found human limbs buried in the sand. The third canoe was found at Massacre Island."

This brought proof that the Frenchmen had put up a brave fight before they were murdered.

The Indian situation grew more and more intense. The Chippewa-Cree decided to invade the Sioux country without delay. They implored Verendrye to give them a commander, and asked for powder, shot and tobacco.

La Verendrye again by strange powers of ingenuity persuaded them to delay indefinitely because of the shortage of ammunition.

But it was agreed that in order to prevent a recurrence of the disaster at Massacre Island, an escort of 50 native warriors would in the spring and fall accompany the French canoe going to meet the merchant fleet from Michillimakinac and escort it to Fort St. Charles.

The situation temporarily made easier, Verendrye sent his sergeant with six men to bring the bodies of his son and Father Aulneau along with the heads of their companions, and the bones of about 13 of them.

They were buried in the chapel of the fort with great solemnity and there they rested for one hundred and seventy years – when the Historical Society of St. Boniface, in 1908, had the precious bones removed to their museum at St. Boniface.

Massacre Island is today uninhabited and thickly wooded. Nothing but a cross remains to mark the spot of the tragedy. And in the generations that followed none but the pagan Sauteux and the beasts of the forests dared tread upon the soil which was red with the blood of the missionary.

How Fort St. Charles was rediscovered is fascinating. In Vendee, France, an elderly man by the name of Aulneau told the Jesuit fathers that he had some 150 year old letters that told about a massacre by the Indians in North America. Interest in the letters steadily increased and soon the letters were published and the Jesuits came to search for the locations mentioned. But to find a specific island in a lake with 14,000 islands was no small task. A Captain Laverdiere and the Jesuits tried to piece together the clues with the fact that the Indians deemed one island to be haunted which resulted in the name Massacre Island. However, no evidence could be located.

Archbishop Langevin again took up the search and was informed by two Indians, Powassin and Andagamigowinini of some exposed stones that may have been the fireplaces of the old Fort. After one unsuccessful search that turned up the home of some adventurer, other stones were found, this time on the American side (Angle Inlet) of the lake. Artifacts like slabs of a fort, fireplaces, knives, scissors, cooking vessels, and finally the bones of human beings were unearthed. The number of them and the accounts in La Verendrye's journal proved their authenticity. The journal read: "He was found with a sort of iron hoe imbedded in his loins" and one skeleton bore this out. The bones were removed to the College of St. Boniface. However, the college later burned to the ground, and with it the relics of the heroes of Fort St. Charles.

Warroad's Catholic Church is a memorial to the Jesuit priest Father Aulneau whose mission it was to Christianize the Indians while he journeyed with the daring voyageurs, the La Verendryes.

It was these stalwart voyageurs who played a major role in the destiny of Minnesota, and as such to our Roseau County. Besides the vast fur enterprise they also gave us explicit and true accounts of our land as it was before civilization changed its face, the kinds of trees and vegetation, the animals, the weather, and the romance of it as a wilderness. Also to the voyageurs we credit the first gardens, the first fields to yield a harvest, the first navigation on Lake of the Woods and Roseau and Warroad Rivers, and the first of the men in our land to receive salary for labor. This all started in 1734, many years before the Declaration of Independence.

Chapter 4

WILDERNESS

Possessing a country is not as simple as flying a flag over it.

North Star Country — Le Seur

Chapter 4

WILDERNESS

The wind rustles the small grasses, fresh and green in the sun of the dawn. The wind rustles the tall brown reeds in the golden diffused light of the sunset. The rhythm of the seasons, spring's sprouting, summer's maturing, and fall's harvest has occurred over Roseau County since the glacial days. Grass that was untrodden, then beaten into trails by animals and red men, ribboned into roads, and divided into agricultural sections became the structure of Roseau County. Upon the little peaceful villages of the Indians after the Sioux were ousted from Warroad and Roseau, the white men appeared over the horizon with his oxen and carts. Here in this grassy valley and forest area he stayed, hewing the logs for his cabin, breaking the soil for his food, and raising his family. Here two cultures met face to face, two breeds, one purpose – survival. This chapter of our history concerns itself with the era from the fur trade up to December 1894, when Roseau County was officially organized.

The end of the French control of the fur trade occurred in the last half of the eighteenth century. In 1805 Zebulon Pike declared the area to be under the jurisdiction of the United States by virtue of the Treaty of Paris in 1783. In the early part of the nineteenth century the American Fur Company under John Jacob Astor took over 40 posts on this side of the boundary, but the golden years of the fur trade were brought to a close by 1850.

What of these dauntless forefathers whose memory we endeavor to perpetuate? Why and how did they come to northern Minnesota where climate and wilderness did not promise an easy and comfortable life? What dreams did they dream, and what did their eyes behold?

The history of Roseau County after the fur posts were set up until the end of the fur trade is sketchy. Most of that time belonged to the first citizens who watched the encroachment of civilization with fearful eyes. A feeling of helplessness created by a language diversity, and the difference in cultural heritage engulfed them. The red man and white man looked at one another each trying to discern the other, and both were full of fear and apprehension. Caution became the byword.

One man, David Thompson, an English surveyor, came to the Northwest as a boy of sixteen, and did more to make locations known through his maps than any other man of the time. He also trapped and traded furs. He located the posts for the North West Fur Co. as he walked from Grand Portage to the Missouri River covering 4000 miles in ten months. The Indian who guided him was called Koo-Koo Sint, the star man. The treaty that ended the American Revolution, and the Louisiana Purchase of 1803 gained for the U. S. the land to the east and west of the Mississippi.

A group of people who walked through Canada and a part of Roseau County in 1818 was a colony of Swiss, Scotch, French, and Italians headed by Lord Selkirk who had been given a block of land by the king to start a settlement. Adversities in the form of grasshoppers, Indian uprisings, and an untamed wilderness proved too much for the itinerants, and they moved south to the protective arm of Fort Snelling. Some of them settled in St. Paul where the founder of that city, Pig's Eye Parrant (so called for he had only one eye) had a trading post which dealt more in liquor than in furs. They left behind the bonanza land of all agricultural locations, the Red River Valley.

In a dramatic way Lord Selkirk became the benefactor of John Tanner, the white boy taken captive by the Indians. Since Tanner spent much of his life in our area before the white settlers came, his story is briefly included.

John Tanner, who lived with his parents on the Ohio River, was stolen by the Shawnees in 1786 when he was eight years old. (He was named Shaw-Shaw-Wa-Be-Na-Se, the Falcon, by the fur traders). He was given to an Indian squaw called the Otter Woman who was grieving the loss of a child. Net-No-Kwa, his foster mother treated him kindly, but after her husband Twa-Ga-We-Nine was killed in a drunken brawl, the Otter Woman, her foster son, and her real son, Wome-Gon-Abiew, suffered from severe hunger and cold. An Indian woman of the Muskego tribe befriended them. Later accompanied by two friends, Peshauba and San-In-Kwub, she managed to get her children through the deep snows of the Canadian wilderness to a place near the present site of Winnipeg. Here she could trap and support her children. For three years they gathered furs, amassing a small fortune for themselves. She then travelled to Fort Mackinac to sell her bounty. Here she met with reverses, for one pack was stolen outright from her, one she lost to a dealer who gave her a due bill which he would not redeem, and another which she gave away for rum and whiskey. Tanner felt a fierce anger toward the traders of the North West Company for so defrauding his Indian mother.

It was the custom of the fur companies to extend credit to the Indians for goods which was repaid to them in furs. Mr. Wells, a North West fur trader disliked Tanner and would not allow him to buy staples for his family. Tanner then had to walk many miles to the Hudson's Bay Company at Fort Douglas stopping at Pembina on his way back in spring with a pack of furs. Wells, the North West Fur representative offered him only a pittance for his season's work. Wells ripped open the pack as it lay on the floor and in derision allowed them to spill out on the floor. Tanner brandished a knife, flipped it into the floor, then calmly went over and picked up his furs, and not a man stopped him.

Tanner became a guide for the Chippewa Indians. He took them to the unspoiled area of Grygla and Gatzke to hunt since the warring Sioux and Chippewa, for fear of each other, had left it as virgin soil. In order not to attract attention Tanner and his friends used bows and arrows, and lived in peace in a village they built and fortified. The Indians later named this region "The Stealing Earth" and it is from this association that Thief River Falls and Thief Lake got their names.

As the fur supply became depleted the rivalry of the trappers became more intense. Hence the North West Fur Company resented any intrusion. Lord Selkirk was, in 1816, trapping with his colony of men along the Red River near the present site of Winnipeg, when the confrontation called the Seven Oaks Massacre occurred in June of 1816 where 20 men lost their lives.

Robert Semple, the local governor for Hudson's Bay Company, died in this fracas which forced the call for troops. Lord Selkirk hired mercenary soldiers of De Meurons to retake the fort. However time ran out on them and they could not use the Winnipeg river for transportation in the winter. The Falcon was hired to guide the men over a route which took them through the frozen swamps of Roseau County. The soldiers took back Fort Daer, and a group of men headed by Tanner himself took back Fort Douglas. Tanner felt that he had thus gained his revenge. So Lord Selkirk gave Tanner a yearly stipend, and helped him to find his white family.

While Tanner lived in Roseau County he spent his time as trapper, guide, interpreter, and teacher. He translated parts of the New Testament into Chippewa. Tanner's son became a missionary to the Chippewa Indians.

It is unfortunate that Tanner could never really become reconciled either to the ways of the white man or to the ways of the Indians. He became acquainted with Henry Schoolcraft (discoverer of the origin of the Mississippi and Lake Itasca) and acted as his guide. However, when Henry Schoolcraft's brother James was murdered, Tanner was accused of having committed it, and he died in disgrace. Ironically, the murderer was found after Tanner's death.

From Tanner's accounts we learned much about the customs of the Indians, the conditions of the fur country, and the wilderness which he knew so well.

It was through the feverish activities of the rival fur companies that routes were established through our county in the early days of the Red River settlements. The waterways for canoes that traveled between Lake of the Woods and the Winnipeg River, and the route starting at Lake of the Woods and then winding through the Warroad River, with a portage to the Roseau River and thence down the Red River were the most commonly used. It was used by Indians, La Verendrye, the explorers, missionaries and settlers.

Delmar Hagen and "Napoleon" who in 1958 retraced the Pembina Ox-Cart Trail to celebrate the Minnesota Centennial. He left Pembina, North Dakota July 10, 1958 and arrived at the Minnesota State Fair grounds on August 23, 1958, going a distance of 420 miles in 43 days, commemorating a century on wheels and Red River Ox-Cart trail travel. It took the pioneers 30-40 days to do the trip also.

However, the glacial Lake Agassiz, having formed a natural arterial highway along its ridge formed a passable overland route. One famous route was the Dawson Trail which started at Harrison Creek at Northwest Angle and ran up to Hudson Bay. Another trail led through Ross and it is said that it is still faintly visible. Near the intersection of Highway 310 at Ross a crucifix was found which presumably belonged to someone in the La Verendrye party. There were also three or four established routes from Pembina to St. Paul which the Red River carts traveled.[9]

The Red River carts were crudely constructed but well engineered for land and even water travel. If a river obstructed the route, the wheels could be removed and the box floated down or across to dry land.

The carts were made entirely of wood and required no special tools in the construction. The Norwegians made a solid wheel called the "kubberulle," but later used the spoked wheel. These carts, which could carry 1000 pounds, could travel about 18-20 miles a day, and were pulled by the patient mule or oxen. The wheels were not greased probably because the dust and dirt would collect on the lubrication to make it abrasive. Charles Mair wrote in 1868, "The creaking of the wheels is indescribable. It can be heard six miles away. It is like no other sound you ever heard in all your life and it makes your blood run cold." It was reported that Sunday services had to be delayed a half hour while the deafening noise of the carts stifled all other sounds.

These carts hauled the precious furs to St. Paul when John Jacob Astor had a post there. On the return trip they brought back the staples such as sugar, salt and flour. The waterways of Minnesota and the land trails played a role in transportation which was vital to the early development of the State. (In 1958 Delmar Hagen of Gatzke traveled from Pembina to the Minnesota State Fair in his replica ox-cart pulled by Napoleon, his faith ful ox.)

The earliest deed made in the area long before Roseau County was formed, was written in long hand and discovered by J. W. Durham in September of 1929. It was a deed to L. Riel after the treaty made with the Pembina and Red Lake Bands of Indians and indicated that it was deeded to half-breeds. The land was in Township 164 N ½ of the NW quarter, NW quarter of SW quarter of Section 34, at Old Cross River, and consisted of 160 acres.

Martin Braaten of Ross was the first to file a claim in what is now Roseau County on June 16th, 1890. There were quite a few squatters in the area at the time that Mr. Braaten entered O. B. Ekman's land office to file his claim for NW of section 35, 163-41 in the town of Dieter. John Krog filed the same day. Martin Braaten told of the hardship to go to Hallock to obtain a marriage license, for it was a 3 day trip over muddy trails with oxen.

Growth from a nucleus of four settlers in 1885 to a little community of 600 people in 1895 with twenty-five businesses was the early record of Roseau. People drifted in in spite of bull flies and mosquitoes, swamps, and undergrowth, severe winters and short summers, unbroken land and little means of communication. Whatever it is that challenges men to explore and subdue the unknown, moved people to establish homes and farms in this new region. It seemed that only the pea vine was the attraction in the beginning for it was good grazing land, but people learned that they could become master of the land if they cared to earn their bread by the sweat of their brows.

One man who traversed the area repeatedly was Ernest L. Brown, taxidermist from Warren who hunted the entire county from

9. Neil Mattson. "Red River Carts." Prepared for the Marshall County Statehood Centennial

1889 to 1915. His accounts give numerous references to Roseau, the Roseau River, the Warroad River, the Indians in both areas, especially Na-May-Puck, Mickinock, and the Cobenas boys. A few sample entries from his diary written in 1900 are:

Sat. Nov. 29 – At Watterman River all open stop over one day and skinned moose heads.

Dec. 2 – On a hunt with Indians of S. Maypuck found a marten up a tree and I shot it in the head with rifle Maypuck tried to shoot twice with Prof (Dyche) rifle but it would not go.

Nov. 17 – Went to Suttons where they had dance.

Jan. 31, 1891 – In the evening Charley Coveness (Cobenas) came with Monkman and brought a moose skin with neat little set of horns. [10]

J. W. Durham, the author of the second account of the settling of Roseau County entitled Minnesota's Last Frontier. He also served as the first sheriff of the county.

It is also to be noted that Brown had a trading post at Warroad near the old Moody place where he traded with the Indians and extended liberal credit to them.

J. W. Durham, first sheriff of Roseau County, wrote about this land from the years 1877 through 1891 and called it *Minnesota's Last Frontier.* It was run in serial form in *The Roseau Times Region* in 1926. He says:

We spent practically the whole night in going over his (Semat's) experiences as a trapper and fur trader in Roseau County before the influx of the white settlers. Mr. Semat was an employee of Commodore Kittson who was an independent trader in this section. . . . [11]

In J. W. Durham's account he mentions another trading post, that of Commodore Kittson.

His trading post in Roseau County as described by Mr. Semat was located on the Roseau River two miles above Roseau Lake at a point situated near what is now known as the "Froid Farm". [12] To verify this account, Mr. William Stafford and myself have found definite markings described around what had once been a building, long ago destroyed or burnt. The description of Mr. Semat tallied with our findings.

Jake Nelson who pioneered Roseau County in 1877 and wrote the account Forty Years in the Roseau Valley. He was born in 1857 and died in 1933.

The Hudson's Bay Post's location has never definitely been found. It has been substantiated that it burned to the ground. Jake Nelson in his account *Forty Years in the Roseau Valley* referred to the post in Roseau: [13]

We finished the raft at the site where the North West Fur Company had the trading post which was burned many years ago where the old pony trail crossed the Roseau River.

Laird told us stories he had heard in Canada of treasures buried there at the time of the fire. When he thought we were not looking, Wood did considerable digging around there. According to the story, papers containing various records and sixteen thousand dollars in gold were placed in a copper can which had a screw top and was water tight. On the top was a loop to which was fastened a copper chain. The can was buried by an oak tree and the chain was fastened around the tree at the ground and covered with earth to conceal it. The man who buried the can was drowned in Shoal Lake and the can of gold was never found.

This is an interesting bit of lore that adds color to the history of our area, but the facts cannot be proved until someone finds the loot.

10The Ernest L. Brown diaries are photostated and are in the Roseau Museum.

11Commodore Kittson came to the Red River Valley in 1843 and helped to form the Minnesota Territory in 1849. He later owned a line of steamboats and was therefore called Commodore Kittson. Kittson County is named for him.

12The Froid Farm is the present location of the Ted Sjaaheim farm (W½ SW¼)

13In order to avoid confusion as to whether the post at Roseau was a North West Fur Company or a Hudson Bay Company Post it should be pointed out that up until 1793 the North West Co. had the monopoly of the fur trade but between 1784 and 1804 the Hudson's Bay Company put up posts along the border, and in 1812 the two companies merged. The American Fur Company put up posts after 1823. So when we speak of the Hudson's Bay Post, it was originally a North West Company post.

Manfred Holm says there are people who search for it to this day.

Jake Nelson further tells about the early conditions in the county under the chapter heading "My First Trip to Roseau Valley."

(September 1885)
In the middle of September, according to promise, the Irishes arrived at Nelson Park. Wood and I were ready. The next morning we loaded our grub box into Irishes' wagon. We travelled about twelve miles on Mound Ridge, and turned off at Two Rivers Crossing, which is in the valley about two miles west of the ridge. We drove leisurely and camped when and where we felt disposed to stop.

The second night we camped at Badger Creek. Next morning we followed the trail down off the ridge into Roseau Valley, and drove thirteen miles across the valley land to the Roseau Lake Indian village situated one and one half miles below Roseau Lake on the Roseau River. Here lived forty Indians – men, women, and children. Often the number was increased to one hundred and more by visitors.

Here I met Billy McGillis, a half breed from the upper Mississippi lumber region, who had married a daughter of Aad Cobenas and cast his lot with the Indians here. He worked in the lumber companies operating in Canada north of the Roseau Valley. Mr. McGillis claimed to be a descendant of Hugh McGillis who was in charge of the Fond Du Lac tributary posts of the North West Fur Company in the early nineteenth century.

Mr. Nelson goes on to tell much about the luxuriant growth of the pea vine and other grasses that made this natural habitat for cattle. He often refers to Pelcher's Crossing where, because of a beaver dam built up at this point, people could cross the Roseau River on footstones. Pelcher was the name of a whiskey trader of the very early days, and

The first creamery built in Roseau. It was located where the Paul Harms, Sr. home on Main St. now stands.

the crossing is where the old or first creamery stood which is now Main Avenue at approximately where the Paul Harms, Sr. house now stands.

He goes on to say:

After a short stay my brother and William Warner returned to Nelson Park (near Stephen) and Wood and I went to work to build a shanty just across the river from the present site of the old creamery (the first one at Pelcher Crossing) in the village of Roseau. We put in long days of hard work for there was danger of snow just at any time. On November 1st, 1885, Wood became the first actual settler in Roseau Valley and from that time on Pelcher's Crossing was known as Wood's place.

Wood was a character in his own right. Inga Billberg in her account entitled *History of the Roseau Valley* from which serials were printed in the *Minnesota Leader* wrote about Wood December 19, 1935. It seems that Wood was an outlaw type reputed by some to have been a member of the Jesse James gang, but this was never proved. However, he provided much entertainment to his guests with his wild and fantastic stories. He had an enviable collection of guns, and when he had guests, he placed his bed in front of the door lest a guest would get itchy fingers. Ole Holm, who came to Roseau in 1888 having been a member of a survey crew, was in the company of Wood since their cabins were closer than most.[14] One day Wood told him that he was very rich and proceeded to get out his strong box which he showed to Mr. Holm. It contained hundreds of railway notes running into many thousands of dollars.

Mr. Wood's long fingers extended to Mr. Holm's gun, but Ole figured out a way to get the gun back. He told Wood that his gun had been stolen and claimed that a bunch of Indians had been there and had no doubt taken the gun. Mr. Holm offered a $2.00 reward and praised Mr. Wood whom he thought would be a match for the Indians. Mr. Wood promptly returned with the gun and reported that the Indians were sleeping off a drunk and he had no trouble retrieving it.

As the settlers came in greater numbers and civilization pressed in on him, Mr. Seward Wood left, never to be heard from again.

Both Warroad and Roseau had well established Indian Villages – Warroad's on the

14It is recorded in an account that Ole Holm brought groceries to the Indians and whites at Roseau in 1882 but found that they had no money. Mr. Holm left his groceries with Mr. Wood, but never saw the groceries or money again. Later he purchased the Martin Blid farm, and homesteaded the Richardson place and the Erick Bjorkman farm.

The old Indian Village at Ross. Note the teepees and the ox cart at the far left.

beach of Lake of the Woods and Roseau's Indian Village was at Ross. J. W. Durham describes the latter this way.

> . . . we came to the Indian Village a short distance east of what is Ross today. The village consisted of about fifty people housed in rude dwellings such as is the custom of the Chippewa tribes. We were received in a friendly manner — After we had made the Indians a visit we continued on until we came face to face with the sparkling waters of Roseau Lake, a magnificent sheet of water, leisurely basking in a warm July sun. The first white man we met after leaving the camp near Duxby was our good friend Jake Nelson. He was on a visit to the Indian village, but his own camp was on the opposite shore from the present Emanuel Holm farm.

The marker for the Old Indian Village at Ross erected by the Minnesota Historical Society. It was abandoned in 1896.

The Warroad Indian Village on the lake shore was in existence long before Warroad became an incorporated village. The account of the early history (in Chapter 9) of Warroad includes what we know about this little community. There was some communication between the two Indian villages from time to time, especially when the settlers feared an Indian uprising. The Cugnet store traded with the Indians and the clerks found them friendly and cooperative. The Warroad Indians perhaps held more religious dances and colorful pow-wows than the populace of the Ross Indian Village.

Threaded throughout the narratives of Durham and Nelson are some of the customs of the Indians in our area that are worthy of note.

Marriage customs of the Indians depended more on the advantages to the bride's father than upon her wishes. Some fathers indulged their daughters and allowed them to make their own selection of mates, but the father had the final say before the marriage could take place. Usually the marriage became legal when the young brave led his bride to the wigwam he had provided for her. If the bride was a lady of prestige there might be a few words spoken by the Chief and some feasting. Many of the Indians practiced bigamy or even polygamy, but the first chosen bride was the favored one. Joe Cobenas got along fine with two wives, probably be-

The summer camp of the Indians at the Indian Village at Warroad. The picture was taken by E. J. Holland.

cause he housed them in separate wigwams along with his eighteen children. However, when Joe went to Kenora to get a government check, he also picked up a third wife more comely than the other two squaws. Joe hoped to continue in connubial bliss, but this was not to be, for wives No. 1 and 2 harassed him constantly; finally in despair Joe took bride No. 3 as far as Warroad so she could return to her own people and he to peace at home.

Burial of the dead was done in true Chippewa fashion. Mrs. Swen Oie and Mrs. Charles Meyers and Ole Oie had occasion to assist the Indians in this rite. The dead was wrapped in a blanket, his knapsack with his most prized possessions was put on his back and he was buried generally in a sitting position. A fire was kindled and kept going on his grave for many days thereafter.

Warroad has evidence to this day of the traditional Indian cemetery with the little grave houses to contain the gifts for the departed brothers. There among others are the graves of Na-May-Puck, Little Thunder, Joe Cobenas, and Ka-Ka-Geesick which are being preserved by the Minnesota Historical Society on land that was formerly the Indian Reservation. Joe Cobenas was the last of the Indians to be buried in a standing position.

Another Indian burying ground was the land across from the old Messiah Lutheran Church. Sad to say that the graves are not marked today and most people are unaware that it was once an Indian Cemetery. In 1920 Laughing Mary came there the last time to lay her precious offering on the grave, but vandals were watching and they soon confiscated them. This ended the practice and unfortunately not even a marker commemorates the site.

It is a known fact that the Indians were highly superstitious. Jake Nelson tells about Mickinock in the year '86 or '87 when an epidemic came to the village and five of the Mickinock children were stricken. Mickinock tore down his house and rebuilt it so that the door was on the east side, and the chimney on the southwest to deceive the evil spirit.

An account of the early history of Roseau must include the exciting story of the Ghost of the Indian Village. Jake Nelson recounts it this way: (1886)

> The ghost of the Indian Village never appeared right in the village but in the immediate vicinity. The Indians had seen it many times and its appearance always presaged the death of someone at the village. This apparition has been known to the Indians for so long a time that they have no traditions of its first appearance.
>
> The first white persons to see this apparition were Edna T. Nelson and her brother, Jesse Nelson. The former Miss Nelson is now Mrs. S. W. Bennett. The children were going to school and about a mile west they met the apparition in the road. When they came nearly up to it they turned off the road and went around it. On they went to G. Davis's claim shanty which was used as the first school house. Edna and Jesse twice saw this apparition at the same place on the road. They described it as being eight feet tall all dressed in white and having on its forehead a large bright star.

It appeared a second time to foretell the death of Mrs. Mickinock's mother who was reputed to have been 150 years old at the time of her death, and was said by some to be the grandmother of all the Indians in the Roseau Village. It was told that Mrs. Anna Mickinock saw Wubagi (the ghost) walking over the prairie toward the house, and shortly

Final resting place for Ka-Ka-Geesick (Everlasting Sky.) Here with the little grave houses to protect the gifts for the dead are the graves also of his two brothers, Na-May Puck and Little Thunder.

thereafter her old mother died. (Unfortunately none of her history was preserved for future generations.) And it appeared again to call Mrs. Mickinock after she had caught a severe cold due to drinking too much cold water and sitting on cool moss. The ghost was seen coming toward her, stumbling a few times, but finally the ghost caught up to her and then it went out of sight behind the east end of the grove on the small ridge on the S. G. Bertilrud homestead. Mrs. Mickinock died the next day.

Nelson records how the Indians tried to catch this ghost but had to give it up. Wood told them that it was too much like playing with the devil.

The Cobenas family did not escape the ghost either. Jim Cobenas told this story to Inga Billberg which she related in another of her series of *History of the Indian Village.*

Jim Cobenas and his family went on an extended fishing trip in early spring. While at the fishing grounds Jim's father became very ill. The mother sent the boys back to the village to get old Osh-Wash (Ay-Ash-A-Wash), the medicine man. When the boys reached the village they heard much wailing and moaning and they saw old Osh-Wash going among the people and asking each if he were sick or not. When the boys made their request saying that their grandfather was very ill, Osh-Wash made an announcement to the people telling them to cease their fears for they were not in danger as the ghost had come to get old man Cobenas. Before he died Jim Cobenas' father made two requests – that he be buried at Buffalo Point and that the Great Spirit should bless his people and cause them to live in peace.

So much of the early Indian history includes the name of Mickinock. His memory should be perpetuated because of his concern for the welfare of all people, be they white or red. Jake Nelson tells some of Mickinock's story:

I, and others had noticed that some of the Indians had hair of decidedly auburn shade. Especially was this true of the Mickinock family. At that time my hair was decidedly red (Jake Nelson's) and when I asked Mickinock how he happened to have auburn colored hair he said, "S'pose some time white man same hair like you scare my squaw."

However the story he told in earnest was later called "The Three Indian Mound Legend," [15]

15One account ties this story in with the story of the Kensington Rune Stone.

Jim Cobenas the stately dignified Indian.

A long time ago all the sand ridges were long islands in a great lake. One fall the lake froze early and then a hard wind which broke up the ice followed. During the storm a large boat was driven against the sand ridge, east of the Two River Crossing and was hurled to pieces by the ice and wind. From the boat there escaped to the sand ridge fourteen whites, seven men, two women and five children, three boys and two girls. After the storm there was quite a long spell of warm weather during which time these people prepared for winter. During the winter their provisions were scant and sickness and famine left only one man and five children alive in spring.

There were Indians living on Cypress Mountains – the high country north of Roseau Valley known as the Pine Hills. The Indians saw the smoke of camp fires on the sand ridge and went down to investigate. There they found the one man and five children and took them to Cypress Mountain where the following winter the white man died. After ten years or more the white boys all had Indian wives, and the white girls had Indian husbands.

This account has never been authenticated, but it presents an interesting possibility.

Because of his kindly attitude Mickinock became a good friend of the pioneers. The children especially liked 'Old Nock.' When he came to visit he would sometimes pretend he would pounce upon them but when they got near he would strut like a "cock of the walk." Another little practical joke that he liked to play was to sneak unseen among the calves and make a horrible howling noise. When the housewife would run out to see what was happening, Mickinock would pop out, and say, "I would like to be one of your

Grant Irish, an early pioneer and Mickinock.

little calves." He would get everyone to laugh.

Mickinock kept a camp at Wannaska especially during the trapping season. A dug-out home that he used was known to many of the older Wannaska residents, and a few of the children later used it as a play house. Beaver were so abundant around Wannaska, and so in demand in New York and Europe for hats for the elite that there was a good business in exporting the pelts. Mickinock trapped all around the Malung, Grimstad, Palmville, Golden Valley and Beaver area. He reportedly sold some of the land to a Mr. Theodore Thompson. At one time the Roseau Historical Society planned to put a marker on the Philip Swenson land in memory of old Mickinock.

An Indian named for his fine character was Honest John. Many still remember how Honest John's widow, who made baskets to sell, would simply have a letter of identification which would earn her food and a night's lodging.

The Indians did not regard themselves as citizens, even though they were the first inhabitants of the land. They pressed on Mr. Durham to get them citizenship papers which would enable them to vote for the "Great White Father" in Washington. In order to satisfy them, Mr. Durham took their names and petitions to Mr. Jadis (for whom Roseau was first named) and for whom all had great respect. Mr. Jadis was at the time the auditor of Kittson county (before Roseau County was organized) and worked for Mr. Sprague in the Sprague Lumber Camp. Mr. Jadis fixed them up with papers that had an authentic appearance, and they were assured that Mr. Jadis was "heap good white man."

In 1883 there were practically no white settlers in what is now Roseau County. Mr. Nelson tells in his account:

> In February '83 I joined the family in their new home (Nelson home was at Nelson Park, in Marshall County) and got out logs to build a large house, where we kept a wayside stopping place for landseekers, hunters, and travelers. Father's place was the outpost of the settlement from Nelson Park to the Canadian Boundary, fifty miles away. There was only one settler fifteen miles north to Two Rivers and to the west there were no settlers. A man could travel from Nelson Park to Pigeon River on Lake Superior and not meet a white man. (The half way house was also a stopping place for itinerants to the Canadian border.)

Peter Sjoberg with Mickinock. Both seemed well armed though the best of friends. The trusty dog lies obediently at their feet.

During these years Jake Nelson was still making periodic trips from Nelson Park near Stephen to the Roseau Valley. About one of his trips he says:

> Early in the evening we camped by the side of the ridge in a heavy spruce grove, known to the Indians as "Ska-Ock-wah" meaning spruce or bush. Here we found shelter for the horses under the spruce trees and a ready madė tent of spruce boughs for ourselves. While James cared for the horses I got firewood and Mr. Wood started a fire in front of the spruce bough tent and prepared supper. We spent the evening talking of the Roseau Valley, the Indians, their village and those tracks we had seen on the trail made by a lone man and a hand sled.

This reference could have been to the present site of Greenbush.

On a successive visit into the Roseau Valley, Nelson had this to say:

> James (Jake's brother) had bought a plow, so first we plowed at the Indian village, then a strip on the river bank on what is now the Strandquist farm and finally a strip on my location where I planted potatoes. These occasions were the first use of the plow in Roseau Valley.

Then during the year of 1884 people began to come into the Valley and Nelson says:

> . . . the Indians had begun to comprehend what this movement might mean to them; but they thought as many of the white people did at that time – that there was not sufficient high and dry land in the Valley for any extensive settlement.

The Indian home was most often a wigwam, but Jesse Nelson relates that the Indians at first dug holes about four feet deep and twenty-two feet across, then bent poles over these holes and covered the poles with birch bark. Soon they changed their architecture to the log house style which Mr. Nelson thinks they copied from Daniel Sprague and his houses across the border.

The settler built log cabins also. Mr. Louis Enstrom says that they had to saw their lumber by hand. It was done by placing a log which had been hewed on two sides on saw horses. They used a two-man saw, with one man standing on top and the other underneath and so cut the log. But Mr. Enstrom hastens to add that the "Swedes were handy with tools" and we must add that the Norwegians were likewise handy since they built log homes for their families as well.

The abundant rainfall caused many problems for the early settler. One problem was the leaking roofs. If the settler was fortunate enough to be able to put a shingled roof on the house he was relatively safe from the elements, but if he had to resort to a sod roof he had a sort of simulated rainfall in his house all summer long. One pioneer lady, Karen Enger, said she had to have the baby sleep under the table, the only dry spot in the house.

Some of the houses had a "loft" which was a cozy place for the children to sleep in at night, but often the family had to manage with one-room cabins until the head of the house could add more room. Dirt floors or rough hewn floors were used entirely. "With oxen, a dog and a cow," Mr. Enstrom said, "they started out from nowhere." From "nowhere" they built a shelter and struggled to add what comforts they could from time to time.

There were times for celebration and rejoicing also in the lives of the pioneers. The four anticipated holidays were Christmas, Fourth of July, Easter, and Syttende Mai. We find we have become somewhat complacent in our attitudes toward our festivities when we compare our days of celebration to the early holidays of the pioneers. The early account of Nelson and Durham give us some insight into typical early Fourth of July events such as July Fourth 1886 when Nelson recalls:

> Mr. Wood, William Dewing and I were at the Indian Village when about ten o'clock in the morning a team arrived from down the river bringing Jim Roe, Elias Irish and his wife, and Byron Ketchel and his wife and three children. Since they were going to Wood's place Wood and I joined the party. Dewing decided to remain at the Village.
>
> We drove to Wood's place accompanied by an innumerable swarm of bulldog flies. After we had put the horses in a makeshift stable which Wood had built, and left the women and children in the cabin we went down to Ryder's place and got a jug of slightly reduced alcohol.
>
> At Wood's place, July 4th, 1886 one hundred and ten years after the signing of the Declaration of Independence, occurred the first celebration of Independence Day in the Roseau Valley. We had a program of the usual sports, jumping, footracing, and swimming and for the tug of war we were to see who could tell the biggest lie. Some of us thought the tug of war would be a snap; we all did our best, but at the end of the first round, Wood was so far ahead of the rest of us that we gave up . . . .
>
> We gave the cabin to the women and children so that they might be under a roof. We built a campfire in the yard and slept on the ground without blankets. Jim Roe set a jug just above his head and began to sing. When we went to sleep he was snoring about as loud as he had been singing during the night. The jug was empty. When we awoke he felt like "the morning after the night before." The rest of us

were happy and realized that the spirit of '76 had arrived in the Roseau Valley only one hundred and ten years after it was born in the original thirteen colonies.

Durham recounts the 4th of July celebration in 1889 thus:

> In 1889 we celebrated our first Fourth of July (Nelson's account differs on this) at my place which at this time was located on the Andrew Vistad farm. I had changed claims since I arrived. We built a platform 50x20. Our women made a flag for the day and it was fluttering on the top of a sixty foot staff. We engaged two anvils for the fireworks which boomed forth its message in the early morning for all to come in memory of those early forefathers who had paved the way for a new nation in the new and great country in the making. Before ten o'clock boats carrying people from up the river as far as Duxby came in. On the trails over the country the Forsythe brothers came riding in on a Red River cart hitched to a little Jersey bull accompanied by a big St. Bernard dog. A speaking program was pulled off after which the best of eats went round. For the benefit of the younger generation I must mention that we were in good style even in this early year. On the platform sat our band consisting of the Holms and Torfin boys. What instruments they played I do not remember, but I do recall that we had some great music which kept the dancers going until morning the following day, when all went home pleased with the first fourth of July celebration in Roseau County.

A later and somewhat less sophisticated 4th of July occurred in 1892 which was described by the late Hube Dieter (mostly told by his elders) of the celebration at the Roswell Waterman place. The Holm boys improvised instruments out of boxes and papers to resemble horns. Cutter boxes were used as a sort of merry-go-round, the power being supplied by R. Waterman's horses.

On one of the trips back to Nelson Park, Jake Nelson mentions Badger and Karlstad which he visited often. He says:

> Then I went down to the Indian Village, had supper with McGillis, slept in the Nelson house and the next morning was on my way to Nelson Park before the Indians were astir. At Badger Creek I kindled a fire and made breakfast. At sundown I was on the ridge where Karlstad is now located. There by the roadside I found a bunch of hay upon which I curled up and went to sleep. Presently a bear came along and I awoke. When I arose the bear ran away. I went on my way and arrived at the Nelson Park at 12 o'clock midnight.

Wolf pelts, which brought a nice bounty, caused a sad experience for some Indians who were working for the Hudson's Bay Company. Poison bait was the most common method of securing the hides, and one day one of the Husky dogs valued at $500 which the Indians had with them, swung off the trail and ate some of the poison which Seward Wood had placed near the trail. Soon the other dogs followed the leader and four dogs were lost to the company. The Indians, who had been reprimanded for indulging in too much whiskey, hated to face "the old man" at the Post.

Mention is made in Nelson's account about Daniel Sprague and his lumbering operation:

> James (his brother) and I returned to Nelson Park for the winter, and Wood having nothing better to do at home went to work at Sprague's Camp at Cypress Mountains in Canada. There he spent the winter.

So far the narratives have mentioned only the first land seekers, but Jake Nelson says that in 1886 two women came to the Valley. "Mrs. James Nelson, at present Mrs. Charles Meyers of Roseau and Miss Kathie Nelson, at present Mrs. William Warner of Roseau were the first white women to visit the Roseau Valley." And J. W. Durham tells that in 1887 he brought his wife and family into Roseau, and his daughter who became Mrs. Art Linder was reported to have been the first white baby to come into the county. Mr. Durham recounts in some detail about the abundance of game, the ducks, geese, and birds of all descriptions, the beautiful scenery, the forests and intervening grassy plains that made him decide that Roseau Valley was to be his future home.

Mr. and Mrs. William Warner and daughter Mabel. Kate was the sister of Jake and James Nelson. The Warners were among the first pioneers. Mabel is Mrs. Elmer Skogen.

In 1886, Durham recounts a great fire starting at the Red Lake in the Beltrami forest and continuing through Roseau County and into Canada. It was a vast fire and burned much of the luxuriant forests and destroyed much of the humus soil. Dufwa's account entitled "Changing Folkways" tells about the fires in this manner:

> A weird sight in the autumn evenings was the prairie fire. One seemed to be encircled with a luminous glow which caused a luminary yet eerie hue to the whole heavens. Abundant rain had produced billowing grass on the prairies. If it remained uncut, the hay the next year mixed with dead grass from the previous year could not be used to feed the cattle. Therefore prairie fires would solve the problem. To protect buildings and haystacks several furrows would be plowed around the buildings called "firebreaks". If the wind was strong, it happened that fires would jump the firebreak, and haystacks or buildings would burn.
>
> After the fires had swept across the prairies the ground appears as black as a plowed field. To a casual observer it appeared that these prairies were dotted with herds of white sheep. If you looked closer, the objects were not white sheep, but white stones. Stones had to be removed before a field of grain could be grown.

At this time in both accounts, Nelson's and Durham's, the name of Rhyder occurs frequently. Mr. Rhyder (sometimes spelled Ryder) had a store 10 feet square on the Dynes (present Magnusson) farm. This part of the history of Roseau is full of drama and intrigue and is actually the first murder mystery that has never been definitely solved to everyone's satisfaction in the county. The story goes like this:

A man named Israel Rhyder came to the peaceful Roseau Valley with a preconceived idea of what business he would establish for himself and he lost no time to begin. The sale of whiskey to the Indians was forbidden by law, but Rhyder did not intend to let that deter him. It was to his advantage to rid the Valley of any influential, righteous men. Rhyder had a plan.

As the men were at work on the Nelson house, Mickinock who had always been friendly and kind to the white men, came down from Rhyder's place. (Rhyder lived on the place that became Andrew Vistad's farm.) When he got near enough he slowly loaded his gun, pointed it down the trail and told the men to get on their way. But James (Jake's brother) who was standing nearest to Mickinock sprang on him suddenly and wrestled the gun from him. Mickinock fell over some logs. In the scuffle the old Indian lost the gun and his clay pipe. Mickinock picked himself up and crept off to his cabin. After a little conference the white men decided to return the gun with the bullets lest the Indian would sense their fears. When they came to the wigwam it was very quiet and Mickinock was lying on his pallet, face to the wall. He would not talk to anyone so the Nelson's gave the gun to his son John who laid it in the cane brake. They laid the pipe inside the wigwam.

Billy McGillis kept the white men informed. He told them that Mickinock felt disgraced. He had accepted Rhyder's bribe of 3 gallons of whiskey to drive out the white men. McGillis was informed to go to Mickinock and tell him that they understood the bribe and knew where to place the blame. Mickinock was quite relieved after that incident.

But Rhyder's monopoly of the whiskey business was not to go unchallenged. There appeared in the Roseau Valley two men who were strangers and seemed not to be interested in becoming acquainted. They set up camp where they could spy on Rhyder and Rhyder caught on very soon that he was their target. So old Israel loaded his canoe with blanket, food and, of course, whiskey, fixed a grain sack for a sail and took off down the river and toward the big lake. A sudden gale came up as is common on Lake of the Woods, and the little craft was pitched this way and that until finally Rhyder was able to get near shore. However, in beaching it he punched holes in the bottom of the canoe. Rhyder tossed the whiskey out into the bush when he saw some Indians camped near by, hoping that he could go back for it later, but when the Indians found the liquor, Rhyder knew it was time to take off and he headed toward what is now Warroad.

Jake and James Nelson had occasion to go to Crookston on some claim business some time later and whom should they meet up with but the two strangers. They struck up a conversation, let the hint fall that they were from the Roseau Valley, whereupon the men immediately tried to make a "deal" with them to deliver Rhyder to them. This incident cemented a strong friendship between Rhyder and the Nelsons since the Nelsons did not betray the whiskey seller.

So Rhyder prospered as he retained the whiskey business against all invaders. Like men who live dangerously, he trusted few other men. Especially, he did not trust bankers or their institutions. So he made frequent trips to get his folding money converted into silver. He would say that he was going to the "front" which meant the Red River Valley. He would deposit his coin in cans and bury them. Once he told Jake Nelson where he had buried his money saying, "I have to go to Drayton, N. Dakota and if I don't come back you are welcome to this money." He said Rhyder's bank was the Roseau River Bank. Anyone for a treasure hunt? Rhyder's money is said to be there still.

The actual report of the murder of Rhyder is in the words of Jake Nelson:

> In November 1887 Rhyder had been away on a hunting trip. When he returned some of the hunters returned with him to his place. In the evening Charlie Cobenas, an Indian from the Roseau Lake Village, became noisy from the effects of liquor and he wanted still more. Rhyder refused to let him have more. The Indian became angry, and as he stood in the yard facing the door, he grabbed his gun and shot. Rhyder, who was standing just inside the door, holding it open with one hand and resting his other hand against it, was immediately killed. The people in the Rhyder house charged Charlie Cobenas with the shooting, but few people in the Valley believed Cobenas to be guilty.
>
> The next morning after Rhyder was killed, Charlie Cobenas at the village packed up a bundle of furs and started up to Rhyder's place to trade them. When he was nearing the place, he met someone who told him that Rhyder was dead, and that he, Cobenas was charged with the shooting. Cobenas returned to the village and told the other Indians. This caused much excitement. Charlie Cobenas could give no satisfactory explanation since he did not clearly remember what had taken place at Rhyder's place the night before. He was not much concerned about this charge, since he remained at the Indian village unmolested until he moved to Lake of the Woods several years after Rhyder's death.
>
> During the two years following Rhyder's death there could have been a great deal of evidence gathered – both direct and circumstantial, concerning this. Forty years hence most of this evidence will be unavailable as there would be few people remaining who had knowledge of the events of that time. Yet there are circumstances of that time remembered by some of the old settlers at the present time, but since mention of them might offend some of the old settlers, I will let them pass and leave it to the world to decide who shot Rhyder.
>
> Charlie Cobenas did not get Rhyder's gold. Rhyder's mother did not get it. Rhyder's estate was never probated. Who did get Rhyder's stake?

J. W. Durham's account of the murder is at great variance with the above account. The circumstantial evidence vindicating Cobenas was that Rhyder was shot in the back and could hardly have been killed by Cobenas' gun if Rhyder stood in the doorway, and Cobenas stood on the outside. Justice did not take its course in this first murder in the Roseau Valley. Jake Nelson has commendatory words about old Israel Rhyder – that he was honest in his dealings, albeit shrewd. That he was a true frontiersman, loyal and just, and that he was a man of far better character than the whiskey runners who followed after his death.

At this time in the history of Roseau County the struggle for existence was often beset with despair, physical exhaustion, sickness, hunger, and loneliness. It was the adversities that drew the pioneers in a kind of kinship that is almost unknown today. Durham often speaks about the valiant women who had to remain behind when the men went for long months at a time to the Red River Valley to earn enough money so that they could exist. Many incidents are told about how they feared the Indians (even though time proved their fears groundless) and how Mrs. Swen Oie became frightened when a red man stood in her doorway, so that she screamed and ran, and the red man merely smiled and walked away. And how a school teacher saw an Indian at her door, became terrified, but grabbed a broom and pretended to be sweeping the house until she got close enough to the door, then quickly brushed past him and ran. Inga Billberg relates that snakes were a pestilence hardly imaginable now. She tells that the snakes made nests in the mattresses and climbed over the sod roofs to dangle into the house when the warmth enticed them. She further tells how Mrs. Gust Johnson scrubbed her wooden floor and the warm water brought beady eyes all over the room. Further she says that Mrs. Meyers was rocking Harry and when she moved closer to the homemade stove she saw a coil of a snake around the pipe. And the gruesome tale is told about Louis Oie who thought he had swallowed a snake during his sleep at night. A bedridden Ross lady said she had a club nearby at all times so she could kill them. Fortunately these snakes were not poisonous. It is hardly surprising that the women often longed for their former life and comforts.

To further substantiate the great hardship and terrifying atmosphere of that era we must include the Indian scare of 1891.

It is told in the words of J. W. Durham:

In the latter part of January of 1891, our new settlement experienced an Indian scare which came near depopulating the country. The whole matter was a false alarm yet matters as they developed looked quite serious for a time. It is somewhat difficult for me to describe just how this scare had its beginning. However, by explaining to my readers that in the year 1890 the Sioux Indians of Pine Ridge, S.D., were planning for a general raid on the whites and in order to make a clean sweep of it their chief, Rain-in-the-Face, visited the Chippewa on the Red Lake reservation, hoping to induce them to join with his people in a general war on the whites. Such were the rumors which passed around. It was further given out that the Indians had purchased all the powder and lead to be had at Thief River Falls and many other stories went the rounds.

Just before the scare developed in the Roseau Valley it was reported that the Indians were having big ghost dances at Warroad with visitors from Red Lake and all other nearby villages. When the settlers heard of this they became quite uneasy as our situation was most unfavorable in case of an outbreak. We had Indian villages to the east, and to the south and to the west of us. Thus everyone can see that the Roseau settlers were completely surrounded by Indians, and if it had come to a clash our chances would have been poor even to escape.

The climax came when one Fred Holmsten and Ole Mattson had been up in the Pine Creek country and had heard that the Indians were about ready to strike upon the settlers. These men were around all night warning settlers of what was supposed to come. At day break they came to John Torfin's place, having travelled all night and they rested there for awhile. John Torfin started to warn the people along the river north of Roseau. He came to my place about sunrise. After he had told his story we both felt skeptical as to these rumors. But as no one could feel absolutely safe under the circumstances we walked down to Roseau during the forenoon and here we found nearly all the settlers in the whole country gathered together for the purpose of organizing a defense. Imagine my surprise when I found that my neighbors and fellow settlers had appointed me to command the defense. My readers will pardon if I say that I felt as proud as Old Zak Taylor when he stood before Buena Vista. Not because of anything I had done, but because my neighbors placed such confidence and trust in me.

Thus far in our pioneer experience we had met with various situations which might be classed as somewhat difficult, now if rumors would come true we would meet with the responsibility of protecting our homes and families from the cruel destruction of Indian warfare. We knew that the odds were against us, but the cause was big – we were to protect that which was dearest to us and would meet any fate to do so. I wish to mention here that Iver Torfin was appointed to be "Secretary of War."

After talking over the matter thoroughly, we called for the names of all those who would volunteer to stay and help defend the homes. Some over one hundred volunteered to do so. The next step we took was to send two men to Warroad as scouts to see what they could learn as to the actions of the Indians. Oluf Efshen and John Henrickson were commissioned to perform this duty. They walked across the forest unbroken by any vehicle. Erick Holm went to Hallock to inform the authorities there of our situation. Further we had ordered a number of scouts who were patrolling the outskirts of our settlements watching for every sign of disturbance, ready to report into headquarters.

The three Cobenas brothers, Jim, Joe (third man) and Charles pose with Tigoble, a Red Lake Indian.

In order that the readers may note that it was not only the Roseau valley which was affected in this scare, but that our neighbors to the south seem to have had some real trouble with the Indians. Some telegrams which went between the governor and officials up here, also a newspaper article are included.

(The telegrams were to Gov. Merriam from T. J. Wikstrom at St. Hilaire, from Oscar Young Green, Sheriff of Kittson County, from John Westerson, Recorder and Ed. H. Love, Major of Kittson County, to the effect that the Indians were holding war dances and the attack was feared.)

The Indian Scare was recorded in the Crookston Times, January 31, 1891 as follows:

There is some excitement and much anxiety among the settlers along the Red Lake Reservation near St. Hilaire and Thief River Falls, over the way Moosedung's band of Indians have been acting during the past few days. For some time past, the Indians have acted in a very sullen and insolent manner toward the settlers with whom they have heretofore been friendly, but no particular attention was paid to their actions until settlers commenced to come in and report that for three or four nights the Indians had been dancing and they had heard the big drums and yells of the savages during the greater portion of the night. Telegrams were at once sent to the governor informing him of the state of affairs and Adjutant General Mullen was dispatched to the scene to make an investigation. He arrived Saturday and took a team and drove to the reservation. He found the settlers very badly frightened, and while he thought there was no probability of serious trouble yet in order to quiet the fears of the settlers he telegraphed to the governor for 100 rifles and 2,000 rounds of ammunition. He returned here Monday and being interviewed by a Times' reporter said that the trouble arose from the settlers going upon the reservation and stealing timber. Many of the Indians, he said had already selected their allotments under the recent treaty and they had only united to protect their timber lands from devastation. He also learned that the Indians had been plentifully supplied with whiskey which had a good deal to do with the trouble. While upon the reservation he witnessed one of the dances and said that it was not a ghost dance at all but that they were dancing for amusement.

Many of the settlers do not agree with General Mullen in the behavior of the Indians that they are not contemplating an outbreak as they say the savages have been very insolent of late. They have been prowling around their houses and have made repeated threats that they would burn them out. They say the Indians have been very unsuccessful in trapping and hunting this season. Game has been scarce and this has caused them to be discontented and quarrelsome. The more remote settlers have become so badly frightened at the threatening attitude of the redskins that they have abandoned their homes and taken their families into the villages for protection. The fact that the Chippewa on some other reservations are making hostile demonstrations tends to strengthen their beliefs that the tribe is contemplating an outbreak. Along the Rainy River near the Manitoba line the settlers have also petitioned for arms and ammunition to protect themselves. It was claimed that the Indians are engaging in ghost dances and that their numbers have increased by large numbers of braves from the Red Lake reservation.

The result of this scare was that large numbers of Roseau Valley settlers hastily packed their wagons and headed south. Erick Holm reported 60 teams on the miserable flight suffering from the November cold, their fears, and the travel over snow covered trails. Most of the settlers returned to the valley when their fears were quieted, but a few left the land never to return. What a surprise and delight must have been their realization upon returning that good old Mickinock had cared for their stock and they could pick up from where they left. He told them also that the Indians had been afraid of the white uprising when they gathered their numbers in the villages.

The first mail was carried in 1888 by John Erickson who had a saloon in Roseau and then moved to Fox where he had a store and a post office. Erickson went to Hallock, first once a week and later twice a week by horseback or team to bring the mail. Sutton's store which was the post office of the region, and Mr. Sutton as first post master of Jadis initiated the postal system in the county. This store was a half mile north of the present townsite of Roseau. The second post office was Badger, established December 28, 1889 with Elias Irish as post master. It was located at the former I. L. Iverson place. This is the oldest post office in the county which retains its original name.

Some "firsts" were established in Roseau County prior to its actual organization in

Esther Danielson Goldner was the first white baby born in Roseau County, June 18, 1888.

The first mail box in Jadis (Roseau) located in the Sutton store located a half mile north of the town of Roseau. It is now in the Roseau County Museum.

1894: The first white baby born in what is now Roseau County was Esther Danielson, who became Mrs. Richard Goldener of Conrad. She was born July 11, 1888.

The first wedding in the county took place in December 1889 when Simon Johnson and Ida Nelson were married. Old Simon, the fisherman, is still remembered by many residents as the congenial court house custodian who had many a yarn to spin with anyone who had the time of day. Mr. Durham says:

> Mr. Johnson has been janitor at the county court house where his genius has taken such a strong hold on the county officials as to make him a sort of captain of all current events, ranging from a general retrospection of all creeds to the prophetic forecast of the future.

In 1887 a first hotel appeared, called the Half Way House. The proprietor Roswell Waterman, a relative of the late Hube Dieter, built it on the river bank one half mile from the present village of Roseau. The officials for the first court session had accommodations there, and although it was termed primitive as were the buildings of the day, it was commended in an account for cleanliness and the host for his hospitality.

J. W. Durham records that the first saw mill was established in the county by John and Lewis Norquist and Louis Haglund in the year of 1888. It consisted of:

> . . . a heavy whit saw, resembling those used in cutting ice. A scaffold was made seven feet high, with four posts and two stringers. After the log had been squared with the broad ax, it was lined in inch spaces, and placed in position on the stringers with one man underneath and one on top of the log to handle the saw. In that way men could cut 100 feet per day.

He describes the shingle mill that they made:

> The shingle mill consisted of a log about twelve feet long, fastened on one end with a heavy steel knife, fastened in somewhat the same manner as a knife in kraut cutters, having the space the thickness of a shingle. One end of the log was laid on the wooden horse three feet high, with a pin through it to hold it in place, but loose enough to let it swing; the other end, with the knife in it was placed on a bench the same height, with a groove to fasten a shingle block in. In that way three men pushing the log like a plane would shave off a shingle.

In regard to the church activities of that year, Mr. Durham gives us a glimpse of the beginnings:

> The Seventh Day Adventists were perhaps the first to enter the field through the work of Louis Haugland and Mrs. Irish, and were aided by Lars Hedin and Andrew Nyquist (father of Gust and Joel), J. E. Holmsten and Paul Wallin. They were followed by the Baptists represented by Andrew Nelson, a brother of Martin Nelson, our county commissioner from this district. The Mission Friends and Lutherans followed close to the above mentioned denominations. Andrew Danielson and Nils G. Risberg were among the first to take the lead in this mission.
>
> Most of the services were generally conducted in the homes of the settlers usually drawing large crowds. The first church was built in 1891 (this was not a church in the true sense, but a barn.) It was located one and one-half miles east of the present site of Roseau on the Nils E. Nelson farm. The church was free to all denominations and earned for its founder the lofty title of "Church Nelson."

J. W. Durham at one of the first houses built in the county near Roseau, the Danielson homestead SE of NW Sec 13 Township 162 N. The house was built in 1888.

Later as this church which was originally intended for a barn, became too small and language caused a split between the Swedes and Norwegians, a church was built in town.

As nearly as can be determined Rev. Askeland was the first ordained resident minister. He had charge of the Lutherans, both the Swedes and the Norwegians. Durham tells how dear to his heart was this genial man who went wherever he felt a need regardless of the weather. When his horse became mired down, he would proceed on foot. He says, "In his zeal for the religious education of the first settlers he conducted services, taught from the good book and shared with others of his scant worldly goods."

The first building built exclusively for a church was in Pinecreek in 1894. (There is an account of it in the history of the towns.)

The first dance was held at the claim house of John Norquist where Swing-Your Partner and Do-Si-Do rang out to the rafters of the house.

There is some difference of opinion on the beginning of the first school. Mr. Ole

Holm says that Mr. Sanders was intrumental in starting the first school in Roseau and that Miss Davis was the first teacher. The late Hube Dieter said in an interview, "The first school in Roseau was held in a building that Andrew Risberg built and it was located just about on the lot where the V.F.W. is now, and a little later it was used as a home for the Risbergs." Most residents remember though, the two school houses located where the Arnold Monsrud and Dwight Roll homes are now on the west side of the river.

The first country school was the Gust Johnson school built two miles north of Roseau where Mike Holm, Albert Kveen and Mr. Tornquist attended school. This building is now the exhibit hall for schools and is located on the fair grounds.

Mr. Durham himself was the teacher in 1890 when he had a class of adults who gathered at the school to learn the English language. In 1893 the position of teacher was taken over by Gustave Erickson. This was when Roseau was still a part of Kittson County. J. W. Durham tells us that he was instrumental in getting the first school district organized when he attended a convention in Kittson County and persuaded P. H. Konzen, the county superintendent, to start a school district six miles square called District No. 27. John Owen, he says was the first teacher but it was found later that he was not licensed so the school could not get state aid. The first school board members were John Marshall, John Norquist, and Andrew Danielson and the first building was said to be a crude structure on the William H. Book property where a few children were taught intermittently. However, he says that a more permanent structure was later constructed two miles north of Roseau known as the Gust Johnson School.

The first legal organization established a voting precinct in 1888 which had headquarters in the Sutton store one half mile north of main street in Roseau. There were 55 votes polled, all Republican except those of Martin Dieter, Roswell Waterman and J. W. Durham.

The first court house building was where the Helgeson Mortuary is now located. It was housed there for a very short period of time, moving soon to the building across the street to the west which later became the

Pupils and teacher of the first school in Roseau County, Dist. #27 of Jadis. J. W. Durham acted as teacher, chiefly to teach the Engish language to these folks. They are standing left to right: John Halvorson, Emanual Holm, Nels Boe, Erick Holm, Mrs. Gust Johnson, Mrs. Erick Bjorman, and Mrs. J. W. Durham. Seated: Mrs. John Norman, Mrs. Ole Dokken, John Thompson, Pete Peterson, Martin Olsen and at the far right. J. W. Durham. 1890.

Threshing before 1900's. Picture submitted by Peter Westlund.

Webster Hotel and the Budd Hospital. As the Webster Hotel it was the stopping place for the famous stage coach.

The county was surveyed in 1888. After the Sutton store a few more stores were established. Charley Steele and Andrew Danielson opened a store on what became the Dynes farm (the present Allan Magnusson farm). Also a brick making factory was started at this site. Sutton's store served not only as a trading post, but also as a jail, council room, post office and carpenter shop.

Jake Nelson mentions that with the influx of settlers in 1888 the necessity for boundaries became evident.

> In 1889 the land was surveyed and the settlers knew their exact location. Concerning this there was little difficulty. It happened that Charlie Williams and Florence Lins took a fancy to the same location. I was present when they met. The location is now a part of the Dalby farm north of Ross. Williams claimed the first right. Mr. Lins said that there was no need for any disagreement about it, because there was land enough for everybody. Thereupon he selected his location, the farm where he still resides in the west part of Dieter township.

The first claim in Roseau was filed June 16, 1890 by James Jester, but the final proof of claim was by Pete Torgerson on NW½ of Section 18 in the township of Stafford. James Jester owned the 80 where the townsite of Roseau was platted. His home was located at the present site of the Children's Home. He sold this land to Rudolph Jacklin who with J. W. Sanders platted the village in 1892. This claim was made on the same day as Mr. Braaten's.

Negroes in Roseau County were virtually unknown. However Jake Nelson records a story about one, who was perhaps the first black man ever to visit the area.

> One cold and stormy day Mat Bush, a colored man from Grand Forks, North Dakota, drove up to the cabin. Mickinock, who was with us, happened to look out the window; he saw the colored man and said, "Blacksmith come." Mr. Bush located a land site a mile up the river, but never came back to settle there.

The first township established in the year 1890 was called Jadis (after the kindly benefactor from Kittson County who assisted settlers to get their citizenship papers). The first officers of the town of Jadis were W. H. Book, J. W. Durham, Iver Torfin, John Torfin, and Amos Ritchey.

Other commercial ventures were now begun in earnest in the general area. Jake Nelson had this to say about it:

> After Rhyder's death, F. W. Kraftha of Thief River Falls came to Nelson Park and arranged for the use of the Nelson house at the Roseau Lake Indian Village for a store. During the winter he hired C. P. Warner to do the freighting between Thief River Falls and the Village. He sent Alfred Drechenfeldt (alias Henry Buck) and Willie Cook to operate the store. Willie Cook had the advantage of being able to speak the Chippewa language. Drechenfeldt, or Buck, as he then called himself, was a younger son of one of the families of the nobility of Russia. To break up a courtship between a servant and him, his father sent him to America.

The log building was the first jail, the building next to it the first Roseau Post Office. The men are left to right, Ed Dieter, Edwin Dahlquist, and Harry Edkins. These buildings stood where the present Co-op is now located.

The trade at the store was profitable since there was no competition in the valley. The Indians brought in good business of furs, especially lynx skins. C. P. Warner made two trips a month, which in all amounted to four hundred miles since travel at that time was by way of Nelson Park.

In the spring the store was discontinued; Willie Cook returned to Thief River Falls; Buck remained in the Roseau Valley for some time and then disappeared. No one knew where he went or how. Some of the settlers had suspicions of foul play concerning his disappearance. There were grounds for suspicion too, as I well know.

Again the Sutton store scored a first since it also became the first newspaper office. The first paper published in Roseau County was the *Roseau Region* which started its publication on Tuesday, August 23, 1893 with Volume one, Number one. The editor was Andrew J. Clark. R. J. Bell started publishing the *Roseau County Times* in July of 1895, and A. M. Pearson started *The Roseau County Press* in Malung in the year of 1905. The Sutton store was also the first jail.

John Nyquist and son Gust came to town in 1893.

The village was platted in 1892 by J. H. Sanders and Rudolph Jacklin and the first building was on the river bank where the former Methodist church stood. (On the north side of the Center Street bridge, across the river from the light plant.)

The Dahlgren home in Stafford. At this home, built in 1889 many of the folks from Malung, Sweden stayed before establishing their own homes. The Lars Hedins were among these early pioneers.

Mrs. Jacob Sonsteng was the first settler in Roseau County to die of natural causes. She passed away in October of 1888. Mrs. Sonsteng had come from Bachelor's Grove near Niagra, North Dakota, and had forded the Roseau River with all her belongings to settle with her husband in Roseau.

Skipping a few years, but also in reference to the firsts in the county, Bendix Holdahl was the first person to be buried in the newly acquired Hope Cemetery.

The next period of time belongs to the organization of the county with city and county government and the growth of the communities or towns within its borders.

Chapter 5

FOUNDATIONS
1895-1908

Enough if something from our hands have power
to live and act and serve the future hour . . .

Wordsworth

Chapter 5

FOUNDATIONS

Riviere aux Roseau the French traders named it, our Roseau River. It was an apt name, for translated it means "river of reeds and rushes" which meant a secure home for the wild ducks and geese that took refuge there. This was the area too that would become home for the settlers who had come mostly from the Scandinavian countries, with few possessions but with a host of dreams and aspirations. On a map belonging to La Verendrye, published in 1737, there is a Roseau Lake, but the river was called Reed River. The grass grew 8 to 10 feet high around the rim of the lake and on the banks of the river.

Roseau County was created from Kittson County, with an addition later from Beltrami County. A legal historical description of Kittson County read:

> Title I of Chapter VIII of the Statutes of 1866, as approved by the State Legislature, listed 76 counties in the State of Minnesota, and their boundaries. Included was Pembina County, which later was reformed and a part thereof became Kittson County. . . .
>
> In 1878, the State Legislature, in chapter 59, established what then became Kittson County with the boundaries described as follows: Beginning at a point where the line between one hundred and fifty eight (158) and one hundred and fifty nine (159) intersects the centre of the channel of the Red River of the North; thence east along said line produced to the point where said produced line intersects the line between ranges thirty-eight (38) and thirty-nine (39); thence northwardly along said range line to the boundary line between the United States and British Possessions; thence westerly along said boundary to the middle of the main channel of the Red River of the North; thence up said river, along the middle thereof, to the place of beginning. This act was approved on March 9, 1878.

Kittson County, by action of the board on April 12, 1879, was divided into three commissioner districts as follows:

District No. 1 consisted of towns one hundred and fifty-nine (159) and one hundred sixty (160), being bounded on the east and west by the county line; District No. 2 consisted of towns one hundred and sixty-one (161), and one hundred and sixty-two (162), and bounded on the east and west by the county line; and District No. 3 consisted of towns one hundred and sixty-three (163) and

First picture of Roseam taken in 1893, before the county was organized. The winter stage coach loads in front of the Hotel. O. B. Ekman's Land Office is across the street, and Lindberg's store has the side stairs. These stores stood where the Penney store and the Red Owl stores are now.

Roseau in 1897. Drug store was run by C. A. Pearson and is located where Gamble store is now.

the fractional part of a town between said town and the boundary line between the United States and the British possessions, and bounded east and west by the county lines. Representing the first Commissioner District was Mr. E. W. Jadis as commissioner.

One can eye a treasure, touch it, long for it, but he cannot possess it until the price has been paid. The first installment on our county was paid in physical discomforts, in terrifying fears, in loneliness, and sometimes in despair. There was strenuous labor and sometimes defeat, but always there was fortitude. The settler's dream of a good life in the new land bred hope, patience, courage and the dream of freedom. All the mental, physical, and spiritual resources of the people were necessary to establish their homes and communities.

The name Roseau County became official after the division of Kittson County. The territory was first called Jadis around the year of 1890 in honor of the kindly auditor from Hallock who befriended the whites and Indians alike. On December 31, 1894, Governor Knute Nelson made the proclamation that the eastern part of Kittson County, consisting of thirty townships would become a new county, which was to be called Roseau County. The proclamation read:

Commencing at a point where the range line between Ranges 44 and 45 in Kittson County intersects the southern boundary line of Kittson County being the line between townships one hundred and fifty-eight and one hundred and fifty-nine; running thence east along said line produced to the point where said produced line intersects the line between Ranges 38 and 39; thence north along said Range line to the boundary line between the United States and British possessions; thence westerly along said boundary line to intersect the line between 44 and 45; thence south on said line between Ranges 44 and 45 to the point of the beginning.

Thus the eastern boundary at that time was actually Golden Valley, Mickinock, Malung, Spruce and Spruce Valley townships. The area lying east of this boundary was unorganized territory and a part of Beltrami County. Leaders in the new county had visions of including the Lake of the Woods area and took steps to have it annexed to Roseau County. By petition to Governor David Clough this annexation was completed on February 11, 1896, when the Governor issued the proclamation detaching fifteen townships, equal to 600 square miles and adding them to Roseau County.

The newspapers of the day chronicled the scant news of local interest, but relied heavily on the syndicated articles to produce a paper. In 1894 when the tax roll listed only 228 names of settlers scattered throughout the area there was hardly enough local news to fill half a page. The printing shop of the *Roseau County Times* was called "The Tabernacle" and it became the favorite meeting place for Roseauites to visit and swap stories of the breaking of the frontier. Here they would try to laugh away the gnawing concerns of the day and to plan together. Oh, how they did plan in those days: They would break the land, raise bumper crops on the virgin soil, raise dairy herds, and build a metropolis! The congenial fiery editor invited folks to drop in and chat as "there is always an easy chair available." Most likely the easy chair was occupied most of the time. Some of the first items in the 1894 paper read:

> P. O. Sutton is working on a stage route to Warroad. it is passable and is at least a frontier path.
>
> A social in the Norquist building. We ask the Pedro Club to meet early and attend the social en masse.
>
> I. Sjoberg is visiting the State Capitol this week.
>
> Falcon and Neil are in town. They have a coal mine on Lake of the Woods.
>
> A Christmas party was held. Everyone got a present except the editor and the "devil."
>
> Chief May Puck of War Road has a son – the first male and will therefore be chief.
>
> La Grippe is in charge in Roseau.
>
> York wants his name in the paper, so here it is. York was in town.
>
> Roseau Rippers beat the Ross Red Caps.
>
> Wish this issue could be the very best the Region ever put out. But it is impossible as everything is in such a mess.
>
> Mrs. Andrew Risberg came from Sweden to Roseau and will make her home here.
>
> Brother Greely Carr of Stephen came to look the county over. Says he may buy it.
>
> Iver Torfin went to the harvest fields in the Red River Valley.

Almost all the men in the area left to work in the Red River Valley during the fall harvest for the settlers were in dire need of cash. It was said that in 1891 during the harvest there were only two men left in the county – a man 80 years old and a merchant. In Durham's book *Minnesota's Frontier* he often refers to the plight of the women left alone in the frontier cabins. They were fearful of the mysterious red men who seemed to be hiding behind each tree as they endured the crude and drafty shelters they called home. They worried about the illnesses of the family, and the scanty provisions to feed them. There was also loneliness. It overwhelmed them when day after day human communication, except with the children, was impossible. So it is not strange, but quite understandable that the women sometimes used their washtubs as boats to ford the streams, and then walked many miles for a cup of coffee with another pioneer wife across the river and down the trail.

As for the men, the trek to the Red River Valley could hardly have been an inviting adventure. Even reaching their destination was a problem. J. Anton Hodik has told of his experiences like this: In the spring of 1904, J. Anton Hodik, Frank Housnar, and J. Kroll from the territory near Strathcona started walking 120 miles to the Red River Valley to work in the fields. Around Breeze there was so much water that they had to build a raft to float down Middle River. They tried to push it with sticks but in the process Frank Housnar fell in and the others had to jump in and rescue him. They had to beg their meals and lodging for they had not even 4 or 5 cents between them. Through mud and water they finally got to the Red River but found it so filled with chunks of floating ice that they feared to cross. They elected Anton Hodik to try the crossing, reasoning that he, being single, would be a better candidate than the married men to try such a risky thing. Finally they got to their destination where they hired out for $135 for 8 months. In the fall Hodik started to walk home. A rain storm turned into a blizzard and the wet clothes froze to his body. He was turned away at two farm houses and was even refused lodging in a barn lest he would smoke and set fire to the hay. At the third home he was given a sheep skin to wrap in and allowed to sleep in the granary. He woke to numb limbs and felt he had to move about or die. He trudged on toward home and finally arrived home. He reported that he felt the effects of this trip when he became an old man.

In September 1897 the Roseau Region reported:

> Nearly the whole male population of Roseau County are now in the wheat fields of the Red River Valley. They will come back well healed (did the editor mean well heeled?) to put improvements on their homesteads.

An article in the paper in 1898 pleaded for the men to stay home and build up their own farms instead of leaving the county to go to the Red River Valley. It was argued that there were now many settlers, and those who had homestead rights ought to make Roseau County their home and work their own fields. Elsie Wenner, in a letter to the editor in an issue of a little later date, went into great detail to point out to the farmers that they would have a good future in dairy farming. As each year the farm report showed increased acreage seeded over the previous year, and increase in the dairy herds, the farmers took heart and the agricultural development in Roseau had begun.

In January of 1895, the government of the county was established. The Governor of the State of Minnesota, David M. Clough, appointed the commissioners who in turn appointed the various officers. As recorded in the **Legislative Manual of the State of Minnesota** of 1895 they are:

County Commissioners:		Charles Hedlund
		Lars Haglund
		Syver Bertilrud
		A. O. Skagen
County Officers:		Hans Erickson
	Auditor	C. A. Moody
	Treasurer	A. G. Lokken
	Register of Deeds	T. S. Nomeland
	County Attorney	R. J. Bell
	County Superintendent	L. P. Dahlquist
	Judge of Probate	O. B. Ekman
	County Commissioner	J. C. Strom
	Surveyor	W. H. Book
	Coroner	I. Sjoberg
	Clerk of Court	I. Torfin

It was January 14, 1898 when the County Commissioners decided to provide convenient rooms in a court house, and also to provide for a jail. They purchased the Webster Hotel where the stage coach made regular stops. J. H. Sanders gave $100 and a lot adjoining the building and 20 cords of wood. The village was to pay $400 and the county $800 toward the total price of $1,300 to make these provisions.

Now the age of business had come to the settlement. The newspaper kept the residents well informed as to the new business ventures which were springing up rapidly. There were news articles on the new stocks of merchandise when they came in. The flowery and flattering words of the editor always predicted success for each new enterprise, adding that with such a fine man at the head of the business it could hardly fail. The papers carried big ads for patent medicines and standard sundries. There was Ayer's Sarsparilla for a disease called scrofula, Cascarets for a laxative, Piso's Cure for consumption, Lydia Pinkham's Tonic for women's problems, a Sapolio cleanser, and Jacklin's White Lily, Starlight and XXX flour from Roseau's own flour mill. Those were the days when large size table plates cost 90c a dozen, straight backed chairs were 45c, a coffee pot went for 5c, a rocking chair (and every grandma over fifty had to have one for relaxation and to sit in while knitting mittens and socks) cost $1.75; a man's suit cost $3.00, and tumblers were 50c a dozen. When in 1899 Ferrier started a saw mill the paper noted that he would do well because he was a great "rustler." (Did he mean "hustler"?) In 1899 Women's Lib started, believe it or not, because the "Rocker" washer which would do away with the wash board was advertised. One could put 100 pieces through the machine in an hour and could sit down while working the agitator by hand.

Roseau County Officers in 1897-98. Back row, left to right, A. O. Skagen, Hans Erickson, Jacob Johnson, Lars Haglund, T. E. Haug. Middle row: O. B. Ekman, Iver Torfin, A. Waag, A. Lokken, J. W. Durham. Front row: R. J. Bell, L. P. Dahlquist.

The Roseau County Board, 1903. From left to right, John C. Spencer, Martin Nelson, Fred Andol, Louis Enstrom, Sivert Bertilrud, and Fred Hanson.

It took more than the flowery words of the editor, however, to settle the country. The Homestead Act, in Roseau County, important though it was, was not enough either, for much of the land was swampy and untillable.

The Homestead Act of 1862 was enacted during the Civil War and was the greatest single factor in the settlement of the entire United States. To take advantage of the Act one had to be 21 years of age, the head of a family, could never have borne arms against the United States or given aid or comfort to the enemy. For the filing and payment of $1.25 an acre, a settler could turn his given 160 acres into his own claim. Between May 1862 and June 30th, 1880, there were 7 million acres in the United States claimed in this manner. In February of 1898 the Free Homestead Law was passed by the senate and secured through the house. This Act provided for the waiver of the $1.25 an acre, with only the stipulation that the settler live on the land for five years. This was a right given to any person coming to the United States if he intended to become a citizen, as well as for the

Gas lights were in use when S. G. Bertilrud and Axel Risberg tended to their duties at the court house which was located where the Moe Floral is today. 1911.

American born. As a result of this law Township 160, Range 42 near Badger, which was opened in May of 1900, recorded 25 claims in person and 40 by mail. Now little settlements with their own trade centers were beginning to develop. However, some sold off the timber on their claims and then left for greener pastures. However, the good high land was fertile and repaid the farmer for his toil. But the good high land was not abundant enough, so there was soon agitation for drainage. This was about the year 1900 and drainage has been a concern to the county ever since that time. There was a law enacted by the Minnesota State legislature at this time that allowed for drainage of lands when a few signers petitioned for it, and the project met with the approval of an engineer. The court could then authorize a ditch against

Roseau in 1904. The Times Office and Benson Candy Store is the present location of the Ben Franklin store. The store at the extreme right is the Holdahl and Foss general merchandise store where the First Federal has recently built. The large store on the corner of the right side of the street is Sjoberg's store, sold to Durgin and now the site of the Penney Co. Dr. F. Norin was located where the old locker plant was beside Montgomery Ward Catalog store.

all other opposition. In Roseau County there were three such ditches with assessments levied against the land that was benefited. The Roseau County Board signed the bonds and the obligation belonged to the whole county. This created a hardship for the people until the State of Minnesota forgave the cost of the assessments.

That there was concern and ill feeling over the drainage problem is evidenced by the report in the *Hallock Valley News*, January 25, 1901, which stated:

> Those who believe that the drainage of the low and swampy land of the lower Red River Valley is slow to come to pass will be pleased to know that the state legislature is apt to do the fair thing in that direction. Senator Myron has his bill prepared for introduction to the senate and we are assured that there is no doubt that it will pass that body as it did two years ago. In the house Albert Berg, member from this district, chairman of the commission on drainage is laying his plans to engineer the bill through the house. (Senator Berg was known as a very corpulent man with a voice to match.) If Senator Jacobson monkeys around too much with the band wagon this year, Senator Berg will turn on him one of his campaign roars and that should be enough to settle it. We confidently predict the bill will pass and become law this time. While this is a good prospect, we glory in the good the State Drainage Commission has done in the way of aiding and developing the Red River Valley. We feel enough interest in Kittson County to rise up at this time to call attention to the fact that Kittson County has not done her share of the good things in the past and it is high time that the citizens of that county insist that they do their fair share. To emphasize this fact we would draw attention to the following statement summarized from the present report of the Drainage Commission. The length of the drainage ditches in miles are: Grand and Traverse 1784, Wilkins, 1817, Clay 23, Norman 18, Polk 16, Marshall 19, and Kittson 5.73.

The Roller Mill which once stood south of the swimming pool does an active business.

There was agitation for a ditch connecting Skunk and Badger Creek to drain a 40 mile swamp at an estimated cost of $20,000. The people argued loud and hard before the County Board that the State had not appropriated any money to date and it ought to do so now. Albert Berg, State Representative had a program he endeavored to promote that would drain 76,000 acres of swampland.

In an article in the September 28, 1906 Roseau County Times the plan to drain Roseau Lake was described. It read:

> For 25 years there has been echoing down the county the cry of drainage. The minions in St. Paul, Crookston, and Duluth have heard at their conferences of

The combination flour, shingle, and lumber saw mill built by Ben Jacklin in 1892. The two small boys are Edwin and Tom Severson with their father Henry Severson, Ben Jacklin on the slab pile, Rasmus Flaa at the saw. The Henry Severson family had living quarters in the mill one winter.

this north country and its great undeveloped riches. They heard of vast acres of state land whereupon swamps and vegetable mold for centuries have been forming and should stamp the sign of agricultural wealth. They heard of the army of settlers growing larger yearly and settlers coming in confident that the state would assist in its development. This sound has gone to the very halls of Washington itself. Geo. A. Ralph is now systematically investigating the Roseau River. He has evolved that the main trunk of the river should be used as a drainage system. The strategic line is the Roseau River and the important point of vantage is calculated in the International Rapids on a line between the U. S. and Canada at a point at the extreme northwestern part of the County. Through the natural action of these rapids some 80 miles down the Roseau River from Roseau City an immense head of water, as of a dam has been held back. General damage is found every fall and spring and the spread of the current is decreased and its death results in bars and shoals that still further hold up the river. The lake is a natural reservoir of fertility and the condition has been endured for centuries. Swamps had formed and mold had gathered and rich grass has grown and has impeded the water. Roseau Lake was once 50 feet deep and has the richest land in the world. The Roseau Lake and Roseau River project would commence at the upper inlet of the Roseau Lake and would cut through the swamp formation in the lake for a distance of 24,000 feet to the outlet. The lower Roseau would continue downward through the rapids and through the obstruction.

The draining of Roseau Lake would provide 80,000 more acres of land for farming, and would cost 15 million dollars to complete. The people were reminded that the government was mindful of the people in Roseau and were doing "the fair thing."

Progress had been made in the area of drainage to the end that there were more and better connecting roads between farm houses, to trade centers, to schools, and to other systems of roads. Also by the draining of swamps, and Roseau Lake (and R. J. Bell and O. B. Ekman feuded over who really did the most in constructive effort to this end) new farm land was created.

The control of the level of the Lake of the Woods by the dam at Kenora also was a concern to the county. In 1907 when Rat Portage was first called Kenora, the Canadian government agreed to lower the height of the water for the relief of Roseau County, but in 1908 the controversy seemed to be renewed.

Sometimes the boundaries of the county were confusing and this led to complications. Sandy Island, now extinct, was located just off the mouth of the Warroad River in 1894. It was timbered with elm, ash, and oak. In 1895 there were two fisheries located on the island owned by the Coffee Brothers.

The *Roseau County Times* carried a story about Sandy Island declaring that a Blind Pig (place were illegal liquor was sold) was doing a flourishing business there selling "coffin varnish." What was more, the article claimed that another such establishment was located on a barge tied up in the Warroad River. There was a dispute about which county, Roseau or Beltrami, must assume the responsibility for the illicit trade. Many argued that it was indeed a part of Roseau County since it was described in the Township proclamation when the area was assumed from Beltrami, and was said to be "bounded on that side by the meandered shore of Lake of the Woods." Worry over the "pigs" was short lived, however, since the Norman Dam at Kenora raised the water level so that the island disappeared into Lake of the Woods, and the Warroad barge sales were discontinued. Representative Marshalk entered a bill to the legislature to keep the water at a lower level in 1904, but the attempt failed.

In 1898 the Red Lake Reservation acres were affected by a decision of the Land Commission, which had a like impact on the homestead lands of Roseau County. The decision denied the settler the right to pay $1.25 on a claim to hold it, and then move to other parts of the area. The settlers were required to reside the full five years on their claim before proving up. This was the era of settlement by homesteading, for 367,000 acres were opened up in the Red Lake Domain in 1899.

In June 1898 (the same year that the State Capitol at St. Paul was built) O. B. Ekman advertised that he could make homestead entries, enter land contests, and make final proofs and do all types of land office business in relation to homestead lands. "My business is done with accuracy and promptness," he advertised. "My maps are up to date. My office is opposite the Sjoberg store. Signed O. B. Ekman."

The day of May 12, 1899, was an exciting day in Roseau County, for homestead land in Town 160, Range 41 was opened for settlement at the Crookston Land Office. A correspondent to the *Minneapolis Journal* describes the event like this:

> The land in Roseau County is a short distance from the county seat, and a large portion is splendid agricultural soil. The first man to apply was Henry Hillman of Mickinock, North Dakota, and he had the right of way over the others owing to the fact that he had sat at the place where he could reach the knob on the door which was the main office during the whole night previous. There was a line all down the hall on both sides and the men sat all night whiling away the hours with stories.

The business of farming was now begun in earnest. In November 1899 in nine townships the threshing rigs for 119 farmers had 42 days of work in spite of a wet fall. It was reported that a record of 950 bushels a day were threshed with a total of 40,000 bushels of grain reaped. The wheat went 18 bushels to the acre which averaged 337 bushels per farmer. It became clear that the land would support the people if they were willing to work at it. But to make a cash profit the grain had to be shipped, and the railroad was nonexistent at this time. This created "railroad fever". Most people thought that a railroad would be built as soon as the need became evident, but this was far from the case. It took nine years of intense longing, pleading, cajoling, threatening, and agitated argument directed to the railroad magnate, J. J. Hill. It seemed that Mr. Hill felt some animosity toward the eastern end of the county and felt vindictive on the subject. Said Mr. Hill in 1899, "I have felt that a milk run is better than a wheat run for your part of the state. Let the Northern Pacific build your railroad." In July of the same year he let it be known that he would have no truck with men who drank or smoked or were of questionable character, so the *Times* admonished the county folk to be ever mindful of their morals. Perhaps the railroad tycoon could be

First dredge used on Roseau River 1906. Dredge was built on the Louis Larson farm. Here the dredge was working at the cutoff at Mickelson's place at the beginning of Roseau Lake. Dredge is 28x70, with a boom 60 ft. and dipper handle 45 ft. long, an "A" frame 45 ft. high. The dipper had 1½ yard capacity. This was the first dredge to go through the lake and into the muskeg.

won over by righteous men of good standing.

From 1899 until the actual date of the initial work on the railroad there were reports that soon Mr. Hill would start construction. But somehow the reports never did materialize — or so it seemed. Then the subject of conversation centered around the route that the railroad would go. As the rumors floated favoring one community or another the anticipation and eagerness for the train grew stronger with each passing day. That all important decision of the engineers could spell the growth or death of any of the little settlements. When Olaf Holdahl, whom Bell called "the father of Roseau County" came back from the state capitol, the rumors he brought back caused a real estate boom in Pelan, and a change in the town site for Greenbush.

In November, 1900 big headlines appeared in the paper:

RAILROAD ASSURED FACT

It didn't happen. In 1902 someone suggested a merger of the Northern Pacific, the Great Northern and the Burlington routes for this area. R. J. Bell hastened to write an article that denounced such a suggestion, and called the idea blackmail. He assured the

First section crew at Badger in August, 1908. From left to right, Section foreman Louis Anderson, Louis Anderson, Jr., Louis Schantel, Ezra Schantle, Ole Peterson. Standing on the hand car are Adolph Ostenson, Ole Monkerud, Adolph Grothe, and an unidentified person.

people that J. J. Hill had done more for the small towns in Minnesota than any other capitalist. In August of that same year the rumor was that the tracks would be laid west from Wannaska on a line ½ circle south from Roseau taking section 7 of Malung and then through Badger. The paper stated that Badger would be the "chestnut." The papers continued to print many articles praising the county's agricultural assets and potential. Perhaps Mr. Hill would read them and be advised.

But in 1904 the electrifying news came — RAILROAD TO GREENBUSH. Everyone rejoiced for the folks in the western part of the county and felt that the system would surely be extended within a year. Again there was disappointment in store for the pioneers. It was another four years before the dream of the railroad into Roseau and Warroad was realized.

In the meantime the farmers got irritable. "We will build it ourselves," they said and meant it, at least at the meeting. To acquire the money, the equipment and the know-how were strong deterrents. In 1907 there was a tone of desperation to their pleading. At a mass meeting the farmers were determined that somehow they must have the extension. "We will have a railroad," they declared.

And it finally happened. Wonderful news was spread across the paper in 1908:

RAILROAD THROUGH ROSEAU COUNTY — A DREAM REALIZED

There were wonderfully happy days that followed. A celebration was held, sponsored by the farmers and merchants of Roseau. The Great Northern was chartered by 100 people from Crookston on December 18, 1908, to be joined by Roseau and Warroad people for a ride on the train with a banquet at the end of the trip. A victory program with speeches, emceed by Billy Clay (whose real name was Wm. Wurschmidt) with flag waving and band playing initiated the Great Northern train into Roseau and Warroad.

Once the problem of the railroad was resolved there were others to take its place. In 1898 there was a war with Spain and there was an urgency for enlistments. Some of the early enlistees were R. J. Bell, Jesse Webster, J. Friend Holmes, John Norman, R. H. Medicraft, William Robertson, Peter Sjoberg, and M. J. Larson. It seems that the war was almost as unpopular in its day as the Viet Nam conflict was in the 60's for the statement "Soldiers in Manila do not believe in the war. Not one would stay a week longer if he could come home," appeared in the paper.

There was domestic rift as well in the little town of Roseau. Controversy over the building of the Pearl street bridge (now Center Street) arose. The project was bitterly opposed by one faction led by R. J. Bell. "It is not necessary," he wrote, "and if it should cost more than $50 it would be a crime." The solution he fostered was to seek donations from those who favored the bridge. Nonetheless bids were let to J. J. Ross on January 21, 1898, and in August of the same year the bridge was begun with village obligations to be $400. The remaining amount needed was to be raised by donations. The opponents did not give up easily for the paper berated the engineers and their work by calling the whole thing a

First train in Roseau October 23, 1908.

Roseau in 1904 looking north. (1) the Sedish Church (First Lutheran) (2) Webster Hotel (Moe's Floral) (3) O. B. Ekman Land Office (Office building) (4) Holm Photography (Wahlberg Pharmacy)

"botch" and said that it would take at least $50 to make the bridge sit firmly on the piers. That time proved them in error is attested to by the fact that the bridge with some repair withstood 83 years of wagon and automobile traffic as well as the buffeting of the ice jams that were almost a yearly occurrence at break up time in the spring. Now Roseau has a new wide and sturdy bridge on Center Street, over the Roseau River which cost $236,000.

But even before the railroad became a means of transportation there was a desperate need for roads. The earliest of the inhabitants in this area had been grateful for the waterways, the pioneers thankful for the sandridge – a sort of trail formed by the early Lake Aggassiz. But even the oxen and horses had a difficult time pulling the wagons on the roads which were really only beaten trails. In 1899 there was a petition for a road to Warroad. Finally some timber was cut to provide a corduroy for a summer road since it was argued that the farmers desperately needed the road to haul their grain to the Canadian Northern (later called Canadian National) railroad. Daily mail service started the first of January 1900, a day that marked progress, for the mail route necessitated a passable road. To build a road the settlers called for volunteer labor and personal contributions. On the 13th day of June of that year the county went on record as being bonded for $500 for better roads with villages shar-

Roseau in 1904. The building to the far right (1) is the blacksmith shop (2) the next shed on the same street after the vacant lot is the Ross barn (3) the building directly across to the north is the Golden Hotel and (4) Ross residence.

The first road grading contract in Roseau County was awarded to N. O. Johnson and Gust Johnson in 1901. The highway is #310. The drivers were Dave Stone, N. O. Johnson, Nels Mattson, Gust Johnson at the controls and John Dahlgren, the back driver. The Risberg house is in the background, later moved to town and is now the Herbert Monsrud residence.

ing the cost. In 1899 there was agitation for a road to replace the "mud" road to Hallock.

Telephone communication began in the county in 1903 when Stokes and Nereson townships erected their own line to the Garland post office and then south. C. A. Pearson in Malung provided a telephone line for Malung with the central being in the Miller confectionary store. In 1905 a big step in the service came into being when Fox-Jowett Telephone strung a line between Roseau and Warroad. Most of the poles had to be set in the winter time. A branch line between Badger and Warroad, a distance of 41 miles came into being in 1911.

The Malung line started by Mr. Pearson was in service for 54 years. Andrew Larson was elected in 1911 to be chairman of the telephone cooperative effort. Olaf Holdahl offered to sell his line from Roseau to Wannaska for $450. The money was raised by share holding. L. P. Larson was hired as "central" at $12.50 per month with the hours of service being from eight until ten each day. The users were to pay 50 cents a month and an additional five or ten cents for calls of longer distances. When Mr. Larson asked for a raise of $20 a month it was granted provided he would keep the switchboard open until midnight. By 1916 a line from Wannaska to Strathcona was operating.

One day Nels Nyhus had a "run in" with the Malung telephone company. His horses got out of hand and ran into a telephone pole injuring the horses. He offered to settle with the company for $150 or he would sell the horses to them for $225. The decision of the board was not reported.

The common practice of "rubbernecking" or listening in on a party line was a part of the entertainment of the day at a time when news was scarce. This was an accepted practice for it added to a spirit of neighborliness.

In 1917 the Northwestern Bell Telephone Co. had completed construction of the work of setting lines in the villages of Roseau and Warroad which would connect them to Crookston, Warren and other "important places." The central was to be located in Heyerdahl's Drug Store.

Civic pride became evident when in 1909 there was a move to replace the board walks with cement. The first one laid was from the depot Holdahl's store on one side, and to the Roseau Hotel on the other side.

The light plant was purchased from C. A. Moody by Mr. Lewis for $1,000 which was to be paid for at $90 a month. For a short time there was some agitation to discontinue using it as it was not a paying business. In 1899 when the heavy settlement occurred in Roseau County the picture changed and although electric lights were not used until 1914 and

The first cement sidewalk from the depot to Highway 11 built in 1909.

Log jams on the Roseau River in 1918. In the background is Sjoberg's store (now Anthony's)

then only on Tuesday and Thursday and turned off at ten at night in the early years, the electric lights were permanent. No more were kerosene lamps a necessity in town, though the rural areas were to struggle for many years before they got the benefit of the REA. In 1913 Warroad combined a light plant, town hall and water works for the sum of $29,925. Badger's effort to get electric lights in 1917 failed until the next year.

The first fire department was organized in Roseau in 1903, and in Warroad in 1906. The system was a volunteer program as it remains today. The first firemen in Roseau were J. J. Ross, Archie Alley, Nick Hagen, C. W. Bell, Paul Buran, Henry Carr, John Howe, John Halvorson, Robert Ross and Mike Holm. In all the villages the first effort to combat fire was mostly the bucket brigade operation and depended heavily on water from the rivers or lakes, which in the winter time posed many problems. Greenbush erected its tower and tank in 1905 and bought 800 feet of hose the next year for fire protection.

The Jacklin Dam held water for the mill race and furnished power for the mill. It provided water for logs which, for many years, were floated down the river. The dam, located just east of the railroad bridge where the Adams house now stands, was an intriguing place for small boys, especially since the Norquist saw mill was located nearby. (Later William Oveson had the saw mill above the dam.) The late John Buran recalled snitching dynamite with which he intended to kill suckers in the river. He tied a few sticks together and then tied them to a rock. Somehow the bundle got loose and floated down stream, but didn't get wet enough before it boomed off, breaking some windows up town. No report on the sucker take.

Lack of transportation was one of the biggest problems in the newly settled country. There were oxen to be had, but little in the way of roads. Mrs. William Warner, in 1902, took the steamboat to Sprague, and then boarded the train to Winnipeg. When the paper reported in 1902 that the Canadian Northern tracks were nearing Lake of the Woods and would run along the south side of Lake of the Woods through Warroad there was great rejoicing.

The **Roseau Queen,** a stern wheeler piloted by Captain Schoonover, and Captain Ritchey, operated on Roseau Lake for many seasons. It was the custom for hunters to hire the boat to take them to their favorite hunting grounds, which in the early days was more a matter of discriminating selection of camp sites than hunting grounds since the birds were so abundant. Sometimes the hunters would stay for a few days or a few weeks in their pitched tents enjoying the bounties of nature. On Sundays the families would picnic near the Emanuel Holm farm and then have an hour and a half ride on the boat with the band furnishing entertainment.

Some kind of records must have been made in those days for the heaviest loads hauled. Tom McKibbon in 1902 was reported to have hauled 6,300 pounds by team. One dramatic experience in hauling happened to Charles Meyer who was moving 4000 pounds of beef on a sled going across the ice of Lake of the Woods. The load proved too heavy and the beef and horses went through the ice. The horses were drowned and the beef lost, but Charles Meyer was saved.

The favorite sucker fishing spot — the Oveson dam (the river in front of Wm. Adams residence). Iver Torfin holds the small net, with Clarence Oie and William Oveson (small boy watching). 1900.

The Roseau Queen owned by Roy Briggs and Amous Ricker at the Emanuel Holm's place on the Roseau Lake.

The Roseau Band is part of the entertainment at a Sunday outing on Roseau Lake.

Holm's boat on the Roseau River in 1902.

Of course the stage coach was the "bus line" of the day. Passengers could leave Roseau at 8:30 a.m., arrive at Karlstad at 6:00 p.m., stay over at Stephen to continue their journey from there, all for a fare of $3.00 which included lodging and meals at the Half-Way House. Jim Reilley, a stage coach driver, was said to have driven 99,600 miles when George Roberts owned the business.

The pulse of the community is its newspaper. To the striving little county the weekly paper served a parent role – advisor, teacher, informant, disciplinarian of sorts, and molder of men's opinions.

In 1892, C. A. Pearson started a paper in Malung named the *Roseau County Press* which was published for three years. At one time, it was said, that when he could not buy printing paper he issued the copy on wrapping paper. Copies of Mr. Pearson's paper in bound editions are in the Roseau County Museum.

The *Warroad Plaindealer* was started in 1898 by W. A. Book and H. Sanders, and was sold in 1902 to Martin Widsten and C. Moorhead, and then shortly thereafter taken over by Mr. Widsten alone. He hired Archie MacDonald to operate it and Paul Buran to print it. When MacDonald later purchased the paper, he changed the name to *Warroad Pioneer* and took Paul Buran into the firm as editor. R. J. Bell commented that Mr. MacDonald was the "second" best looking editor in the county.

E. R. Umpelby was the editor of the *Greenbush Journal* which was welcomed by all so that the western part of the county could be heard from.

In 1895 the *Roseau Region* was started by C. Clark, but because of ill health he found he had to sell the newspaper he had just started. It was purchased by R. H. Medicraft who hired Paul Buran and Ray Gilbertson. Another paper called *The Roseau County Times* was started by R. J. Bell. Young Bell, an attorney, was volatile, fiery, and pitilessly frank as an editor. He never failed to speak out loud and clear on all issues, and published his opinions whether popular or not. The newspaper business was attractive to many in those days as there was a $5.00 fee for publishing the necessary proving up of claims, and the newspaper equipment was almost portable. The *Crookston Daily Tribune* carried this article in 1897:

> The village of Roseau which has perhaps 700 people and is 90 miles from a railroad has two lively newspapers – better in fact than is warranted by their surroundings. But each publisher has a side issue – from which good revenue is derived. One publisher operates a drug store, while the other has a lucrative law practice besides. Now comes a third fellow – a William Book who is president of the village council and he has purchased another newspaper outfit and is going to publish a third paper there to be called the *Plaindealer.* Mr Book has evidently got a grudge against the other two newspaper men and is going to have an organ of his own. A newspaper will soon be a necessary adjunct to every well regulated family up there.

By the beginning of the 1900's there were eight county papers:

The Pelan Advocate	G. H. Brenden, Editor
The Greenbush Journal	E. R. Umpelby
The Roseau County Press	C. A. Pearson (Office in Malung)

The Warroad Plaindealer	Book and Sanders
The Roosevelt Record	C. W. Bell
The Roseau County Times	R. J. Bell
The Roseau Region	R. H. Medicraft
The Badger Herald Rustler	J. Novotny

R. J. Bell was an editor who thrived on controversy. However, the more he "kept the pot boiling" the more he increased the circulation of his newspaper. People understood that behind the caustic tongue and opinionated articles was a staunch, intrepid editor whose main concern was the promotion of Roseau County. Bell advertised the county as a Garden of Eden, a young man's bonanza, and the fulfillment of the American dream.

In 1898 the *Roseau County Times* had an article which called all the lesser newspapers in the county "7x9 outfits." He begged the people to pay their subscriptions in cash or cord wood, and reminded them that he did the county printing for $200 when actually $400 was the estimated cost. In spite of this however, the *Roseau Region* got the printing business in 1898. The editors would sometimes feud among themselves and lend juicy bits to the readers. Once the *Roseau Region* accused R. J. Bell's paper of doing slip-shod work and editing. The *Roseau County Times* promptly replied that when they needed a "Practical Printer" they would call on the editor of the Region.

There was animosity between Roseau and Hallock for Mr. Bell read in the Hallock paper that a surveyor from their town was surveying the Roseau **swamps.** Said Mr. Bell, "Just when a good feeling had begun between Hallock and Roseau, this had to happen."

The Crookston Times noticed that Mr. Bell was on vacation in Illinois and Iowa, and reported in their paper: "He must have a locomotive in his grip, a passenger car under each arm and plans in his vest pocket. Now Roseau can expect railroad facilities."

The vitriolic pen of editor Bell was used on the author of an article that appeared in the *Svenska Posten* written by a Malung man who signed his name "A Good Populist." Bell used these adjectives to describe the incident thus: "The contemptible act of a disreputable man whose moral code is as black as his deceptive lies, and his lustful practices. Populist!"

Incidentally one surveyor (may have been the one Bell took exception to) seriously suggested a canal be dug from Lake of the Woods, through the chain of rivers and creeks to Roseau. Bell said "It would be a great saving in the expense of freighting besides being an inducement to fisheries to send their production to Roseau." History might have been changed had the idea materialized. The targets of Bell's pen were never spared, and there was always a feud raging. For example there was Sam Fullerton –

Friday, December 3, 1897 report from the Roseau Times:

> Mr. Sam Fullerton, State Game Warden accompanied by a deputy swooped down on Roseau last Thursday, took Thanksgiving dinner at the Roseau Hotel, and proceeded to do business. His watchful eye discovered a barrel of birds in the stage being shipped by J. H. Comlins. Joe was there, so was the deputy and Sam. In the name of the State and by virtue of the law for the preservation of game for the benefit of sportsmen Sam seized the barrel of birds. Joe proceeded to wipe the floor with the game officials and a short but decisive battle took place. Mr. Comlins was subdued and arrested and on the following day paid his fine. The jig was up. If there was any game of the contraband kind in town it was soon hid away. The officers on the following day went to Sutton and Benson's camp south of Haycreek but found nothing. The boys in the camp put up a job on them. They came in from the woods and taking in the situation drove at great speed past the camp to Roseau. The two officers quickly got their teams hitched up and pursued in hot haste but it was no go. The boys came in several miles ahead. They had no game in the wagon. The joke was on the warden. On Monday Sam swore out search warrants and searched the business places but got nothing for his trouble. The visit of Fullerton might prove of great benefit. What game we have here is fast decreasing and the killing of it ought to be stopped, not for the benefit of the city sportsman but for the benefit of the residents. Mr. Fullerton said that he would appoint a game warden for this section of the country and it is to be hoped that he will select a good man.

That was the start of it. No doubt Mr. Fullerton easily surmised where Mr. Bell's

A day's catch on Roseau Lake in 1902!

Salesmanship in 1900! The J. R. Watkins products are vended by the J. R. Watkins man, N. C. Husted as John Holm prepared to enter his jewelry store.

allegiance was placed and the feud really flared up. Bell said that Fullerton had heard that a moose was killed in Alaska and that he (Fullerton) was wondering what part of the state that was in. Fullerton said that Bell had been arrested when in St. Paul, and fiery R. J. refuted it and "told him off." Bell said that Fullerton arrested people just to have money in the state coffers and to make a good name for himself, and that Sam had knots in his head not created by study. March 18, 1898, Fullerton questioned Bell's honesty, and Bell reported that Fullerton himself was arrested at Wahpeton for shooting game illegally. Fullerton said that Bell should be arrested for eating moose meat out of season, and Bell reported that Fullerton had been punched in the nose in the state capitol. All this made for spicy reading and no sooner did this feud die than Bell had another target. For instance, G. H. Mattson, Superintendent of Schools got a great many tongue lashings from Bell, who declared him incompetent and an opportunist. The Methodist minister, C. E. Saunders had two deer which he had tamed. R. J. Bell's boys had a large Chesapeake dog that was trained to pull a sled. One day Rev. Saunders shot the dog, claiming that the dog had attacked his deer. The Saunders-Bell feud which started in 1916 went on for some years.

However, Bell was not always the fault finder, and always he was the loyal booster of his home county. He wrote:

> Roseau is an organized village of 700 inhabitants in the center of Roseau County established in 1895 and is the county seat. It is 65 miles east of Stephen, the shipping point of the G. N. Railroad, daily mail and stage line. The county has a population of nearly 5000, the greater portion of which does business at Roseau. There are many acres of free homestead land subject to entry in the county and 200,000 in the Red Lake Indian Reservation is also open to settlement. Principal industry of the farmer is cattle raising. The soil is rich, sandy loam with a white clay subsoil and there are immense quantities of meadowland producing the best hay to be found in the state. The county presents splendid inducements for the projection of a railroad from Crookston, Thief River Falls, and some points in the Vincent branch of the Great Northern or an extension of the Northern Pacific. The manufacturing in Roseau is flour, lumber, lime, brick, leather, and shoe pacs. Recent improvements include a water power of 100 h.p. built by R. Jacklin, proprietor of the flouring mill which has a run of 16 rolls. Roseau has an electric light plant owned and operated by J. Marshall, a practical electrician. A stage line carries the mail twice a week to Warroad on Lake of the Woods. The fisheries at Warroad do much business in this town.

The populace of the county took for granted that Roseau was the county seat — took it for granted that is, until Badger, an up and coming, flourishing community wondered why it might not have the honor. At least it was worth fighting for. On January 22, 1904 the battle for the county seat had reached the proportion of an out and out show down, and the Times reported:

> Judge Grindeland dissolved injunction suit and an appeal will be taken. Word came yesterday that the injunction in the county seat case had reached the stage when nothing remained for the county board of commissioners to do except to order an election to vote upon the proposition of the removal of the county seat to Badger. At this point an injunction was served restraining the commissioners, before this could be done, for further action until the court study the case, and decide on certain legal phases. Case will no doubt be appealed to the Supreme Court which sits in April.

Bell really worked on this issue. He warned Badger citizens that should they get the county seat they would have to produce a $20,000 court house. He also told them that the eastern part of the county would no doubt want to be cut off, being so far away from the county seat. So he concluded that a vote for Badger was a vote to divide the county, and he begged the people to think hard before voting. "Do not cut off your nose," he said, "to spite your face." The county seat remained in Roseau.

One story which Bell printed to hasten payments to the paper concerned a minister who announced to the congregation, "All who do not pay their debts, stand up." Only the editor of the paper stood up. The minister was about to ask why he did not pay his debts, but said instead, "Let us pray."

It was a bitter defeat for Bell when in

1907 he ran for County Attorney and lost the election. He was further embittered when in the same year O. B. Ekman took credit for bringing drainage benefits to the county.

On the 20th of December, 1907, the first colored picture appeared in the *Roseau Times*. It was a picture of Santa Claus being pulled by two bears with many animals in different poses watching on the side lines. Not only was the picture apropos for the season, but it was truly an innovation for a county newspaper.

Some interesting notes in the paper in those days were:

Girls, want to be a bride in a month? Red lips and rosy cheeks – Drink Rocky Mountain Tea.

Cow for sale – ¼ short horn – ¾ coyote – named Lillie. Attached to present abode by a stay chain. In May she goes away and returns with a red calf with wobbly legs. Will throw in double-barrel shotgun. Rather sell to a non-resident.

September 1898 – My wife having left my bed and board without just cause or complaint, I will not be responsible for her debts.

Advice on darning stockings – draw holes in stockings with stitches. Sew across hole, but the first problem is to get the stockings.

The well-being of the citizens was of concern to all in the new settlement. As early as November 1897 the paper carried a warning to the people to boil the water to guard against the danger of typhoid fever, after three new cases had been reported. The paper also had an article explaining the necessity of quarantines for families afflicted with the disease.

Dr. Oyen was in charge of the health of the young town so he was ever watchful for an epidemic. One issue of the paper included this note: "Dr. Oyen has not lost a case. He has a dead cure."

J. I. Adams, an optician, appeared upon the scene about this time and advertised that he had a large stock of gold and steel rimmed glasses, with the note: "I have a pair for all kinds of eyes. No charge for the examination." Another note in the paper was: "Nothing will improve your complexion like housework." This was in the days when a tanned skin did not indicate leisure time.

The wonders of Lydia Pinkham was commonly taken for granted. An arresting ad in the September 1897 *Roseau County Times* had a bold faced caption which read:

STOP WOMEN! (here was a picture of an amply bosomed woman holding up her hand). You are asked to consider an all important fact. You can talk freely to a woman like Mrs. Pinkham but it is revolting to confide in any man. Besides a man does not understand simply because he is a man. Many women suffer in silence, drift along from bad to worse knowing full well they ought to have assistance. You can talk feely to Mrs. Pinkham who has more experience than any physician. A woman's natural modesty impels her to shrink from exposing herself. Without price a woman can write to Mrs. Pinkham who has more experience than any woman in existence.

In the paper of November 1898 it was stated that Roseau County had been without a physician for three weeks and the health of the community was generally improved. The paper also had a suggestion that sulphur should be taken for the grippe since the Doctor was away. E. C. Chase advertised public bathrooms and added that this should solve many health problems.

That certain diseases and affliction had social status was indicated by this humorous note: Was Beatrice weeping because her husband had appendicitis? No, she said he didn't get it until it was out of style.

Some of the sure cures were St. Jacob's oil for relief of muscular problems, Bromo for a cold (and money back from the druggist if it didn't cure). There were Doan's Pills for backache (still on the shelf as a drug item), Swamproot, Crazy Crystals for constipation, Dr. Page's Catarrah remedy (with $500 reward for any case it couldn't cure), and a face bleach to remove sallowness, sunburn, suntan, and freckles. One ad stated that Peruna caused a Mr. Buck to live to be 114 years old.

In 1899 Dr. Hanley came to Roseau County and practiced for a year, after which he left to go to Cass Lake. In 1899 the schools were ordered to assume the responsibility for vaccination for small pox.

While there is often humor to be found in relation to most problems, so there is pathos to many. One such case was the plight of a man of German descent who, on May 4, 1900 brought his little daughter, who was suffering from pneumonia and a weakened heart, into Roseau by team and wagon. The father couldn't speak English and could not communicate his need in time to find the location of the doctor. The little nine year old youngster died.

And other diseases were a constant worry to the people. The disease we call tuberculosis and have fortunately conquered

Dr. Laurence Parker the musician-doctor who pioneered in medicine in Warroad and thrilled many with his traveling medicine show. He practiced a few years in Roseau, but spent from 1900 to 1940 in medicine in Warroad.

in a large measure, was the disease then called consumption. Anyone with a constant temperature, a dry cough, and continuous weight loss was in great fear. Chief Mickinock lost a daughter and a sister to the disease. Chicken pox, small pox, and mumps were rampant through the country in 1901. When in 1902 the paper related that the diseases were under control there was a great sense of relief. But in 1908 there were numerous cases of typhoid fever as well as diphtheria. A woman from Barto came to town with her sick children, stopping at the home of Iver Torfin. When the doctor saw the children and instructed the mother as to their care, he required that the household be quarantined and the Torfin home fumigated. A warning that all persons with a sore throat were to remain at home until the doctor could advise them, appeared in the paper.

The dental surgeons were mostly itinerant at this time. One ad read, "If you need teeth see Dr. Right." Doctor Gibson (father of Mrs. George Marvin) had an office in Warroad but made periodic visits to the other towns in the county. Some Warroadites can still remember his office situated where the Standard Station is now, especially because there was a set of false teeth clicking in the window.

It was comforting to the people when Dr. Norin installed a six bed hospital over his office which was located where the Hayes accounting firm is now. He hired a nurse, Miss Scott to assist him. This hospital served the people until 1904 when Dr. Muir built a home which for 20 years was also used as a hospital. This is the present James Helgeson residence.

Smoking was considered not only a detriment to the health of the individual but also a sad state of moral degradation. The paper included this item in the December, 1906 issue:

> A word to the little boy 12 or 13 smoking on the sly – What do you want to be when you grow up? A strong stalwart lad or a little puny dude? Do you want to be a thing to be pitied by parents, despised by girls, or do you want to be a man, strong, with hair on your face and muscles on your limbs. Do you want to end up in an asylum? Then quit smoking.

There could hardly have been a more flamboyant philanthropist in the entire history of Minnesota than Dr. Laurence Parker who lived and worked in this area. The great physiognomist from London, England was also a physician, a surgeon, a composer of music, a pianist, an entertainer, the owner of a traveling medicine show, a pharmacist, and a poet.

The education of young Laurence was carefully planned. He was given the opportunity to be in contact with musicians, the theater, and writers. His own grandfather wrote *The History of Rome* in fourteen volumes and received royal recognition from Italy and from Pope Pious IX. When an illness threatened the eyesight of the boy, it was deemed wise to send him to America.

Young Parker studied medicine in Iowa when he first came to this country, but soon he was eager to see what lay beyond, and he traveled north. In Roseau he set up a practice and later in Warroad and for a time all went well until both the *Roseau Times* and the *Roseau Region* reported that Dr. Parker might be a fraud and there was a court hearing to substantiate the fact.

The paper reported in the May 30, 1913 issue:

> Dr. Lawrence Parker of Warroad charged with a misdemeanor was given a jury trial before Justice W. H. Alley, Tuesday afternoon. The jury was about equally divided and could not agree. The court discharged the jury. The complaint made by Fred Hoyez charged that Dr. Parker in August 1910 prescribed electrical treatment for Mrs. Hoyez for which he charged a fee, Dr. Parker not being licensed to practice medicine. The prosecuting witness practically admitted that the action was brought up to get even with Dr. Parker who had quarantined his home for scarlet fever – the case will likely be re-tried.

Dr. Parker played the piano like a virtuoso. He entertained in his home and for groups. There are some who recall how the dignified gentleman with the flowing white hair would seat himself at the piano and with a great flourish begin his concert. He would not only play the best of classical music but would include his own compositions, such as "Lake of the Woods," and "Hurrah for the Red, White and Blue," or he would improvise music that thrilled his audience. Some of his tunes are being revived now by ensemble groups from Warroad.

After Dr. Parker had learned to concoct medicine with a "kick" to it, he assembled a traveling medicine show. He called the medicine "Kickapoo Indian Remedy" which was known to be a sure cure for almost any ailment, but especially for advanced cases of melancholia. With his flair for the theatrical and credit from Noyes Brothers and Cutler, he set up a company that could put on a real extravaganza. There were some eight or nine performers, most of them with circus acrobatic abilities. The colorful troup included tightrope walkers, trapeze artists, trained dogs, and he even included some freaks from the animal world. Dr. Parker kept an audience enthralled with the acts, his sales pitch, and his lively piano numbers, and the Kickapoo medicine sold by the cases. His itinerary included all of northern Minnesota and much of North Dakota.

In 1900 he was persuaded to settle down in Warroad and practice medicine. What goods he had in Roseau were shipped by steamboat to Sprague and then by railroad to Warroad. While this mode of life might have been less glamorous, it was surely not less arduous for the doctor. His services were sought through the countryside and in Canada. With money from his family he built a 14 bed hospital in Warroad. In order to visit the sick he traveled any way he could, by horses, by "hitching" rides, or by going on the hand cars of the CN. Later he got his own Model T, and then an Oldsmobile. Surely the horse and wagon must have been the preferred modes of travel, for when he had a driver he could catch forty winks in the back of the buckboard.

Dr. Parker's son Irvin related how the doctor often told the story of how the wolves had followed his wagon on a return trip from Roseau, frightened the horses until they became a wild run-a-way team. The wagon pitched this way and that until Dr. Parker finally threw his bag of instruments at them and went back for them the next day.

Perhaps one of his most gruelling experiences came about when he was called by his friend Paul Marshalk (later to be representative from this district) to go to Zippel Bay with him as Mrs. Marshalk was very ill. It was bitterly cold and the Marshalk home was located some fifteen miles across the frozen Lake of the Woods. Most men would have deemed such a trip sheer folly, but Dr. Parker with Mr. Marshalk and two other men loaded up the Oldsmobile and set out. The ice ridges on the lake caused the men great concern and finally the car got hung up on one of them. A block and tackle which they had included with supplies disengaged them. Dr. Parker performed an appendectomy in the kithcen of the home, and thus saved Mrs. Marshalk's life. In due time they started back home and encountered more trouble in a fierce blizzard. The men could do nothing about the car in the deep snow so they started out walking, each fearing this would be the last walk of their lives. Finally they got across the lake, sighted an old cabin in the woods and took possession. Here they built a fire, boiled some used coffee grounds and stayed secure until daylight.

Dr. Parker was a friend to Indian and white alike, and got paid for his services only in a minority of cases. However, he risked all to help people and never counted his bad debts, but reckoned his pay in helpful services. He built a large building across from the CN depot after he had lost four other buildings in fires which also took many of his instruments and his medical library. In the new building he put a hospital upstairs, had a theater and salesroom down stairs and stocked about 25 pianos for sale along with glassware and dishes.

The illustrious doctor died March 16, 1956, at the age of 88. His son said that he remembers the hordes of people who came to pay their respects to the family at the time of death, and among them almost the entire Indian population. All had been a friend of the good doctor. Dr. Parker's widow still resides in Warroad.

The first official mail service in the area which is now Roseau County dates back to April 12, 1888, when the Jadis post office was established onc half mile north of the present town site of Roseau. Horace W.

Sutton, who operated a store at that location, was the first postmaster. Since this whole territory was then in Kittson County, the mail was carried from the county seat, Hallock, by the same teams that hauled the freight for Sutton's store. With no regular schedule, mail deliveries were often as much as two weeks apart. Settlers would call at the store for their mail, and usually for that of their neighbor and neighbor's neighbor. Thus the mail was relayed from one to the other until all were served. (This relay system, by the way, was often a deciding factor in the establishment of postoffices throughout the county as the number of settlers increased.) The original post office boxes used in Mr. Sutton's store are now the property of the Roseau County Historical Society and may be seen at the County Museum.

The post office at Pelan was established on the same date as Jadis, April 12, 1888; however, when Kittson County was divided in 1895 to form Roseau County, Pelan remained in Kittson County. Later (sometime after 1912) Pelan post office was moved across the line into Roseau County.

The second post office to be established was Badger, on December 28, 1889, with Elias B. Irish as the first postmaster. This is the oldest post office in the county retaining its original name. (Jadis post office was moved and the name changed to Roseau on February 16, 1895.)

Many of the early settlers located near the Roseau River. This was true in the Ross community where the third post office was established on June 30, 1890, with Ole Johnson as the first postmaster. Since early post offices were usually located in the homes, their locations would change from time to time as the postmasters were changed. Thus one of the early locations in the Ross community was about one half mile west of the community's present site. A short time later it was located near the Indian Village east of Ross on, or near, the George Jorgenson farm. Later when mail came to Roseau by railroad, it was brought to Ross by the star route carriers.

During the time that Roseau was a part of Kittson County, five post offices were established. Of these the first three have already been mentioned: Jadis, Badger, and Ross. Fox was established on November 15, 1892, with Tollef S. Nomeland as postmaster, and Greenbush on September 15, 1892, with Fidelia Hedges as postmaster. The original Greenbush post office was located at what is now known as the "Old Greenbush" site, about two miles east of the present location. Four of the first five post offices established were still operating in 1959.

"Coming for the mail" at the Goos Post Office.

There was unofficial mail service prior to the establishment of the first post offices, but very little is known about it. This lack of information may be attributed to the fact that there were very few settlers receiving mail. These people were occupied with other things according to J. W. Durham, who, in his book, *Minnesota's Last Frontier*, speaks thus of the summer of 1887: "Our nearest post office was located at Fir, some sixty miles away, so our mail did not worry us a great deal. Daily papers and magazines did not intrude upon our time. We were living in a world all our own with other things to occupy our time."

Fir, by the way, was located south of Karlstad where the Stephen trail came in. The relay system was in use at that time too. Mail would be picked up by the stage drivers or others visiting Hallock or Stephen, brought to the usual stopping places, and relayed again to other destinations.

After the division of Kittson County in 1895, the mail came from Stephen instead of Hallock, then through Pelan to Greenbush, Badger, Roseau, and Warroad. This was a much improved service, as the mail now came in once a week. Some of the early carriers were John Erickson, 1896; Andrew Olson, 1897; George Roberts, 1900-04.

Malung (now discontinued) had the distinction of being the first office to be established in Roseau County proper (the first five being in late Kittson County). This office was established July 23, 1895, with Daniel Garighan as postmaster.

The eleven year period from 1895 to 1905 saw the establishing of twenty-eight new post offices throughout the county. Over half of these were established in the years 1897, (6), 1899, (4) and 1901, (5). It may have been only coincidence but thirty-one post offices were established in odd numbered years and only fourteen in even numbered ones. There is, perhaps, no special significance in this fact unless it might have been a politician's way of saying "thank you" for his election in the even-numbered year. Politics did play an important part in the establishment of post offices . . . and the appointment of postmasters.

As the population increased and new post offices were established, each township could have an office if its population warranted it. Records show that there have been at least forty-five postoffices organized in Roseau County, some of which lasted only a few years. Mandus was in operation less than one and one-half years, and Dawd and Boobar only a little over three years. Some places thought of as post offices were really only "half-way places" where a carrier or some other person would bring the mail to have it distributed by the "relay" system; thus, their designation as post offices was incorrect. In general, all the early offices were operated in connection with stores, and became a general gathering place for the immediate community.

The establishing of Eddy post office is typical of the manner in which many offices originated. Mr. J. E. Budd obtained thirteen signatures to a petition circulated among the homesteaders. This petition was forwarded to Congressman Eddy of Minnesota who took over from there. The office was established March 1, 1897, (by the Post Office Department) and was named in honor of the Congressman. Mr. Budd was the first postmaster. This office was located seven miles south of Roseau.

The establishing of the River post office illustrates another typical method. Patrons petitioning for an office or the postmaster-to-be must guarantee carrier service from the nearest source of mail supply to the location of the proposed office. Often the postmaster had to carry the mail for the first six months, a sort of probationary period, or until the need for service could be established and a regular carrier appointed.

The five settlers who had petitioned for a post office at River needed a carrier to bring the mail from Pencer to River; hence they met and nominated Mr. Albert Hayes as the carrier for the trial period of ninety days. Each of the five agreed to pay him ten dollars for his work. Mr. Hayes accepted and carried the mail, on foot, a distance of ten miles, three times each week. That was in 1907 – over fifty years ago – and Mr. Hayes now deceased was never paid.

Charles Peterson, an Icelander living in the Duxby community, found it impossible, at times, to cross the big swamp to the south to get his mail and that of his neighbors at the Lolita post office (located on the Andrew Gordon farm in Moose township). The need for a post office at Duxby thus clearly demonstrated, permission was granted, and the Duxby post office was established November 2, 1897, with Mr. Peterson as the first postmaster.

Flossie was the lady-about town in the early days. Some senior citizens still can remember how she came to town all gussied up and splendid in her bustles and feathered hats.

One citizen recalled that Flossie once bought a case of beer at the local tavern, requested delivery of the beer and a lift home for herself. The gentleman who recalled the story was a small boy at the time and often accompanied the delivery wagon. However, he felt some tinge of embarrassment to be seen in such company so walked a half block behind the entire distance.

R. J. Bell, who never minced words and was known to give the readers many a juicy bit, wrote in 1900:

> A masquerade gave the notorious Flossie a chance to appear among respectable people. She came out of Dagan's beer parlor.

However, the names of the other citizens who came out of the saloons did not get newspaper space.

On June 22, 1900 Flossie's house burned at a loss of $600 and then on the 28th of the same month the newspaper reported that she had been fined for keeping a house of ill fame. Not all the pioneers were without reproach.

There were many spirited citizens who were dedicated to the good of the county, but they are too many to write about in detail.

However, one such outstanding gentleman was Israel Sjoberg who was something of a Beau Brummell; always fastidiously dressed in the best fashion, with even a hint of artificial coloring to his cheek and lips, he cut a colorful figure. The Sjoberg brothers, Israel and Peter, had many enterprises – general merchandise stores in Roseau and Badger, a general store in Salol, a saw mill, a cheese factory in Badger, a snuff and cigar factory in Roseau, a flour mill in Badger, and perhaps there may have been others. He wrote to his people in Sweden singing praises of the new land, the general area and the new town. "I am mayor here," he wrote, "and this is like being a king in Sweden." R. J. Bell accused him of pretending to be a Republican, but he denied it and wrote articles for the *Swenska Posten* declaring that he was a Populist, first and always. In one election he showed something of racial prejudice and egotism for he declared that a mere Finlander could not defeat him. Mr. Sjoberg made many trips to the State Capitol in behalf of the county, especially during the battle for the railroad, and the struggle for aid for drainage in the county. He wrote numerous articles for the paper showing how situations that were similar were handled in the "old country." Being as aggressive as he was in politics, he found some dissenters to his causes and his methods. One incident that brings a little chuckle now was the story about the time he was accused of desecrating the American flag. Ole Rice, it was reported, came to the rescue. Mr. Sjoberg was said to have paraded through the town with a shoddy, torn flag and nailed it to his store. When he was accused of a misdemeanor he stated that he had a right to do so since it was his birthday.

The "king" felt that he had unerring judgement, for when his carpenters were at work on his buildings he would inspect and dispute some of their engineering processes. He said he cared not a whit what the ruler might indicate, because he could see that it was not straight.

A debonair figure he was, self-assured, a bit egotistical, but always a firm believer in the prosperous future of Roseau County.

In the chronicle of the era it must be noted that the settlers had their vicissitudes in the form of suicides, murders, and accidental deaths. Without going into any detail on the events it might be noted that Erick Nystrom was murdered in 1897, Albert Jensen and Josie Johnson both met tragic ends, and a man was found dead in a closet of the Hotel Roseau in 1903.

Two burglars who had robbed stores in Badger were caught in Two Rivers, and were apprehended for a hearing, jailed and then escaped on the way to the Crookston jail. Then we have the story about a Mr. Lewis who was put in jail but protested his innocence, and was allowed to leave the jail upon promising to turn up for the next term of court. He did so, and was found innocent.

One of the most tragic happenings occurred to Frank Tuber, who when as he was dispensing drugs happened to drink from a glass that had a few drams of carbolic acid in it. He died in agony.

The obituary notices were full of flowery commendation. When L. M. Murray died (he was the father of Mrs. Harry Sanders) it was reported thus:

> ". . . blood went out of the body and soul at the advanced age of 4 score years and 6 months – death due to no cause except that years of vigorous life had dimmed the spark that held the departure of immortality from the body. He had lost his faithful consort in 1852."

Olaf Holdahl, one of the first pioneers, came to Roseau County in 1887 from Nelson Park in Marshall County. Mr. Holdahl owned land where the Ross creamery was located and in 1896 entered into partnership with A. H. Foss and a brother, Bendix Holdahl. In 1905 he incorporated the bank called Citizen's State Bank. He had an interest in the flour mill, helped Pearson to organize a telephone company and he served on the school board in 1890. Besides his business interests he was president of the council and was active in the Roseau County Historical Society. He says of himself in his own account entitled *Milestones from my Life:*

> "In 1893 I was sent to Warroad to trade with the Indians. I had a load of goods for them and I was to buy fish and furs from them. There was a demand for fish if one peddled it to North Dakota. I set up my place of business in the home of Chief Na-May-Puck. There were others later, but I was the first merchant in Warroad.
>
> I was the first buttermaker. During summer season we bought butter, both salted and unsalted. It was my duty to work the butter, salt it and color it, and it was put in a cache until fall. We had a carload by fall but we lost money on it – paid 12½ cents and only got 9c for it.
>
> I was the first Register of Deeds – Nomeland asked me to go to Hallock to transfer deeds from Kittson

County Register to Roseau. I did it willingly. I completed it in 1896, and A. H. Foss and I were offered a partnership with brother Bendix. We homesteaded land on which Ross creamery now stands, and I turned this in on the deal and signed a note for $15,000 and I became one-third holder in business of Holdahl Brothers.

This was also the age of prospecting. The paper carried these interesting notes:

Dec. 24, 1897 – Ole Johnson was down from Lake of the Woods and returned home Friday. Mr. Johnson was prospecting for gold and has five well defined loads. (lodes?) He placed them on the market and was offered $1500 for them but refused saying that $5000 was more like it.

February, 1899 – Rainy Lake – Gold experts say that there is $100,000 worth of gold in the mines of Mikado, the Sultana, and the Regina. (These names later were used as names for beer – Mikado Pale Ale, Sultana Lager, and Regina Beer.)

October, 1900 – Pat McCoy discovered a vast vein of Iron Ore. R. J. Bell, Oscar Nelson, and Joe LaFond have an interest in it.

January 4, 1907 – Gold and silver found on the Louis Larson farm. Specimens were sent in. Assayers say gold goes 1/10 oz. to the ton and is worth $3.00. Silver ¾ oz. to the ton and is worth 52c. Therefore it is not enough to mine.

Though the story of the big fish did not occur in Roseau County, it did come out of the Roseau River. So spectacular was this event that it was written about in all the papers of the area, and photographed by a Mr. Barraclough from Winnipeg. Mr. Waddell, a miller from Dominion City hauled in a fish weighing 400 pounds, which measured 15 feet in length. Mr. Waddell and his son Jim were out to make some collections for gristing from the farmers when they decided to stop for lunch and tea. As young Jim went to the river to dip his pail for some water, he noticed a commotion in the middle of the deep pool from which he was going to take water. It had been a dry summer and there were just a few deep pools left in the slow moving current. Jim got his father, and by encircling the spot and poking with a stick, they got the fish to put his head out of the water. They could see it was a monster. The elder Waddell armed with an ax was able to strike the fish when he raised up again. It was necessary to hitch the team to a rope pulled around the gills of the fish, and they brought it to dry land. It was the largest known sturgeon ever to come out of the river.

On the 5th of May 1906, the first park was donated to the village of Roseau by Olaf Holdahl. It was a one acre plot, directly in front of the former Messiah Lutheran Church. This is the site, incidentally, of the old Indian graves to which in the very earliest of settlement days the Indians came with their gifts for the dead.

First hockey team organized in 1908 on the rink where the power plant is now located. From left to right: Selmer Oie, Oliver Oie, Bob Ross, E. Jacklin, L. A. Thompson, C. Peterson, and Carl Von Rohr.

An agricultural society was formed on the first of June in 1904. The first directors in this new society were: Dean Benson, Israel Sjoberg, A. A. Waag, A. L. Alley, Roger Bell, Bendix Holdahl, John Ross, Ed Olson and S. T. Holdahl. This was the first attempt at organization for the betterment of farming in the county. It is interesting to think about what strides have been taken through federal, state and local effort to make agriculture the science that it has become.

Since Roseau County is an agricultural area, it was natural that the early pioneers should want a county fair to celebrate the harvest and motivate the farmers. In August of 1906 the Agricultural Society decided to buy 35 acres in the northwest corner of Waterman's farm for a fair grounds. They decided to sell stock in the corporation for not less than $2000. One block of land was to be kept for either a courthouse or a schoolhouse. There was no problem to raise the money for this project. The capital stock was $5000. The first fair was scheduled for September 20, 21, and 22, but had to be postponed to October 11, 12 and 13th.

The people of Roseau County have always been sports minded; it is recorded that in 1903 there was a bowling alley in Roseau, and one soon thereafter in Warroad. John Amundrud scored 199 as the high bowling score the first year.

Even as early as 1908 the people were interested in hockey. The first hockey rink

Fourth of July in 1895. Mike Holm was the bicyclist.

in Roseau was built by volunteer labor, of course. Members of the first team were Selmer Oie, Oliver Oie, Bob Ross, E. Jacklin, L. A. Thompson, C. Peterson and Carl Von Rohr. It must have been a problem to find competing teams out of town, but they played Hallock and Warren, and soon thereafter Warroad.

In spite of the fact that the settlers had much work to do simply to establish themselves, they had time for cultural activities as well. In 1898 a band was organized in Roseau with the village supplying the instruments. The director was Joe Baugh, county surveyor. Members of the first band in Roseau were Mike Holm, O. A. Holm, L. P. Dahlqust, J. Cornes, L. Spence, J. U. Skoglund, C. W. Bell, Harry Miller, Ole Sjoberg, Richard Sjoberg, Joe Baugh and Claud Bell. This band was called on to perform for many occasions, chief of which were the Fourth of July celebrations. In December of the year 1898, Mike Holm started an orchestra. Mike played a violin concert as a benefit to get the organization financed. In this concert Boyd and Jacklin played a clarinet duet, and a cornet solo was played by Joe Baugh. The orchestra personnel included Mike Holm, Morris Goodwin, Alex Jacklin, Mrs. John Spencer, J. H. Baugh, Robert Ross and Edward Jacklin. Carl von Rohr joined the group a little later.

Probably the most talented musician to come out of Roseau County was Henry Spencer. He was a most accomplished clarinetist and won recognition also as a composer and for his orchestrations. A few of the early citizens of Roseau can still remember hearing the virtuoso Spencer on the clarinet and they agree that he was superior to almost any other musician they have ever heard.

Among other cultural events was a gramophone concert given in 1902 at Eddy's store which was well attended. Professor Paulson directed the evening's entertainment. In 1907 the Malung Singing Choir sponsored a literary and musical evening in the I.O.G.T. Hall.

The Fourth of July celebrations started as early as 1894. The programs included an early morning gun salute, a speech often given by a local dignitary, races for the children, a baseball game, and a bowery dance. These celebrations were much anticipated by children and adults alike. Then the tasty potato salad, home baked pies, lemonade, and all the wonderful delicacies that the good Swedish and Norwegian cooks could produce were on hand. A popular speaker at several of these celebrations was G. M. Stebbins, and the music was the band or orchestra of the villages. All the little girls had new dresses for the big day and the boys had a new pair of home made knicker pants for the event.

As early as 1906, the people in the county were fully aware of the wisdom of preserving what they could of the past for posterity. The first Historical Society of Roseau County was formed on the 30th of November of that year. Later the Fryklund museum (discussed in a later chapter) which contained an enviable collection of artifacts and memorabilia, not only from Roseau County but from various parts of the world, was purchased by the society and became the nucleus for one of the finest museums in the state of Minnesota. At present the Library-Museum complex is under construction, located beside the Municipal Building.

There were many bombastic speeches and articles in the paper relative to the political climate of the period. The people did not take lightly their privilege to vote. Even as far back as 1887 when there was an election on the question of liquor and the result was for a dry county, there was much dissension and a petition for a recount was circulated. The result, though, was the same as the first count. In 1905 the village marshall fined a saloon keeper in Roseau because he had pulled the shades of his saloon through Sunday, and the complaint read, "Fined for not letting the full light of the Sabbath shine across the bar from the front window."

R. J. Bell had no time for the Populist Party, and vented his anger in his paper saying in June 1898, "When an ignoramous is allowed to dominate a party it is time to leave it alone to die a natural death." However, R. J. Bell was in favor of Albert Berg when he ran for speaker of the house and he wrote many articles to praise him. One of his favorite puns was, "He is big enough and strong enough for the position." (Berg weighed close to 300 pounds.)

All the settlers were dismayed when I. Torfin resigned as Clerk of Court on July 22, 1904 and R. J. Bell said, "We are all surprised because Torfin is such an upright man."

In September 23, 1904 when Bell was defeated by Mike Holm for Judge of Probate, Bell was disappointed in his fellow pioneers. He reminded the people of how hard he had worked for the county. He said of Holm's election and his defeat, "Such is greatness. I was hit hard by friend and foe alike. I am sure that the opposition (to Holm) shed tears in every part of the county."

In September 1907 N. E. Wold carried on a spritely and humorous campaign in his communications to the paper. He stated that while he was canvassing, his son did the farm work including the shocking of the grain, and the hired girl pitched in to help, and "wasn't this a shocking thing to do?" He also composed poetry which read:

If you turn me down
I will not frown
But thank you all the same
That you another one did name.

If down you will tilt
With anyone my vote to split
Why not be brave and true
In building somebody's waterloo?

If not in office my bread I earn
Unto my acres I will turn
And though I and my faults are fifty
I will scratch my farm like sixty.

He ended the letter by saying: "I do not like the primary law running around cigar in hand seeking to devour each one you meet. No siree; but you can swallow me if you think you'll not get sick of it."

The first decoration Day parade May 30, 1901. John and Mike Holm are leading the band. Ole Oie is the sdrummer. The parade started at the Webster Hotel and proceeded east.

The first officers of the village of Roseau were:

President	W. H. Book
Recorder	James Webster
Treasurer	H. W. Sutton
Trustees	Harry Howe
	J. H. Comlins
	Olaf Holm
	A. O. Skagen

Township Clerks were:

Jadis	Iver Torfin
Skagen	A. G. Lokken
Pohlitz	Charles Peterson
Dieter	E. E. Olson
Malung	L. O. Peterson
Moose	Hans Erickson
Barto	P. P. Kukowski
Spruce	E. W. Sehlstrom
Stafford	Nat Eilertson
Soler	E. Nelson
Stokes	B. C. Satter
Grimstad	T. Knutson

In 1900 there were seven parties in the gubernatorial race which were: Republican, Democratic, People's Prohibition, Midroad Populist, Social Democrat, Socialist, and Labor.

There were so many public spirited citizens of the past who have contributed immeasurably to the development of our county, but it is impossible to record even a small part of those accounts. One, though, who contributed not only to our county but also to the state of Minnesota must have some mention. In the Encyclopedia of American Biography an article about Mike Holm is included. It reads in part:

> A record of public service unique in the annals of his home state of Minnesota was that of Mike Holm, who held office longer than any other man in the history of the commonwealth. He also established a record in receiving a higher percentage of the vote cast in any single election than any other Minnesotan. "Mike" as he was known to literally thousands throughout the state, possessed a genius for making friends. He was a public office holder throughout the years of his mature life, but his executive and administrative abilities represented but one phase of his versatile nature.

He was born at Ringvattnet, Jamtland, on June 17, 1876. He and two brothers took "squatters claims" in Roseau County. During his early life he bartered with the Indians for venison and furs, and a mutual trust was enjoyed.

He kept his legal residence in Roseau throughout his career. He was first elected justice of the peace in Roseau County when he was twenty-one years old, and then served as councilman, and later as Judge of Probate.

Mike Holm who was Secretary of State for 31 years.

He became Secretary of the State of Minnesota in 1921, was re-elected to the office every biennium for the rest of his life. He was urged by many to become a candidate for the governorship of the state, but he declined saying, "I have only one ambition and that is to serve conscientiously and with all my ability in the office to which the people have elected me several times. If my services here merits my continuance in this office, I am extremely gratified and happy."

Mike Holm also served as an officer in several organizations, namely Association of Secretaries of State, American Association of Motor Vehicle Administrators, the American Institute of Swedish Arts, Literature and Science and the John Erickson League of Minnesota. He managed the county exhibits at the State Fair to do great credit to his own people.

The little old red school house, scene of nostalgic memories for many of our older Roseau County citizens, has passed from the educational picture, but never to be forgotten are the educational experiences that bring a twinkle of merriment or even a tear to the eyes of the teachers and students of those days.

Mrs. Jens Jenson (Anna Torfin, daughter of Iver Torfin) was a pioneer school teacher in 1916. A typical school day in Mrs. Jenson's career went like this: She had to arise early, around five o'clock in order to get to her school (which was district No. 44 first and then district No. 62) to get the pot-bellied stove going so that the school children could be warm when they arrived around nine o'clock. The wood was always cut and plentiful, thanks to the fathers or the big boys in the classroom. The school was not fortunate enough to have a caboose over a wagon to transport the students as some schools had, so Miss Torfin's students arrived cold and sometimes frost bitten from their long walks to school. Each student carried his books from which he had done his assigned homework, and a syrup pail which contained his lunch. Each one said a cheery, "Good mornin, Miss Torfin." If they were early they helped with the preparations for the day – to sweep the floor and to carry water for drinking and washing. (They had a common drinking pail and dipper, and a wash basin into which they poured water warmed on the stove.) The coats and sweaters hung on pegs in the "cloak room," and at nine o'clock they sang the opening song, "America," and said the pledge of Allegiance to the flag. Then they settled down for the routine lessons of the day. Miss Torfin heard at least 32 groups recite while the others were studying. They sat at home made desks and tables, wrote on blackened board, and assiduously learned their ABC's and language and sums.

Then it was lunch time – a welcome break after a long hike and a morning at lessons. By rows the children were ordered to stand, turn, and pass to wash their hands for the noon lunch. It was interesting for the youngsters to peer into the pails of fellow students for exchange of food, or just to share. None went hungry.

After lunch, lessons were resumed. It seemed as if the children could concentrate in spite of the loud recitations of older or younger school mates, for each was absorbed in his own studying unless there was a good joke to be shared. The children had heard about the time when instead of a lamb that came to school with Mary, a ram came with Sam when Lydia Hetteen (Mrs. P. A. Larson) was the teacher and held school in a church building. The ram had been teased by the boys, and when he butted his way into the school the naughty boys scurried on top of the desks and the teacher had to catch the ram by the horns and hold him until they came to the rescue and pushed him out the door.

Baseball and king of the mountain were some of the favorite games of the children during recess and at noon hour.

A few older boys had taken to chewing "snus" and the parents asked Miss Torfin to use her influence to make them stop this practice. "I promised I would do this in school," said Miss Torfin "but since the boys are bigger than I, I am afraid that I will not have much success at recess."

Once when Miss Torfin came to school at the beginning of the term and was busy getting things in order at her desk she was confronted by five gangly youths, one of them a year older than herself, who were going to enroll. A shiver of fear ran down her spine at the thought of ordering these older boys to do lessons, and she confessed that had the school house had a back door she might have run through it, but the boys respected her and all went well. It seems the same then as now – the students respond to a sympathetic teacher.

Christmas time at school was special for then the students would "show off" for their parents. The usual recitations and singing were on the program as well as pantomime of the Christmas story complete with bathrobes for the shepherds. One boy who was wearing long pants for the first time did not learn the recitation his parents insisted he should have, but he was declared the best performer of all as he stood and twitched and turned in embarrassment on the stage.

How the students crammed for the State Board Examination! This was the final test of the year and it meant passing or failing so it was in fact, "the moment of truth."

At this time the requirements for the schools were that each one be held for one month. Each pupil must attend at least one day per term. This was the basis for state aid. The age of the students ranged from five to twenty-one years, and each district was required to have a definite enrollment to be financed. It was not surprising then that often the mothers of pupils would enroll to enable the school to be established. But sometimes the parent enrolled in order to learn English.

Before the beginning of consolidation of schools in 1950 there were 112 school districts in Roseau County. The difficulty of travel coupled with the severe northern climate were the two factors that prompted every small settlement to create its own district. In spite of the close proximity of the schools the students still had to walk long distances to attend, and the attendance requirement in the very early days was sometimes only a 30 day period. O. A. Roberts in his book on the history of schools entitled *Footsteps in Education* has compiled data from the various districts that would provide the reader with more information. Only the schools created before the 1900's are included in this history.

In the memoirs of Lydia Hetteen Larson who was an early teacher in Malung and Stafford townships, she records that the Malung School was first held in the Pher Hetteen log home. The family had to move upstairs to accommodate the 36 pupils who attended the school from time to time. It was in 1893 that a school board was formed: K. A. Sireness was clerk, P. E. Roseen, treasurer, and Henry Severson acted as director. The teacher, Anna Johnson, taught for a monthly salary of $30. Her pupils sat at home-made desks, and long recitation benches. In 1894 the school was moved to a bachelor's home, Daniel Peterson, who got $4.15 per month for rent.

Spruce township had its school before Roseau County was organized. It was on July 30, 1894 that Isaac Winterhaus was elected clerk, Halvor Shervin and L. Lofstedt, directors. The school was first located on the H. E. Bjorkman farm and later moved to Section 28 where it burned to the ground. Ida Coombs was the first teacher.

Roberts has recorded in his history the beginning of District No. 39 in Pohlitz Township which organized its school in 1895 in the John Vik home at Duxby. It was recorded by Ernest Schmidt who started the school

The first school in Malung, also the home of Pher Hetteen (father of John Hetteen). Those pictured are from left to right, David Johnson, Reuben Larson, Joel Olson, Sylvia Lisell, Marie Johnson (Evelyn Elling) Harriet Olson, Lillian Eklund. Lloyd Olson sits on hood of the hood of the Ford.

that in the first school the taller boys could reach the dried moose meat hung up in the school, and often cut off a chunk for a snack. The first teacher was Henry McCormick.

Dieter Township had two of the earliest schools, District 11 of Pinecreek organized in 1897, with Anne Knutson as clerk, Fred Larson as treasurer, and K. T. Oien as director. District No. 20 was organized January 1, 1899 and had as its officers George Davis as clerk, Syver Erickson as treasurer and Martin Braaten as director. Also organized that year was District No. 36 with Hans Haugen as clerk, Thor Vik as treasurer and G. T. Haugen as director. About this same time District No. 25, which was located forty rods north of Dewey Township in Section 23 came into being, with Ellert Hanson, clerk, Asle Asleson, director and Helge Willemon, treasurer.

In the territory known at the time as Kittson County there was also the Johnson School, District No. 27, two miles north of Jadis (Roseau) which bears the distinction of being the very first organized school district. This was the very beginning of the pioneer effort to educate the children.

Perhaps there were other school districts which could date back to the 19th century, but the records and dates are incomplete and this is the only authentic data in regard to the school district formation.

A unique school was one which was used only one year for one pupil and had only one teacher. This was the U12W school in Section 34 of Township No. 159. Miss Enrose Dallum was the teacher and the only student was Robert Thorkelson, son of the late August Thorkelson. It was later consolidated with District No. 2 of Wannaska.

The county superintendents were:

L. P. Dahlquist	1895-1901
G. H. Mattson	1901-1909
Anna C. Olsen	1909-1915
Eddy Billberg	1915-1935
Charles Christianson	1935-1967
George Rinde	1967-1968
O. A. Roberts	1968-1970

These are a few insights into the foundation upon which Roseau County was built. If the edifice is to be substantial the foundation must be straight and solid. If the mighty oak is to mature and spread its branches it must have good roots. The hopes, dreams, sweat, tears, labors, victories, defeats, but always the fortitude of a dedicated people banded together by necessity, by spiritual zeal, and just plain goodness of heart was the foundation, the roots of Roseau County. But there was joy in accomplishment, and the realization of dreams coming true as the County took shape. From paths to roads, from ox carts to trains and finally to automobiles and planes, the future of Roseau County was developing.

The Roseau County Board in 1900. Atlantus Austin, Sheriff, Mike Holm, Judge of Probate, J. C. Spencer, County Auditor, S. G. Bertilrud, Deputy Auditor, John Johnson, County commissioner, Andrew Pearson, County Commissioner, L. P. Dahlquist, Superintendent of Schools, Mike Johnson, County Commissioner, A. G. Lokeen, County Treasurer, Ole Peterson, County Commissioner, Iver Torfin, Clerk of Court, George Davis, County Commissioner, G. M. Stebbins, County Attorney, and Ole Oie, Register of Deeds.

Chapter 6

INFANCY
1909-1918

And now I know that we must lift the sail
And catch the winds of destiny
Wherever they drive the boat.

George Gray
Edgar Lee Masters

Chapter 6

INFANCY

The long lonesome whistle of the Great Northern had barely started to echo down the ribbons of steel through Roseau County when the staccato blasts from the rubber horns of Henry Ford's first autos scattered the chickens and dispersed the cows in the street. A notice was published that cows would be impounded if allowed to roam freely in the business district as they were a hazard to automobiles. The hogs too, who foraged on the "slop" (which was disposed of at any convenient spot) now would have to be penned away from the main streets. The rules of the road had to be posted in 1908. They read:

> If an automobile meets a team, the driver of the auto must put a tarp over the machine to match the surroundings.
>
> The speed limit this year on the country roads will be a secret. Offenders will be charged $10 a mile for every mile in excess of it.
>
> In case an auto makes a team run away there will be a fine of $50 for the first mile they run, $100 for the second, and $200 for the third, in addition to the usual cost of damages.
>
> The speed limit over the planked bridges was 4 m.p.h. in 1914 and the people were reminded that for keeping the bridges in good condition they should cooperate on the speed laws.

Yet there was no stopping the daring adventurers in this new mechanical contraption. Speeds of 25 miles an hour were recorded through the town and even over crossings, when everyone knew the limit was only 8 miles an hour. Even though the oxen were to be bought for as little as $140 a team, and horses did not use gasoline, it seemed that the so-called menace of the roadways continued to increase in number. By 1915 there were 139 automobiles in Roseau County, more cars than miles of passable roads. Jonas Sjoberg was selling Maxwell Roadsters for $670; these were advertised as "2 seaters, fast, powerful and can hold the road at 50 miles an hour." And then there were the deluxe Overland cars which sold for $1075 that had 35 h.p. engines, electric lights and starter, and electric horn, high tension magnetic speedometers, roadrails and curtain boxes.

It was reported that Pete Gunderson of Roosevelt bought the first automobile in the county, and Mr. George Roberts the second one, a Buick for which he paid $1250. Gasoline in those days cost 35 cents a gallon.

A M. Landby drove the first auto into Salol and had as his passengers his son Martin, Mr. A. E. Lins and A. Able. They dined at the Hotel Anderson and made the trip on the Cedarbend road and along the ditch road to the lateral No. 6 to a point one half mile south of Salol from Warroad in one hour and 15 minutes.

In 1915 five Warroad automobile owners made the trip to Greenbush on the summer road and used the new state road on the return trip. They made the trip down in three hours and the return trip in two hours. Ed Cantelon, Jack Jowett, George Roberts, Bill Rader, and George Marvin made the trip and reported the road from Roseau to Salol to be safe for automobiles. In 1918 Dr. Delmore

The Hodgeman Livery and Feed Barn with Ben Hodgeman looking over his stock. Now the Chevrolet Garage is located at this site.

The Crookston auto club of over 100 cars came on a good will tour in 1910. The cars are parked in front of the Pioneer Drug Store and Lindberg's General Store.

was credited with making the best time on a trip to Warroad and back when he averaged 40 miles an hour.

As early as 1911 there were 100 autos from the Crookston Auto Club that made a trip to Roseau as a part of the activities of their club as well as to honor Roseau and visit the county fair.

In 1907 Greenbush handed out bills urging the salesmen to hire livery automobiles "for a high rate of speed." However this story to inspire the driver to take care appeared in the Greenbush Tribune:

> Hartwell who operates an automobile in Greenbush, appears to be a menace to travelers between this city and Greenbush. Monday while Bob Ross was driving his car, with 8 persons on board toward Roseau, Hartwell came up along his auto at a furious rate of speed and turned sharply to the right in front of the Ross machine, which was traveling about 15 miles an hour. But for the quick action of Mr. Ross who turned his car abruptly to the left, a terrible mix-up would have ensued. His machine went crashing through the brush and timber along the road until it was brought to a standstill by the emergency brake. Seems to us that the driver of a livery automobile should be sane, sober and familiar with his machine and a man of discretion. A reckless driver is just as apt to kill as get killed.

Bumping along in the automobiles over the trails that could scarcely be called roads was taxing, even in those with underslung springs, and cushioned seats. Soon there was agitation for better roads. The pioneers did not sit around and moan for lack of funds. If they needed better roads then it was up to the civic minded citizens to get busy and build them. It was proposed that all able bodied farmers should spend a designated number of days donating their time and teams, or to donate a few dollars to make passable roads in the county – a poll tax system. In 1911 it was reported that the road to Salol was almost completed. The old winter road from the west side of Hay creek connecting with Salol and the road east from the main bridge were repaired. This was done by raising $400 by popular subscription.

In 1914 a system of state aid roads in all counties was authorized and engineers were appointed to construct, supervise, and maintain them, Roseau County was one of the first to have an engineer. V. B. Chapin held that position until 1937. The road system planned and laid out by the Board of County Commissioners with the approval of the Highway Commission and later the State Highway Department became the pattern for highway building in the state. It was the first tangible effort to provide an adequate system of roads at the county level. Under rules promulgated by the state these roads were constructed according to minimum standards and were required to be surfaced and to have regular maintenance. In general, they originated at or near the several villages, and extended out into the rural areas. They have justified the judgement of their originators in that they were almost without exception still the most intensively used roads in the county. Perhaps the most noticeable weakness of this road system resulted from the fact that they were built prior to the need for snow plowing. Most grade lines were so low that it was practically impossible to keep them free from snow. It might well be noted that at first snow plowing had considerable opposition since it was thought to be detrimental to the sleighs and cutters which had been the principal vehicles for winter travel.

As the program to up-grade the roads progressed, certain roads would be singled out for special maintenance on "good roads" day. In 1913 the road east from the bridge through the village of Roseau to the Spruce line was so designated. Twenty teams were required to haul gravel. In order to get the job done, supervisors S. O. Lindquist was assigned to the village, Martin Nelson for the county and Nicolai Nelson for Spruce, who in turn would work under the direction of Engineer Chapin for the state.

Wooden bridges were built from native lumber, and the roads had "fills" created from peat taken from the side ditches. This material was cut into sections with a spade or hay knife and were thrown into the roadway with a fork. Later the peat would be covered with clay or gravel from adjacent higher ground. What an ordeal it must have been to sit precariously on a lumber wagon while the team lunged to pull the wagon over a rutted, almost impassable stretch of road.

On the township level road building was done under a contract. It consisted of building up the grade by using the natural soils in the ditches along the roadway. Teams and "slip scraper" were employed, and by virtue of repeated trips the road was compacted. In the earliest period oxen were used for this work, and no small part of the job was to get the oxen to move. One writer suggested that some of the tainted language in vogue at the time originated as the result of this type of road building.

About every three months R. J. Bell, editor of the *Roseau County Times*, would print a glowing account of the resources of the fledgling county. The article in the Dec. 15, 1916 paper read:

> Roseau County soil cannot be excelled. There is good water from numerous flowing wells. The county is well drained. There are no hills, and there are more graded roads than any county in the state. For successive years the Roseau County exhibit at the fair has been a prize winner. The highest yield per acre of wheat was 54 bushels, for oats, 97 bu. and 600 lbs. of potatoes to the acre. The county abounds in natural tame and native grasses. The bank deposits are over one and a half million, a gain of over one half million a year. There are three high schools in the county, one of which is a state approved school, 7 consolidated districts, and 102 county districts. The high school in Roseau cost $142,000 and has 12 teachers, 3 industrial arts departments (manual training, domestic training and agricultural). The county fair is held on 35 acres which has good buildings, and has a one-half mile race track that is within 5 minutes walk from main street. Roseau is the county seat. What will make Roseau County wealthy? The answer is the cow. The county will become a great dairy center because there is no better forage, and this will make Roseau County farmers wealthy, the richest in the U. S.

We perhaps can forgive some ambiguities from an over zealous editor. But the "well drained" county was constantly fighting the battle for better drainage. While the river and its tributaries were a ready made highway of travel so instrumental in the discovery and pursuit of the fur trade, and an unsurpassed convenience for the important lumber business, yet water in Roseau County was a constant problem. The rivers and streams too often became swollen with the abundance of rain in the area and the results were catastrophic. Good farm land lay under the swamp and marshes.

The natural waterways in Roseau County (in addition to the six judicial, eight state and nineteen county drainage systems) are:

(1) Willow Creek, located north of Roosevelt and partly in Lake of the Woods County, flows into Lake of the Woods.

(2) The Warroad River with its east and west branches serves the area south of Warroad (in general) and an area as far east as Oaks Township, south of Roosevelt. It drains into Lake of the Woods, and serves as an outlet for Bull Dog Run in Moranville Township as well as several county systems.

(3) Hay Creek starts eight miles southeast of Salol and flows northwesterly into the Roseau River about three miles north of Roseau.

(4) Lost River lies about five miles to the north and west of Salol, with Judicial Ditch No. 61 as its outlet.

(5) Mud Creek commences at the Canadian Border, due north of Roseau and flows in a southwesterly direction into the Roseau River about six miles north of Roseau.

(6) The North branch of the Roseau River being near the Roseau County-Lake of the Woods-Beltrami line, flows northwesterly to a point north of Malung where it joins the South branch of the Roseau River. The North branch serves as an outlet for Sucker Creek and Bear Creek, both in Malung Township.

(7) The South branch of the Roseau River has its beginning at a point near Skime and flows northwesterly and north to a point joining the North branch and north to Roseau, and is an outlet for Cow Creek in Spruce Township.

(8) From Roseau, the Roseau River flows north for a distance of about six miles before turning westerly through Ross, where it acts as an outlet for Pine Creek, and west and northerly into Kittson County and into Canada where it empties into the Red River of the North.

(9) Skunk Creek commences at Fox and flows southwesterly for a distance of about eight miles, draining into Lateral Number One of the State Ditch System.

(10) Badger Creek starts at a point east of Badger, and flows through Badger in a northwesterly direction and empties into Whitney Lake Ditch.

(11) The South Fork of the Two Rivers starts south of Badger, and flows southwesterly along the south side of the ridge running from Badger to Greenbush and into Kittson County.

The three main drainage systems were established from the date of organization until July 12, 1921, a period of about twenty-six and a half years and the total cost was $1,486,651. The total acreage that benefitted from the extensive systems are about 865,793 acres, exclusive of the township ditches.

When the drainage of land had been effected, new lands were sold in Roseau County. In 1910 Auditor Iverson sold 830 acres in a spirited sale. One of the big buyers was a man named Oscar Zipf who bought land at the average price of $6.20 an acre. The total amount taken in for the sale was $52,037. It was reported that in June of 1911 at another sale 250 buyers were on hand and the lowest priced acreage went for $5.00 and the highest for $22 an acre. At this sale 17,000 acres were sold. And then in 1912 the biggest sale on record took place when 24,500 acres were sold at an average price of $12.50 an acre with buyers coming from Illinois, Iowa, the Dakotas, and western Minnesota.

Farmers Co-operative Creamery in Greenbush, in 1910.

There had been many enticements for the farmers to lean toward dairying instead of grain farming. One report in the paper said that the lake bottom was alive with teams and men cutting hay. There were also yokes of oxen hitched up, some driven by women who "pitched in" to cut the luxuriant water grass which they said was renowned as a nourishing food for cattle. In 1914 the farmers were advised to forget about raising wheat or flax as the land and climate were not well suited for grains.

Now the great back-savers, the farm machines, began to appear on the scene. In 1919 S. K. Bergland was reported to have a new aid in farming which consisted of a tractor which could pull a plow and a rake. The picture of a threshing machine appeared in the paper in 1910 and a two plow tractor was introduced by a Dr. Donnelly whose son had spent a week at the factory learning to use it properly and to teach others. It had a 45 h.p. engine, and was advertised as a means of saving horse flesh while it did the work in much less time.

Elevators and creameries became a necessity to the farming people. Greenbush had its creamery in 1904, and its cooperative elevator built by 100 farmers in 1907. Five years later there were 137 patrons under the leadership of A. G. Lokken and Peter Forness. In December of 1912, the Ross farmers built a creamery, and in 1933 built a second one to replace the first. Buttermilk could be purchased at 35c a keg at the time. The Warroad creamery was completed in April of 1908 and was declared by the folks in that section to be in the best spot in the whole county. The same year Roseau built a creamery by selling $25 shares to farmers and patrons. Since that effort met with success an elevator was built by the same plan of fund raising — three years later.

Fox also built a creamery about the same time and later Hanson and Barzen and Co. built an elevator there and engaged T. Nomeland to manage it. George Marvin's elevator No. 1 was built in 1921. It was at this time that butter sold for 28 cents a pound and the Roseau Creamery paid out $607 in the month of December to the farmers.

Both Warroad and Roseau had potato houses built in 1918. These warehouses handled about 20,000 bushels of potatoes a year. In Roseau, Benjamin Franklin and son were busy men at potato harvest time for they had a new machine that would sort the potatoes for storage and selling.

Robert Storey wrote an impassioned plea which appeared in the paper, imploring the farmers to meet and exchange ideas on farming procedures, pointing out that the co-operative creameries and elevators were the result of the combined efforts of the farmers. In April 1913 a Farmer's Institute was held at the Opera House. O. A. Berg spoke on the subject of crops and soils and a Mr. Carlson lectured on livestock. The meeting was sponsored by the Commercial Club and resulted in a permanent farmer's organization. By 1914 there were 11 such clubs throughout the county. At a mass meeting of all the clubs held that year the problem of finding ways and means of settling all the vacant land in Roseau County was the topic of interest.

The Commercial clubs which have played such a strong part in promoting the various communities drew large and enthusiastic memberships. Through their efforts the various promotions, Badger's Flax Day, Greenbush's Sheep Days, Warroad's Timber Days, and Roseau's Clover Festivals, had their inceptions.

In 1914 a group known as the Roseau County Development Organization was started. The main function of this group was to promote legislation for the northern part of the state, and to advertise this area, using the county fair for this purpose. All towns in the county worked together to this end.

The Roseau County Farm Bureau which is still active today was organized in 1918 chiefly by A. M. Landby from Warroad, and had Walter Anderson, from Badger, as its first president. This farmer group has worked steadily and enthusiastically for the welfare of the county farmers.

The state fair was used to its fullest potential to advertise the county, with exhibits set up by Mike Holm, under whose directorship the exhibits won four first, and three second places. Once the ingenious Secretary of State even included a 125 lb. sturgeon in a tank to advertise Lake of the Woods.

Cow testing programs were started in 1916, and were systematically and scientifically carried on in the county after that. On September 28, 1917 the largest shipment of stock that was ever shipped out required a special train. The train had 32 cars of stock with Warroad furnishing 8, Roseau 6, Fox 4, Badger 6, and Greenbush and Middle River with 8.

Haying in 1913. Martin Malmskog, C. A. Malmskog and Arthur Malmskog using a Milwaukee Binder.

The Red River Valley Shows had their initial start in 1895 and were annual events from that date on. The purpose was chiefly to disseminate agricultural information but they also provided entertainment.

During this period many of the less stable newspapers had disappeared from the scene, but each community retained at least one official written spokesman. Roseau continued to have the *Roseau County Times* and the *Roseau Region*.

One of the early exhibits at the Minnesota State Fair set up by Mike Holm which won a first prize.

By 1910 the Roseau County Times took on a more sophisticated format with fewer purchased news articles, but with more local news, and news from surrounding communities, stories in serial form (usually with a buxom swooning maiden falling into the arms of a moustached gentleman), and an interesting "How-to-do-it" article for a farmer or his wife. In this year R. J. Bell celebrated his 16th year of editorship with this article:

> The Times has had only one owner and one editor. The aim has always been the settlement and development of Roseau County. To this end the Times has built a railroad every year for 13 years. For many years it looked as if Jim Hill would never reach heaven on the strength of the prayers of the county people, but now we are permitted to ride on coaches no more crowded than the old stage and almost as comfortable. The Times was the second newspaper in the county. There are at this time six newspapers with creditable editors. Fifteen years ago the assessed valuation of Roseau County was less than $75,000 and now it is about 3 million and the actual wealth of the county will reach over 20 million, and that is going some, but actually the development of the county is only started. Ten years from now there will be 30 creameries instead of seven, and the population will be 30,000 with a valuation of 40 million unless some fools succeed in dividing the county in an attempt to get the county seat. Roseau County is destined to become the best agricultural section of the state.

As a business the newspapers had as much trouble with credit as the stores up and down the street. Their buildings, too, were surrounded by cord wood in exchange for a year's subscription, but even these piles diminished and the poor editors had to beg via the printed word:

> This is the season for planting seed
> Also the time for the printer's need
> Sow radishes and lettuce too
> And pay the printers what is due
> Of watermelons you'll need a patch
> Editor's pants need one to match.

The 1909 paper reminded the people in a most dramatic way of their most fearful problems – that of disease. The June 25th edition of the paper came out edged in black to mourn the passing of G. H. Medicraft, editor of the Region, a victim of typhoid fever. After his death P. H. Buran took over the paper with Ray Gilbertson assisting.

The fear of disease and epidemics was all too real for the early settlers who at that time knew nothing of the antibiotics we take for granted. To get specialized care the patient would have to travel to Crookston or Warren with horse and buggy, over roads that were little more than trails. Little wonder then that each community in the county yearned for its own general practitioner to care for the families. Throughout the early years several doctors came to the little towns, but with so little in the way of facilities to take care of the ill, they found the heavier populated and more settled communities more attractive. Some of them came to look and left immediately, others stayed for only a short time, so until about 1910 there was a great turn over in the medical personnel.

The first doctors in Greenbush in 1904 were Dr. Hjelstrup, and Dr. Torgerson, who were followed by Mr. and Mrs. Clark (both were doctors) Dr. Houg, Dr. Mork, Dr. Hanson and Dr. Summerfelt. The old school was remodelled into an office, operating room and patient's room. The pharmacists of the early days were Carl Engelthrope, Tom Torgerson and Andrew Clay.

In 1896 the first doctor came to Badger. He was Dr. O. J. Berg, who was followed by Dr. Lea Murphy Sr. and then Dr. N. C. Davis who came in 1907 and stayed until 1922. In 1909 Dr. Simon came to Badger and in 1912 Ray Gardiner located in Badger and stayed until 1915. Dr. Joseph Stratte came in 1915, but stayed only two years. The dentists in Badger were Dr. Lea Murphy, Dr. H. Krogh and W. Cram. The druggists were Drs. Murphy and Davis, E. Y. Wilson, H. E. Brown, E. R. Wright and J. J. Kirchener, who sold his drug store to Amos Fikkan in 1921.

Dentists who served the Roseau territory in 1901 were Dr. W. J. Wright of Hallock, Dr. Gibson from Warroad, and Dr. Vandersaal who were itinerant dentists. It was Dr. Brandelin of Warroad who came in 1910 and stayed for several years. He was followed by Dr. Brandt.

In Roseau, Dr. Per Oyen was the first doctor, to be followed by Dr. Parker in 1897 and Dr. F. L. Norin in 1900, followed by Dr. Brown.

Dr. Norin brought not only his family but also brought a nurse, Miss Scott, and established a 6 bed hospital over his office which was located where the old locker plant stands. He trained Minnie Larson, Hildur Johnson and Mrs. Anna Dahlquist, who later on did practical nursing and was known affectionately as "Mother Dahlquist."

Dr. J. B. Muir, who came in 1904, built his home and office at the north end of town, now the James Helgeson residence. He returned to Hallock in 1907 but came back to Rsoeau in 1912 and practiced here until his death in 1929. The hospital, established in 1912 was equipped with an operating table, a portable sterilizer, and 4 hospital beds. It was lighted by kerosene lamps, as there was no electric light plant in Roseau at the time.

Lack of nursing assistance was the big problem at the time. Miss Holmquist worked at the hospital a year, and Miss Mary Dahlquist nursed occasionally. Since there was only one nurse on duty, Dr. Muir would relieve the nurses in order that they could get some rest. In 1915, Mrs. A. E. Lundquist established a maternity hospital, which she operated until 1950. It was licensed for three patients.

Perhaps the first hospital board ever organized met in 1914. It was composed of Dr. J. L. Delmore, Sr., Dr. Norin, Dr. Stuart Leech, Dr. Muir, Israel Sjoberg, Rev. B. A. Birkeland, Olaf Holdahl, and Knute Lee. The first piece of business was to consider the purchase of the Muir property. Dr. Muir was asking $6000 for the house and there was a promised subscription from townspeople for $2000. The year's report given that day showed that 43 patients had been treated and there was an average stay of 13 days. There were 33 operations. Receipts from patients were $1,039 of which $609 had gone for nurses salaries.

Mr. and Mrs. Budd came to Roseau in 1911, and Mrs. Marie Budd, a graduate of the Warren Hospital Training School of Nursing gave what time she could to nursing in Roseau. The Muirs decided they could no longer cope with help shortages and other problems of a hospital and closed it in January of 1915.

The problem of maintaining a hospital was an acute one, so the County Commissioners finally encouraged the Budds to start a hospital in 1914, giving them the lease of the old courthouse (now Moe's Floral) with option to buy. To clean, remodel, paint, and replace almost all broken windows, add a cistern for water so that carrying it from across the street could be avoided, were obstacles they took in stride. The hospital was called the Roseau County General Hospital and opened for service May 12, 1915. It was equipped with a portable U. S. Army operating table, a sterilizer, and two hospital beds with bedside tables and a few chairs. There were four rooms for patients, an operating room, a kitchen and dining room on second floor. Ole Bergstrom made cupboards for the surgical instruments and Dr. Delmore Sr. placed his own instruments in it. Hospital beds were added until there were ten beds at the beginning of the new year.

Miss Hilma Osterlund was trained by Mrs. Budd to assist, and she later became Dr. Delmore's assistant and office nurse and stayed with him for several years. Miss Ethel Strandlund, who had been employed at the Nopeming Sanatorium, came to assist at the hospital. The hospital could not be licensed however, since there was no sewer or running water, but the institution was allowed to operate since it filled a need in the community, with the provision that when these facilities were available in town the hospital would be the first to have them.

In 1910 when the epidemic of typhoid fever broke out the settlers were advised to put calcium hyperchloride in the water according to the directions the pharmacist would give them. There were 15 cases of the disease and two deaths. Three children of Nicolai Nelson were ill at one time.

In 1912 the editor said that people should give credit to C. O. Heyerdahl for introducing a simple Buckhorn Bark and glycerine mixture called Adlerika which had accounted for many cures.

Another "cure" that occurred in 1912 was promoted by a company which called itself the Quaker Medicine Show, and which advertised that there were cures for any illness, be it appendicitis, rheumatism, gout or tapeworm (which took 2 hours to remove). For two weeks they held shows at the Opera House, and besides selling their fake medicines they put on shows to draw big crowds. On the 24th of March, however, the paper reported that they had gone – with several thousand dollars.

A report of the death record on June of 1911 was: T. B. – nine cases; pneumonia – seven; cancer – three; diphtheria – four; whooping cough – five; small pox – none; scarlet fever – four; measles – one; typhoid fever – four and accidents, eight cases.

A young doctor with a certificate from the University of Minnesota and financial resources of $13.00 came in 1909 with Dr. Muir to Hallock to look over the country. They hired the Hodgeman livery for a trip to Roseau and were afraid all the while that Mr. Hodgeman would ask for the money in advance. Dr. Delmore Sr. looked around him and liked what he saw. He declared to his friend, "This is the place I want to live."

Roseau had three doctors at this time but none were surgeons, so there was a great need for his services. The spirit of the people also appealed to him. He thought of them as high-minded, justly proud of the rewards of their labors, and friendly.

The good doctor set up his practice in Roseau in 1909. On June the 10th he mysteriously disappeared. Worried conjectures were made as to his whereabouts, but finally it somehow became known that he had gone to Minneapolis to get his bride. His friends were quite ready for him when he returned. They had a buckboard all decorated and had an ox, and a small pony hitched up to pull it. They met the train and hoisted the beautiful Mae Frick Delmore and her husband to the driver's seat for a ride through the town. The populace formed a parade behind them shouting good wishes and hurrahs. The entourage stopped in front of the Heyerdahl Drug store and the merrymaking went on in the street. Mrs. Delmore ducked into the drug store, but was immediately escorted back to the happy people. Thus the Delmores began their life in Roseau. Mrs. Delmore, a nurse, assisted her husband whenever she was able to leave her household. Some of the narratives that "Doc" had to tell should be preserved for posterity. Here are some of them in his own words:

> I was born in Elroy, Wisconsin in 1886 near La Crosse. When I came to practice in Roseau it was just as hard to figure out how to get to a patient as to know what to do when you got there.
>
> In the summer, I went by horse and buggy. It wasn't too bad. Sometimes I rode a railroad handcar to Warroad. In the winter I used a "jumper", a low sled pulled by two horses. We made about 8 miles an hour. Once I used a dog sled. The biggest problem was the cold. I remember a 19 mile trip when it was 55 below zero. I wore sheepskin and heavy underwear, and the sled had a footwarmer – a felt-covered metal container with burning charcoal inside. A little later someone invented a sled caboose. It was a box with a small stove and stovepipe.

Somehow the doctor acquired a driver, Emmet Dahlquist, who recalls that it happened that the two of them spent many days without their clothes off as they took turns driving and sleeping in the wagon. Once the driver also had to act as the anesthetist as a man had accidentally shot himself and the hotel room had to become an emergency operating room.

The late Milo Peterson needed surgery when he was a youngster after falling out of a tree and rupturing his kidney. The operation was performed in the Peterson home after Milo's mother had sterilized everything she could with Lysol and even dipped the sheets in the antiseptic. Paul Buran Jr. was the first baby Dr. Delmore delivered August 27, 1909.

Another experience in Dr. Delmore's words:

> A young fellow's wife was expecting. She had already lost a baby in Minneapolis and this was her second pregnancy. During the delivery I looked up and there was the farmer pointing a rifle at me. All I could do was to go ahead. The baby and mother were fine, and when the farmer came in to pay his bill he said, "I was planning on shooting you. I am glad I didn't.

Doctor Delmore Sr. worked hard for an adequate hospital in Roseau, and helped the Budds to set up a hospital in the old court house. He established his office over the bank building where he started the Delmore Clinic.

Another experience the Doctor told was:

> I had to go to Roosevelt on November 8, 1917 for a patient with acute appendicitis. I had my own car (he bought it in 1912) but when I got to Warroad there was six inches of snow on the ground. I made it to the patient and put him in my car, but seven miles west of Warroad we got stuck and I broke an axle. I left the patient and walked five miles to Salol to get help. I called the mail driver and persuaded him to come and he arrived O.K. but when his truck broke down a block from the hospital, I carried the patient the rest of the way. The patient recovered and I never got paid.

In 1918 the deadly flu epidemic hit northwestern Minnesota. He said:

> From October 1 to March in 1919 schools and theaters were closed. People wore masks on the street. Five people died in one family.

Another epidemic hit the town in 1910 when 19 persons from Ross and Pinecreek died of scarlet fever.

Dr. Delmore Sr. held a golden life membership certificate in the Minnesota State Medical Society. A 4-H plaque was presented to him by County Agent Radway with these words inscribed on it:

> "Recognition for meritorious Service to 4-H, Dr. J. L. Delmore."

But deeper than a plaque or a certificate is the deep love and gratitude with which

Badger School 1902

Warroad 1908

Greenbush 1910

Roseau 1912

the memory of Dr. Delmore is revered. It was a sentiment echoed by many citizens of Roseau County.

Education took great strides ahead from 1900-1920. In Roseau there was a question of building a new school, and the main point seemed to be where it should be located. It was argued that since the courthouse was on the west side of the river, the school ought to be on the east side. A straw vote was cast in 1910 which resulted in 267 in favor of the east side and 135 in favor of the west side. On July 4th the cornerstone for a new building was placed.

Short courses were offered in Roseau for the benefit of those who could not enter in the fall. These courses started in November and continued until March, and included arithmetic, agriculture, and government. In March of 1915 there was a move to make their high school a state accredited school by meeting certain course requirements. The school was receiving $1250 in state aid and this was to increase to $2000 with the upgrading of the curriculum. (R. J. Bell's glowing accounts of Roseau appealed to the public awareness of the situation and helped to swing the vote to the affirmative.) Quite a stir was caused in 1913 when the Roseau School Board was criticized for being extravagant in wanting to add classes in gym, manual training, sewing and cooking. The editors argued again that in order to get more state aid these courses were necessary. Proof of progress was evident in that Professor Bengston who had started in 1909 with 5 pupils had in 1913, 29 high school students. The new courses were added. In 1911 Salol got $800 additional state aid through the efforts of Superintendent of Schools Anna Olsen since its school building had burned in the fire of 1910.

Consolidation came early in progressive Roseau County. The small schools in the Swift area consolidated into one unit as early as Jan. 19, 1912. The Greenbush school had begun in 1901 with only a few children and was then taught by a fifteen year old girl. Later classes were held in several locations. But in 1920 a fine new building was erected. The first building to house a high school in Badger was built in 1918 and the first graduating class from high school included Florence Geroy, Ida Iverson, Nellie Medhus, and Anna Sunderland. Fewer men went to high school in those days, due no doubt, to the demands of the home farming operation. Newell Lee was the first boy to graduate from Badger. The Superintendent was Krein Bring. Roosevelt had a high school in the early 1920's which was disbanded in the 1930's.

Sixteen persons in Warroad voted in 1904 to establish District No. 12 there. Rena Gilbertson was the first teacher at the log school. For lack of room some classes were held in the Baptist church. The first school house at the present location was built in 1918. It was enlarged in 1952 and in 1957 a gymnasium was built; a new elementary complex was added to the school in 1967. The first graduating class consisted of Viola Carlquist Hanson, Etta Bergland Holland, Isobel Carlquist Marvin, and Olive Flozdal Sweet. Members of the board of education were E. L. Hillis, C. E. Carlquist, L. B. Hedlund, Albert Berg, F. N. Brown, and C. A. Moody. Other early teachers beside Miss Gilbertson were Mae MacDonald and Basti Fitzpatrick.

Forensics were an important extra-curricular activity. One debate on the public ownership of the telephone and telegraph was held between Roseau and Warroad. Debating for Roseau were Olga Wold, Signe Heyerdahl and Ethel Clark. For Warroad were Arthur, Edgar and Jerry Truax, and Jerry Southwick. The editor of the paper advertised the debate thus, "Remember the debate tonight. One night only. Better than two nights in the bar rooms." Another subject for debate was "Resolved that women should not be given the ballot."

Mail and Post Offices

The first post office, Jadis, was established April 12, 1888. The last one, Conrad, on January 2, 1913. During the period from 1911-13 only three new offices were established. The postal service of Roseau County was about to begin a new era – that of the Rural Free Delivery service. One route had already been established, namely Route Number One out of Roseau, begun on February 1, 1910.

The early carriers were Star Route or "contract" carriers. They often sub-let a part or parts of the route to others, indicating that the "relay" system was employed here, too, to speed mail delivery to all parts of the county. Lack of roads, abundance of wilderness and swamps, high water and mosquitoes were

Post Office at Oak Point in 1909. The man is the husband of the postmistress Emma Poirier.

summer hazards for the carrier, and winter brought little relief with its snow, ice, and cold weather. The early carrier often traveled on foot – aided in winter by skis and snowshoes. Riding horseback was a common mode of travel, often handicapped however, by deep mud or snow. Oxen were often used in summer since they could travel better in mud and swamp. (This was not a very speedy service compared to our so-called "jet generation", but it served its purpose well for a generation that took "time out" to live.)

Getting the mail through to its destination was often a real problem. Tennes Thompson, one of the early carriers to the Benwood post office, found the water on part of his route so deep in places that both he and the mail would get soaked, in spite of the fact that he rode horseback. Ole Dokken, the first carrier to Juneberry, piled the mail on the seat of the buggy and then stood on top of it in order to get through some swampy places. This was the only way he could keep the mail above the "water-line" and keep it from falling out of the buggy while he was busy driving his horses. This was also the experience of an early carrier at the Herb post office, according to Mrs. M. J. Kotochevar of Greenbush. The fact that Charley Skog, the carrier to Dawd post office, used a totally blind horse did not prevent his getting the mail through, related Mr. P. O. Nelson. Nils A. Johnson, one of the early carriers between Falun and Malung, tells of leaving home in Falun at 6 A.M., walking about ten miles to Malung, waiting for the mail (sometimes all day), and walking back to Falun with the mail in a pack sack. He encountered the usual snow, ice, water, mud, too, but his pet peeve was carrying the Sears catalogs – sometimes as many as thirty at one time.

Contract carriers were also permitted to carry passengers and merchandise. When the carrier was on foot there was, of course, a limit to what could be carried — at least no one is known to have carried passengers that way. Merchandise was another matter. Albert Hayes, the "charitable" carrier mentioned earlier, tells that he would often carry a fifty pound sack of flour on his back in addition to the mail, and that women along his route would often times either borrow or buy flour as he delivered the mail. Sometimes there would be no flour left when he reached home. It must have been quite a temptation, at that, to lighten the load a bit after the first three or four miles. Mr. Hayes seems to have been left "holding the bag" in more ways than one.

Another "flour carrier" was Knute Kompelien who lived northwest of Ross, near the Canadian border. Edward Erickson related that he (Mr. Kompelien) would often carry a hundred pound sack of flour on his back from the Ole Moen place (about two miles east of Edward Erickson's to his own place — a distance of ten miles.) It was necessary, of course, to rest occasionally on such a trip, but, with the ground wet much of the time, he couldn't set the flour down. The method he devised under such circumstances was to get down on one knee and to lean the flour sack against the trunk of a tree while he caught his breath for the next lap of the journey.

Contract carriers in early days also included stage coach drivers who, in addition to carrying passengers, brought mail into the county in pre-railroad days.

Points on Lake-of-the-Woods for many years had mail service differing from that of the rest of the county. Before the Canadian National Railway came to Roosevelt in 1901, the mail was brought from Warroad to Arneson P. O. (Rocky Point) by boat, and then carried by Alvin Norton to Roosevelt. When the Canadian National Railway was completed through the eastern part of the county, a second source of mail was opened. Mail was carried between Warroad and Roseau by stage coach following the old "summer road" (the old Indian War Path) and served three post offices along the way: Goos, Pequis, and Cedarbend. Even the stage faced difficulties, however, for at times the water was so high the stage had to be abandoned and the mail brought through on horseback.

The first major change in the county postal service came in 1910, when on February first a rural free delivery route was established out of the Roseau post office, with August E. Roadfeldt as carrier. In 1913, two more routes were established, these out of Badger: Route one on March first, and Route two on August first. S. T. Hagen served as temporary carrier for two months and then Harry T. Gaetke was appointed regular carrier. In 1914 two more routes were added, these at Greenbush. Sanky Dufwa was appointed carrier serving both of these routes on alternating days.

In 1913 the Post Office Department inaugurated parcel post service. Together with the rural delivery service, here was a combination mobile post office and general merchandise store all rolled into one. While the star route carrier had been charged with transporting the mail, the rural carrier could transact, right at the patron's mail box, all business normally done only at the post office before. The patron had but to reach for the trusty Sears catalog, make out an order, purchase a money order through the rural carrier, and then sit back and wait until the merchandise was delivered to what was practically his doorstep. (Sometimes this step would be a couple of miles long, but this was real service!)

With the coming of the rural routes and parcel post service, the need for so many post offices was ended; consequently, many of them were discontinued by the Postal Department. The four year period from 1913 to 1916 saw seven offices closed. More followed each year.

The plight of the early rural carrier was much the same as that of the star route carrier. He traveled an average of 23 miles a day on non-existent, or extremely poor roads through summer rains and winter storms. His spirits were sometimes sustained by the promise of new roads, but hope grew dim when that promise was delayed for many years or completely forgotten. Horses and a variety of vehicles were the accepted mode of travel, though some carriers still had to resort to the oldest means of locomotion known, walking. Jalmer Wellen, one of the early carriers at Badger, (appointed March 16, 1914) did considerable walking whenever the quantity of mail permitted it or the condition of the roads made it necessary.

The trusty old Model T must be given much credit for the mechanization of the rural route. It served well in the summertime but had to give way to horses again when the snow became too deep. Then in the late 20's came the snowmobile, which was considered the ultimate for winter travel. It, too, had its drawbacks, as it was heavy and cumbersome in loose snow. It worked best when the snow on the road was packed by its own daily travel and that of sleighs.

The transition period from winter sleigh roads to snow-plowed roads caused considerable concern to the carriers. When the County first began plowing some of the roads, the snowmobile with runners in place of front wheels was unable to travel on the bared roads. A combination wheel-runner on the front was a partial solution but proved quite unhandy.

Carriers were not stumped for long as new and ingenious modes of travel were devised. The principal one was the propeller driven sled, such as had been used on Lake-of-the-Woods for hauling mail and freight. Where the roads were snowplowed, these sleds would travel on the fields. Heating the cab on sled was a problem as these cabs were usually canvas covered. The engines were air cooled aeroplane type and created quite a blast of cool air, especially at 30 below! Other carriers equipped Model A Fords with donut tires that would ride over snow or mud with a fair degree of success. When the spring break-up arrived, some parts of the roads would be bare while others would have three feet, or more, of snow. Finding suitable equipment for making the appointed rounds was a real problem. One carrier had a car, a wind-sled, a snowmobile, and a tractor as equipment, and still there were many times during this transition period when he could have used a horse!

"Neither snow, nor rain, nor heat, nor gloom of night stays these couriers from the swift completion of their appointed rounds."

The present system of maintained roads presents quite a contrast. A few carriers resort to the use of a Jeep occasionally, otherwise regular cars are used exclusively.

There have been trends and changes in the type of mail handled during this period of history. The volume of mail has, in general, increased. Good roads, trucking service, and the ability of local merchants to stock a greater variety of merchandise at competitive prices has led to the decline of small parcels from mail order houses.

Delivery of baby chicks by truck, direct from the hatchery in many cases, has greatly reduced the number of chicks sent by parcel post. This is a welcome change for most postal employees, as this type of parcel post could – and did – present many a problem. Before the present star route from Thief River Falls was established, many a postmaster had the "headache" of deciding what to do with a carton of baby chicks consigned for rural delivery – but arriving on a Saturday afternoon! Frequently they were for a patron who had no telephone. Quite often there were dead chicks in the carton, and on a hot summer afternoon – draw your own conclusions! (Usually the postmaster, in desperation, made a "Special Delivery") If the chicks were refused by the addressee (most of them came C.O.D. and could be refused) and if they could not be returned to the sender within 72 hours from the time of hatching, the postmaster would have to dispose of them to the highest bidder. Those who were employed at the Badger Post Office will not forget the day in the spring of 1939 when a shipment of 2300 chicks arrived at one time.

Another class of merchandise – now gone but never to be forgotten – was dry lutefisk shipped via parcel post. It arrived in bundles, sometimes wrapped in burlap, but often simply tied with a strong cord. This, too, like some of the chicks mentioned, had a certain air about it that would linger long after the bundle had been delivered. Unlike the baby chicks, though, this class of merchandise was anything but perishable, and seemed to be able to "live on" forever! It was often necessary to keep this item at the post office over night, and sometimes over the week end. It demanded real courage to put the key into the lock and open the door the following morning. Here was mail the employees needed protection FROM. It did have one redeeming feature, though in that it was absolutely indestructible. The Post Office Department has yet to receive a claim for damaged, or spoiled, dry lutefisk.

One of the merchants in the county was in the habit of ordering a 50 pound bag of coffee and a bundle of dry lutefisk from a certain wholesale house each week. Soon his coffee sales doubled, and people would tell him that his coffee had an added flavor they had never tasted in any other brand. Too, it took less coffee and yet it seemed to give them that added "lift". The merchant proudly advertised the fact he had the "beste Kaffe i byen" ("best coffee in town"). When, for sanitary reasons (or could it have been for the protection of the weaker postal employees?) lutefisk was shipped in wooden tubs, his coffee sales declined.

From the first regular mail service in 1895 until June 2, 1952, when the present star routes were established, one sees that there has been a constant aim at improvement in service. In 1895, weekly service was provided by stagecoach from Stephen; in 1952, daily morning service by truck from Thief River Falls made possible delivery to rural patrons the same day.

The early stage drivers relied on the best and swiftest horses they could possibly provide. The automobile was just about to replace the horses, at least part time, when the railroad came to the western part of the County. An item from the August 11, 1905 issue of *The Times - Region* of Roseau, bears this out:

"George Roberts pulled into town Wednesday afternoon with his fine new automobile, bringing the mail with him. The large car is like the ones the *Minneapolis Journal* uses for touring Minneapolis, is a four seated covered rig and a comfortable carriage to ride in. Mr. Roberts is doing everything in his power to give the patrons on his route from Karlstad to Roseau the best service possible and the mail service is as good as anyone might desire at present. The auto will henceforth carry the mail from Karlstad as far as Badger, and from the latter place to Roseau it will be conveyed by fast horses."

Then the article went on to say that Mr. Roberts had a separate stage for carrying passengers and express between Greenbush and Roseau. The incoming mail would arrive at Roseau at 3 P.M. The outgoing mail left at 8 A.M. Not a bad schedule, considering how many years it took to greatly improve upon it! The county now had two sources of mail. From the east, the Canadian National railway brought mail to Roosevelt, Swift, and Warroad. Very little mail came this way, however, as the service was round-about and slow. Another item from the *Times-Region,* dated July 31, 1908 bears this out:

"The people of Warroad and Roosevelt are clamoring for better mail service. They ask that the mail be brought via Duluth over the Messabe, Rainy Lake and C. N. Railways. They are now getting the mail thru Winnipeg and the service is very unsatisfactory."

On Monday, January 18, 1909, the Great Northern Railway brought the mail for the first time. Thus ended the old way of bringing it by stage. The star route between Roseau and Karlstad was discontinued. The problem of adequate mail service was now settled for many years to come. As one editor put it, "it was as good as the best".

The most faithful and dedicated servant in Roseau County's postal history could well be the Knute E. Lee of Wannaska. (The title of "Mr. Postmaster" would be well deserving and very fitting for him.)

Mr. Lee was appointed postmaster at Wannaska, August 24, 1904, and served until his death, October 21, 1945. This is a period of 41 years, 1 month, and 28 days! During that time, Mr. Lee was in direct contact with, and helped institute, the many changes that have been mentioned. The post office was at all times, and still is, operated in connection with a general store business.

It would be impossible to estimate the amount of service Mr. Lee gave during his time. Much of it was above and beyond the requirements of the Postal Laws and Regulations. In the early days the mail would be dispatched to Roseau at 6:00 a.m. The incoming mail would often be as late as 11:00 p.m. In reality, the office was never closed. It was not uncommon for a patron to buy a money order or perhaps take out a C.O.D. and for payment say, "Charge it, Knute". Mr. Lee would thereupon advance the amounts needed and charge them to the customer's account until such time as he was able to pay. Service of this kind certainly does make history! Leland M. Lee was appointed postmaster upon his father's death, continuing also to operate the store, in the same building where it started in 1904.*

One of Minnesota's great natural resources is its great, beautiful, and productive forests. At one time more than half the state was covered with forest where no axe had cut. In 1820 the first saw mill was built at the Falls of St. Anthony, and saw mills grew in number until there were 300 commercial saw mills and an undetermined number of smaller ones in the more wooded areas. Roseau County had many such mills.

This was the age of the logger. At the beginning of the 1900's lumbermen were hired to "log off" an area. A camp was set up for the men, and then the work began. Each lumberjack had a definite type of work to perform. The "axman" or "undercutter"

*Postal Information by Obert Wammer

An early lumber planing operation on the Emil Hedlund farm.

notched the tree on the side of the trunk toward which the tree should fall. Then two "sawyers" using a cross-cut saw stood on opposite sides of the trunk and sawed toward the notches. "The "swamper" came in then to chop off the branches and clear them away. The "skidder" was next, he hitched the log to a team of horses and dragged it to the pile, to be loaded on a wagon or sled to a river. The ruts for the sleighs were kept slick by watering them at night for icing and easier hauling. Going down hill the "road monkey" had to put hay or straw on the ruts to prevent catastrophe. Piling 2,000-4,000 lb. logs one on top of the other on a sled was no easy task, and was accomplished with a heavy chain pulled by horses. The "scaler" had to keep the books on how many board feet of lumber were cut each day, and then the logs were stamped with a stamp hammer as a sort of brand. In spring when the river was running high, the log drives began. Men used spiked poles to get the logs in position to float, and many took an icy dip in the river. Log dams were built up to allow the poles to go through in controlled fashion, and some long drives became floating rafts, being tightly enclosed by the outside chained logs. Rafts were especially built to tow some of the drives that had not sufficient current to get to their destination. Some large crews were fed from wanigans or floating kitchens so that no precious time was wasted in spring. Along with the saw mills, the planing mills came into operation.

Timber operation was big business in the county from 1900-1915. There were many large and smaller mills in full swing. Henry Vog from Warroad sawed 700,000 feet of lumber annually. From 1908-1912 the Swift Lumber Company owned by Joe Ault and Randolph Sperling along with two other men, King and Brown from Indiana, sawed a million feet each year. The Norquist brothers from Roosevelt operated in 1906 to 1915 with an annual cut of about 400,000 while Jack Russell also from Roosevelt, operated a mill from 1915-1928 with an annual cut of 400,000. Halvor Robberstad and Conrad Brohaugh cut out 250,000 feet of logs each year for two years. Altogether the larger mills sawed out 3½ million feet per year and the smaller ones an estimated two million feet. Most of the lumber from the larger mills was shipped out to the western planers in Canada, and our own western states, while the lumber from the smaller mills was used for home consumption. There were also several lathe and shingle mills in the county at the turn of the century which provided material for local use as well as products to ship to other markets.

In 1909 William Oveson built a planing mill at the end of the Jacklin mill race in Roseau. The evidence of the grounds for his mill in the Roseau River are still visible at the railroad bridge below 7th Ave. S. E. Mr. Oveson employed 17 men and two teams to cut the 1 million feet of lumber for the St. Hilaire Lumber Company in 1909. The log drive from Penturen took three to four weeks to reach Roseau.

Timber products worth $150,000 had been marketed in Salol in 1918. The Sjoberg brothers planned a large store there as they expected it to become a "wood metropolis" of the northwest. Dr. Parker reported on one of his visits to Roseau that 60 teams were hauling wood to Warroad regularly during the winter of 1908. The C.N.R. reported a timber business in 1919 of $500,000 from this area.

Then in 1910 came the tragic fire in Baudette and Spooner. This year was the driest ever recorded in the state. A terrific

Lumber operations on January 1, 1911 in Roosevelt. Louis Larson is the second man from the right.

wind on October 9th fanned the many smaller fires into major ones, and both towns were virtually wiped out. People fled for their lives. A Duluth paper reported:

> The horror of the devastating fire that swept along the northern Minnesota border is revealing itself in all its horrible consequences. Never before in the history of the state has such a calamity hit so large a section. The intolerable agony under which the stricken people had to go is incomprehensible. Mothers burning to death to save their babies clinging to their breasts and fathers dying while trying to save their families reached the depths of the tragic in human life. It is estimated that the strip 75 miles long and 25 miles wide is consumed in forest and the dead. Baudette and Spooner, Graceton and Cedarspur, and Triple Creek are wiped out. Other villages are in grave danger. Last Friday hurricane winds whipped the fire and in less than an hour smoldering ruins were left to mark the spot. Rainy River is just across the river from Baudette and Spooner. A train was hurried across which carried the terror stricken people to safety. Those who lingered or got bewildered burned in the street and those too sick to get out met death in their rooms. The fire rushed on into forests beyond where a large settlement of homesteaders lived. They had no way of escape but to face the seething flames and the roads leading out of this settlement were the next day found strewn with charred bodies while farther into the country entire families met death. Those not too far away rushed on to the railroad tracks only to find they were hemmed in. They ran along the tracks until clothing caught fire, and death ended their agony. The loss of life is estimated to be 300-500. (This was found later to be a gross exaggeration as there were actually 42 people who died.)

> The thrifty settlement of Salol was overrun by fire Sunday. A relief train from Crookston rescued settlers. Much hay and timber and some buildings were destroyed and several settlers lost part of their stock. Several men from around the territory also helped fight the fire. Gov. Eberhard who was scheduled to speak in Roseau cancelled, and rushed up to Baudette to help the stricken area. Later Gov. Eberhard decreed money and seed relief for the destitute farmers in the Baudette area.

All the communities came to the aid of the stricken families with shelter, food and money. Malung alone contributed $98.00 to the cause.

The Oveson Dam south of the railroad bridge.

The P. G. Larson and Thortsen Haugen saw mill at Pinecreek in 1897. The men are from left to right: Ole Alton, second and third men unidentified, Fred Haugen, Oscar Haugen, Gilbert Flaten, Ole Ranstad, Hans Haug, Knute Springen, Thorsten Haugen, Fred Larson and Ole Stromstad.

The last fire was responsible for the establishment of the Minnesota Forest Service of 1911 to supersede the legislative act of 1895 with William T. Cox as the first state forester. The authority was transferred from the state auditor and placed under a forestry board. Mr. Cox with his secretary General C. C. Andrews devised the system of forest rangers, who in turn hired patrolmen.

For Roseau County a network of fire protection sites were set up. Dick Willems became the first deputy warden with an office over the bank in Warroad. As time went on look-out towers were erected at Northwest Angle, Clearriver, Norris, River and Malcolm (Grygla). Besides the important responsibility of fire protection the Forestry Department was also to care for forest management so that a continuous supply of timber would be forthcoming. This system was hardly a haphazard tree cutting program but rather one that has become highly specialized and scientifically calculated.

Fire was also a fierce enemy of the early settlers, destroying their buildings, sometimes even the greater portion of their towns. With lumber the main building material, and wood-burning space heaters the chief means of heat, and with poor fire fighting equipment many a holocaust resulted. It would be difficult to record the buildings that fire consumed, but suffice it to say that Dr. Parker alone lost five of his medical buildings by fire. Greenbush had a fire in 1908 that took five stores. Warroad had a major fire in 1905 and again in 1917 when the Warroad school building was burned. When the last business place in Pelan, the Lofgren store burned in 1912, the town was no more. The early settlers had every reason to feel the need of good fire fighting equipment.

In 1913 the Roseau Commercial Club met with the village council concerning the water and electric light systems. Mayor G. M. Stebbins said that he would not act unless it was the express wish of the business men and taxpayers, but urged that the town put in these two improvements, especially the water which was so necessary for fire protection. He mentioned that the fire engine was in good repair and could draw water from the river, except in the winter when it was hardly feasible. In 1913 the fire hall itself burned and the new hoses with it, and this stimulated the people to work for a new fireproof engine house. In Warroad the ladies raised $200 by sponsoring a benefit dance, which money was to be used for fire protection. Both towns got electrical lighting systems, Roseau in 1913 which showed a net profit of $501, and Warroad in 1918 with a profit of $300. Warroad converted the old log jail into an engine house and someone said: "Now if the fire department will see that the proper tests are made with the fire engine and holes are kept in the ice, all will be well."

.Scene of tragedy in the 1910 Baudette-Spooner forest fire in which holocaust 27 people lost their lives.

"Necessity is the mother of invention," goes the saying and Roseau County had much necessity and many creative people. In 1909 J. W. Durham, first sheriff of Roseau County, invented a fireless cooker and installed one in the home of the editor. R. J. Bell advertised it by saying that everyone should have one. Another of Durham's inventions was the "wonder lamp" which gave incandescent light at one-half the cost of using kerosene.

In 1911 A. O. Homme invented a thermodynamic fire alarm. At a certain heat the alarm was supposed to sound and some magnifying device would make it loud enough for the surrounding area. Homme announced that he would not seek a patent, but he would install one in his own home and would sell to anyone who wanted this fire protection.

In 1912 Dr. Stuart Leech of Roseau was granted a patent on a device for testing the purity of air which he called "aemoeter process." It was recommended by the state board of health. It had liquid through which air was forced by means of a single bulb instrument. Carbon dioxide and the impure air acted on the liquid to destroy the color. The rate at which it lost its color was indicative of the amount of impurity in the air. This seems to be somewhat of a reversal of the present air pollution problem in some of the metropolitan areas where the air turns to almost violet color in the dense smog.

In 1908, the paper carried directions for making a home refrigerator – for ice, of course.

Around 1910 the popularity of the Populist Party decreased being supplanted by the Socialists, who were at this time looking for a charter for the county.

The result of the election in 1914 found Ole Rice, sheriff, Paul Marshalk, representative, L. P. Dahlquist, treasurer, and Eddy Billberg, superintendent of schools. There could not have been so much attention to

Women's Lib in 1912, for the total male votes cast that year were 2033, and the female vote was 439. Taft received 278 votes in Roseau County, five of those coming from the town of Roseau. Wilson received 229, with 10 from the village. One humorous note in the paper read: "It turns out that the President was a Presbyterian while all the while he posed as a Democrat."

There was a controversy preceding the November 1912 election on redistricting. The County Board was beseiged by leaders from the county to have the board rescind the redistricting plan. The voices were especially strong from Greenbush and Badger.

The political campaigns were conducted in the same bombastic manner as we know them today. It seemed that the editor felt it his duty to evaluate the candidates which he did often. In 1908 he wrote:

S. G. Bertilrud is a necessary fixture for auditor.
A. S. Houkom is more reliable than anyone for County Treasurer.
A. O. Hagen has three years experience and has perfected his knowledge of his duties and the work of his office, and to elect a new Clerk of Court would be sheer nonsense.
Mike Holm should be Judge of Probate. He is wise, and a good official we should keep him for many years to come.
G. H. Mattson has now come to be appreciated. (Bell unmercifully attacked him as Superintendent of Schools)
Ole Oie is a deserving soul and worthy of the good things of this world, and we should keep him as Register of Deeds.
Mr. Stebbins has done so well that there is no opposition to him for County Attorney.
Mr. John Richmond also has done so well that he should not be opposed. [Richmond died in October of 1908].

On August 14, 1908, Bell had this to say about G. H. Mattson — "If he should be representative he would knock the railroad. We do not want any bumkum representative of the Mattson stamp. If this overgrown youth wants to go down and fight the railroad the best thing we can do is to keep him at home. We are talking to you, Mr. Republican voter."

Some of the election returns around the county in 1910 were interesting. William Oveson was elected mayor of Roseau with 140 votes cast. *The Roseau County Times* accredited the Socialist party for electing Oveson, and A. O. Homme and M. Tostenson on the council. P. H. Buran Sr. became the clerk, while T. C. Petterson was elected trustee, and T. D. Thorson, treasurer. Jess Webster became the justice of the peace and Emil Anderson and J. Wurschmidt were elected to become the constables.

In Warroad, C. A. Moody became the mayor. The report on the election was that C. A. Moody swung the vote by renting a hall "to stump." The vote was 88-53.

Roosevelt elected Beibenheim as president, and the trustees were Waldo Hamilton, Lars Oseid, Ernest Harwood, and the Clerk, C. W. Bell. A. H. Hamilton became the treasurer and Whorley Oaks the constable.

Malung elected Atlantus Austin as supervisor, Louis Enstrom as clerk, and P. D. Peterson as treasurer. Erick Erickson assumed the supervisory position in Stafford with E. G. Backlund the clerk and the constable position went to Andrew Berg.

The records of two men in Roseau county for outstanding politcal service were those of Edward Erickson, and Martin Nelson. Edward Erickson served 44 years on the County board. He was first elected in 1909 and he served continuously for 44 years except for one term. He held the record at one time for having served the most years of any county commissioner. Martin Nelson, father of "Cap" Nelson served on the same board for 37 years. For 27 of these years he was elected chairman of the board, and he served on many committees. He was the first county official to act on a newly formed child welfare program.

The vote on the liquor question raised a great amount of controversy and agitated comment in the years from 1909 through the election year of 1972 when the county went wet. In 1909 Bell wrote:

The question is whether the town is any better since it went dry or not. Seems the young men get liquor from some place for down at the pool hall there is some drinking. No one is accusing anyone of selling liquor, however.

The paper also included this note:

When the Scotsman was asked why he didn't keep a supply of liquor in his home instead of going to town to buy it, he replied, "Liquor won't keep."

In 1909, $100 worth of booze was confiscated in spite of the recent dry vote. In the 1910 election, Roseau went dry while Warroad, Badger, and Greenbush (by five votes) went wet. The paper commented:

Since Roseau County went dry there has been no material change in activity or business, nor has the population decreased. In fact it has increased.

Roseau County Courthouse built in 1914.

The liquor license in those days cost $12.50 and each town had more than its share of saloons. One of the strict rules was that the blinds were not to be pulled in a saloon on the Sabbath day, and in two instances the law was enforced and a fine imposed.

Someone sent a case of beer to R. J. Bell. He sent it back to the shipper saying that if anyone kept his eyes open he could see it was available in Roseau if it were wanted.

The Anti-Saloon League was founded in Roseau County on August 12, 1910. A Mr. Quist spoke in Wannaska, at the Melum Church, and at Pinecreek and on the final day a mass meeting was held at the Opera House in Roseau.

The people of Roseau County became enthusiastically civic minded during these years. Roseau had electric lights as of 1912. At first lights were allowed only on certain days, and the plant was shut off at ten o'clock. Gradually as the profit picture for the light plant became brighter, the lights were allowed for longer periods of time.

The need for a new courthouse in Roseau was acutely felt following the settlement of all the feuds. Calculations on assessments needed to build the structure were made and it was found that for an additional revenue of 50 cents on each land owner a courthouse could be built for $30,000. At the vote held in 1913 there were 1131 for and 1042 against the new building. Subsequently bonds for $25,000 were sold. Since the east side got the school building it was the west side that got the courthouse. A peony bed planted by Mike Holm on the lawn of the building the next year is still growing! Sidewalks too were a part of the improvements, and in 1909 Roseau built the walk from the depot to Holdahl's corner (Main street and Highway 11) on one side, and from the tracks to the Roseau Hotel on the other.

Like improvements were appearing in the other communities as well. Warroad got its electric light system in 1913. The bridge over the Warroad River was built in 1917, and the village fathers announced that they would build a mile of cement sidewalk the same year.

Greenbush got its system in 1915 with a bonded indebtedness of $3000, and made plans for the sidewalks which were built two years later.

Badger worked on plans for electric lights, gearing their installation for 1917, but had to wait another year for a Chicago firm had not sold the bonds.

The depot at Swift was built in 1917, and Mr. Carlquist assured the people that the C. N. would make a stop there to provide for passenger service.

Proudly the county residents can point to their early interest in culture and the aesthetic in their lives. Many of the communities had early instrumental groups. Even as early as 1894 the Malung Singing Choir was active and gave many concerts, sometimes featuring the Mission Friends and singing in the Good Templar Lodge Hall of Malung.

There were opera houses in Warroad, Roseau and Wannaska which featured lyceum courses in 1910 under the sponsorship of the Wilkinson Co. The courses consisted of educational lectures, readings, and musical numbers. A band called the Homolka Band, after its originator, Anton Homolka was sometimes invited to supply additional numbers.

Bands were initiated in many of the small towns. The Badger Cornet Band, organized in 1903 by Morris Goodwin, performed for 4th of July celebrations and other activities in the county. The members of the band were John Burkee, Adolph Hannestad, Bernad Johnson, Johnny Nelson, Martin Hannestad, Dan Goodwin, Jr. and Morris Goodwin. After Mr. Goodwin left Badger in 1907, G. A. Hannestad started a band called the Norman Band.

Morris Goodwin was the director of a band started in Warroad in 1910. Joe Ault took over the leadership in 1912 when the band consisted of Earl Eisenrich, Burt Roberts, Shorty Joyce, Dwight Gorham, Doc Sanderson, George Sperling, Martin Akre, Conrad Brohaugh, Ted Spreiter, M. Rayner, John

Pryor, Halvor Robberstad, Chet Carlquist, Elmer Doyle, Les Sprieter, Joe Ault, Jr. and Reggie Middleton. Later Mr. Amidon took over the band, which staged minstrel shows and local talent musicales in the Opera House. This building was located where the present Memorial arena is now. Later, in 1920 Warroad added an orchestra to its musical groups.

Roosevelt had a band organized in 1909 which was directed by Mr. Monroe, a Spanish American war veteran. Some of its members were George Hannestad, Conrad Brohaugh, Fred Ault, Bob Carpenter, Alvin Norton, Halvor Robberstad, Charles Turnbull, Peter Sherwood and Worley Oaks. Haug had a cornet band in 1914.

The Rev. C. P. Lewis agreed in 1912 to start a band in Roseau. A basket social was held to get a fund for the music for the organization but the director agreed to work without pay. In 1916 the town hired Al Seifert of New Ulm to come to Roseau to direct a Municipal Band and to give lessons. This proved to be very successful as Mr. Seifert taught the youth and adults alike and had a band of 40 members that did a creditable job. An orchestra was formed at this time also which consisted of Ray Gilbertson, drummer, Chester Dahlquist, trumpet, Rudy Holm, saxophone, Dewey Jacklin, saxophone, and Dorothy Holm Wangenstein, pianist.

Swift organized a band in 1918 with Peter Floe as director. Nordahl Carlson sponsored the band and bought the instruments. Some of its members were the Greens (Clarence, Ray, Alfred and Charles) and Lenus and Martin Landby.

Badger had an orchestra too consisting of Newell Lee, Obert and Helmer Wammer, Gerald Deitz, Herbert Strandsland, John Sjoberg, Ross Sjoberg and Eugene Goodwin.

Piano lessons were given by Miss Josie Oie of Roseau a few days a week at the T. G. Durgin residence.

In 1912 the Roseau Choral Club was formed which was composed of any willing singers from all denominations of churches. Their first sacred cantata was "Ruth." A second town orchestra in Roseau was organized about this time which remained in existence until about 1940 when O. G. Gunderson left for California. The members were O. C. Gunderson, violinist, Ed. Johnson, violin, Elmer "Cap" Nelson, flute, and Mrs. Elsie Johnson, piano.

A ladies' quartet consisting of Mrs. G. J. Brenden, Mrs. H. E. Lockrem, Mrs. J. G. Nelson, and Mrs. L. W. Swanson, and directed by Morris Goodwin was formed in Badger in 1906, and was on hand to sing at many important functions in Badger and Greenbush. A male quartet with A. S. Haukom as director, B. C. Christianson, Theodore Haug, and his son Evold was also a popular group around this time.

The Oak Leaves Study Club, an organization of women in Badger, met twice a month for more than ten years. They studied a wide variety of subjects ranging from child care to political problems of the day. One or two meetings a year were devoted to entertaining the youngsters. Grace Reed, sister of one of Badger's founders, taught school in Badger and added much to the cultural and musical life of the town until her retirement in 1911. Mrs. Brenden was one of her voice pupils. Another lady to contribute to the culture of the community was Mrs. Walter Anderson, later known as Mrs. Alma Lind.

The Zion Lutheran church altar in Warroad was long graced with a picture painted by O. M. Berglund which was a donation by the Willing Workers of the town.

The Roseau County Museum has instruments made by Henry Paulsburg of Wannaska in 1918. One is a two headed bull fiddle, and the other a hand made cello with a case.

The colorful pow-wows of the Chippewa

Roseau Orchestra composed of Ray Gilbertson, drummer, Chester Dahlquist, trumpet, Rudolph Holm, saxophone, Dewey Jacklin, saxophone, and Dorothy Holm Wangenstein, piano.

Indians of the area added another cultural note to the life of the residents.

Hockey early became the game of the north and spurred the towns to build arenas and sponsor first class teams. Today Warroad is known as Hockey Town, U.S.A.

There were some trials connected with the sport, for when Roseau scheduled games with Hallock and Warren, Hallock agreed to pay toward expenses, but Warren could only pay $17, so the games were called off. When the game was rescheduled for the 30th of January 1908 the final score was Hallock 7, and Roseau 2. The paper reported that the reason Roseau lost was that the boys were not used to playing by lamplight.

Roseau built its first skating rink south of the firehall and had a band appear at the grand opening. Sub zero temperatures of 40 degrees did not deter either Warroad or Roseau fans and having to clear the outside rinks as they played in a snowfall seemed to be no problem at all. The game between Roseau and Warroad on January 31, 1908 resulted in a tie. This time the paper reported that Warroad refused to play off the tie. The members of the Roseau squad were D. Jacklin, D. Oie, Maurice Dahlquist, Chester Dahlquist, Roy Hagen, Sabin Durham, Carl Von Rohr and Henry Hagen. Players for Warroad were J. Jowett, R. Smith, Soderstrom, T. Gerrie, F. Hagen. The referee was T. G. Thompson.

February 11, 1910 a ski club was organized. The editor must have been feeling a bit facetious when he wrote:

The 1920 hockey team. Standing: Dewey Jacklin, Maurice Dahlquist, Chester Dahlquist, Roy Hagen and Dewey Oie. Seated, Sabin Durham, Carl Von Rohr, and Henry Hagen.

The baseball team of 1912 with Paul Buran as manager. Standing are: Alex Welch, Charles Hafner, Ray Gilbertson, pitcher, Paul Buran, manager, Fred Halvorson, Cliff Rice, and Paul Hafner. Sitting: Laurence Dahlquist, Dick Sjoberg, Carl Von Rohr, Oliver Oie, and Archie Alley and "Slug" lying behind Lawrence Dahlquist.

To qualify for the Ski Club: Scandia Club of Roseau will be the name of the club. To become a member a person must be five times as tall as his waist measure or their circumference twice their height when sitting. Twenty qualified. It was decided that a hill of snow could be built with an abundance of hay at the bottom. Skies could be either barrel staves or from Sears and Roebuck. To raise funds members would be fined whenever they loop-the-loop. The director was Dr. Norin.

Baseball continued in popularity from the time the county was organized. The members of the team in 1912 in Roseau were Alex Welch, Charlie Hafner, Ray Gilbertson, Fred Halverson, Cliff Rice, Paul Hafner, Lawrence Dahlquist, Dick Sjoberg, Carl Von Rohr, Oliver Oie, and Archie Alley. Paul Buran Sr., was the manager. The baseball diamond was where the Roseau Arena is now situated. Warroad played ball on the diamond north of Cal's on Lake of the Woods. Their roster included Roy Smith, Joe Gibault, Phil Huerd, Otto Hassenstab, Adam Lawmaster, Clayton Whaley, Archie Meyers, Sam Meyers, and Clarence Green. The Ross community called its team the Red Caps. Greenbush, Salol, Roosevelt, and Strathcona also had baseball teams, and these teams would meet twice during the summer and there would be a special game the Fourth of July.

In 1917 Salol organized an athletic and improvement club with Mrs. B. S. Johnson as president. The club took care of arrangements for competitive games. With basket socials and evening performances they earned enough money to provide a piano for the town hall.

"Little Jake", the spirited race horse is being held by Burt Bassett, Sr., while Joe Holland rides the sulky.

Tennis was popular at this time also. Both Warroad and Roseau had tennis teams in 1908 which played competitively. Earl Eisenrich was the president of Warroad's team, and Dr. R. V. Harris of Roseau.

There was interest in horse racing in those days. Joe Holland from Warroad had a race horse which won second place in competition in Thief River Falls in 1909. Small boys found it a delight to help Joe clock the horse and work with him. Art Alley owned a horse called "Little Jake" that was the talk of the town. He was so spirited that it was difficult to put a bit in his mouth. This was Little Jake that only the brave dared to race. He was later sold to Joe Holland.

Up here at the top of the nation hunting and fishing have always been popular, game and fish being so abundant as to almost be taken for granted. It was the favorite pastime during the time when it was common to take the gasoline launch, the Knute Nelson up the river, pitch tents and camp out for a week at a time to hunt the ducks and geese that lived in swampy land. There was never any question of getting one's limit; however, hunting and fishing were illegal on Sundays up to 1917.

Commercial fishing was a lucrative industry in these days. In 1911 the Armstrong Trading Co. managed by Paul Marshalk had a fishing business amounting to $42,288. In 1909 the fish catch between June 2nd and July 3rd totalled 455,625 pounds of fish of which 93,933 lbs. were white fish, 192,493 were wall-eyes, 65,076 were pickerel and 18,305 were sturgeon. The rough fish taken amounted to 84,621 lbs. of bull heads.

In 1912 the first fish haul netted 229 boxes of fish from Oak Island, 310 from Bigsby and Zippel for a total of 6 car loads.

In 1916 a sturgeon weighing 240 lbs. was caught at Oak Island, and one weighing 236 lbs. was caught at Long Point. It measured 8 feet. The fish was caught by Louis Palm and his assistant Fred Peterson and brought into town on the Isobel.

It was no great trick to catch fish in the Warroad River and if one were not fortunate enough to have a boat one could fish from the jetty. When the good old summer time came around, this occupation consumed much of the time of released school children. The Wahlberg children fished tubs full of fish and peddled them for a few cents a pound to make money to spend on the Fourth of July.

Deer hunting in the north country in 1910. Earl Eisenrich, Victor Lundbohm, John E. Wahlberg, and Jens Martin.

The Fourth of July! This was the day of days for all pioneer children. The little girls all had new dresses for the day, and the boys would wear their new knickers. The pennies and nickels that had been cached for this day

Dog sledding on the Roseau River in 1908. The Chesepeake dog team belonged to G. M. Stebbins. On the picture are from left to right, Les Bassett, Carl Von Rohr, G. M. Stebbins, Lou Thompson and Pat Ross.

Fourth of July in Roseau in 1919.

had been totaled many times and saved to buy goodies from the stands on main street. What woe-begone children should the 4th turn out to be rainy, but oh, what joy when the sun shone down and the events could take place. The day always started with a gun salute in memory of the war dead. There was always a colorful parade led by the dignitaries of the town. At the end of the parade there was a hay rack for the children to ride in. In the Warroad celebrations the children kept a wary eye out for George Marvin who threw out nickels for them to scamper for. A special guest at the Warroad celebrations was Pat Moran, a Civil War veteran, who lived in Warroad until his death.

The fun part of the Fourth included the races, for which the children had practiced for weeks. There were water sports with high dives, greased poles and boat races — rowing of course, in Warroad. All the celebrations included speeches held either in the center of town or in a park. In the evening there were fireworks, ending with Old Glory in sparkling lights. Some of the speakers for this great occasion were J. W. Durham, Charles Thompson, Hans Tellefson, Israel Sjoberg, and G. Stebbins. Later in the evening the children were taken home and the bowery dance began.

The float in the Fourth of July parade prepared by Bruss and Haberberg on May 30, 1915. Cigars were offered for sale for 5c and included New Life, Sage-Guard, and White House, while Extense, Don Amile and Big Duke cost 10c. Notice the big cigar on the float.

Chautauquas were in vogue at this time too. The program sounds stimulating with lectures on such subjects as "A Good Neighbor," "The Basis for American Civilization," or "What it Means to be an American." There were well known bands who played for the large audiences, the Mac Dowell singers, and usually there was a group of bell ringers. Comedies were enacted with titles like "Glory in the Morning," and "The Bishop and the Convict."

April 6, 1917: The United States was involved in World War I. The chilling news with all its ramifications called forth the urgent call to duty for all Americans in whatever fields they might be able to serve. Roseau County responded with vigorous and enthusiastic patriotism.

There was a picture in the *Roseau Times Region* of a glider type airplane with a caption that read: "Is America prepared for an invasion?" At the state fair in 1917 a thrilling preparedness demonstration was performed with airplanes, parachutes, first aid, soldiers and nurses being a part of the show. It awakened the citizens to what was demanded, and of the horrifying possibility of war on our own land.

On June 22, 1917 a list of the Roseau County draft eligible men was published and recruiting for the army was in full swing. The notice to start drafting had been received from President Woodrow Wilson. Minnesota was to supply 17,854 inductees of which 1141 on the draft list were from Roseau County. The first name to be drawn by lottery was that of Gilbert R. Thompson of Ross. A Zippel man evaded the draft. The punishment for that was 15 years at Leavenworth.

By August 119 men had had their physical examinations, and there were 56 who passed. However, on the basis of need at home they all claimed exemptions.

The first group of men who left for camp on September 21, 1917 included Axel Sun-

A sad scene in 1915 when the soldiers marched through town just before leaving for the war.

sten, Harry Norland, Gustav K. Williamson, Clayton Whaley, Stephen Gust, Carl Moen, Calvin Carlson, Eddie Polezinski, Fred Goslein, Carl Henrickson, James C. Green, Lars Pederson, George Roetman, David Lofgren, Andrew Mattson and John Mork. The second call for 102 men left for Camp Dodge, Iowa, on February 23, 1918.

At home there were war time measures adopted to help the effort. Every community and township had their own Red Cross Chapters. Vilda Stebbins was the county secretary of all the Red Cross Chapters. Money to the amount of $2,663 had been donated to the Red Cross by the 4th of April, 1918. The citizens observed meatless and wheatless days in order to conserve food for the army. A mass meeting was held on October 12, 1917 to promote the Liberty Loan Committee throughout the county. Packets for the soldiers were being prepared for the boys overseas which besides food also included warm knit sweaters. Many meetings were curtailed to save fuel, and flour and sugar was rationed. Thrift stamps went on sale. The county subscribed $174,850 to war bonds. There was a great deal of fervor to win the war and get the boys safely home.

All the newspapers carried a weekly digest of the war news. These reports were avidly read and discussed. There were no radio or TV stations to relay the news.

There were the inevitable tragedies. Clarence Helliwell from Warroad was the first man to give his life in the war. He did not die in combat, however, but from pneumonia he got while at Camp Dodge. Kaleb Lindquist was reported missing in action on the 16th of August in 1918 and later reported dead, becoming the first man from Roseau County to die in combat. Another war casualty was Andrew O. Mattson who died in combat, and it is to honor these two men that the Roseau and Warroad American Legions named their posts. Other men to die in combat were Charley Doesser, Louis Hendershot, Oscar Hammer, Louis Besserud, John Krzoska, Stephen Gust. Those who died from disease or accidents while serving their country were Edward A. Roadfeldt, Theodore Jallo, Severin Brager, Peter Johnson, Mike Grugal, David G. Welch, Gilbert Hagen, Erick O. Erickson, Adolph Lindgren, Jentof Anderson, Anton Anderson, Thomas Dahl, Arthur Sjodin, and Nestor Oberg.

No one's patriotism was questioned in the county, but a mass meeting was called by the Mayor for the purpose of discussing how Roseau County citizens could better assist in winning the war. There were addresses and a band concert and Ole A. Rice issued this proclamation:

> As Sheriff of Roseau County I wish to assure all citizens of foreign birth that in this time of crisis, they need not fear invasion of their rights so long as they go about their business in a peaceful and law abiding manner. The U. S. has never confiscated any property of foreign born citizens unless the foreign born of their acts make it necessary. I take this means to assure all citizens that are foreign born that they will be protected.

But finally on November 11, 1918 the armistice was signed. Ten boys on their way to camp heard the good news when they got as far as Crookston, and returned home. Church bells rang, whistles blew, a parade led by the band happily marched through the towns. Now the wounds of the war could begin to heal and Roseau County with the rest of the world could begin a new era.

Chapter 7

ADOLESCENCE

1919-1945
(Between Wars)

Take up our quarrel with the foe!
To you from failing hands we throw
The torch; be yours to hold it high!
If ye break faith with us who die
We shall not sleep, though poppies grow
In Flanders Fields

In Flanders Fields
John McCrae

Chapter 7

ADOLESCENCE
1919-1945
(Between Wars)

Many wise men have observed the truth of the statement – hardship is good for the soul. Roseau County had, during this era, its share of hardships and was tried in the fires of adversity to emerge stronger and wiser. The agricultural economy of the time was at first promising, and later disappointing, beset with problems of weather and unstable prices. The county had only one promising industry, the clover. It was the age when the young people "seeking their fortune" left for more lucrative positions away from home. War had its effects too, with a feeling among the people of emotional depletion and apprehension. The adolescence of Roseau County was unstable and became a slightly stormy period – a tempering for the years to come.

"In the clover" was both literally and figuratively true of Roseau County during the early part of this period. The luggage of the high school hockey players carried the casual slogan, "We are from Roseau where clover is a weed." No section of the country could compare with Roseau County in the production of sweet clover seed. Greenbush was rated as the most important sweet clover center in the world, shipping out twenty to thirty carloads of seed which netted the community an average income of one hundred thousand dollars each year. In the eastern part of the county the red clover and alsike grew like weeds. Alfalfa, too, was an abundant crop. The acreage for alfalfa was extended from 500 to 4000 acres in six years. Buyers from the south and east found Roseau County their best source of clover seed which was then so much in demand.

Swift became an alfalfa center. A. M. Landby with sons Lenus, Martin, and Andrew M. Widsten, Gus Anderson, J. W. Taylor, and Martin Erickson started an alfalfa meal factory. It was a $3000 investment that could process a ton of alfalfa in one hour. It was called the Landby Dehydrating Company; it was later taken over by A. J. Landby, who sold some interests to Canadian operators who relocated the plant near Winnipeg.

A. M. Landby, one of the pioneers of Swift, was a man of foresight and enthusiasm for the agricultural development of the area. He came to Roseau County in 1898 and homesteaded a quarter section of land, dug ditches, sought scientific ways to improve his land, and was instrumental in improving drainage around Swift to produce more farm land. He invested in prize stock and raised his own silage. He helped to organize the Livestock Shipping Association, and helped to build the Warroad Creamery, and started the Farmer's Elevator.

Enthusiasm for farming was keenly felt during these years. The county boasted 8 new silos in 1922 with 18 more on order; the goal was 100 silos by 1923. The need for diversified farming was stressed by farm groups. Professor Crimm, of the University of Minnesota, held meetings on crop diseases. Velvet barley, Anthony oats, and Marvel wheat were endorsed for seeding. As early as 1942, A. R. Lee, International Harvester dealer, displayed a self-propelled combine for demonstration only.

However, all was not progress, for the grasshoppers were having their day too, along with the army worms. The county agents working with the federal government set up the creameries as distribution centers for insecticides. A concentrated effort eradicated the pests.

In 1933 the wheat relief plan was put into effect. It was a temporary organization set up in each county to reduce wheat acreage. In 1928 through 1932, Roseau County seeded 5000 acres of wheat. The average yield was 14.3 bushels to the acre with yearly production of 71,560 bushels.

The second creamery building in Roseau.

With the good yield of hay crops the dairy farmers took renewed interest. A test for TB on all dairy herds was made in 1926 through the U. S. Department of Animal Husbandry. It was found that 26 head of cattle were infected with the disease. But by efficient programs the county was declared free of TB in all dairy cows by 1929.

With advances in agriculture and dairy production the need for creameries and elevators was acutely felt. Experience had proved that cooperatives efficiently handled the produce. At the end of the first quarter of the twentieth century there were farmer's cooperatives in Warroad, Roseau, Badger, Greenbush, and Wannaska.

In 1920 when W. J. Miller was president of the creamery association in Roseau, and Elias Grahn, N. E. Wold, Peter Strandberg and Carl Von Rohr were on the board, the annual report showed an increase in produce revenues over the preceding year. There were at this time 606 patrons who received 12 cents more for their butter fat than they had in the previous year. 91,552 pounds of butter had been produced, of which 3000 pounds were sold locally and 88,552 pounds shipped to New York. On July 14, 1924, when W. A. Lindahl was buttermaker, the creamery was so swamped with cream that one batch had to be churned before the rest could be accepted. In 1920 S. T. Holdahl donated a piece of ground on Highway 11 for a new creamery building, which was completed in 1923. In 1929, additions were built to the building for refrigeration machinery and a buttermilk dryer. A produce building and a milk pasteurization department were added in 1936. The Land O' Lakes Drying Plant in 1945 required major expansion because of a demand by the government for more outlets for dairy products.

Efforts were made to establish more creameries, and one was set up in 1921 in Warroad, a good central location for the eastern part of the county. The building was a frame building with a wooden floor, a churn, open vat and paddle for hand cooling and agitation, a small boiler, cool room and ice house. For a short time the creamery had to close for lack of cream, but in 1922 when there was an increase in dairy cattle, the forward looking farmers took steps to build a more modern creamery. This was a cooperative venture, and at the initial meeting Harry Sanders was elected president, Elmer Brandli, vice president, E. F. Kennetz, secretary-treasurer, and Adolf Olson, Bert Myers, Martin Landby and William Gould, directors. Fred Schultz was elected as manager of the Warroad Cooperative Creamery Association. When the Beltrami forest area was depopulated and the people relocated at other locations there was a temporary setback to the creamery, but the ground lost was regained after only a few years.

It was at this time that the identifying butter carton with the picture of the beautiful Indian maiden became Minnesota's trademark for Grade A butter. The name Land O' Lakes was selected in a state wide contest. Now this excellent butter can be bought in most grocery stores around the nation.

Warroad had an establishment owned and operated by Pete Heppner to pasteurize and homogenize milk. The business was begun in 1948.

Continued interest in livestock raising and breeding resulted in the erection of a new shipping yard with six new stock pens, along the Great Northern tracks. The Roseau Commercial Club took steps to promote the dairy industry, and one of their most effective programs was to encourage the 4-H members to raise purebred animals which were generally raised by the youngsters to market condition and then purchased by the businessmen. In a county-wide testing program in 1940 for Bangs disease it was found that 28,820 head of cattle were infected with the disease. But this disease was also eradicated from the herds.

The practice of artificial insemination was introduced and an association was formed called The Northwest Breeders which used prime Holstein stock, and became a vital factor in the upgrading of herds.

The second Minnesota Sheep Palace in Greenbush, scene of the annual Sheep Days Shows.

Long before the state of Minnesota in 1921 issued a grant in aid to the Greenbush Sheep Days promotion the farmers around Greenbush and south of Roseau had been holding a "Sheep Day" as an annual event to upgrade and increase interest in wool production in the area. Men from the Department of Animal Husbandry of the University of Minnesota were invited to speak and demonstrate such phases of sheep raising as, prime fleece sheep, building of market pens for lambs, judging quality sheep, and the science of sheep shearing. A wool pool was organized in 1927 with John Dynes as president. In 1926 there were 720 sheep shipped into Roseau County from Faith, South Dakota to let out to 18 farmers in the county as first grade animals. The Roseau Wool Growers Association was formed in 1926. Its records showed production of 4000 lbs. of wool the first year which increased to 58,000 lbs. by 1932. At the annual Sheep Days held in Greenbush there is a contest on shearing of sheep, which has been a factor to perpetuating the skill of shearing sheep.

The Minnesota Sheep Producers Association was organized and incorporated in 1954, which assists the farmers in all phases of the sheep raising industry. The county committee which belongs to the state association is composed of Bernard Nelson, chairman, Stanley Evans, Belmar Thompson, Don Wicklund, Arthur Giese, and Stephen R. Evans, all farmers or businessmen from Greenbush.

In 1930 the value of farm products in the county exceeded 2 million dollars. Butter, beef and grass seed were the most important agricultural commodities. Roughly the statistics were: butter, \$800,000; cattle, \$300,000; grass seed \$225,000; sheep \$175,000; wool, \$30,000; flax, \$150,000; poultry and eggs, \$114,000; fish, \$125,000; timber, \$75,000, and miscellaneous \$50,000.

The raising of hogs, pigs, and chickens, never a big cash crop in Roseau County declined during the years 1900-49 at a rate of 7% over the previous five years.

The trend in agriculture during this period was from smaller farms to fewer, but larger ones. Thus in a five year period the total of 2433 family type farms in 1940 with average acreage of 239 decreased to a total of 2272 farms with 261 average acres. This trend has continued since that time.

Gross income from agriculture rose 55% in the period of 1945-59. In 1940, 59% of the farm sales dollars were spent for operating expenses, whereas it was to rise to 70% in 1959, thus demanding more efficient farming operation. With the second World War came increased crop sales and higher prices. Also there was a trend toward more full time owners, and less tenancy.

In Roseau County, the climate, the prime factor in agriculture, has extremes in temperature varying to 159°. The lowest recorded temperature is a -52° and the high 107°. There are usually 105 days of growing weather. January usually averages a 1° F, and the July temperature usually averages 67°. There is usually precipitation in Roseau County of about 20 inches per year, with Warroad generally having an inch or two more rain than the rest of the county. May through August receives about half the precipitation, with the other months averaging ½ to ¾ inch per month.

It was fortunate that the county had an alert and energetic county agent, J. W. Taylor, through whose effort agriculture took great strides at this time. In 1923 there were experiments on the Wallace Merrill farm to test for new and better fertilizer. The new wheat varieties were used in experimental plots on the A. R. Miller farm. Peat was considered at this time as a commercial product.

With the slogan "not profits, but service to the farmers" the elevators of the county have built enviable businesses. In Roseau the Roseau Farmer's Elevator started in 1911 with the first organizers being Erick Backlund, O. B. Ekman, C. E. Brandt, R. E. Boen, John W. Johnson, Carl Dunseth, and C. A. Olson. These directors were anxious to have a business owned and run by the Roseau County farmers, so they approached the Red Lake Milling Co. and Hanson-Barzen Milling Co. to sell them their establishments. In 1934 the old building was torn down and a new 35,000 bushel capacity elevator was erected. In 1938 increased business necessitated the construction of a 35,000 ft. annex. A feed mill was added in 1944 along with a new office. The next addition in 1946 included the coal sheds renovation, a seed processing plant and a warehouse, together with a 100,000 ft. annex. The company handled 782,000 bushels of grain in 1949. The Farmers Co-op Elevator processes its own grain and feeds and markets its grain, and does custom grinding and mixing. The Northland Elevator came a few years later.

It was the Northland Grain Co. of Badger that was the first elevator in Badger, having purchased the business from the Red Lake Milling Co., and renaming the elevator. A custom feed grinding was added in 1943.

Warroad, Salol and Roseau operate Farmers Union Elevators. The Salol elevator was completed in 1941 at a cost of $12,000. The Warroad elevator was built the same year. In the eight years after it was built the amount of grain handled increased from 100,000 bushels to 450,000 bushels annually.

George Marvin came to Warroad in 1903 to run a Canadian company's grain elevator for the Warroad community. The job lasted only a year since this elevator was torn down and the business moved to Saskatchewan. However, Mr. Marvin bought the other elevator from a Thief River Falls firm and operated it for the town of Warroad. Marvins then bought out the firm and in 1938 and 1939 they erected two seed cleaning plants. The Marvin Seed House run by George Marvin and sons was approved and accepted by the Crop Improvement Association for the handling of certified seed.

In 1918 farmers who recognized the need for improvement in farming practices and livestock breeding organized the Roseau County Farm Bureau. Since the state required a sponsoring agency for a County Extension program, the Farm Bureau assumed this obligation and the County Extension Service was initiated in Roseau County. The primary object of this organization was to help coordinate the work of the federal government, the state, the county, and the division of agricultural extension of the University of Minnesota in promoting the county extension work in agriculture and home economics. The first officers were Walter Anderson, president; A. M. Landby, vice-president; P. H. Buran, Sr., secretary-treasurer; and the directors were Martin Widsten, Benjamin Franklin, Fred Nordine, Mark Searson, E. L. Thompson, Louis Enstrom, C. B. Goodrich and A. L. Rodeman. A share in the Farm Bureau could be bought for $5.00.

In 1918 O. M. Olson was hired as the first county agent of Roseau County. In 1953 the State Legislature relieved the Farm Bureau of extension responsibilities.

The optimistic report of 1922 that 90% of Roseau County was under some system of drainage and that 91% of the swampy land was in the process of being reclaimed was heartening, and cause of rejoicing. The news about the flooding of the Roseau River, an almost annual event, however, was disheartening and the steps to correct the situation were less than adequate.

To sense the futility of the attempts to solve the problem, the following are just a few of the news reports on the situation:

Flood time in Roseau April 17, 1918. The Methodist church which stood at the east end of the Center Street bridge is inundated.

May 10, 1926 – Manitoba says it will dyke the Roseau River on its side to prevent floods and protect farmers at a cost of $150,000.

August 8, 1929 – International Joint Commission hearing to decide what can be done about the flooding of the Roseau River will meet.

June 5, 1931 – Drainage was being considered via Two Rivers to stop flooding. Felt the project could get by with only 20 miles of digging.

February 6, 1932 – Roseau River Drainage Committee to study Pinecreek and Mud Creek at the border to help control flood in times of excessive rains.

October 2, 1937 – War Department continues hearing on Roseau flooding control. Lt. Colonel Fleming to preside at the meeting.

April 2, 1942 – River flood one foot higher than highest last year.

July 7, 1945 – Hearing set on river matter for June 22. Board of engineers for rivers and harbors to be present. They requested that the 1936 report of flooding be brought up to date.

May 23, 1946 – Proposed dike along north side of river from northerwestern point of county to eastward into Pohlitz by E. H. Nelson, Committee Chairman. Ditch 17 is involved which would drain Pinecreek, Duxby, and lower Roseau River. A mass meeting has been called.

May 6, 1948 – Canadians have plan on Pinecreek. Propose a diversion of Creek into bog area given at meeting. Minutes presented a map and survey. It includes a dam 2½ miles north of a line to east of Pinecreek and a ditch 18' wide to cut diagonally SW 6.7 miles to border and to enter U. S. in Sec. 26 north of Duxby. Cost to Canada $50,000.

January 1, 1949 – Army working to re-survey for river control project. Congressman Harold C. Hagen has information.

A common occurrence in Roseau in spring. The old Pearl street bridge (now Center street) shows the height of the water. The Baptist church to the right and the Methodist church on the left have since been removed.

And this is how the flood control project started back in the early 1900's and has progressed since. To date there remains only the problem without any concrete advances to solutions. Roseau has thrown up dikes along the river to protect its homes, but the problem of the flooding for agriculture still remains.

Yet the agriculture of the county did progress. To express their pride in accomplishment there have been annual festival days held in some of the communities. One of the anticipated events in Roseau was the annual Clover Festival. Part of the program was educational with University of Minnesota experts sharing their expertise with the farmers of Roseau County. The other part of the event was the festive parades, various contests, and dances that rounded out a two or three day event. Now with less emphasis on clover seed production the celebration of the Clover Festivals has ceased.

The beautiful Roseau River!

"The patron shall keep the approach to the mailbox free at all times. . ." except . . .

Clyde Dowers in the 1940's gets the mail through to Badger.

In Badger a festival called Flax Day is held annually. With the raising of flax crops the threshing days could be extended when necessary into the colder weather, so it became a major crop in the central and western part of the county. Both festive and educational features were a part of the celebration.

In Warroad during the 30's and 40's the Labor Day week-end was the time to celebrate Timber Days. The money raised at this event was used to sponsor the Laker Hockey team, and was a cooperative town endeavor. Later the Timber Day idea was given over to an event called Water Frolics, but the hockey benefit has remained.

The weather in Roseau County played many tricks in the area in the period from 1920 through 1945 that were frightening and costly. Perhaps the biggest rainfall of all time fell in 1919 when 8 inches fell in 48 hours causing a widespread flood, Peat chunks floated up and several people walked out on them, but found when they tumbled off that there was four feet of water beneath them. Again the unpredictable Roseau River was rampaging.

One of the wildest windstorms in the county occurred in 1925, flattening many buildings. Warroad holds the record for cold when in 1936 the temperature read a -52° below zero.

The blizzard in late spring, May 1941 was the storm of the century, for in the northwest 72 people lost their lives. Twenty-eight of these victims were from Minnesota and among them was Sidney Bonaime of Roseau who died near Dugdale, Minnesota when he left his marooned car to try to find help. On this particular night there was a basketball game at Stephen. Many parents and fans had gone earlier in the day with the band and had escaped the blizzard. When the players attempted the trip in the cars of Superintendent Hollister and Coach O. Lindberg, they became marooned. The level-headed thinking of the men probably saved the lives of the boys, for they insisted that the boys stay with the cars, and that they all get into one car and to stay sitting and holding one another for warmth, and that they keep telling jokes and singing. A happy reunion occurred the next morning when the snow plow was able to release the cars so the players could join the waiting folks at Stephen.

The Roseau Memorial Rink, built in 1924, was blown down in a windstorm in 1943 as were 100 barns in the county. In 1939, M. J. Hegland became the official Mr. Weatherman. In that year the Weather Bureau installed instruments on his property so he could record and transfer information on temperature, air pressures, wind velocity and precipitation.

The Memorial Arena in Roseau, built in 1925 and destroyed by high winds in 1943.

The William Crooks train, the first wood burning type, made a historical run through Roseau County in 1937, commemorating the first years of settlement in this area. On board were dignitaries from the Minnesota Historical Soceity on tour of the northland.

In 1929 there was a total eclipse of the sun in June and again on December the 24th. That year there were 7 comets visible in the sky. The total eclipse will not occur again until the year 2024.

The year was 1937. A special pioneer train, the **William Crooks** passed through the area to commemorate the 50th anniversary of the white man's settlement in Roseau County. The train was of historical importance, evoking many nostalgic memories with its coal burning engine (the very first ones burned wood), the red plush seats, the well worn wood floors, a pot-bellied coal heater, and its swaying back and forth that didn't lull anyone to sleep. Only 28 years ago the favors of J. J. Hill had been won over to extend the line to Roseau and Warroad.

The tour which originated in St. Paul was planned by the State of Minnesota Historical Society and the Roseau Historical Society cooperatively. The train, under its own power left St. Paul, June the 19th, with the following passengers on board: W. P. Kenny, president of the G. N.; Dr. Theodore Blegen, superintendent of the Minnesota Historial Society; Senator Victor Lawson, editor of the Willmar Tribune; Willoby Babcock, curator of the Minnesota Historical Society and archaeologist; Edward Gale, president of the St. Paul Historical Society; Harold Lathrop, director of state parks; Dr. Grace Nute, curator of manuscripts of the Minnesota Museum; Mike Holm, secretary of state; and Eddy Billberg, president of the Roseau County Historical Society. A group of old timers met the train at Fox, and for an extra 13 cents all the passengers proceeded to Roseau. Here the band and a large group of Roseau and Warroad citizens met the train and all participated in the dedication of the Roseau County Museum. A Lake of the Woods tour was arranged for 60 interested persons for the next day to visit the site of Fort St. Charles, on Magnuson Island, Lake of the Woods.

The last passenger train ran through the county in 1950, but the role of the G. N. to open and settle the northland had its heyday in the early 1900's. George Marvin was a passenger on this last train as he was on the first one through the county.

The agitation after 1920 for more and better roads, a need felt throughout the state, was a part of the problem of good transportation in the county also. An amendment called "number one" brought the Trunk Highway System into existence and for Roseau County with its 1454 miles of "passable" road it had a twofold effect. It helped make contacts between the counties and various centers of the state and greatly stimulated automobile travel with the result that many miles of our state aid road systems became incorporated into the Trunk System. Perhaps the most striking change in road construction came with the passage in 1921 of the county aid system by the State Legislature which was known as Chapter 323. It provided funds for construction and maintenance from gas tax collections. One feature of this system was that unlike the state aid road system, all roads were designated, constructed and maintained by the County Engineer, entirely by mandate and under authority of the County Board.

With this new source of revenue and having no back-log of responsibility for maintenance the new system developed quite rapidly. There were several other factors that contributed to the rather phenomenal growth of the system. Perhaps the most important was the extremely low price paid per mile of construction of roads, especially during the 1930's when costs were as low as a few hundred dollars per mile. It was also the practice to permit the townships to build a section of road after which it would be taken over and maintained by the county as a part of the county aid network. This practice, started in 1930, continued until recent years. Another factor was the use of the elevator grader or "mucker" which when controlling construction practices were not required, could move dirt rapidly and inexpensively. There were some problems in the road building program that were detrimental to Roseau County, however, in that many ditch grades were included in the county aid system. Since the base for these roads was often a conglomerate of peat, topsoil, stumps, clay or sand, the adverse weather conditions created maintenance problems.

At the township level there was continuous improvement of roads, especially after the consolidation of schools occurred so that a good transportation system was necessary. The cooperation of the county and township boards, however, made these country roads not only "passable" but entirely adequate. The road from Warroad to Roosevelt was established in 1920.

As the travel to and from Canada increased, the feasibility of a better road between Roseau and South Junction was initiated by A. O. Beaudry. A hard surfaced road was built in 1930 between the towns, and the roads to Pinecreek and Middlebro came at a later date. In 1924 there were plans to put a road from Sprague to Northwest Angle, which didn't materialize until 1972.

In 1930 when Roseau County had 3000 automobiles, $35,000 was designated by the county for roads, but the amount jumped in 1931 to $80,000. The depression days of the '30's created the WPA (Works Progress Administration) which provided a proportionate amount of money and labor for county road building. In 1938 when Harry Paine was the County Engineer, there were 142 miles of state aid roads and 327 miles of county roads, and 90 miles of graded roads built. In 1939 the bridge over Highway 11 was opened with due ceremony. The bridge cost $37,147 to build. In 1941, 60 miles of new roads were built in the county, and in 1942, Highway 89 was to get a coat of gravel. These were the preludes to our great highway systems of today.

Telephone communications took strides ahead in 1921 when Northwestern Bell Telephone Company bought many of the county systems. In March 1938 there was a drastic change in the technical aspects of the telephone when a cut over from the magneto to the common battery type telephone was made. The new equipment for the western part of the county was housed in Roseau. Now no one needed to "crank" to get central. Instead by simply raising the receiver one could hear a friendly "number please."

In 1930 the Fox-Jowett Telephone Company which had erected the line from Warroad to Roseau, and offered telephone service in the Warroad area was sold to the Northwestern Bell Telephone Company. At this time there were 174 telephones in the Warroad area but expansion came about so fast that by March 1957 it became necessary to build housing for the common battery type equipment and switchboard. Milt Fish had planned to stay only a few years, but these years extended until he retired in Warroad in 1964. He died in 1965. There were at this time 320 town telephones in Roseau and 200 in the rural area. Badger was served by the Wickstrom Telephone Company and had some 181 telephones in 1933 and 205 in 1944. Now it was no longer necessary for the farmers to maintain the lines and to find centrals who would be willing to take on 24 hour jobs.

In 1923 the radio made its appearance in Roseau. The hospital installed headphones for the patients, and the Nelson Garage and Delmore Clinic were the first to install radios in their establishments. In 1926 the radio fans were hoping for "quiet air" so they could hear the Minnesota-Michigan game. An appeal was made in the paper that no electrical motors be used at this time to avoid static.

Dr. Delmore, Sr. reported in November 1923 that he had heard the voice of Captain McMillan on short wave from the North Pole. This unusual experience as related by the doctor was received much as we received the voices of the astronauts when they were on the moon. McMillan had a relay of news from Chicago. He reported that it was 15° below zero at the North Pole, with only two hours of twilight. He further related that the Eskimos had come aboard his ship and were quite confounded by the voices that came from nowhere.

Dr. Delmore also related that he was able to hear the heart beat of a man who was lying ill in the hospital in Pennsylvania. A new and intricate device had made this advance possible.

Erling Mikkelson built a plane in 1931. The paper stated simply that "the tests showed that the machine needed improvements." He used a Model A Ford engine. The days of air travel were fast approaching, however, and the towns made plans for their own airports. In Roseau an 80 acre plot was purchased in May, 1945, which was a mile and a half from town in the northwest corner of Section 14. Another 80 acres was added the same year to the original site. Dan Carver was engaged to instruct the would-be air birds. In 1946 the town got a federal grant of $15,550 from the state appropriation of $600,000 for airports.

Warroad secured the option on land in January 1934 for an airport for $1000. In 1949 the construction of a $26,000 airport was begun with the help of a federal grant. Greenbush received a federal grant of $20,000 for its airport. For the folks at the Northwest Angle the airplane was termed a "god-send" for mail deliveries and emergencies. Rudy Billberg was the pioneer pilot.

The newspapers of the county were now becoming more sophisticated with the trend toward less syndicated news and more variety of local news and features. One of the first pictures which appeared in the paper back in 1923 was one of Earl Melick, courtesy of the *Minneapolis Journal;* he was pictured with the purebred calf that won him a free trip to the International Boys and Girls Club in Chicago. Cartoons made their appearances and there were fewer serial stories. By 1937 the paper closely resembled the type of newspaper we are accustomed to today. It carried a pictorial supplement called Northwest Pictorial Monthly which included in a few issues, articles on Lake of the Woods and areas around Roseau. In 1940 Verner Nelson started a paper called *The Minnesota Leader,* which he published for several years. *The Roseau Times Region* was purchased by Dan Carver in 1944.

It was not until 1935 that the light plant operated at a profit. Up until 1910 the village of Roseau had to use kerosene lamps for light. The first steam engines were installed shortly thereafter and operated until 1928 with electricity being sold at 16c a kilowatt. The village allowed light only on certain days

Roseau in 1920.

and service was severed at 10 o'clock. For a short time the first diesel and steam engines were operated simultaneously. In 1932 a diesel with 120 h.p. was replaced by one with 210 h.p. Five years later a 375 h.p. and then in 1946 a 556 h.p. engine was installed. The plant showed a profit of $8000 in 1936. It was a proud time for the little village when it could boast a "white way" in 1932. At each intersection four poles for light were erected on Viola Avenue (Main Street). The kilowatt hours increased 100% from 1944-49, so that in 1942 the light plant was out of debt. The plant made $514,650 in 1948 and on November 10th of that year a 1600 h.p. engine was installed. The light plant has shown a steady increase of profits from that time on and has aided the village not only with excellent service but also with grants and gifts for municipal projects.

Other civic improvements in Roseau included a municipal building, erected with the aid of WPA labor in 1936. The Roseau Auditorium was dedicated May 13, 1937.

Main Street in Roseau, then called Viola Avenue, was paved in 1939, and new storm sewers were constructed on Pearl Street (Center Avenue.)

In Warroad in February, 1913 a special election was held to vote on two questions (1) Shall the village issue bonds in the sum of $20,000 for an electric light plant, and (2) Shall the village issue bonds in the sum of $8000 for public water works. A decided majority in favor of both issues started that village on its way to progress. A generating plant for the REA was started in May of 1940 and completed in December of the same year on Highway 11 just out of Warroad.

In Roseau a zoning committee was appointed in 1940 with R. J. Knutson as chairman, and E. H. Nelson, J. P. Grothe, and A. R. Lee as directors.

The banks, barometers of economic growth, numbered 16 during the time period of 1918-1958. Each town boasted at least one bank and some of the villages had two or three banks at the same time. Even the smaller communities had their own banking institutions hopeful that the winds of good fortune might make their town a center of trade.

The oldest bank in Roseau was the First National Bank with H. T. Thorson, T. D. Thorson, and Israel Sjoberg as promoters. In 1905 the Citizen's Bank was founded by Bendix and Soren (Sam) Holdahl and was located where the Reese Variety store now stands. The Farmers and Merchants Bank, with the new innovation of safety deposit boxes, was set up in 1907 by D. E. Tawney, A. H. Foss, and Carl von Rohr. The Roseau County National Bank, housed in a corner of the Sjoberg Mercantile store was the last to be started in 1920.

There were two banks in Warroad. The Security State Bank, with D. E. Dixon, and T. H. Spreiter as founders, was begun in 1912, the next year Peter Alldrin started the First State Bank with Frank Brown and Amend Soderstrom.

Greenbush residents could claim three banks in their town. There was the Farmers and Merchants Bank started in 1913, followed by the State Bank of Greenbush which was liquidated after a short time and lastly the People's Bank of Greenbush.

Badger also had three banks. One was called the Scandinavian-American Bank; one which existed for only a short time was the Badger State Bank, and finally the First State Bank with N. O. Folland, I. S. Folland, and N. B. Gustafson as officers.

Many of the little inland villages had their banks as well. The Farmers State Bank of Wannaska was begun in 1915 and operated until 1926 with Olaf Holdahl as president and Ed. G. Johnson as cashier. Later Almer Skrutvold acted as cashier. Roosevelt's bank was begun in 1927. The Strathcona State Bank was begun in 1931, and Salol's State Bank with E. M. Broughten as cashier. The Wannaska and Salol Banks merged in 1922, with the Citizen's State Bank.

The Pelan State Bank, with Kelso as president must have done a thriving business with Roseau County citizens who traveled by stage to Stephen from the eastern part of the county.

Chester Dahlquist has the distinction of being the first and only 50 year banker in Roseau County. He started in 1916 as bookkeeper at the Farmers and Merchants State Bank of Roseau and continued there until 1926 when the bank was liquidated. In 1927 he became the president of the Citizen's State Bank and continued there until 1966 when he retired.

Starting in 1929 a depression became

nation-wide. By 1931 the situation was becoming a desperate one for most of the people in the nation. Unemployment was at an all time high, machines were idle, and industry was at an all time low. It was then that the CCC (Civilian Conservation Corp) was formed to give young men out of high school or college some kind of purposeful employment. They were set to work on reforestation, on other timbering pursuits, or in some regions in fighting forest fires, as was the case in Warroad in 1933. The CCC camps in the area were at Norris Camp, at Clear River, and at Faunce.

Another government endeavor was the WPA (Works Progress Administration) which had the program of building schools, or public buildings, constructing roads, creating and maintaining parks, and staffing recreational pursuits. Roseau County benefited during this trying time, with the construction of schools and the work done in the county on the highways.

In March of 1933 the government declared a bank holiday to avoid a money panic in cases where some banks were unstable. After the bank was examined and found to be sound it was allowed to reopen.

There was a chick hatchery in Roseau which was started by a Mr. Swanson and Burtweser in 1929 and which ran for two seasons. They planned to hatch 3000 chickens and about 100 turkeys in incubators. Somehow the big plans for the business failed.

An interesting addition to the usual businesses in Roseau was a peat factory started May 9, 1924 with proprietors from Bagley. It operated like this: a dehydrator was set up on the field, and the peat was carried to the dehydrator and ground to powder and then heated to temperatures of 300 degrees. Then it was elevated to a silo-like tower and expelled at 125 degrees. The idea was to convert the peat into a useable type fuel.

In 1927 Turnquist sold out his stock to L. B. Hartz, and the Co-op building had to be vacated for the J. C. Penney Co. who then held the lease. This was the smallest town in the nation for a Penney store. That year Paul Tweet opened a variety store in the Lauring building and the post office was moved to the first floor of the Farmers Merchant building. The Commercial club was reorganized with 65 members with G. M. Stebbins the elected head.

The first store of the now famous L. B. Hartz Wholesale, Inc. opened in Roseau on July 6, 1925, in what is now the Penney Store. Another store was started in Badger, and a third store was begun in Ross. One unique incident was that the heavy rains that occurred at the time the Ross store was to be opened necessitated stocking the store by boat. Olaf Arneson built a foot bridge from the road to the front door so customers could get in on the opening day. Middle River was the site of the fourth store and Warroad of the fifth in 1928. These stores were general stores, carrying clothing as well as groceries. The first store carrying only groceries was opened on June 20, 1931 in Thief River Falls. The first independently owned store was located at Karlstad in 1933. Now the stores are all agencies and number above 300.

One of the first, and one of the very few strikes occurred April 8, 1937 when the employees of the American Arc Cast and Welding Co. in Roseau staged a "sit-down" strike as they demanded 30-50% increases in wages. The strike lasted only a half an hour with many employees demands being satisfied.

In 1933 a business known as the Feldspar Products Co., was established by Wm. Rader near the C. N. tracks in Warroad. The raw product, feldspar used in producing porcelain was mined on an island in Lake of the Woods.

In 1940 a factory to rejuvenate old mattresses was started in a building near the Nelson Chevrolet Garage. Malung had a business in 1939 with Ed Larson and his son-in-law Howard Skyberg manufacturing concrete building blocks. This business continued for several years.

An interesting crop that became marketable in war time was typha or cattails, which was used by manufacturers of life vests. In 1944 Albin Helstad bought typha and paid pickers a total of $1200 for 30,000 pounds of the product. Vernon Hovda came in with 1892 lbs. for which he received $75.

The electrifying news in 1929 that there was oil under the ground in Roseau County resulted in 53 oil leases filed in the office of J. A. Burkee. Malung, the report went, was floating in oil, especially on the T. Johnson farm. The oil land was reputed to be a strip of land 12 miles wide extending from Laona and Oaks townships through the central parts of the county to Strathcona. A Mr. Dahlgren, representing a New York firm felt there also was oil in the Warroad area, south as far as Roosevelt. A. M. Pearson (editor of Malung's newspaper) invented a sort of "oil witch" patterned after the common forked willow stick used to detect water well sites. The metal oil witch is in the Roseau County Museum.

The fur trade of the early years was resumed during the 30's with the domestic raising of mink around the Warroad area. The start of the business came about almost by accident. In December 1927, Shorty Joyce bought a live mink from a trapper and kept it in a cage behind his barber shop. Surprise of surprises! One morning Shorty had mamma mink and four little kits. This is how it all started in Roseau County. Shorty built up a small ranch and kept enlarging it. Dr. Warta came to Warroad to set up a mink ranch employing George Heinen as manager. Here the food for mink, consisting of burbot and tulibee from Lake of the Woods, horse meat and jack rabbits, could be easily and cheaply obtained. It wasn't long before the mink farmers began breeding the darker mink with the shorter silkier fur. As the litters increased the mutations appeared and some beautiful different colors, such as the Silver Blues, the Pastels (really the brown mink) the gunmetal colored mink called the Aleutian Palomino appeared. The mink offered a good study in Mendel's law of genetics, for the mutations when bred to standard dark mink produced hybrids. Then to breed the different mutations produced what was called dihybrids and by mating these one out of every 16 kits was new colored. This resulted in a mutation called the Heinen Buff which was famous for its color and texture.

During the height of the industry the larger mink farmers generally had about 450 breeder females and 100 males for which they needed 550 breeder cages and 1700 pelting cages; three men were needed to operate the ranch. The Heinen ranch grew to be about double this size. Mink farmers in Warroad received $70,000 for mink pelts in 1939 with 10,000 being marketed at one time, followed by another 13,000 in 1940. Fur buyers from New York and Chicago came to Warroad for the prime pelts. The mink could at this time be raised at a cost of $8-$10 whereas the costs now have risen to over $15 an animal in many cases.

Dorrance Johnson with a prime mink from his ranch near Warroad.

Besides the mink ranches already mentioned others in the business included Dorrance and Al Johnston, the Linders, the Brewsters, Hans Selvog, Percy Gilbert, Lewis Spotts, Jens Martin, Shorty Henderson, John Lawson, John Pick, Julius Anderson, Bill Holmes, Happy Floe, Frontie Parker, the Kvarnlov brothers, and Frank Glessner. Frank Glessner had 150 mink and 38 silver fox in his fur enterprise in 1933.

Another enterprise in Warroad has always been its commercial fishing. The rules regarding commercial fishing were set down by the Minnesota Board of Game and Fish Commissioners in their recommendations to the state in 1895 and they remain much the same today. In 1896 more than 300 pound nets were allowed in Minnesota and Canada, and in 1905 size limit regulations were enacted. Fyke nets were allowed in 1911 and gill nets came into operation in 1913. By 1941 there were certain species that were protected such as muskellunge, bass, crappies, walleyes, saugers, northern pike and whitefish. It was at this time that the individual commercial fisherman was allowed 10 fyke nets, six pound nets, and 4,000 feet of gill nets.

Some of the pioneers in commercial fishing were the Selvog brothers and Paul Marshalk. In 1908 Paul Marshalk came to Warroad as District Manager of the Booth Fisheries. In 1900 he married Lillian Zippel (from whose family Zippel Bay takes its name.)

He was elected to the legislature in 1913, 1915, and 1917, and worked diligently with the United States Federal Committee on lake levels. He was active in community affairs, and served as school board member and as mayor.

Hans and Sivert Selvog were associated for a long time with the commercial fishing industry. Records show that the Selvog brothers were issued a license to fish with three pound nets in 1908. After operating the Lakewood Hotel and the Warroad Hotel, Sivert Selvog became the superintendent of the State Fisheries at Redby which he had started as a war conservation measure, for Red Lake had not been fished commercially before that time. In 1927, Sivert Selvog took over the fishery at Warroad and named it the Selvog Fish Company, a name synonomous with commercial fishing from that time on. Other early fishermen were the Ringling brothers and the Brewster brothers.

Lake of the Woods has yielded abundantly for commercial and sports fishing and is renowned for its walleye catches, but unfortunately since 1940 there has been a decline in catches. In 1935 the walleye catch was the largest with a record of 1.2 million pounds. The catch in 1969 was the lowest with only 79,000 pounds. Northern pike have shared the same fate, with a record high of 525,000 in 1915 and a low of 270,000 in 1916.

During the early years of the fisheries, the sturgeon was the most valuable of all species of fish. Since 1925 it has been the walleye that has had the spot light, contributing 30% of the total value of the fish taken from the lake.

Burbot and tulibee are harvested for the mink ranches, being an excellent and nutrious food for the mink diet.

The trawlers used experimentally during the later part of the '60's have been studied and recommended by the State Department of Fish and Game. However, there has been a great deal of controversy about their usefulness and effect on the catches from the hook and line sports fishermen.

People from all over the U. S. come to Lake of the Woods for its excellent fishing. It remains one of the few large lakes to be free from any appreciable amounts of mercury as detected in the fish catch experiments.

In August of 1936 a fish meal factory began to operate in Warroad, and in 1938 a fish hatchery was proposed. The state went on record as saying that they would not issue a license until fish fry were returned to the lake. Mr. C. Milne was to find ways and means to rid the lakes of rough fish to provide for the future of both commercial and sports fishing.

One of the most dramatic experiments in the resettlement of farmers occurred in 1934 when the U. S. Government found hundreds of people homesteading in the sandy or swampy lands of Lake of the Woods and Red Lake Counties, and the wooded areas around Bemis Hill. It was obvious that the farmers could not eke out a living on this unyielding land, let alone carry their tax burdens. While in some cases the land had been cleared and other improvements made, yet the land was far from adequate for agriculture and was better suited for raising of timber and wild life. Most of the land had been drained and heavy ditch taxes were levied, but with an average yearly income of $317 per family, the legislature found it necessary to resettle the farmers on more fertile land. 310 families representing 1,050 people were settled in new areas, and the land they left is now the beautiful Beltrami Island State Forest consisting of 476,718 acres, with 109,645 acres in Roseau County.

After the settlers left the forest area in 1936, the Forestry Department began to establish a fireguard around the outer perimeter of the forest and elsewhere as needed. Roads and telephone lines were built connecting the various towers and ranger stations for better communications and the roads were used not only by the Forest Service to move heavy fire fighting equipment such as bulldozers, plows, discs, fire engines, water tanks, trucks and man power with a minimum of time and effort, but were also used for the convenience of personnel on routine work. The roads were excellent for winter timbering operations. There are today 150 miles of roads in the State Forest in the Warroad area, that are improved and gravelled and maintained. There are also 76 miles of telephone lines.

Besides the headquarters set up at Warroad there are five ranger stations and five lookout towers all connected by radio and telephones; each station also has fire fighting equipment on hand.

During the past, forest management has been practiced in Roseau County, as in other counties, under trained foresters. The timber sales are based on a sustained yield cut. A timber survey is made and an allowable cut taken each year so that only as much timber is cut as should be harvested each year and replaced by an annual growth.

At present we have two types of timber sales, the larger auction sales in isolated parts of the area and the smaller sales, known as Sec. 1 sales, in the more accessible areas. The latter are sold to small operators and farmers in urban and rural areas. These small sales cannot exceed $500 per sale, and have been a means of a great deal of employment and revenue to local people. During the season 1956-57, 455 such small sales were made from the Warroad office. Some of this was clear cut and a great deal was marked timber depending on what method was best. All told some 70,000 cords of timber were harvested including federal, state and private timber land, supervised by the Warroad area. Approximately one-third of this amount was cut in Roseau County. The total value of all products cut in the area at this time was approximately $1,228,000 and Warroad gained the distinction of being the largest pulp shipping station in the United States during the 1956-57 season. Most of the cutting in jack pine was in over-mature stands. In the younger pine stands which are 5-6 years old, the trees are marked for correct spacing to assure a better crop in the future. Black spruce was at this time the highest in demand but over the years jack pine became more desirable. With better forest management and excellent control of forest fires, the stands in Roseau County have had excellent chances to mature.

Cutting practices vary with the condition of timber, but generally rim cutting or strip cutting tends to hasten reproduction. All timber sold by the state is supervised and rigid cutting regulations are set up to insure sustained yields. Reforestation has been given every consideration. Since 1938 slightly over 3 million trees have been planted in Roseau County and adjoining areas.

For our neighbors across the border 1919 was still a big year for the timber business as they floated 75,000 logs down Mud Creek in that year.

The words "hockey teams" and Roseau County are practically synonymous. Of particular pride to the people of the county are the Warroad Lakers which started in 1947. The idea was conceived by Cal Marvin and Ed Holland when they drove home one night from Thief River Falls after a hockey game. It seemed to them that the name "Lakers" would be an appropriate name for the new team they had in mind, since they had two Zippel boys and Clarance Smith from Williams beside the Warroad players that should make up the team.

Laker Hockey Team of Warroad, Hockey Town, U. S. A.

The extraordinary success of this team is due to cooperative effort to be sure, but without the enthusiasm and constant effort of its chief promoter, Cal Marvin, it could never have become the consistently high calibre team with the fine reputation it has enjoyed. The first team was composed of Dick Roberts, Ted Wilson, and Wes Cole all returned from the navy, and Cal Marvin from the marines. George Dickinson had been a paratrooper, Gordon Christian had been in the army and Bob Murray in the air force. All these boys were from Warroad. The Zippel boys, Bill and Keith from Baudette had just come from the army, and from Williams came Dan Mckinnon, a navy man. Clarence Schmidt was also on the team and he had played with the Boston Bruins at the age of 18.

In 1945 Cal Marvin and Richard Roberts called the first meeting which resulted in organizing the Warroad Recreation Association which sponsored the Lakers and was instrumental in building the covered Memorial Arena with a seating capacity of 2000. Contributions from individuals, profits from town celebrations were part of the community effort which has kept the Lakers in the play. Ed Christian, father of the famous Christian brothers, organized the volunteer labor to build the arena. All three of the Christian boys, Gordon, Bill, and Roger played on the U. S. National team which played in the World games at Oslo, Norway. A deserved feather in their cap was the Lakers win over the U. S. Nationals after that team had won the gold medal. The score was 6-4. The town of Warroad played host to the Swedes, Norwegians, and Czechoslovakians in 1960.

"The Clover Leafs" was the name chosen by the Roseau people and hockey club in a contest for the reactivated hockey team in Roseau. It was submitted by Ralph (Scooter) Erlandson. The first team under this name was Stanley Alley, Merle Alley, Carl Dahlquist, Luverne Dahlquist, Philip Anderson, Charles Habstritt, Reuben Skoglund, Leonard Sundin, Roy Hagen, Lloyd Nelson and Donald Grothe. Since the first rink was blown down by a windstorm in 1943 a new rink was soon planned. The Legionaires in Roseau solicited funds and labor for the project. Spearheading the effort were Knute Grahn, Milo Anderson, Nick Johnson, Les Paine, Rudy Rice, John Grothe, Ray Gilbertson, and many others. The Legion donated $2000 to begin the project and volunteer labor made the project a reality in December 1949 when the Clover Leafs met a Winnipeg team before a crowd of 3,000 spectators. The arena also became the scene of many ice revues directed by Mrs. Bernie (Nancy) Burggraf. These revues involved most of the children in town who were organized into a Skating Club.

The Roseau High School hockey club, for 29 years under the coaching of Oscar Almquist, won four state championships, were runners-up four times, and gained 14 regional crowns. Under his leadership, Roseau teams noted 404 victories, 148 defeats, and 21 tie games. State championships were won in 1947, 1958, 1959, 1961. In his reminiscences the coach recalls that at Fosston the team played in a blizzard and the game would have to be stopped at intervals to clean the ice. At Williams a game was played in 50° below zero weather.

Warroad High School has been represented at the state at six tournaments, and were runners-up in 1948, 1953 and 1969.

The menace of fire was truly a problem for the people of earlier years. The Roseau Volunteer Fire Department was organized in 1903 after bucket brigades had been the only system available to the people. The next development was the purchase of an 18 h.p. engine to pump water. This new addition to the fire fighting equipment was a source of great pride to the people, but it was itself destroyed by a fire in the old fire hall. Finally a pressure engine and chemical fire extinguisher were added. Iver Torfin was the first president of the fire department. A party was held in honor of the gallant fire laddies who volunteered for fire duty, and was emceed by Mike Holm, on November 16, 1923.

The individual fires destroying homes and businesses are too numerous to list, but we could mention one at David Palm's saw mill south of River destroying 50,000 to 70,000 feet of lumber. In 1931 a fire occurred in Roosevelt when the Curtis restaurant and pool hall burned due to inadequate fire fighting equipment.

On September 18, 1931, a hot high wind fanned the fires in Beltrami Island State Forest causing three deaths. The fire swept from Malcolm northward toward Warroad, Roosevelt, and Baudette. Fire fighters helped settlers to get out of the area. Six sets of farm buildings were destroyed and much livestock was lost. The relief work for the stricken area was headed by Carl Listug, and the Red Cross supplied 14 dozen sweaters for old and young in the fire swept area.

In 1947 the Northwest Breeders Association lost their barn at the fair grounds. Fortunately no records, and no registered sires were lost in the fire.

A mild tornado was raised in Roseau in 1919 when Dr. Muir, member of the school board, proposed that high school athletics should be abolished. Much discussion followed with G. M. Stebbins and A. O. Hagen actively opposing such action. Athletics remained.

Hockey, since its introduction to the northland, has always held high priority on the list of entertainment. The merchants of Roseau decided to close shop on a Saturday afternoon in 1929 so that they could attend the double header of the Northwest Minnesota hockey tournament held in Thief River Falls. Perhaps the skating prowess was developed from such feats as performed by Jack Starren and Philmore Nelon who in 1942 skated from Northwest Angle to Warroad, a distance of 60 miles. Another sports record must have been set in 1942 when Gustav Nelson biked 50 miles into town on a 1902 bicycle which had been in constant use since it was purchased on that date. It was noted that he beat the record of a Rochester man who was still using a 1904 model bicyle. He was a bit perturbed when he was unable in 1942 to buy parts from the mail order house from which he had purchased his bicycle.

Roseau joined the other high schools in the area when they added football to their list of extra-curricular activities in 1946. Headlines in the paper that week read: "Extra! Roseau High School football team played its first game in history at Williams. Roseau won 45-0."

Other sporting activities for the county included golf, tennis, curling, and of course hunting and fishing. The golf enthusiasts in Roseau prior to 1932 had to play golf on a make-shift course on the fair grounds. At first it was a seven hole course, but since it interfered with fair time activities, it was deemed advisable to find another location. In 1932 the village got title to 67 acres south of the railroad bridge which had previously been owned by W. A. Book and was used as pasture land. On this site the village laid out a rather elaborate and ambitious plan for recreational purposes. There was to be a golf course, a park complete with picnic tables and an available pump, tennis courts, and a swimming beach along the river bank. Archie Lee, mayor of Roseau at the time, issued a decree that no one was to swim without a bathing suit, subject to arrest!

Establishing the nine hole golf course in the wooded area south of the tracks was not an easy task. The land was heavily wooded, and the first piece of business was to clear it of trees and stumps. The first year after this phase was completed, the links (as it was called in those days) was seeded into crop and grass. The course was designed by Cal Larson, with L. B. Hartz as the first president. The initial membership of 30 included a few women. On the 31 acre course nine substantial sand greens were installed, and a small clubhouse built with a tiny kitchen, and a screened in area no larger than many living rooms. Here the women served dinner to the tournament players without benefit of running water or stoves (hot plates were pressed into service), and of course there was no modern plumbing. Some of the early "pros" who lent their enthusiastic support to the club then and are still enjoying the good game of golf are "Cap" Nelson, R. J. Halvorson, Carl Listug, E. O. Anderson and Paul Buran, Jr.

When Dr. Bob Harris was a fledgling twelve year old golfer he would sometimes borrow Rex, the Carl Wahlberg's brown Labrador dog who had gained fame for finding golf balls. It was interesting to watch the dog get a scent of the ball, circle the spot, and close in on it where it lay. Once Bob reported 20 "finds." Carl Wahlberg, who had lost 5 balls one day, took Rex out after the game and gained 18 golf balls.

The Warroad Golf course was first located on land donated by Halvor Robberstad where a nine hole course with sand greens was maintained. It was later moved to a location near the Bloom school where it is at the present time.

Tennis as a community sport was much in prominence from 1930 to 1940. In Roseau new courts were built in 1934 south of the bridge in the recreational area. Regular tennis tournaments were held. The late Dr. R. V. Harris was chairman of the tennis club.

In Warroad the tennis courts were located on Lake street near the present location of the hospital. They were clay courts. Two enthusiastic tennis stars were Jens Martin and Jack Jowett. It was in 1919 that the baseball diamond and bleachers and the park was laid out near Lake of the Woods.

The Roseau Rifle team often took honors in their meets. Ed Johnston and Obert Lillo were high men in 1938. Curtis Stennes, Ed Johnston, and Leo Vilz won third place in a state meet in 1942.

Trap shooting was also a popular sport in Warroad and Roseau. Some of the most avid of the trap shooters in Warroad were John Wahlberg, Earl Eisenrich, Elmer Carlson and Jack Jowett. In Roseau "Cap" Nelson, Oliver Wold, Seth Gavelin and Carl Wahlberg instigated the sport.

A beautiful swimming beach was made possible at Warroad in 1934. The beach area was enlarged and bath-houses and playground equipment were installed. A park adjoining the beach was equipped for campers and picnickers. The area on Lake street half-way between the beach and town, sometimes called Hospital Bay was also called La Verendrye Park as the noted explorer was thought to have landed there.

Hunting and fishing are two sports that are taken for granted by the Roseau County populace and our opportunities envied by many others. It was not a feat of skill to row up and down the Warroad River and have a stringer of 3-5 lb. pike in an hour in the '30's. However, for Charles Neumiller the fishing was unusual in 1931 for he caught a 215 lb. sturgeon. Jim Helgeson made the news when he hooked a 30 lb. muskie across the lake and in 1942 Carl Wahlberg came in a close second with one weighing 29 lbs. Simon Johnson, Roseau County's expert fisherman, caught many pike weighing 14 lbs.

Vic Johnston and his party had an exciting experience in 1919 when they were set upon by a pack of timber wolves. At a point on the high ridge near the Algoma swamp a dozen or more wolves followed their car, and the leader of the pack got his front paws on the running board of the car on the driver's side and jogged along with the car. They speeded up the car and the wolf had a ride of about ten rods before he fell off the running board.

Lloyd Hilborne was attacked by a bear in the early '30's and received 207 wounds. Friends finally managed to ward off the bear as they stabbed him with a pocket knife. Lloyd recovered from this terrifying experience.

Warroad Municipal Hospital built in 1940.

The first municipal hospital at Warroad was the home now occupied by the Andrew Landins. Dr. Leitch was the first doctor to practice in this hospital although Warroad had been served before by Dr. Elliot, and Dr. Setzer. Dr. Leitch promoted the present municipal hospital and he himself drew the plans in 1937. It was completed in 1940 with much of the labor done through the WPA. The hospital board at this time was composed of A. E. Cantelon, Conrad Brohaugh, E. O. Doyle, Halvor Robberstad, and G. R. Sperling. The Hollands served the Warroad community with a drug store.

In 1927 free clinics to detect TB were established in Roseau and Lake of the Woods counties through the schools, with funds from Christmas Seals. In 1929 the Oakland Sanitarium with its 56 bed capacity was overcrowded with TB patients, but in 1931 the county was declared free of TB and the Oakland Sanitarium could be converted to other uses. The school children are still being given Mantoux tests.

The war against polio was likewise dramatic. Inspired by President Roosevelt, our county along with the nation promoted programs to eliminate the disease. After the Salk vaccine came into use the victory was won. Much credit must be given to the March of Dimes for this blessing.

One humorous episode happened in August of 1931. A band of Indians (natives of India) came to Roseau in three cars and set up a type of underground clinic. One woman was told that she had heart trouble and was not long for this world. However, the strangers assured her that for $125 they could heal her. The money must be put in a sack, rubbed over the heart, put in a pillow and slept on, and the cure would be complete after a few days. The desperate lady did as directed. She brought the money in the sack to the healer and after he had put a cloth over her eyes, he rubbed her heart – gave her the sack and she started the last part of the cure – putting it under her pillow for some consecutive nights. However, friends convinced the poor lady that perhaps the sack had been tampered with, and rather reluctantly she investigated before the date of the cure was to be completed to find only a wad of paper inside. The band of embezzlers was apprehended in Canada later.

When the State Department of Health decreed in 1930 that the Roseau Hospital's facilities were inadequate, steps were taken to rectify the situation. By 1936 a non-profit association was set up with doctors loaning $5,000 at 1% interest to erect a fireproof brick building according to state specifications. The new hospital was called the Budd Hospital, Mrs. Budd having furnished the lot on Highway 11. The name was a memorial to Mrs. Budd for her devoted years of service for the health of county residents. Organizations such as the American Legion and its Auxiliary, and private businesses donated furniture.

In spite of the fact that there were still dedicated people like Miss Ina Bloom who took over management of the hospital, prior to this time, the nursing problem was always acute. A maternity hospital started by Mrs. Hildur Chilgren on her farm home (present Gordon Halverson home) operated from 1935-1943. A public health nurse was hired for the county, Miss Lila Hemstock, who served until 1945. Dr. Delmore, Sr., Dr. Rice and Dr. Berge staffed the hospital at the Budd Hospital during the '30's and into the '40's. The pharmacists during the time were Oscar Lauring, Amos Fikkan, C. A. Heyerdahl, (who sold his Rexall Drug Company to V. E. Lumdbohm who was later joined by his son Jack.)

Dr. A. J. Button arrived in Greenbush in 1925 and established a hospital and office in a building formerly used as a school house. Dr. Button and his wife (she was also a physician) continued serving the hospital until 1933 when Dr. G. Knutson took over. The building was burned beyond repair in 1943, and the town was without a hospital until Dr. Klefstad arrived in 1944 and a new hospital was built in 1949. Carl Engelthorpe, Tom Torgeson, and Andrew Clay were the pharmacists in Greenbush.

The Badger community was served by Dr. Joseph Streatte who came in 1915 and stayed two years. He was followed by Dr. Olaf Kittelson, Dr. H. R. Rice, and Dr. Drumm. Dr. H. Marcome came in 1943 and remained in Badger for three years.

The terrible epidemic of Spanish flu swept the country in 1918, and in November of that year the report was that all of Salol was down with the flu. There were eighteen homes that were hit with illness and one death reported. The train from Vassar and Sprague was not permitted to stop in the U. S. because of the epidemic.

The Welfare System with which we are familiar today, really came into existence in 1920 when an agency was created by Roseau County that was geared especially for well-being of the children. Monthly donations were made to families in cases where either unemployment, or the size of the family made it difficult to adequately feed and clothe the children. Martin Nelson was put in charge of this operation, and from this start we have the coordinated system of aid to the unfortunate.

P. O. Fryklund is the one name that stands above all others in regard to preservation of history in our county. Furthermore he inspired many to be interested not only

P. O. Frylund who started the Roseau County Museum. The collection was first kept in the Badger School, then the Roseau Court House, and after it was purchased by the county, in the Municipal Building. In 1975 the 10,000 articles were displayed in its own beautiful building which it shares with the library.

P. O. Frylund (left) and John Dahlgren search for sea gull eggs for the museum collection.

in their own history, but in the history of the world in general, for in the collection that he built up, there are now some 10,000 items, most but not all from Roseau County. It is hard to imagine that one man could have collected so many fine artifacts and memos of the past. As Earl Chapin, former Warroad newspaperman now deceased, has said, "It is where history becomes visible." He went on to say, "Here history is not left to perish with the minds that contain it. It is not even relegated to scholarly obscurity between the covers of a book. It is brought vividly alive by the collected works of a shadow legion of artisans that, over the centuries, plied hands and minds to fashion a culture, a heritage, and a modern civilization for one small but locally all important part of this state called Roseau County."

The Badger School was the first repository in 1920 for P. O. Fryklund's collections. It was moved to the court house when Mr. Fryklund became Clerk of Court. To enrich his interest in preservation of valuable items for posterity, he became an expert ornithologist. Today there is in the museum a cabinet of drawers filled with the skins of hundreds of birds.

The collection has been augmented by contributions from citizens and friends of Roseau County who are eager to enlighten future generations about their heritage. Some items are rarities. An ivory spear that was created 10,000 years ago (verified by the University of Minnesota) is perhaps the most unique artifact. Archeologists have testified that it is from the tusk of the wooly mammoth that roamed this area around the time that Lake Agassiz covered the major portion of northern Minnesota. Other interesting items are points of arrows made of copper that attest to the migration of the Ojibway from the east through Michigan. Many artifacts of the Chippewa, arrowheads, mauls, stone hammers, pottery shards are in the museum.

The museum could easily tell the history of farming in this county with its examples of early type plows, a flax hackle, and yokes for the oxen. The visitor will find butter churns, spinning wheels, candle molds, hand made candles, and a hand-painted bytte (this was a container in which the good neighbor packed a gift of food and sent it to the mother of the newborn infant.) There is a whiskey bottle with two necks in the museum which perhaps suggests some wild tales. Implements and articles are not confined only to the U. S. but also come from the Scandinavian as well as other national backgrounds.

From the beginnings of Roseau County we have the first typewriter used at the Court House which at that time was called a calligraph; the first operating table, an antique pencil sharpener, and the first boxes for mail that came to the Jadis post office. The first newspapers printed in Malung are in bound editions at the museum as well. In addition one can see some excellent examples of Indian beadwork, basket weaving, and the Indian feather headdress.

There is one artifact, the Roseau Stone, which was in Mike Holm's possession, and which he loaned to the Minnesota Historical Society for study. John Jager, who was a student of stone-age literature and paleography made a two year attempt to decipher the script on the stone. He reported: "There is no doubt that the script is archaic. There are virtually two lines of text in evidence, the upper one distinct and pronounced, the lower fragmentary or interfunctioning with the other . . . much as observed in runic characters. The stone seems to be a miniature human head with an inscriptional ribbon contouring the entire face as a seam or head gear." Unfortunately after the stone had been subjected to an acid bath much of the patina seemed to be lost, and more unfortunately, the stone itself is lost. The author of this history attempted for two years to track it down but without success. A picture of the Roseau Stone is in the museum, and John Jager's description is in the appendix.

Mike Holm reported this about the stone in relation to finding it:

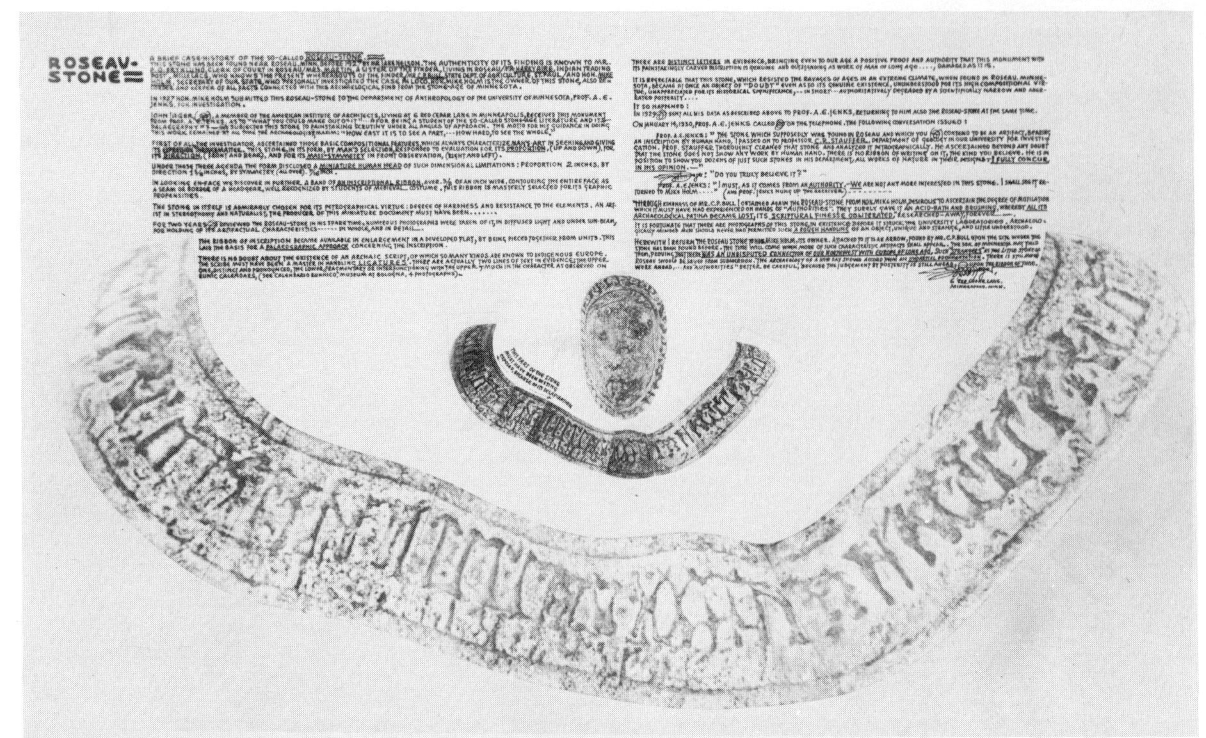

The Roseau Stone found by Jake Nelson, and turned over to Mike Holm. Unfortunately an acid bath destroyed the inciveness of the stone. Now the stone itself is lost.

Found by Jake Nelson (Yankee Nelson) in the northeast corner of NE¼ of Section wr, town 162, range 40, about 1916 or 1918. This location is now just within the limits of the village of Roseau.

Jake kept a garden and while working in it came across this stone, which attracted his attention, and he picked it up. Later he gave it to Mike together with an Indian club also found in the garden. Arrow heads were also found. A stone used to scrape hides were also picked up. Mike now has this scraper.

This garden is or was half mile or more from the river and on the east side of a little depression. Indications point to the probability that the Indians came here and camped or assembled preparatory to crossing the river. They probably came up across the lower ground (on the way to Warroad, or the "big water," Lake of the Woods) to this higher spot, then crossed over and on their way. Thus the two spots seem to be identical, viz: the garden and the assembling ground.

The museum has had several curators, but none as ardent or zealous as Ingvard Sunset who served for 25 years. Someone said that to talk to Mr. Sunset was like reading the history of Roseau County from an interesting book, for his knowledge and enthusiasm were so vast. He retired from a job he loved in 1973.

The Roseau County Historical Society was formed April 29, 1927 when E. E. Billberg was elected president, and J. W. Durham, and P. O. Fryklund, directors. At its inception it was termed "an infant that needs nourishment." The constitution was adopted June 19, 1927.

For years it has been the hope of many people that the exact site of the Hudson's Bay Post could be located. To that end the late Mr. Fikkan, and E. E. Billberg spent much time on research. On August 6, 1931, there was a notice in the paper to the effect that J. W. Durham and E. E. Billberg with the help of Jim Cobenas had located the site on the Mikkelson farm northwest of Roseau. The Indians called it Ka-bo-geo-nay-go-dea-og. Interpreted it means a place where one could see for a long distance. However, that this is the exact site has never been official and the search goes on for proof of the exact location.

The County Historical Society was instrumental in putting three bronze markers on historic buildings. The Pinecreek church and the rose church were marked for historical value. The plaque on the Pinecreek church reads:

FIRST CHURCH BUILDING IN ROSEAU COUNTY . . . built by Norwegian Evangelical Lutheran Congregation at Pine Creek in 1894. Organized 1890.

On the Rose church these words appear:

FIRST CHURCH ORGANIZED IN ROSEAU COUNTY July 16, 1888 by Norwegian Lutheran Free Church at Ross.

Ingvard Sunset who was curator of the Roseau County Museum for 25 years. He and Mr. Fikkan (deceased) have done more to preserve the history of the area than anyone since Mr. Fryklund.

The oldest school house in Roseau which was then called Jadis, and is now in Jadis Township, has a marker which reads:

> First school building in Roseau County organized January 8, 1889. First school board John Marshall, John Norquist, and Andrew Danielson. First teacher Frank Irish.

The Minnesota Historical Society placed a marker at the probable site of the first trading post in the county believed to have been erected in 1880, in Warroad. This is the bay sometimes called Hospital Bay since it is located by the first hospital in Warroad, which is now the Andrew Landin home, and is across from the present hospital. The marker reads:

WARROAD

> The name Warroad bespeaks the Indian heritage of the town. One of the largest Chippewa villages on Lake of the Woods. The Chippewas fought long and fierce war against the Sioux for the Lake's rice fields. Occupying the prairie of the Red River Valley, the Sioux invaded the territory by way of the Red and Roseau Rivers. A route which ended at the mouth of the Warroad River. This was the old "War Road" from which the river and village derive their name.
>
> Erected by Minnesota Historical Society and Warroad Chamber of Commerce, 1968

The site of the Indian Village in Ross was appropriately marked with a plaque mounted in a large boulder. It has these words:

> Site of
> Old Indian Village
> abandoned 1896

The marker was erected in 1947. The site is now the George Jorgenson farm directly east of the bridge at Ross.

A normal training department was added to the Roseau School system in 1920 to better qualify the rural teachers for their positions. It was later moved to Warroad. This department was ably handled by Miss Myrtle McBroom whose pupils felt they had earned a full college degree after having graduated from a one year course. Certainly the caliber of rural teachers was greatly upgraded after her normal course was instituted.

A step forward for education was also taken in 1925 when free textbooks were given the county students. The school apportionment in 1920 was $4.20 per pupil for state aid. There were 162 teachers (144 women and 18 men) at this time. The average teacher's salary was $1000 a year. Warroad then employed 14 teachers and Roseau had 11. The cost of textbooks was 50c a pupil. There were 130 school houses in the county, and the estimated valuation was half a million dollars. By 1938 the average salary for high school teachers had been raised to $1500. In 1926 the state appropriation was $67,684 for the 3454 pupils in the county.

The school house which had been built in Warroad in 1898 was put on a concrete foundation in 1921 and kept on the present school grounds. However, it will become a part of Warroad's planned Pioneer Village in the near future. At the Warroad school reunion held in July 1973, Pete Pearson was present and he reported that he had been a student in this first log school. Other persons in the county that attended that school were members of the Saurdiff family.

The Warroad High School Orchestra of 1921-22. John Lawson, saxophone, Ross Goodwin, horn, Gladys Marschalk, piano, George Jaros, violin, Supt. John Theilvold, cornet, Edna Holland, drums, Clarence Weitemier, violin, Garnet Merrill, violin, and Minnie Vog, xylophone.

An annual event in the county has been the Rural School Play Days which was started in August, 1924, when it was first called the Roseau County Olympics. The first years it was held at the fair grounds where some of the activities were running high jumps, standing broad jumps, and 40 yard dash contests which were held for both boys and girls before a grandstand filled with parents, teachers and friends. It was decided in 1932 that the fifteen highest students in each rural school could compete. By 1947 the event was held at the Roseau School, and kittenball, dodge ball, and volley ball were added to the events. The name was changed in 1954 to Rural Play Days. Charles Christianson, county superintendent worked tirelessly for these events which have retained enough interest for it to be an annual event.

During this period the people were agitating for bigger and better schools. In 1929 a school bond was voted on for Roseau with 93 for and 47 against. The amount called for was $81,880 with bonds amounting to $45,000 and the balance to come from the WPA fund. A two story addition was built to accommodate 800 elementary pupils. Strathcona dedicated a new school in 1937, built chiefly by WPA funds at a cost of $11,900. The Greenbush school was destroyed by fire in 1939, and had to be replaced. The new building provided more rooms for the Greenbush system, at a cost of $50,000 for which the village sold bonds for $28,000.

The Roseau County cultural organizations continued to be active in the period between the wars also. Mr. Goodwin from Badger organized an orchestra in 1924 which played at programs and social events. Members of this group were Newell Lee, Obert and Helmer Wammer, Gerald Dietz, Herbert Strandland, John Sjoberg, Ross Goodwin, and Eugene Goodwin. In 1928 there was a men's chorus under the direction of Mr. Sanderson, a high school teacher of music whose group sang at Roseau and Badger functions. A Music Study Group was formed in 1936 with Inga Billberg as president. Wannaska had an opera house in 1932 for their cultural functions.

Audiences have thrilled to the united efforts of church groups who sang, "The Seven Last Words of Christ," and this cantata was first presented in 1923 when Redeemers church of Badger, and the English Lutheran church choirs sang it for the first time. From this initial effort a Roseau Choral Society was organized in 1950 in which all choirs of the Protestant churches were invited to participate. Each year on Good Friday the same cantata was presented. In 1936 the annual Christmas Candlelight concert by the English Lutheran Church choir was first sung, and it has been a part of the season's presentation ever since. It has been prepared mostly through the efforts of Mrs. Rudy Rice and Mrs. Reuben Halvorson.

The first band in the Greenbush area was the Pelan Band, organized in 1926 and directed by Arthur Anderson. Another band was the Haug Band. In 1940 the Greenbush community put on an outdoor pageant or operetta called "Wanda and Wannaska," depicting the legend of the Indians in the Wannaska area. Mrs. Haug was the director, and Mrs. Tennes Halvorson sang the leading role of Wanda. The Roseau County Historical Society staged an historical pageant in 1926 and again in 1928 depicting the days of the early settlers about the year 1899 in Roseau County with the Warroad Indians participating. Carl Listug, E. E. Billberg, and P. O. Fryklund directed it.

True works of musical art were performed by the Warroad High School Choruses under the direction of Paul Chase when he staged several Gilbert and Sullivan operettas. two of these were "The Mikado," and "The Pirates of Penzance." The Roseau Orchestra assisted in some of these productions.

Other annual events of cultural value were the annual pow-wows put on at Warroad by the Chippewa Indians. In their full regalia, and with authentic Indian drums, the sagas of love, war, peace and harvest were chanted to an enthralled audience.

The last Sun Dance was held by the Indians at Buffalo Point in 1921 but was forbidden by the government after that time. Some of the spectators watched from boats around the Point and were witnesses of the passing of an era in Indian culture.

A part of the fourth of July celebrations included excursions to Buffalo Point in a boat captained by Henry Vog, or on the **Defiance** piloted by William Rader, and in later years run by Captain Fay Young and his trustworthy **Resolute.**

The Fourth of July was still a day that was celebrated patriotically with lecture and ceremony, and for the children it was anticipated as a day for fun and frolic. The Syttende

Mai Fest was observed annually. On one such occasion Pastor Ernest Ekeberg was the speaker.

The Chautauqua and Lyceum courses were still a part of the life of Roseau County in 1925. Such presentations as Gilbert and Sullivan's operettas, the La Salle Singers, the Beth Bell Ringers, Dunton Charmi, Bavy's Opera, Hadley's Concert Co. and lectures were a part of the entertainment. The University of Minnesota and North Dakota supplied the talent and the shows were put on in the Princess Theater in Roseau and the Opera House in Warroad, and the public halls in Badger, Wannaska and Malung. In 1925, a duo of note appeared at the First Lutheran church: Foellinger, violinist, and Berggren, pianist. Olle Skratthult appeared quite regularly in Roseau County and was a great favorite with the public.

The Princess Theater, the former opera house which was located where Bradley's Appliance store in Roseau is now, provided its attractions such as "The Unpardonable Sin" and "The Grapes of Wrath" for 25 and 50 cents. There was a storm of protest from the public concerning the latter with many in favor of censorship. The Princess Theater also offered a weekly golf series. In 1931 the Princess Theater was temporarily closed by the owners Bell and Johnson, so that it could be converted to the "talkies." Hardly anyone in town missed the first pictures following the remodeling. It should also be recorded that the Princess Theater gave one evening's receipts to a fund for relief of needy people in the county in 1931.

The interests of the youth have been well served in the county for many years. Each church has carried on extensive youth programs in their behalf, both spiritually and recreationally. Summer Bible camps proved a valuable asset for both purposes.

The Boy Scouts and Girl Scouts have been active in Greenbush, Badger, Warroad, and Roseau. The educational program of Girl Scouts through a system of merit badges is a wide and diversified program. There have been summer camps for this activity too. The Brownies, the beginner scouts, have had their introduction to scouting in the day camps and the group participations. The emphasis in scouting has been toward the development of the whole person, spiritual, physical, mental and cultural. Civic projects are stressed and patriotism is also a key emphasis.

The Boy Scouts of Roseau County have from their earliest inception in 1920 developed well defined programs that have graduated many county scouts to the highest honor of Eagle Scout.

The 4-H Clubs, which interpreted means head, hands, health and heart really started back in 1910 when the club was called "The Industrial Workers" and was started in Roseau County by Mr. D. Peterson. The organization, though mainly geared to the rural youth, accepts all willing club members into its wide program. Delores Andol became the 4-H director on April 8, 1946. The growth of the club work is reflected in that there were 19 clubs with 399 members when Miss Andol became director. Today it takes 150 adult leaders for the 579 members enrolled in the program. Whereas in 1940 there were some 458 exhibits by 4-H members at the fair, there are now around 1500. The biggest change in the program is in foods, for formerly there were 3 different divisions, and now there are 7. There are now practically no chicken raisers among the young club members. The Junior clubs include the Citizen Short Course in Washington, D. C. and the district work shops. Betty Johnson was the first state and county president of the 4-H Federation. In 1967 Miss Andol was honored as one of seven directors for distinguished service by the National Association of 4-H clubs.

Creativity in Roseau County was apparent in this era as in the past. Andrew Johnson, Jr. in 1921 invented a type of washing machine that moved in a rotary motion so that the suds could run through the clothes. Shades of the modern washing machine and the liberated women!

W. C. Rader in the early 20's rigged up a type of wind sled that worked. Even though he tested it in a blizzard he was able to go from Warroad to American Point in 2 hours and 45 minutes. No account was given as to how he made it over the pressure ridges. Details are lacking, but in 1927 Ven Hovorka invented a machine that could be placed on a cream separator which could quickly cool the cream. He expected that each would sell for $2 or $3.00, and he took out a patent on it. It was reported that there was an iceless refrigerator, but no details given except to say that it could keep ice cream.

Otto C. Johnson with an early type snowmobile which he built in 1917.

The first snowmobile, built by Otto C. Johnson.

One inventor who did big things with his creative brainchild was Gust Nyquist who, in 1929, invented a riveting machine for which he got a patent. Gust Nyquist and Andrew Johnson were in partnership at the time. The gadget was bought up by the Vega Separator Co. It weighed 35 pounds, and stood 15 inches high. It could rivet harnesses, cut rivets from sickles and would sheer iron to one quarter inch. The same year Gust Norquist invented the new all purpose welding rods. He set up a factory in Roseau which he called The American Arc-Welders, just west of where the swimming pool is located now. Mr. L. B. Hartz, now of Thief River Falls, believed in the invention and plant and invested money in the operation. The firm was moved to Mason City, Iowa and then later moved back to Roseau.

In 1934 Stanley Willcox invented a gravel locator. This electrical detecting device could locate gravel by means of impulses sent through the earth by noting the amount of resistence. Information on this invention was included in the State Highway Bulletin of that year.

One man who saved the county a great deal of money by his ingenuity was Tom Gardner, who was an engineer affiliated with the highway department. Mr. Gardner made a machine which could be attached to any tractor and converted it into a road machine which would otherwise have cost the county $6000 to own. This invention was used by the Roseau County Highway Department for about two years.

A man who had the reputation of being able to build about anything mechanical was Edgar Hetteen. In 1944 Mr. Hetteen manufactured a power lift. One of these machines was used at Springsteele Island to raise the boats out of the water to drain them after a big rainfall.

Back in 1919 Andrew Landby breezed into town in a new vehicle that ran on snow – a winter vehicle that was made from a motorcycle frame, and used two big wooden wheels in back, and a single ski in front. It was said to travel in deep snow as well as on hard surfaces. Otto C. Johnson built his own snowmobile in 1917.

Even the good earth from Roseau County held possibilities for a new industry back in 1942. Clay from the Lindford Hackman farm was sent to Pennsylvania and tested as a material for earthenware, and declared to be excellent. Perhaps this enterprise died for want of promotion.

December 8, 1941 – day of one of the most ignoble acts in history! Radio announcements and headlines of papers read: "U. S. Officially Declare War on Japan!" "Japan Attacks Hawaii", "President Roosevelt Makes Statement about Pearl Harbor," "Large Losses Suffered at Pearl Harbor." "The Arizona and the Utah Sunk." So with only one dissenting

An answer to the mail delivery problem in 1950. The sled is parked in front of B. J. Borgen's implement building.

vote Congress declared war on Japan. This was the start for us of World War II.

As in the previous world war, the Korean War and later the Viet Nam conflict, the people of Roseau County responded to the war effort. All male adults registered for possible war duty.

A draft board was established which would serve without pay. On this board were I. A. Sunset, J. Stanislawski, and Lenus Landby. In a national lottery the first number to be drawn from the pool of 2011 in the county was number 158, which was Raymond Tofte's number. Eddie Polezinski was the first man listed as missing in action in Roseau County.

Members of Roseau County Local Board, second World War, October 11, 1940. Joe Stanaslowski, I. A. Sunset, R. M. Holt, clerk and Lenus Landby.

In April of 1942, thirty-nine men left the county for duty to their country. At home the effort consisted of energetic selling of war bonds, rationing of commodities such as sugar, tires, gasoline, and coffee. Tin cans were saved, and victory gardens were encouraged.

The Roseau County "crop" train was the altruistic effort of farmers in the area to lend a helping hand to those across the seas who because of the war were in hunger. The slogan was "Send Hearts to the Hungry." A miniature box car was put on display as filling up with donations of wheat. Roseau county sent several box cars to other lands.

The Red Cross geared itself to possible emergencies and boosted its membership in the county to 700. The American Legion was mobilized for action. A full page ad in the paper read, "Honestly now, what have you done for your country?"

One of the most dramatic stories of local interest concerned Homer Gilbertson, son of Ray and Aaget Gilbertson. He was listed as missing in action, taken to Battaan and forced to participate in the death march, and finally freed on September 27, 1944. From a picture in Life Magazine he was identified by Roseauites before his release which gave hope to the parents.

Some of the pot-pourri from page 2 (as Paul Harvey would say) include these interesting items:

October 27, 1925 – The village council passed a resolution that the younger generation were not to be on the street at late hours – "cutting up." Parents better watch lest home fires go out.

January 1, 1936 – Leon Plante spurned relief. He bought a creamery churn, placed it in the park across from the old Messiah Lutheran Church, and lived in it. He won national recognition in Ripley's "Believe it or Not."

November 5, 1936 – Two Roseau County residents went to hell - and liked it. Peter Sjoberg and Seth Gavelin just returned from Hell, Norway.

June 4, 1942 – A model prisoner locked the official in the cell meant for himself. C. F. Corry, check forger, came into the Wahlberg Hardware, wrote out a $30 check, which Carl Wahlberg cashed, and then recalled that the man's picture was in a hardware trade magazine being wanted for general forgery throughout the country. Mr. Wahlberg trailed the man over to Ulvin's grocery (which is where the Golden Shears beauty shop is now) and had the sheriff close behind. Mr. Corry (or Reverend as he wished to be called) was locked up in the local jail. But the Deputy Sheriff Brandt went past the cell, and Corry grabbed the keys, locked the sheriff in the cell and escaped, using a car he found on the street. Rudy Rice opened the cell to let the sheriff out.

September 4, 1944 – A posse composed of Sheriff Sillerud, Carl Wahlberg and a few other men hunted four bad men near Pinecreek. These men were wanted for burglary in Canada, and eluded the Mounties. When the Mounties shot their tires they took off on foot down the river bank. The American police were alerted and the hunt was on. The Americans waited on this side of the bridge, flashed the lights on the fugitives from justice, but they again escaped. The next day Wahlberg's dog, Rex, flushed them out of a cover of hay.

September 12, 1924 – The schoolhouse at Elkwood was moved during the night. It seems that the ground on which the school was placed was deeded to an unorganized school district and dances were not permitted. During the night a crew of young people removed the school house to another site so it could be used as they wished, for dancing. This matter could easily have been settled by an appeal to the law, and a restraining order was issued. However, it seemed more expedient to some husky lads to take the matter into their own hands.

December 25, 1924 – The body of immigration officer Robert Lodbell was found Christmas Day at 9 o'clock lying face down on Highway 11 near the Dahlen place, by Robert Norris of Williams.

June 22, 1928 – A second Indian grave was found on the Theodore Johnson farm and also one on Sam Evans land in the gravel pit.

April, 1937 – There are still some Roseau residents who remember the genial peddler, C. A. Malmskog. (His satchel is in the Roseau Museum). He was a familiar figure as he trudged from house to house selling his wares and having a cup of coffee and a friendly chat with all his friends. One day he was beset by two women bandits. One jumped on his back and the other made a dive for his satchel. But Malmskog was not to be outdone, and in spite of his 80 years he sent the women sprawling. So familiar was the leather cap that he wore that the children all begged to buy a "Malmskog cap." He was the father of Lena Anderson, former resident of Roseau, and Mrs. John Eklund of Badger.

June 1937 – More old graves are found by Alfred Erickson, son of Ole Erickson of Malung, in the southeast corner of northeast quarter of Section 16. Beside two skeletons, 16 arrowheads, and 2 flint knives were found four and a half feet below the surface. These artifacts were given to P. O. Fryklund for the museum, who said that since this section is part of the ancient Campbell beach once the shore of Lake Agassiz, these finds are likely to date back a long time. The bones of the skeletons were broken into many fragments due to the frost in the ground.

November 28, 1940 – The paper carried news that a municipal liquor store would possibly be built in Warroad. There was much curiosity over this since Roseau County was dry. The municipal liquor store was built – on land dredged up from the Lake of the Woods, since the shoreline is the boundary of the counties.

Three Civil War veterans are mentioned in the paper as having their residence in Roseau County. They are Edwin Evans, Pat Moran, and Henry L. Howe, father of Harry Howe of Roseau.

C. A. Malmskog of Badger. The last peddler in Roseau County. 1920.

Edwin Evans was a native of Davenport, Iowa who was a stage coach driver, and chauffeur for a doctor in Drayton, North Dakota before joining the army, and knew about Roseau County at that time. After his army life where he had attained the rank of Corporal, he came to Jadis and requested to live with the Iver Torfin family. The hospitable Torfin family took him in on the condition that he would not indulge in liquor, and he lived with the family until his death August 27, 1920. He was affectionately called Uncle Ed by the family, and Old Ed by his many other friends.

Pat Moran settled in Warroad after his war duty and Moranville was named after him. He was always an honored guest at the Fourth of July celebrations. He died August 23, 1908 at the age of 82 years.

Major Henry L. Howe was a prominent figure in the Civil War and resided where the Lofstedt farm is now located. He was from a prominent English family, who disowned him because of his marriage to an Indian lady. He remained in Roseau County to raise his three sons and a daughter. He died in March, 1910.

The date of May 6, 1935 was a day of days, not only for Roseau County but for the entire rural population of the United States. On this day President Franklin D. Roosevelt created the Rural Electrification Administration. It was truly "the night they turned on the lights" as the author Harold Severson who wrote about the R. E. A. systems entitled his book. It revolutionized the rural style of life.

In Roseau County as in many areas, the skepticism of the farmers was the major obstacle to initiating the program locally. The concern was over costs, government rights to foreclose on farms, and directors' liabilities. Many educational meetings were held to reassure the people.

The persistence and foresight of men like Jalmer Wellen and a few of his fellow board members back in 1938, made electricity a reality for Roseau County farmers. After an initial meeting at the courthouse at which only a half dozen appeared, a house to house canvas was made for signers. The issued died for two years for lack of support, but was revived again upon evidence of other county installations. In Wannaska no one appeared for a scheduled meeting and at another meeting only nine farmers attended, and only one signed on the dotted line. A lantern hung at the meeting place became the symbol of the effort.

However, led by Spruce Township, the idea caught on and the torch bearers, Albert Brandt, Jalmer Wellen, Henry Jensen, Ernest Johnson, Ernest Klema, Henry Hamlin, William Wilson, Archie McMillan, Clarence Lian, Delmar Hagen, Martin Ellingson and others brought in signers who paid their $5.00 for a share in Roseau County Rural Electric's project. On August 21, 1941 the government approved a loan of $218,000. To overcome the obstacle of exhorbitant bids for line construction farmers were hired to set the poles themselves, and construction started January, 1942. The cooperatives used their own equipment. The Warroad and Baudette farmers used the Border County Power Cooperative (a generating co-op to supply power for the two distribution co-operatives.)

The great day finally came for rural electric lights. The first farm to receive power was the Roy Bloom farm in Warroad. Forrest Ammerman was the first employee of the REA.

The work of the R. E. A. was held up for some months due to the shortage of government specified poles, but when the Canadian cedar poles were approved the work progressed to the point of 260 farm homes lighted by 1942. In 1945 Bert Hoffman became the head lineman.

Upon resignation of Henry Jensen, the reins of direction fell to August Bourque. With characteristic determination, congeniality, and efficiency, he promoted the work over any obstacles. Many people remember how he convinced the irate farmer who stood over him with a shot gun into allowing the pole operation on his land, and how he talked strong and powerfully to the forces in Washington. Through his efforts he got the Roseau Electric Cooperative and the North Star Electric Co-operative to become members of the Minnkota Power Company.

Meridith Haslerud succeeded Mr. Bourque and is the present director. He has worked tirelessly not only for the REA but also for community interests. The office of the REA was originally in the courthouse, but now the cooperative has its own neat and spacious office building on Highway 11.

Today the REA not only serves the farmers of Roseau County but also the villages of Strathcona, Wannaska, Grygla, Gatzke, Salol, Ross, and Pinecreek. It also serves Polaris and Springsteel Island. It has better than 1629 miles of line and 2,500 patrons in Roseau County, Beltrami, and Marshall County. In 1964 it purchased 17,800 kilowatts. In 1972 the REA had 3000 customers, and purchased 41 million kilowatts of power from Minnkota.

Roseau County was the first in the state to secure a rural area development loan from REA for the Marvin Sash and Door after that firm experienced a devastating fire. Through their Section Five Financing Program, loans have been made which have boosted business and given employment to many persons. Furthermore the REA conducts educational programs that keeps an informed membership.

The big 1973-74 project for the REA was to set up a station at Northwest Angle and lay lines into Lake of the Woods to give service to the islands. This will extend to Oak Island and American Point and islands along the way. Also in the plans are lines to energize the Northwest Angle Indian Band territory, in Ontario from Peterson Island. It was in executing this project that Robert Vickaryous lost his life when the freighter he was piloting turned over in the stormy Lake of the Woods and reels weighing 3000 pounds were sunk. These reels were later recovered, and in June of 1974 they were loaded on to a pontoon boat, and the cable was laid to Lambert Island, Brush Island, Flag Island, American Point, and up to Bear and Harrison Creek.

At ceremonies in August of 1974, the station at Northwest Angle was dedicated and named in honor of Meridith Haslerud, who had piloted the entire project.

There are many conjectures as to the source of power to be used by this cooperative in the future. At the present time the actual power used is generated at Garrison Dam in North Dakota. It is delivered to Grand Forks by transmission lines and substations provide the remaining link.

It is a thrill to drive through the country side at night, or fly over the area and see the many blue mercury lights that are a symbol of the dawn of a new age for the farmer.

Chapter 8

MATURITY

To every thing there is a season, and a time to every purpose under the heaven.

Eccelesiastes 3:1

Chapter 8

MATURITY

Imagine Roseau County 20,000 years ago, for that is about the time of the last ice age when the topography of the area was formed by the vast Lake Agassiz as it receded, formed its waterways, its beaches, and left its moraines. Then as the aeon of time passed man invaded nature's lonely wilderness. What these years were like can only be conjecture, for climate, the molder of nature and man, worked its slow but sure magic of change. The skeletal finds make us certain that man lived in Minnesota territory about 15,000 years ago, but not until the record of Groseillers and Radisson in 1654 do we have recorded history. From that time until the present, this year, this day, this hour to which our pioneers have brought us we have been pleased to note strides in progress. And we enjoy the ring of the word "progress' as we think of it in terms of bigger, better, easier, more beautiful. Ironically, though, there has recently been a spirit among people to yearn nostalgically for the simplicity and sensitivities of the past. With the new born spirit has also come appreciation so that we feel with the American naturalist and essayist, Henry Thoreau that we come closer to the truth as he says:

> I went to the woods because I wished to live deliberately, to front only the essential facts of life, and see if I could not learn what it had to teach, and not, when I came to die, discover that I had not lived. . . . I wanted to live deep and suck out all the marrow of life, to live so sturdily and Spartanlike as to put to rout all that was not life, to cut a broad swatch and shave close, to drive life into a corner, and reduce it to its lowest terms, and, if it proved to be mean, why then to get the whole genuine meanness out of it....

AGRICULTURE

After the late fifties, Roseau County could no more be called "the County of Clovers" for the market for clover seed had disappeared. What followed after this era was a series of wet years that found the farmers struggling to reap the staples, wheat, rye, oats, and flax. The farm market was depressed.

However, over the farm horizon in the early sixties there appeared a bright promising crop that fired the imagination of the farmers. It was a crop that could well rename the county to "the County of Bluegrass." It was nursed, and tendered and experimented with by experts from the University of Minnesota on experimental plots on the Tollefson, Wold, Bjorkman, and Kveen farms. Actually the story of bluegrass started back in 1937 when Dr. H. K. Hayes, and Dr. H. L. Thomas from the University of Minnesota started their intensive research. From the work of Dr. Thomas, Dr. Hayes was able to select fifteen strains that would be the most hardy for the Roseau County area. Nor has the research relaxed, for Dr. Laddie J. Elling has continued the constant experimentation.

Bluegrass, or Kentucky bluegrass as many know the product, is a fine strain of grass desireable for exquisite lawns, golf courses, parks, airports, and roadside landscapes. Grown in Roseau County beside Park, is also Marion, Nugget, Penn, Primo, and Sydsport (this strain is exported exclusively to Sweden) and Newport.

The agronomists and farmers involved in promoting this new crop early recognized the need for controlled situations for the new product so fields were of necessity isolated from noxious weeds, or other existing lesser strains. For some years the product was raised by contract with the farmer thus controlling the yields and protecting the market. With the increased demand, the contract system was relaxed. Whereas no bluegrass was grown in 1955, there were 31,345 acres in bluegrass by 1973.

The greatest credit for the early production of the new product in Roseau County must go to Gustav Kveen who seeded the first 12 pounds of bluegrass on a six acre plot in 1953. This was the beginning of a yield of 4½ million pounds in 1973. An association called the Northern Minnesota Bluegrass Association was formed in 1957 which included Leo Hipsher, Gustav Kveen, Jack Janzen, Leland Lee, Chester Dahlquist, Robert Bergland, and Stanley Roadfeldt.

In 1956, Charles Habstritt designed a bluegrass cleaning plant in Roseau which cleaned the seed to 70% purity. Mr. Habstritt, himself an extensive bluegrass farmer, has since built another plant on his own farm that cleans to 98% purity.

It is interesting to note that whereas at the outset 80% of the seed was exported to England, Scotland, Denmark, Holland, Japan, Norway, Sweden and Switzerland, the figures today are exactly reversed, with the domestic use 80% and the export 20%. Bluegrass yields over the years have been as follows:

1959	350,000 pounds
1960	1,125,000
1961	205,000
1962	900,000
1963	650,000
1964	365,000
1965	1,250,000
1966	1,500,000
1967	1,600,000
1968	1,250,000
1969	3,250,000
1970	2,200,000
1971	2,000,000
1972	3,200,000
1973	4½ million

To add to the bright farm picture, Northrup King, Inc., has experimented with timothy and promoted it in Roseau County to the point where Roseau County can boast of being the largest timothy producing county in Minnesota, supplying some 40% of all timothy produced in the U. S. for domestic and export purposes. The seed is raised on a controlled contract plan. Northrup King, the largest processing plant in the northwest, has a broad research program which has produced strains that are new to the area and have broadened the diversification of farm crops. In 1964 there were 17,545 acres of timothy harvested in the area which increased to 33,695 acres in 1971.

Another lucrative farm enterprise in the county is the raising of turkeys. Production started in 1936 when it became apparent that it could be a successful large scale operation. Tony and John Burkel, the A and M Ranch, Glen Jaenicke, and Martin Hedlund are perhaps the largest of the turkey growers.

The Burkels built a turkey processing plant in Greenbush in 1951. The rate of growth is reflected in the figures of 1959 when 430,000 birds were raised for a return of some 2½ million dollars to 1973 when 610,000 birds brought 5 million dollars into the county. With modern advance in genetics and antibiotics the strains are constantly improved. It now takes the hens 17 weeks to reach a weight of 14 pounds and the toms 20-21 weeks to become 20 to 25 pounds.

Harvesting blue grass in Roseau County.

In the early sixties when moisture in Roseau County was excessive and spring flooding common, emergency help was solicited from the government. In 1962 the farmers received $507,374 in emergency loans. The ACP (Conservation of Soils and Water) received $113,462 for distribution and the CCC received $544,900 for grain storage.

The Soil Bank, a plan to cut down on production in an effort to create demand, was enacted during this period. It paid the Roseau County farmers $1,048,391 for the 117,210 acres not in production. In 1956, prices of grain were as follows: dark northern spring wheat $2.06, flax, $3.09, and rye $1.23 a bushel. There were two types of soil bank, the first used for allotment crops which carried reserve acres, and the second conservation reserve acres. In 1959 the Soil Bank was used by 266 farmers who received $1,442,816 of federal money. In 1961, 300 had signed up for the benefits. There was controversy over the shortage of pasture land, and after some protest, the soil bank land was allowed to be used for pasture.

The phenomenal growth of elevators and creameries levelled off during this period, but improvements and additions were noted. In 1958 the Roseau Creamery was unionized and the first strike occurred in August of that year but was settled four days later. In 1961 the Roseau Creamery voted the sale of its products to Land O'Lakes with a depot at

The third creamery building in Roseau — the Land O'Lakes Drying Plant.

Fosston. The creamery managed by Clifford Skime, moved from what was the second creamery building in Roseau to the Land O' Lakes building.

Oscar Nelson won the highest possible score as butter maker in the years 1966-67 with a score of 99.3, and in '67 the score of 99.83, and in September of 1967 at the State Fair his score was 100% in competition!

Interest in the formation of a Soil Conservation District in Roseau County began in 1955 when Bill Provance, acting county agent led the initial promotion work.

Meetings were held in Roseau and outlying communities to inform the public of district organization and operations and to determine need and interest. These meetings were organized by the Roseau County Extension Agent and carried out in cooperation with the State Soil Conservation Committee on December 27, 1955. A favorable hearing on the petition was held in Roseau on January 25, 1956, and a referendum occurred on February 17. The vote was favorable and organization proceeded. The certificate of organization was issued by the Secretary of State of Minnesota on March 13, 1956.

Arnold Hattling and Robert Guyaux of Salol were appointed by the State Commission to the first board of supervisors of the newly organized district. James Njaa, Ben Christianson and Sam Bergland were later elected. These five men served as the first board of supervisors.

The first official board meeting took place on May 10, 1956. Under Minnesota statutes governing soil conservation districts, all land in Roseau County is now included in the district.

In 1956, a memorandum of understanding was entered into between the Roseau district and the U. S. Soil and Water Conservation Service. Under the terms of this agreement, SCS provides the necessary technical assistance in soil and water conservation, working through the district organization to carry out its program.

Harold Grothem was assigned to the Roseau County district in September, 1956 as its District Conservationist. Art Weiss, Soil Conservation Technician, was added to the staff in 1957. The Soil Conservation Service provides assistance to the county in engineering, agronomy, biology, woodland conservation, and administration from the area office in Thief River Falls and the SCS state office.

The district was formed to provide an organization through which farmers and other land users may secure on-site assistance in planning and application of conservation practices. On March 13, 1973 the district completed seventeen years of operation with a total of 529 cooperators having holdings amounting to 248,740 acres.

The present board is made up of Ben Christianson, Odin Lisell, James Njaa, Jay Estling and Arnold Frosaker. Board members serve six years and are elected at the general elections.

The ASCA, the original Agricultural Adjustment Administration, was formed in 1933. The first committee was DB Franklin, Virgil Laznicka and August Kukowski. It was called the Corn Hog Committee and had its office in the Court House with the County Agent, John Taylor, as the director and the clerk Carol Hagen Schwichtenberg. The name was changed from the AAA to the PMA (Production Marketing Administration) in 1943. In 1954 the name was again changed to the ASC and in 1963 to the ASCA (Agricultural Stabilization and Conservation Administration). The present director is Joel Olson. The purpose of the organization is to implement the farm programs for Roseau County as they are issued from the United States Federal Government.

In 1937 the Farm Security Administration was formed to consolidate the assets of the Resettlement Administration and the Minnesota Rural Rehabilitation Corporation. An office was then established in the Roseau County Court house under the direction of Arthur Johnson. The Farmers Home Administration, a supervised credit agency of the United States Department of Agriculture, achieved its present form in 1946 as a result of predecessor agencies.

Several directors have served the area including Chris Nash, Burton Olson, Charles Geddes, Arthur Skull, and Albert H. Mattson who served for 18 years, James R. Moen, and presently Egidie Scherr.

The office has been housed in the Sjoberg building, the Budd building, the Hagannah Hotel, Walter Bell building, Berge Clinic building, Citizen's State Bank building, and the Yon building where it is at the present time.

The Roseau office has always been known as a training office for supervisors, due to the size and diversity of the case load that has existed through the years. The Bankhead-Jones Act of 1937 permitted Tenant Purchase loans which enabled farmers to purchase land. Among the first in Roseau County to use this service were Ole Vistad, William Baumgartner, Merle Bassett, Albert Bizek, A. E. Sando, Alvin Fugleberg, D. S. Heppner, Gilmore Gregerson, and Palmer Hogan who were also among the first in the United States to take advantage of this authority.

The NFO of Roseau County was formed in April of 1963 with Norman Wahlstrom as president. Brynolf Grahn promoted the organization. It was formed for the purpose of with-holding produce in order to force better prices.

The NFO dumped 35,000 lbs. of butterfat from the Grade A milk on the Randy Lofstedt field to gain 2 cents per hundred weight for the product in an action that was nationwide.

In 1968 the holding action was extended to grain and there was a threat that meat and milk would be the next farm products to be affected by the plan.

Land valuations were a source of discontent beginning in 1966. Farmers were seeking a reduction in valuation of 30,000 acres for tax purposes due to flooding effects on the land. Special meetings were held in 1972 in Greenbush, Warroad, and Roseau, for the purpose of airing the discontent. Land classifications were defined as "a systematic method of taking inventory of the land."

The farm picture in Roseau County reflects the effect of bluegrass and timothy production, and the increase in wheat production. There is an increase in beef production and a decline in dairy cattle. The farm product prices were a dream come true for the farmer in 1973. It was the hope of all Roseau Countyites that at long last the farmers all over the nation were coming into their own.

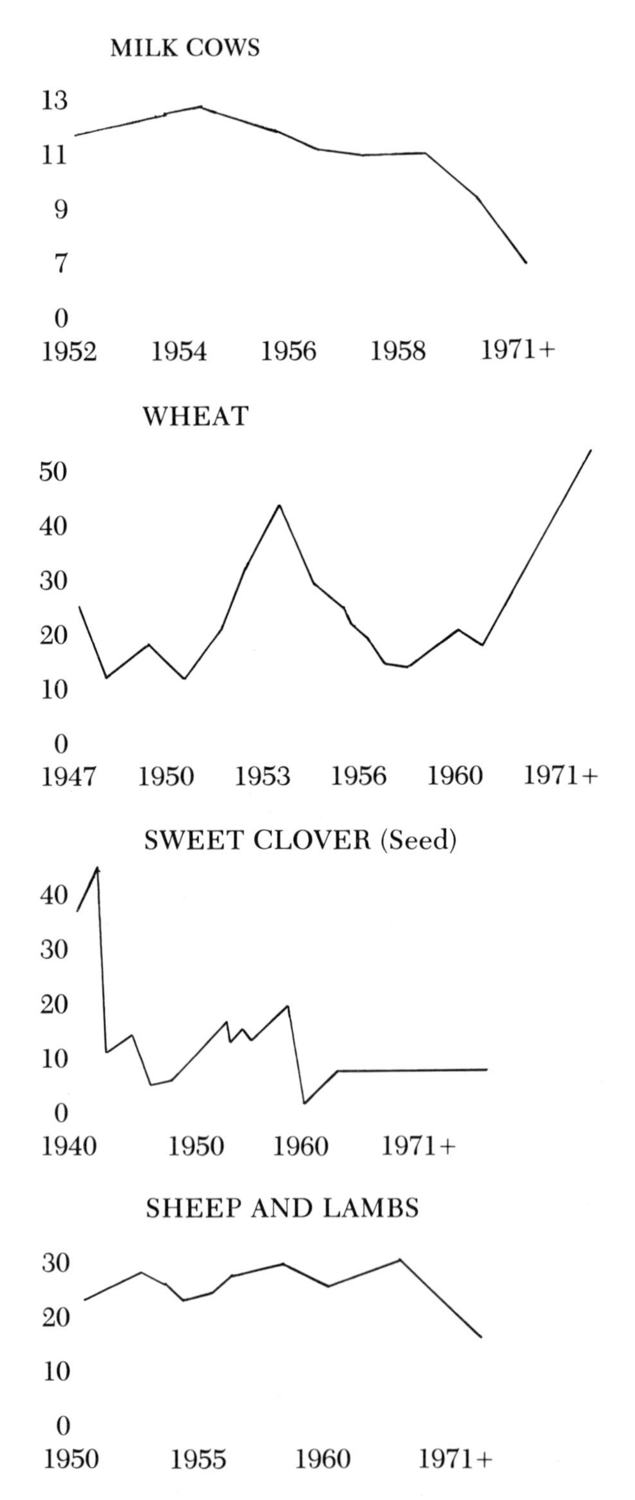

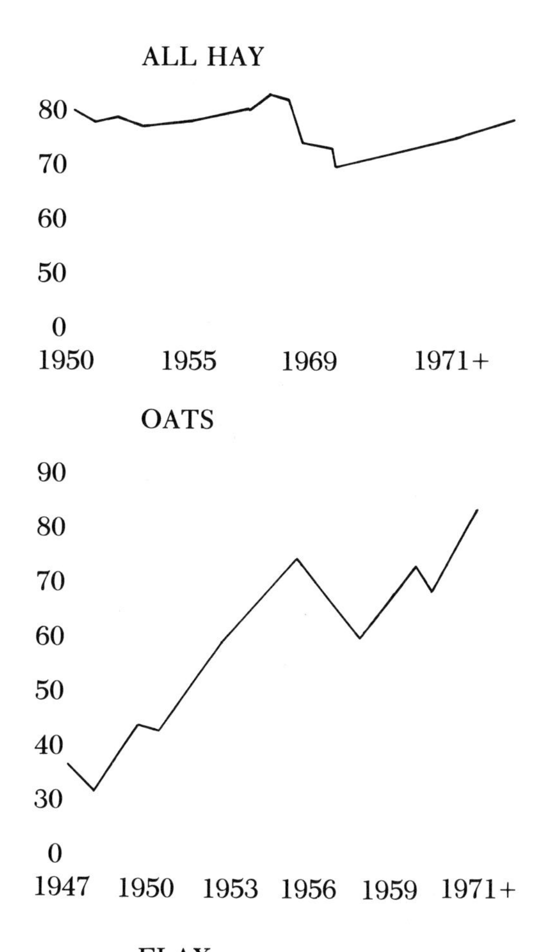

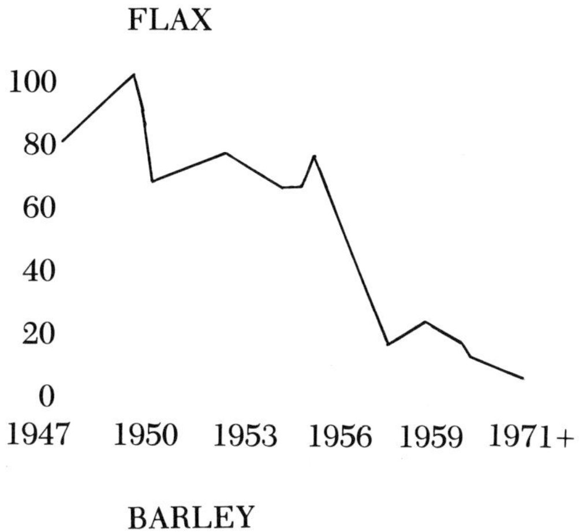

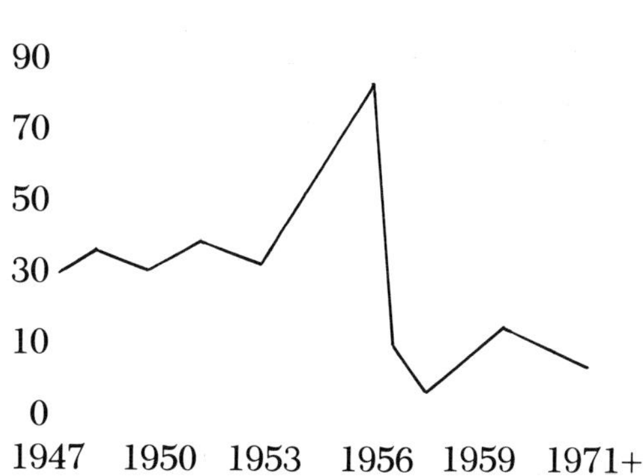

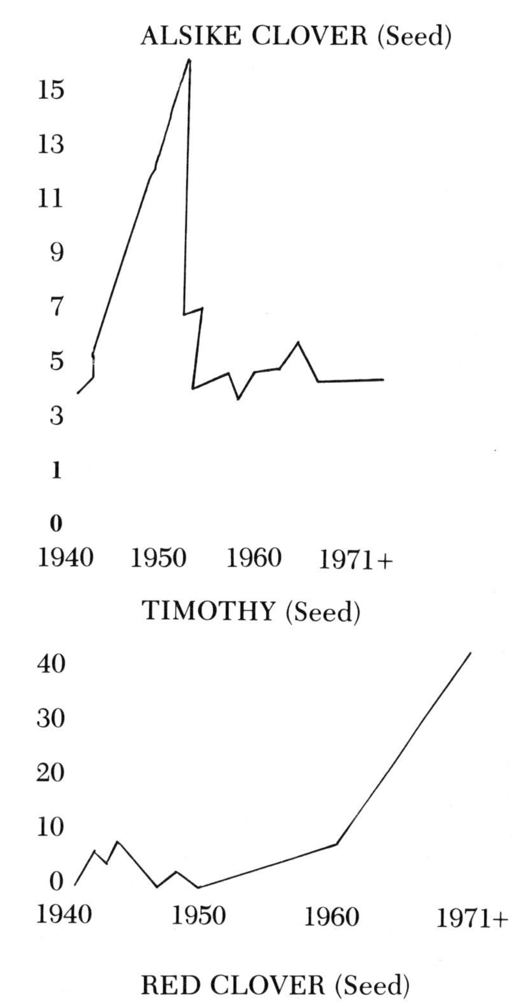

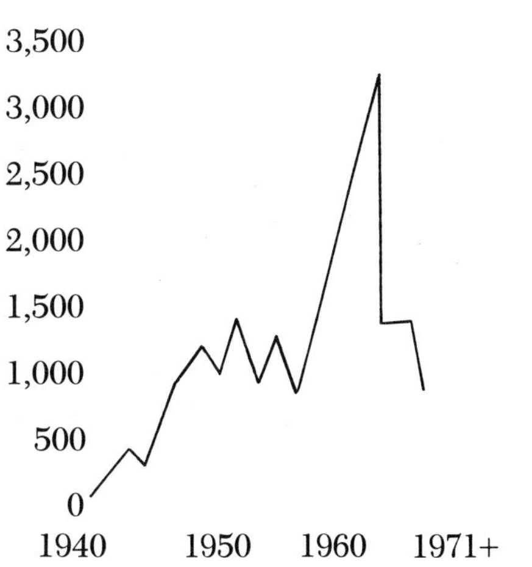

Note: All figures are on the basis of thousands (thousands of acres, or thousands of animals)

The 1971+ figure for all graphs are an estimated figure from the County Extension Agent, Mr. Hilbert Pfeifer.

Graphs are taken from "Looking Ahead in Extension Work" prepared by Roseau County Extension Committee and Long Range Planning Committees.

Perhaps the best way to describe the evolution of farming is by tabulation. Trends in farm sizes and numbers in Roseau County.

	1940	1945	1950	1954	1959	1970
Total No. Farms	2433	2272	2347	2132	1700	1400
Commercial Farms			2013	1878	1220	900
Other farms			334	215	500	500
Farm Size Group (In Acres)	No. %	No. %	No. %	No. %	No. %	Trend % of Farms
Under 10	39 2	45 2	29 1	22 1	11 1	Decrease
10-49	210 9	127 6	114 5	83 4	61 4	Decrease
50-69	29 1	21 1	20 1	18 1	14 1	Decrease
70-99	246 10	176 8	154 7	112 5	77 5	Decrease
100-139	131 5	130 6	148 6	89 4	63 4	Decrease
140-179	568 23	484 21	435 19	295 14	255 15	Decrease
180-219	178 7	190 8	219 9	188 9	123 7	Stable
220-259	203 8	212 9	255 11	209 10	191 11	Increase
260-499	626 26	678 30	763 33	815 38	651 38	Increase
500-999	192 8	192 9	194 8	268 13	232 14	Increase
1000	11 1	17 1	16 1	33 2	22 1	Increase
Average Size Farms in Acres	239	261	266	312	320	390

Commercial Farm – A farm selling over $2,500 worth of products per year, or $50-$2,499 if the operator was under 65 years of age and did not work off the farm for over 100 days, or if his off-farm income was less than value of farm products sold.

Source: County Auditor and County Highway Department

FLOODS

Water, water everywhere, could have been the theme of this era in Roseau, for the extensive drainage projects while solving some problems, created others and the relentless rains and spring run-off caused the Roseau River to rampage all too often. All the intensified efforts of committees appealing to the government, the studies made by the Corps of Engineers, and the petitions of the citizenry did not, and has not to date initiated action to solve the problem. Joint commissions with Canada and proposed appropriations have not motivated any change.

The years 1916, 1920, and 1950 will be remembered as the flood years, but 1965 was called "the flood of the century." All volunteer help dug in to pump, and sandbag. The Red Cross was called upon for aid when the townspeople very nearly were threatened with evacuation. True, the government did provide aid to stricken farmers and helped build the dikes through the town, but the actual solution was not started.

Melvin Jordahl and the Corps of Engineers recommended, after a detailed study, the widening and deepening of the river with three sections of levees, and a two mile extension of the Canadian floodway level. Automatic flood gates were to be constructed. Federal funding was to be forthcoming for the project except for the bridges and the maintenance. Meanwhile the cost of the project is expected to continue to escalate from the 1970 proposal of $6,080,000 with $250,000 to be raised locally, and an appropriation by the U.S. of $644,000 to Canada.

The August 30, 1973 issue of the *Roseau Times Region* stated: "It may be time for the 'big guns' to be used in the river matter." The Canadians claim to want to spend more time on the engineering and environmental studies. Perhaps only another ice age will settle the matter of the Roseau flood waters.

Roseau County has known some disorders of weather in this period besides floods.

In 1966 on March 4, 5, and 6th the county endured its worst blizzard. Fifteen inches of snow was dumped into the area and there were winds up to 60 miles an hour. Schools were closed and 100 persons were marooned in Roseau for the better part of three days. Snowmobiles were pressed into service to bring the doctors and nurses to the hospital. The snowbanks literally blocked off the front of most of the stores.

July 7, 1973 was the date of the worst wind storm the county has ever experienced. Described by Bill Adams, editor of the paper as the "Hammer of Thor," the winds destroyed numerous barns, steel granaries, uprooted groves of trees, snapped off poplars by the hundreds, and ripped off the front top of the Malung Hall. No lives were lost but a trailer home belonging to Dennis Kofstad was completely demolished. Some fields with swathed bluegrass lay bare with the precious seed blown into ditches, and around high wires.

HIGHWAYS

The various avenues of communication changed perceptibly during this, the modern period. Established hard surfaced roads replaced the mud or gravelled roads to facilitate the mounting numbers of automobiles in the county. The highway between Roseau and Pinecreek was built after a misunderstanding was cleared up. The bridge at the Richardson crossing was first erected in 1956 and replaced in 1972 due to a shift in the pilings. Now there was a direct route to Highway 12 leading to Winnipeg on a black-topped all weather road. Albert Johnson was the first man to cross the new bridge which is notable since the first road to the border had been built with the help of Gust Johnson, Albert's father, using a horse and scraper. Young Albert had hitched rides on that scraper.

The sum of $458,953 was spent in Roseau County in 1964 for highways. There was a request for a road through the swamp land to Northwest Angle to serve all seasons of the year and give access to a port closer to the islands in Lake of the Woods. The funds were not forthcoming, but the road became a reality by the efforts of some of the citizens at Northwest Angle, using private funds.

The final link of Highway 310 was built in 1967 to complete the thoroughfare to Winnipeg. The theme "Hands Across the Border" was used at the dedication and is indicative of the spirit that has always prevailed between the people of northern Minnesota and their Canadian neighbors.

The Mississippi Parkway or "Great River Road," a proposed route from New Orleans to the Trans-Canada Highway was a project assiduously worked on by many Roseau County men, none more zealously than Amos Fikkan and Julius Anderson. This route will be 2,740 miles long, have 80 lookout stations and over 1,000 historical markers. Though born in 1950 its progress has lagged until 1972 when Minnesota's Representative Blatnik, Chairman of the House Public Works Committee has revived the plan with due promise that all ecological aspects and preservation of natural beauty would be a prime consideration. This Great River Road has forty miles newly constructed in Minnesota with 69 miles a part of the interstate highway, and with 226 miles yet to be upgraded. This road will lead through Strathcona, Greenbush, Badger, Roseau and Warroad and would become a gateway to the proposed Voyageur National Park.

The Voyageur National Park was created in 1971 but cannot be finalized until the government gets the land rights. It will cover 219,000 acres which includes 80,000 acres of lakes and streams. Waterways will be the chief mode of travel, and will be a means to preserve the wild life in the area.

COMMUNICATION

In other fields of communication there were changes as well. John Reese, depot agent and former mayor of Roseau took the last message on the old style telegraph line in March, 1967, and in May of 1952 the passenger service was discontinued on the Great Northern Railroad. In 1973 many in the area would have welcomed the "Galloping Goose" when car travel was curtailed due to the energy crisis.

Something the natives called "snow", whether apparent in June or January, was the fare of the TV watchers in 1960. Pembina was the one station available but reception could only be called fair, depending on the weather. A relay station was installed in 1963 but the improvement left much yet to be desired. Then came cable TV in 1967 installed in Roseau by Sjoberg of Thief River Falls. The 480 foot tower was erected northwest of the county garage. There were nine miles of coaxial cable which provided the

Roseauites with almost perfect reception. In Warroad the cable was municipally installed a few years later.

Perhaps the most dramatic improvements were made for the telephone in this era. A microwave system went into effect in 1959 for long distance and military communications. One relay tower was built between Roseau and Warroad, and another erected near Wannaska. The storm proof system became a part of a nation-wide hook-up. A new telephone building was built in Warroad in 1965 and one in Roseau in 1966. It was Mrs. Emma Carlquist from Warroad, and Mrs. J. L. Delmore Sr., who received special recognition for having made use of the telephone for the longest period of time. Special recognition was given also to Othelia Gaukerud and Mabel Gregerson for the long years spent with the company. In their reminiscenses they told about how calls were made years past by giving the name of the family rather than the number, and how they were expected to track down a desired person. One humorous incident told by Miss Gaukerud was about a man who was the first to get an upright type phone, which he thought had to stand on the floor where the instrument had been placed. He got down on his knees to place his call. "Central" as the operators were called were the first link for help in all emergencies – fire, sickness, and death. This was changed when the power plant in Roseau and later, the sheriff's office, and the hospital in Warroad had incoming type call telephones for such situations.

In 1966 the dial systems were installed, and in 1973 the area was hooked up for direct dialing for long distance. Mr. Glenn Fossum, manager for the Northwestern Bell Telephone Co., was commended by D. M. Wiley, district Manager, for the smooth and competent change-over from the operator to the dial system. There are 2344 telephones in Roseau with 1552 main stations in Roseau, and in Warroad there are 1268 telephones with 861 stations. Badger, Malung, Wannaska, Roosevelt, are also served by Northwestern Bell Telephone Co. while Greenbush and Strathcona are served by the Wickstrom Telephone Co.

An effective means of communication in the county is the radio station called KRWB (initialed for Roseau, Warroad, and Baudette) which was built by private interests in 1963.

The Roseau Municipal Airport.

It serves the communities with advertising and announcements, as well as broadcasts of athletic games and church services. The station was sold in 1974 to William Rendell.

AIRPLANES

Interest in plane travel came to the county in the early sixties, although Pinecreek had an airport in 1959 located south of the custom house. It was capable of handling 20 planes. At the dedication Mike Holm was the speaker, and Edgar Hetteen was the first to use the airport.

In 1959 the village of Roseau asked for a bond issue to relocate the airport east of the village. Interest in getting an adequate airport was heightened because the corporation Fly-Lite associated with Polaris needed a landing field for testing airplane skis. An allocation of $88,000 from the Federal Aviation funds was secured through Congressman Odin Langen. The village bonded itself for $42,000 to make the airport possible. A 3,700 foot runway was constructed and lighted and ready for use in August of 1962. It was dedicated in September of that year with Governor Rolvaag as speaker, and with a spectacular show of U. S. Air Force planes staging maneuvers for some 5000 spectators. Warroad has had its airport for many years and is at the present time expanding the runway to 4000 feet to be ready for modern development in plane travel.

The commercial passenger air service has been disappointing, with companies like Gopher, Red Baron, and Fleet Lines each trying to establish service. At present the three towns, Roseau, Warroad, and Baudette are attempting again to put in daily air service to the Twin Cities. However, the airport is used enough to warrant the FAA to approve the visual Omni-Range station which was installed in 1970. A master plan for improvement and expansion of the airport was proposed by the Federal Aviation Agency and the State Department of Aeronautics.

NEWSPAPER

The *Roseau Times Region* celebrated its 83rd birthday in 1974. The reminiscences of the pioneer newspapermen, R. J. Bell, R. H. Medicraft, A. J. Clark, Paul Buran, John Grothe, Jake Snustad, and Ray Gilbertson have been colored with the hardship of the early days, as well as the satisfaction of mutual concerns. The mud roads, the mosquitoes, the first log homes, the frame business places, and the struggles to progress have all been a part of their lives. All type had to be set by hand in the earlier days with headings being the same size as the regular print. In 1917 the *Roseau Times* and the *Roseau Region* were consolidated. In 1923 Jake Snustad, John Grothe, and Paul Buran, Sr. became partners and operated the paper. Mr. Grothe left soon after to become postmaster of Roseau. In 1941 William Adams became co-editor with Jake Snustad when Dan Carver bought a share in the paper. Jake Snustad retired in 1953 after 30 years of faithful service to the community through his newspaper work and his community interests. Mr. Snustad took an active interest in Boy Scouts, the skating program and arena, and he worked on the gathering of material for a future historical record for the county.

Ray Gilbertson (deceased 1972) recalled that he came to Roseau in 1909 for a brief stay but somehow made that stay last the better part of his life. He operated a complicated "wire baby junior" as it was called. It was a happy day when the line-o-type was installed. Ray will be remembered best as a newspaperman, but also as a true sportsman and a friend to all.

In 1958 the paper had a supplement called "Majestic Minnesota" which featured early methods of farming, early types of newspapers, and the Mississippi environs of former years. In 1960 the editor revived the idea of a special Christmas edition printed as if from Bethlehem with the news of the birth of Christ.

The newspaper now edited by Mr. William Adams has been developed into a sophisticated weekly paper, much anticipated by its wide circulation. Such additions as his own "Corner Post", Paul Harvey's columns, and quite frequently features by his wife Maggi, improvements on lay-out and print, and numerous news pictures has added flavor and charm to the chronicle of history.

The threat of Communism to our country became a poignant reminder to many in Roseau County of what freedom in America really means. The editor of the *Roseau Times Region,* Bill Adams, together with Gustav Kveen and others planned and executed programs to make the public aware of what a communistic take-over could really mean to us. Programs for the public and for school children were planned at regular intervals in the 60's. Typical of these was the one in which W. P. Strube participated. It was an all day seminar and involved the entire school and public. Eleven organizations assisted in this educational and patriotic endeavor.

POLARIS

On the lot where Hodgeman shod the horses at his livery barn (now Nelson Chevrolet) stood an old dilapidated building. One summer day three boys were busy erecting a home-made sign to the amusement of the spectators. The sign read "Finklestein's Auto Parts". The Hetteen boys were involved in this enterprise and this is perhaps where the Polaris story should begin, for it was with these two boys, Edgar and Allen Hetteen, and David Johnson that the snowmobiles in the United States got their start, in 1944.

Edgar Hetteen started Hetteen Hoist and Derrick with David Johnson offering financial assistance while he was with the armed forces and joining the company in 1946. In 1948 Allen became a partner in the business adding car salvage and car repair to the services. The company made a variety of items such as electric hoists, corn and grain elevators which they sold to Midland Farmer's Union, small fishing boats, oil heating gun type furnaces, grain boxes, field sprayers, straw choppers and did much engineering for major manufacturers.

A type of snow machine was made by several men in the county, including Otto C. Johnson, John Elton, Leonard Johnson, Andrew Landby and Albert Peterson to mention a few. The owners of Hetteen Hoist and Der-

Eliason

Polaris

The first snowmobiles! Carl Eliason from Sayner, Wisconsin made the first model. The first type Sno-Traveler made by Polaris shown below was the beginning of the industry in the U.S.

rick envisioned a small, more maneuverable machine operated on an endless track. Cap Nelson secured some specifications from Carl Eliason in Sayner, Wisconsin who had built a machine similar to the one built by Otto Johnson, and these ideas laid the groundwork for the building of the first snowmobile of the marketable type in the United States.

The first snowmobile as we know it was built in 1945 and was called a Sno-Traveler. H. F. Peterson insisted on buying the first machine with which he aided the young company by doing extensive testing over different terrains and conditions of snow. The machine made between 3-5 miles an hour.

Allen Hetteen wanted a machine for himself, and built one, which when completed he parked in his yard. One day when Allen and Albin Erickson were delivering straw-choppers Harley Jensen chanced by, saw the machine and wanted the machine for his work in cutting pulp at American Point. There went the second machine the boys had built. The next machine to be produced went up to The Pas. Then came a sizeable order from H. C. Paul in Winnipeg, which suggested the marketable product and its potential. This happened in 1958. Mr. Paul saw the machine as an ideal vehicle for out of the way installations that needed attention.

What to name these vehicles? Sno-travelers, snowmobiles, which was the general names they carried were not identifiable with the company. But an appropriate name was suggested by David Johnson which had been used for the straw choppers. A fitting name would be Polaris! The name means the north star, and that star is the anchor point for direction. What better than to call the new machines Polaris which would find the way for all snow vehicles in their pioneer-endeavor.

The next years were hardly the glory years for the struggling company. Manufacturing with all its problems, the demand for research, the necessity for markets, advertis-

Allen Hetteen, former president of Polaris who with his brother Edgar Hetteen and David Johnson built the first snowmobiles in the U. S.

ing and organization needed immediate solutions. And the greatest problem was money. The inventors dug in, did much of the manual work in the factory, tested the machines after the day's work, traveled far and wide for markets and investors, and tackled the gargantuan task of interesting people in the snowmobile business. The machines were hardly accepted at first for this was an altogether new concept in winter travel. The snow posed many problems with its versatility of being sometimes deep or sparse, sometimes soft to slush, sometimes crusty or crystalline, and uneven as it blanketed the land. Many people seeing the machines standing idle could scarcely figure out what kind of a contraption it could be. When some rather reluctant investors did come to the rescue the problems were far from solved, for with increased interest and business came, of course, increased costs.

Edgar Hetteen left the company in the early '60's to go to Alaska and then later to Thief River Falls where he founded the company called Arctic Enterprises. The Polaris Company bought out the Fly-Lite corporation and began to manufacture skis for that company in 1959. As the snowmobile business began to develop, the ski business was sold. Carl Wahlberg joined the company in 1962. There was an obstacle of grave importance about this time, for the company had produced a number of Comet machines which failed to fulfill its claims. In order to keep the good name of Polaris and keep the company operating, the management decided to recall all the Comet machines with full refund. When the later machines called the Colts, Mustangs, and Super Voyageurs rolled off the line and not only lived up to all expectations but proved to be a superior line of snowmobile, the integrity of the company was proven and business began to boom. With money from the Roseau Research and Development Corporation a new building was erected, and from time to time more sophisticated manufacturing was established. As the sports world took over the whole idea of snowmobiles, other companies sprang up all through the snow belt.

The worth of the machines was demonstrated sensationally when Edgar Hetteen, Rudy and Bessie Billberg and Erling Falk went from Bethel, Alaska which is on the Bering Sea, overland to the Yukon, and on to Fairbanks, a trek of 1,500 miles. People were

David Johnson, who with Allen and Edgar Hetteen founded Polaris, Inc. This is the Sno-Traveler, the first type machines to be manufactured.

astounded at the durability of the snowmobile and their maneuverability in all kinds of snow and climatic conditions. The newspapers and magazines had a whole new editorial field. Roseau was spotted on the map as "Little Detroit" and the Alaskans called the machines "an iron dog that doesn't eat fish" while the Easterners called the sport "pungin".

Snowmobiles became the attraction of the winter. The idea of racing the jaunty little machines was a natural trend. At first the races were done just for "the fun of it," with the company men, Allen Hetteen, David Johnson, Edgar Hetteen, and H. C. Paul winning many. Often the prizes were in winter clothing with the winners going from store to store to collect. Naturally the races became more sophisti-

One, two, three, go! and they're off — racing the machines to victory at the Sno-Mo-Cade. 1969.

Polaris Sno-Travelers at the South Pole. Picture taken for the National Geographic. 1959.

cated, and the endurance race from Winnipeg to St. Paul was initiated. This was called the "500" and had its premiere in 1966 with Herb Howe from Larson-Olson winning the first race. Polaris machines have dominated the races since. Allen Hetteen, president of the company, raced his big water-cooled Polaris over ten miles in 22 minutes and 3 seconds in Beausejour, Canada to win a pioneer race.

The man who has been the most consistent winner of all races and holds the World's Championship as well as the Canadian Power Toboggan Championship is Robert Eastman of Roseau. Eastman was the first to be named to the Snowmobile Hall of Fame. Other racers who have continued Polaris' winning ways have been Jim Bernat, LeRoy Lindblad, Greg Grahn, Stan Hayes, and Larry Rugland.

On July 1, 1968 Polaris was sold to Textron, a conglomerate with sales of $1.7 bil-

Roseau Thrill Team. Spectaculars were featured in 1970-71 featuring driver Dennis Olson, Ted Otto, Allen Kukowski, Loren Miller, and Roger Dick (not pictured is Larry Rugland).

Polaris Racer — won the speed record at 110 miles an hour.

lion a year. A five year plan for expansion of facilities for manufacturing purposes, and warehousing was initiated. The main plant was built in 1963 with another warehouse added. In 1967 an addition to the north and one to the main production plant was erected. Another building for accounting was added in 1967, and more additions to the main plant in 1968. More warehouse was added in 1969, and a third building for engineering was added in 1969.

An International Snowmobile Association was formed to upgrade every aspect of the sport with Allen Hetteen as its first president. Clark Dahlin and Jim Langley, riding Polaris machines, were the first to cross the continent on snowmobiles a distance of 4,018 miles touching the Pacific and the Atlantic oceans. Polaris was the first to publish a trail guide for snowmobiles over Minnesota's 2000 miles of trails through some million acres of winter wonderland. Safety schools for young drivers, ecology studies, noise and speed studies have been made using money from owner's registrations. In the study conducted by the Bemidji State College, the results showed practically no harm to the ecology created by the machines.

The snowmobilers have come to the rescue of men and animals alike in times of need. In Roseau's worst blizzard in 1966 when the town was virtually sealed off from the outside world, it was the men on these machines who took doctors and nurses to the hospitals, brought groceries and supplies to families and took care of other emergencies. Many a snowmobile has been called into action when there have been accidents. The deer that face starvation in winters of high snow are fed by the Conservation Department on snowmobiles. Whoever has not thrilled to a ride on these speedy, jaunty little wild horses has a thrill awaiting him.

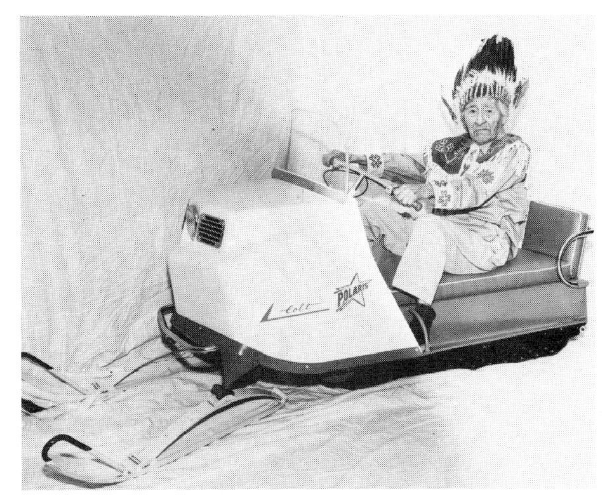

Ka-Ka-Geesick who at the age of 120 years said, "It's a good iron horse."

MARVINS

The destiny of Warroad was profoundly affected in 1903 when George Marvin came to operate the first grain elevator in town. When that elevator was torn down and moved to Saskatchewan, Mr. Marvin decided to stay. What a fortunate decision it was for the people of Warroad, as well as the Marvin family.

George Marvin bought a small retail lumber company and bought and sold pulp wood. The lumber company was engaged to build ammunition boxes during World War II, but at the close of the war they searched for other outlets. It was then the plant was converted into a sash and door factory, and then finally to a window manufacturing firm. Other enterprises under the Marvin name were the grain and seed, the pulpwood, a hardware retail store, marine outlet and model home construction.

At first native lumber was used for the window frames, but soon, with experimentation, it became evident that good kiln dried western woods were necessary to produce quality windows. Today the market for Marvin windows stretches across the land and into Canada. The firm does its own hauling with a fleet of 26 tractors and 30 trailers.

The Marvins were undaunted by two devastating fires, one in 1955 (when the temperature was 35 degrees below) and one in 1961 which completely wiped out construction, leveling a 200 foot square building, and putting all 175 employees out of work. Fortunately, they had their roots in Warroad and did not consider the possibility of quitting or moving.

The new building was started immediately after the fire and built to the north of Warroad on the curve of highway 11. This was a 90,000 square foot building which soon required an addition of the same size. In 1967 there was additional contruction which gave the Marvin plant another 86,000 square feet of manufacturing space. Then a third and fourth addition to the plant added still another 85,000 and 114,000 square feet of building to the plant complex. There is now a total of 10 acres of manufacturing facilities.

The Marvin Lumber and Cedar Company is a family owned business with Bill Marvin as President, Randolph (Tut) as Vice Presi-

The Marvins — Randolp "Tut", George, and Bill Marvin.

dent, and Jack as Secretary-Treasurer. The father, George, is 92 years of age. Until recently one could find him at his desk carrying on the business affairs of the company.

Local people are hired to operate the plant. During the summer months summer employment is available to many college and high school students.

There is a spirit of congeniality in the plant with a home town atmosphere. There is an annual cash profit sharing plan that has been in effect for some years. In 1971, $225,000 in cash was divided among the employees. In 1972 the amount shared was $375,698 and in 1973, $552,651 in cash was divided among the employees of Marvin Lumber and Cedar Company.

The history of Warroad has been profoundly affected and the town is justly proud to be the home of the Marvin Lumber and Cedar Company. The Marvins have not only contributed economically to Warroad and the entire area, but the community and sports interest of this enterprising family has been an influential force in the lives of many people.

SMALL BUSINESSES

Besides the two large manufacturing plants, Marvins and Polaris, there are a few other establishments. The Christian brothers, renowned for their hockey prowess, started a hockey stick factory in 1964. With increased interest in hockey and the trend toward artificial ice facilities, the hockey fever has become wide spread. This plant adds more than $100,000 to the community in payroll money. Producing something like 151,158 sticks in

Marvin windows are manufactured in volume.

The Christian Bros. Hockey Stick factory in Warroad.

6 months the twenty-five employees have a busy season. There are 22 models of sticks with laminated handles that are imported from Finland, and some from Wisconsin which are finished at Warroad. There are 475 stockholders in the corporation with the Christian brothers and Hal Bakke as the officers and directors. The hockey sticks are exported to Canada and have wide acceptance throughout the United States. The sticks are distributed through 175 dealers.

A business which started in the basement of Allen Hetteen's home and which was engineered by Mrs. Hetteen soon grew out of its quarters, moved temporarily to a garage, and then to the new building on Highway 11 near Roseau. This business first made cushions for Polaris, and later for Arctic Cat snowmobiles as well. The company branched out into assembly of Hi-Fi radios, and stereos. From this project the company began to deal in furniture, constructed according to special orders, and then into building the more conventional models for sale. The line was named Gallant Furniture. Upholstery was a specialty of the company. In 1970 the Polaris distributorship was added and also a surplus business. In 1972 the Trailmaster line of campers was added through a merger with Trailmaster Co. of Red Lake Falls. The camper company moved back to Red Lake Falls after the tragic death of Allan Hetteen. The business was first known as Northern Upholstery and later AMCO.

The Progressive Tool and Engineering Co. came to Roseau in 1969, owned and operated by Neil Pearson. The company makes dies and parts of the machines and the metal stampings for cleats, slide rail suspension, throttle levers, and other sundry articles.

North Star Transport is the name of the company started in Roseau in 1964 when a truck owned by Jon Miller and William Hagen picked up a load of snowmobiles (called sno-travelers at the time); they have been hauling ever since on an ever expanding scale. The offices for the company are where the Roseau Machine Co. was formerly located. The practice of hauling Polaris snowmobiles to the Twin Cities and other points and hauling back materials became a good business for the boys. Soon they added Arctic Cat to their freighting. Mileage of 80-120,000 miles is common for the trucks. Each semi can haul 45 snowmobiles which now have sophisticated packaging to insure perfect machines on delivery. The company instituted an on-the-job-driving training program to make an attractive situation for the drivers.

The huge yellow bugs that one sees around the county are not Martian infestations but rather a creation called Mr. Litterbug which were designed to contain trash and aid in the anti-pollution campaigns. It was first built and engineered by Alder Pederson and Udell Nelson.

EDUCATION

A leading figure in education in Roseau County during the time of consolidation of the schools was Charles Christianson who was active from 1935 until his untimely death in 1967. Besides his leadership in the educational field in the county he held many offices in other educational organizations such as being Chairman of the State School Reorganization Committee, Chairman of the Northern Minnesota Education Association and also Chairman of the Minnesota Association of County Superintendents. His civic interests included membership in the hospital board, the fair committee, and others for which he worked for many years. It was under his direction that the 112 school districts were consolidated into the four high school districts of Badger, Greenbush, Warroad, and Roseau. Wannaska and Salol and Malung became a part of the Roseau district, while parts of Wannaska and Ross all of Haug-Leo and a portion of Grass Lake were consolidated into the Badger district. The Malung and Wannaska communities retained their own facilities. Roosevelt became either a part of Warroad or Baudette. Each town maintained a bus line to the four high school districts to enable every student the privilege of attending a high school.

Deloris Andol, 4-H Club director, presents a plague to the late Charles Christianson, County Superintendent of Schools in recognition for the outstanding cooperation he extended to the program.

There was a concentrated effort to expand the school plant facilities in the high school districts. Warroad built in 1955 and again an addition in 1965. A bond issue was passed in Roseau for a new gym and eight class rooms in 1948, and an additional grade school in 1955. Greenbush dedicated a new school in 1965, and that same year Badger started on their new facilities.

The educational services of the county were greatly expanded not only with additional buildings but also in the diversity of educational opportunities.

The need for vocational education was felt in 1952 when Roseau added a Vocational-Agricultural building. But the big impetus for vocational education for high school students came in 1968 when the federal government along with the state gave financial aid. Joe Freeman was the man who coordinated the work in the county, and classes were held in Badger, Greenbush, Warroad, and Roseau in such subjects as typing, shorthand, bookkeeping, knitting, Norwegian, sewing, cooking, drafting, home repairing, and G. E. D. (General Education Diploma) for adults. For the student the curriculum was expanded to include courses in small engines, electric and electronic courses, cooking for boys and welding.

In 1938 the American Legion Auxiliary created a library for Roseau. A grand opening was held with appropriate readings and music. The library had, even at that time 1211 volumes of adult non-fiction, and 2779 children's books. The library was housed in the Municipal building, and served the community well until funds were made available by the county and the state for bookmobile service to the entire area. Now other services were added besides books, such as film, records and slides. The library in Roseau is at present located in the Budd apartment building, but by the summer of 1975 a beautiful new library will be in operation to be located in a museum-library complex beside the Municipal building. Since joining the Regional Library System the collection in Roseau has been increased.

The youngest taxpayer in Roseau County is Neal Novacek of Greenbush who resides in Polonia Township. Retiring after 40 years of service is Willie Strandberg, County treasurer, shown with his wife Mathilda.

Greenbush has an adequate library which is located in the rooms beside the clerk's office and is serviced by the Regional bookmobile. Warroad also maintains a library in the rooms formerly used as a doctor's clinic.

Besides delivering books and other materials to the established libraries, the bookmobile makes stops at several other communities in the county and so creates a library on wheels for young and old. By request a patron can secure any book in the Regional Library.

It was disappointing news to learn in 1971 that Roseau County had lost population on a 4.9% basis over a ten year period. The figures recorded a drop in population of from 15,103 in 1961 to 11,560 in 1971.

The Vocational Carpentry class who built the club house at Oak Crest Golf Course, under the direction of Ernest Wicklander (first man seated in second row.) Vocational Education is directed by Walter Pederson (first man third row).

In September of 1967 the personal property tax was eliminated, but on April 1, 1971 by invitation of Jerry Deal, the taxpayers crowded the auditorium to air their views on the lowering of the real estate taxes. Inasmuch as the sales tax came into effect at this time with a rebate to the counties of 35% from the state the taxes were lowered, but not through the efforts of Mr. Deal, who managed thereby to increase his personal income. In 1974 the rebate to the county was raised to 45%. The revenue sharing in 1972 amounted to $224,752 for the county.

William Provance was made the head of a survey for area development with a four-point emphasis on (1) youth activities, (2) family living, (3) agriculture, and (4) public affairs. The planning firm of Aguar, Jyring, Whiteman, Moser, Inc. was hired to assist in comprehensive town development to coordinate with the county unit. Such problems as zoning, forestry, parks, industrial development, roads, and housing were to be considered.

The State of Minnesota sent twelve engineers to study the topography of the area for the United States Geological Survey. The purpose was to establish a basis for study of the earth problems, urban planning, farm and industrial sites for development.

In spite of the decline of population, the progress of the county communities was evident in many ways. Most of Warroad's improvements have been made since 1965. A building project under the federal H.U.D. produced a low cost housing called Young Manor. A pipeline was built north of Warroad from the Trans-Canada system to International Falls with Warroad putting in its own municipal line. Another village project was the TV cable. The bridge across the river was replaced at a cost of $326,706.

Warroad has two new apartment buildings; one with twelve apartments is located on highway 11 and a new apartment building with 18 apartments is the Robert's Apartments which is located on the Warroad River. Water and sewer lines have been extended on the south side of the town. There is a new trailer park built by Tut Marvin capable of accommodating 50 trailers. A new road called the Taylor Road (after Morris Taylor) is a part of the park expansion that connects Lake Street with Highway 11 from branch highway 313. An interesting development is being built on the lake shore across from the airport called War Road Estates. A nine hole golf course is nearing completion which will be expanded into an 18 hole course. There will be some 300 or more lots sold around the course for resort cottages. This development is being promoted by Robert Anderson of Grand Forks, Sammy Grafstrom and Mike Marvin from Warroad.

Roseau's improvements have included village water and sewer extensions, three trailer parks, a swimming pool, four new tennis courts, plus two at the school, completion of a new tourist park on the south side of town, and a wayside park area west of the village. The Baptists, Methodists, Catholics, Moe Lutherans, and Messiah Lutherans have either added to their existing churches or built new edifices. The Spruce church which burned the winter of 1972 was rebuilt, and plans are being made for rebuilding the recently burned Concordia Church at Ross. Two apartment houses, the Anda and the Garden Court Apartments have been added to the town.

The law enforcement center building in Roseau was built in 1963. It has facilities for 18 prisoners, and was erected at a cost of $53,000. It was a point of pride for the county when in 1967 the Roseau County Sheriff's office was tied nationally to the computerized crime information hook-up and to the State Bureau of Criminal Apprehension and thus to the FBI. The record of apprehensions of County Sheriff Knochenmus was better than the state average since the state records 80% and Roseau County 86% of crimes solved. It might be noted that offenses in the county were up from 64 in 1963 to 73 in 1974. The

Robert Bergland, Congressman from Roseau looks over his farm at Roseau.

Sam Bergland, pioneer of Roseau County looks over some bills with son Bob Bergland who is a congressman from this district.

first municipal judge was Arnold Hildahl. Donald Shanahan is Judge of County Court. A conciliation court for petty grievances was started in the county in November of 1973.

Greenbush has a new series of low cost homes for the elderly built with H.U.D. funds. This is a 20 unit structure with many fine features such as a fireside room, conversation centers and a kitchen suitable to be used when occupants have guests.

Both Roseau and Warroad have new bank buildings. Warroad's bank, built by Harold Heneman in 1963 had its dedication on the 50th anniversary of the first bank in Warroad. The Citizen's State Bank in Roseau with Robert Foley as president, has a new bank built in 1967. It is one of the first banks to hire a full time agricultural assistant, Mr. William Provance. It uses computerized bookkeeping systems.

The sanitary landfill area a mile east and half mile south of Salol became operative in 1972. This facility serves Roseau, Salol, and Warroad. The sewage lagoon started in 1972 at a cost of $482,500 was completed in 1974.

In 1973 Roseau County found itself in the newly formed Region One Planning commission. This includes Roseau, Kittson, Marshall, Norman, Pennington, Polk, and Red Lake Counties. Roseau County has four representatives on the regional board: a county commissioner, a representative of the municipalities, a representative of the townships, and a representative of the school boards. This group will do the regional planning within the area.

Robert Bergland, United States Congressman, is a native son of Roseau. Robert, the son of Selmer and Mrs. Bergland was born in Roseau July 22, 1928 and at the present time has a farm south of Roseau. He is married to the former Helen Grahn also from Roseau.

Being active in politics from 1960 when he was co-chairman of the Farmers for Kennedy Campaign in Minnesota, he has always been aware of the part government must play in agriculture. He was elected to the Congress in 1970 and has served on various committees including: House Committee on Agriculture, House Committee on Science and Astronautics, and the House Select Committee on Small Businesses. He served as Regional Vice-Chairman of the Democratic Study Group with responsibility for six mid-western states in addition to Minnesota, and also co-chairman of the Study Group's Task Force on Rural Development. He served as an assistant to the Secretary of Agriculture, Orville Freeman. He was appointed State Chairman of the Agricultural Stabilization and Conservation Service in 1961.

Bob says: "Roseau County will never be as heavily populated as areas nearer the Twin Cities but the per capita income of Roseau County residents coupled with the modest increases in population, and the better farm prices will create more prosperity than ever before – that plus our proximity to some of the best fishing and hunting in the State will insure a comfortable future for our County."

CIVIL DEFENSE

The Civil Defense in Roseau County was started in 1951, shortly after the state recommended its establishment. It was started in Pinecreek by Mr. E. G. Simmons, who was requested to form a Ground Observation Corps under the Air Defense Command. The plan, which proved to be a model for other units, appointed one person to watch from his own residence for one week. Mr. Edward Erickson, county commissioner, delegated Mr. Simmons to set up a countywide organization. Mr. Simmons who had helped write the Civil Defense Law when he appeared before the State Legislature succeeded in setting up a structure that would also use county funds for maintenance.

Roseau County was the only county in Minnesota to receive help from the American

Red Cross to teach instructors to train people in home nursing care. Miss Ginnestad from St. Louis trained eleven instructors throughout the county, who in turn instructed some 660 women. Amos Fikkan trained many in First Aid in the County at the same time. Roseau County, because of its efficient program, became eligible for government hospital emergency equipment in 1957.

The first International Conference between Minnesota and Manitoba Civil Defense was held in Roseau, September 24, 1958. Other persons concerned in the Civil Defense program were Mayor Reese (who was set up to send a national warning system capable of sending messages nationally in less than three minutes), Bert Hanson, first Civil Defense Director for the village of Roseau, Mr. Radway, in charge of emergency operations in Kittson county and later transferred to Roseau, Edward Erickson, Edgar Wold, Jim Jaros of Warroad and Ernie B. Miller.

Mr. Simmons received a commendation from the State Auditors and Governor Elmer L. Anderson and from President Eisenhower for his work, and became an honorary member of the Air Defense Command.

PORTS

Roseau County has always been on friendly terms with its Canadian neighbors. There are three ports to our friends to the north, all upgraded in facilities and services during this time. The Pinecreek port was first established as a Customs Station in 1899, and is unique in that it is on the exact location of the Old Indian Trail. The first office was in Gulbrand Haugen's store, and the first Customs Officer on record was Mr. John J. Thompson. He received a salary of $3.50 a day with 50c allowance for horse and feed. The office was moved to Knutson's store and then to a house owned by Mrs. Rudy Nordengen, and then moved to the border in a house owned by Gilbert Skogstad. After considerable effort by the Ross-Pinecreek Association and through public law 194 permanent buildings were erected for living and office space for custom officers.

The Roseau port is located north of the village. When this port, a "station" was opened on April 4, 1930, it was located on the Richardson farm, north of the bridge. This office was an old building, used as a chicken house in former times. In 1956 the office was moved to the border and a house was used that belonged to Mrs. Richardson. The first officer was Edward C. Collins. The Sprague road was abandoned after a bridge near the Westling farm collapsed, and when a detour was installed, it was felt that the port should be at the border. Permanent residences and offices were then built there.

The port at Warroad has always been the largest and busiest port in the county, since it has railroad, highway, water and air traffic. The port came into existence July 1, 1900. Charles A. Moody, the first Deputy Collector of Customs was in charge at a time when Warroad was still spelled War Road, which was 1905.

For some time all passenger trains were convoyed by an Immigration Officer who rode the east-bound train until it met the west-bound from Fort Francis and then returned on that train. The practice was discontinued in an economy move at the time the force was reduced, and trains are now cleared for inspection at Warroad.

In 1915 the Deputy Collector moved the office from a box car on the CN track to the New Canadian National station in Warroad where quarters were maintained until the port south of Middleboro on highway 310 was built.

HEALTH

Medical services were expanded after 1950. In that year the Greenbush Hospital was deemed too small and a building program added eight rooms; in 1963 another 20-bed unit for convalescents and nursing care was added. In 1971 the administrator, Morris Bertilrud, presented a certificate of need to the state department and after some confusion the administration was certified to proceed on the new building program. This resulted in a $430,000 addition which provided 20 skilled nursing beds, and 20 beds, a remodelled X-ray department, dietary laboratory and laundry department.

In 1973 Dr. Klefstad, who has served the Greenbush area for 27 years was honored by the community for his long and faithful service. Besides his dedication to his profession he has been interested in numerous civic projects. He also set up a clinic on his Chris-Craft and each summer served the people living on the islands of Lake of the Woods.

Mrs. Budd assumed responsibility for the Roseau Hospital which had been built

The Roseau Area Hospital addition in 1973.

in 1937 on Highway 11. The doctors were repaid their loans, and things were going well with peak loads of 35 patients and 15 babies being cared for at a time. The shortage of nurses was a constant problem and it was felt that proper housing would offset that need, so in 1950 a nurses' home, modern in every respect, was built. The hospital was enlarged and updated.

The school board decided in 1953 that a nurse should be added to the staff and Mrs. Alice Patton acted in that capacity until 1955, at which time Mrs. Vivian Anderson took charge. Following her death Mrs. Velma DeFrates has filled the position of School Nurse.

It was decided to have the hospital become community owned property, and with pledges and commitments and a down payment of $60,000 the property changed to community ownership and was named "Roseau Community Hospital Association." Mrs. Chapman, and later Mrs. Ruby Halvorson acted as administrators after Mrs. Budd sold the hospital and retired. The hospital board at this time was composed of L. A. Ross, Herbert Monsrud, A. R. Lee, J. A. Helgeson, Carl Jackson, Norman Flagstad, and Robert Thorkelson.

In 1961 several Roseau professional and business men became interested in a project to provide a home for the elderly of the county. Headed by Dr. Berge as chairman of the board, and Rev. Lindholm as assistant, a drive was made for funds to make this dream a reality. It was stressed that it must be a county-wide project, and in a short time the board had raised chiefly by donations, the sum of $43,000 and aimed for $60,000 before beginning the home. Large ads appeared in the papers stressing the fact that the older folk were the pioneers to whom we owed a great debt which could be expressed in some measure by our thoughtful care now. In September 1962 work was begun on the home which was eventually called Sheltering Oaks, and was located west of the golf course. It was at this time that the nurse's home on the highway was converted into a home for the elderly ambulatory patients and called Eventide.

The Senior Citizen's program was started in 1966 sponsored by the O. E. O. with Esther Snustad the first director. Now the program is sponsored by the village with Mrs. Hulda Roadfeldt in charge. The Senior Citizen's Organization gives the elderly outlets for sociability.

In 1969 greater expansion was planned to enlarge the facilities of the hospital and the Commission of Accreditation was awarded to Harold Kloempken, hospital administrator. In December 1971, the construction of an $844,000 addition to the hospital was begun. This new facility added 20 more beds to the nursing home unit, an out-patient addition, expanded X-ray facilities, a physio-therapy occupational unit, and more office space. No bond issue was needed as it was financed by the gross revenue bonds and cash reserves. The complex was completed in 1973 and dedicated on September 1, 1973 with Congressman Robert Bergland as speaker.

An organization called "Doctors for Roseau" was started in 1966. Although Roseau has had many doctors their stays were short. They included Drs. Wheeler, Gisvold, Berg, Vidinli, and Pinnsonnealt. The Lion's Club, Commercial Club and other organizations donated money to help finance medical students who were then obligated to practice in Roseau for a period of time after their internship.

Dr. John Leo Delmore, more affectionately known as "Dr. Jack" has served Roseau County since April 29th, 1937 when he joined his father in the Delmore Clinic. Having been released from the army with the rank of Captain, he was free to practice, and wanted nothing more than to serve his home folk.

A special commendation was given to Dr. Jack Delmore in 1944 for his service to his country. The plaque reads:

The U.S. of America to all who shall see these presents, greetings. This is to certify that the President of the U. S. of America authorized by executive order, February 4, 1944 has awarded

The Bronze Star Medal
to
Captain John L. Delmore
for
meritorious achievement in Ground Operations in European Theater of Operations against the enemy.
Given under my hand in the city of Washington
This 3rd day of February
Signed: Edwin Withers, Major General, The Adjutant General

A license plate familiar to people of the county bears the letters WOMAK, and everyone recognizes "Jack's" car, for his hobby is "hamming". He passed tests for Federal Communication Commission in 1952, enabling him to use frequencies available to all amateurs. He belongs to the Sioux Amateur Radio Association in Grand Forks, and also to the Lake of the Woods Radio Amateur Network.

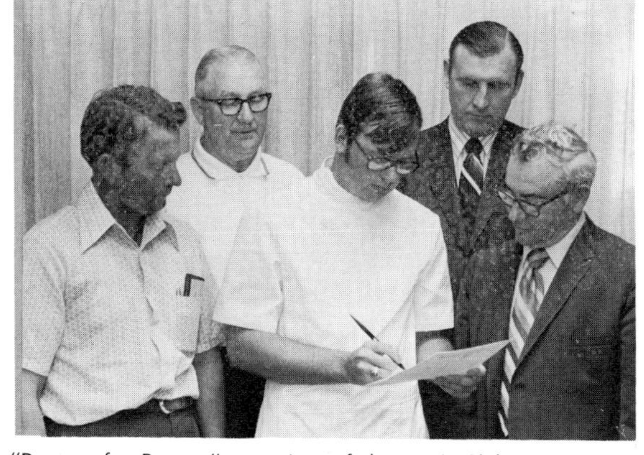

"Doctors for Roseau" a project of the Lion's Club was started in 1966. Meredith Haselrud, Oscar Almquist, David Willey, Bob Foley and Bill Provance look over the agreement David is signing.

Dr. John L. Delmore affectionately known as "Dr. Jack" who started to serve the area in 1937 continues to head the Delmore Clinic.

In 1947 Dr. Robert Delmore joined the clinic. Later he moved to California to continue his practice. He died in 1962.

Dr. Mike Metcalf joined the Delmore Clinic in 1972, and Mike Rossner, physical therapist joined the staff at the hospital in 1973.

The Warroad Municipal Hospital which was built in 1939 was added to in 1962. Twenty-two more beds were made available and an out-patient clinic was also established. The Drs. Janecky, Pearson, Schuneman, Potts, Nelson, Russ, and La Tonn have served the community, but at the present writing the hospital is closed for lack of a resident doctor. Dr. Larson has been a dentist in Warroad for the past 28 years.

The Children's Home owned and operated by Mr. and Mrs. Albert Olson is another medical facility in Roseau County. It serves children from all over the state of Minnesota. In 1943, Marie Mortenson took foster children into her farm home, some of whom were retarded or handicapped. The Mortensons bought the Leslie Norman home in 1955 and opened a home for retarded children. In 1964 the Olsons (nee Mortenson) built new facilities for the children, which was under the direction of the Minnesota Welfare Department. At one time there were as many as 90 children cared for, but the number has now levelled off to around 50. In 1970 the home was sold to Mr. Sam Levy and Associates from Milwaukee, but in 1972 it reverted back to the Olsons who are operating it at the present time.

A clinic which has been active for many years under sponsorship of the Crippled Children's Service and the American Legion Auxiliary of Roseau, Greenbush, and Baudette is a free service to the children of the county. This clinic is staffed by pediatricians, speech and hearing specialists, dental specialists, and nutritionists. The clinic is well received for each year more than 50 children have been screened for possible further attention, and it has been found that 5-8% have a need. Mrs. Carol Schwichtenberg has acted as local chairman for several years.

Dr. R. V. Harris, Sr. started his dental practice in Roseau in 1922, and his son Robert joined him in the Harris Clinic in 1952. Dr. Schurke joined Robert in 1972 after the death of Dr. Harris senior.

The county was declared free of TB in 1954 with an appropriate celebration which was held in the Roseau High School at the January P.T.A. with the program under the direction of Charles Christianson. The next year the anti-polio shots were started in the county, and the annual Mother's marches for the cause of polio eradication were in progress. Cancer crusades have been an annual part of the county's fight against that disease.

In 1971 the growing concern over drug abuse resulted in public seminars to alert the people concerning the problem. Sheriff Knochenmus was on hand to give first hand information. In March of 1971 more than 200 people gathered at the auditorium for an informative meeting to learn and disseminate the information.

Ambulance service is part of the Roseau Area Hospital's program.

Through the NWCA for "Operation Medicare Alert" a grant of $7,463 was given to the county under the Social Security Amendment of 1965. Thus the county residents have had advantage of fine and adequate health facilities and programs.

SPORTS

Not all the good hunting in Roseau County is a matter of a fortuitous environment. It is this surely, but much more, for good stewardship of the wild fowl can be credited to the Roseau County Conservation Club through the foresight of Elmer "Cap" Nelson. When the sportsmen became aware of a plan by private interests to create a private hunting club in the bog area, they appealed to the Roseau County Board to withhold the sale of the bog land to outside interests. Fortunately the Roseau County Board realized the rationality of the request. The proposal was called the Roseau River Wildlife project and later the name was changed to Roseau River Wildlife Management Area. The plan called for 5 miles of diversion of Pine Creek from Canada as a source of water for impoundments. It was presented first at a meeting at Ross in June, 1946. In August of that year it was approved and the proposal for a public hunting ground was presented to the Department of Conservation at a Camp Fire meeting at Hutchinson. Division of Game and Fish biologists field-checked the bog in August and in November the ground work was done, and a plan provided to develop the north side of Roseau River so as not to involve drainage problems.

At the ground breaking ceremony on October 7, 1948, at which outdoor sports writers from the Twin Cities and the local area were present, the work was officially begun. The Division of Game and Fish acquired almost all of the 51,760 acres of land in the project in 1951 with approximately 6,189 acres purchased from private land holders, about 3,030 acres turned over to the project by the Roseau County Board, and the remainder purchased from the State of Minnesota. By early 1952 a contract calling for three impoundments and the diversion of Pine Creek into the bog was let, as well as for the diversion of Pine Creek from its natural channel near Piney, Manitoba, to the International Boundary north. In 1968, approximately 12,000 acres of trust fund lands, known as Juneberry supplement, was acquired so the present acreage is now 61,333 acres.

The 23 miles of dikes enclosing pools of 2,200, 3,700 and 4,600 acres and the diversion of Pine Creek as a source of water was completed in 1953, and water began to accumulate that fall. A refuge manager was assigned to the bog and in 1955 construction of personnel quarters were completed. The project cost about $850,000 and was paid for by the federal aid to wildlife restoration popularly called the Pittman-Robertson funds.

It is interesting to note that in 1951, the year before the development, there were about 95 hunters present at the Pine Creek pothole and about the same number in the remainder of the bog. Pool 1 which includes the old Pine Creek pothole alone had over 600 hunters on it on the opening day of hunting after the project was completed.

In 1969 a check was made as to the use of the area. The result given in "man days" is as follows:

Waterfowl hunters	7,000
Deer hunters	500
Upland game hunters	300
Fishermen	7,000
Picnickers	400
Boy Scouts	200
Bird Watchers	200
Students	100
Sightseers	3,000
Trappers	100
Rifle trap shooters	200
Boating	500
Snowmobilers	500
Total	20,000

The development is favorable to mallard ducks, blue-winged teal, and especially to geese. Although water fowl propagation is the primary purpose of the bog, it has many other useful purposes as the above list will attest. One use not often known is that it is a natural spawning water for northern pike. There are 100,000 northern pike ranging from minnow size to 2 lbs. which are transferred to deep water lakes all over Minnesota annually. This is a highly beneficial practice for since the water is too shallow at the bog for the pike they would freeze out annually if not moved.

The deer in Roseau County are beautiful and provide challenge to the many hunters.

The Roseau River Wildlife Management area is under the supervision of Jack Jensen.

Lake of the Woods with its 950,000 acres, is the 40th largest lake in the world. It has 14,000 islands, is 60 miles wide and 70 miles long. The United States owns 32.5% of the lake, or 307,020 acres. During the years 1955-68 the United States catch of fish was 34.3 million pounds; this represents 19 different species of fish. However, one-fourth of the fish were the very edible walleyes. The mink were fed 85% of the catch of rough fish which the 30 commercial fishermen brought in. Most of these fish were caught in gill nets. The trawlers were licensed for 1963-1964 but were removed due to public pressure after the 1964 season.

A gun safety program to teach the young to be cautious with firearms was instituted in 1967 with John Kennedy, a former teacher and Stanley Roadfelt as first instructors. The course was given initially to 183 youngsters, and has been taught annually since.

A full and satisfying sport program is carried on in the high schools of the county, offering to the students football, hockey, basketball, track, golf, baseball and other sports. The Lakers continued to play for Warroad, the Cloverleafs were revived during this time to play for Roseau. Jim Stordahl, Larry Stordahl, and Donald Ross played for the Nationals in Ljubljana, Yugoslavia. Henry Boucha from Warroad, and Earl Anderson and Mike Baumgartner from Roseau all play professional hockey at this time.

Moose in Roseau County are quite a common sight.

One rather unique record occurred in Roseau High School in 1966 when four regional championships were won at Roseau in different sports. Coach Kramer led his boys to victory in track, Ray Kavanagh in baseball, Oscar Almquist in hockey and Pete Groschupf in golf.

Robert Harris and his sons have won distinction in golf during the late '60's and early '70's when Robert and son John won the Northwest Father-Son Golf Tournament in 1968, 1969, and 1970, and Robert and son Robbie won it in 1971, 1972, and 1973. He was honored by the Sports Illustrated Magazine for having won this tournament five years in a row. Bob has also won the Vandersluis Labor Day tournament in Bemidji twice and was also medalist at the Birchmont. In 1974 John Harris was named to the second All-American Golf Team and won the Minnesota Big Ten Golf Championship.

Ever since 1950 Roseauites have enjoyed winter festivals that featured their home product the Polaris snowmobile. These festivals attracted large crowds and featured parades, international cross county races, and many other featured races. In 1965 Carla Augasta King and King Boreus XXIX from the St. Paul Winter Carnival reigned over the event, now called the Sno-Mo-Cade. One feature that thrilled the audience was the stunts done on the machines. Other features were jumping machines from a ramp over several cars with Wayne Burkel winning the long jump for a world's record of 841 and 911 feet. Running through a burning hoop was another thriller. Running the machine around an 18 foot loop was the crowning thrill of the spectacular. There were more than 6,500 people who saw these stunts performed by the Thrill Team. They were presented for two years but then discontinued as they were deemed too dangerous to the riders. The Polaris machines raced to a speed of 110 miles an hour.

Ice Revues, which were started by Margaret Bell and Maureen Flagstad as Girl Scout leaders were later directed by Mrs. Nancy Burggraf and for 13 years she directed the extravaganzas.

Warroad which has the only natural swimming site in the county has maintained a beach and play area there for many years. A park for picnickers adjoins the beach. Roseau realized its dream of having a swimming pool in 1961 when the village agreed to assist in the construction of a municipal pool which was located south of the power plant. A fund of $30,000 which was raised by the citizens was matched by the village making the construction possible.

The rural play days which was called the Junior Sports Meet and was anticipated by children and parents alike was discontinued after the consolidation of the schools. Formerly Malung, Pencer, Wannaska, Skime, Swift, Roosevelt, Salol, Ross and Strathcona participated in these events.

Although baseball has lost some of the glamour of the early days it has nonetheless been kept active. Softball and little League games have also become part of the sports program. A baseball park named after Roseau's outstanding player is called Gilbertson Field.

In 1972 a popular fund raising project was used in the area which was called "Walk for Development". The walk, from Roseau to Wannaska was open to any participant and was a project to raise money for medical purposes. The merchants were the donors.

One problem in the sporting field that remains unresolved today is the controversy over the trawlers, the commercial fishing and the anglers. The state, after studies made on the subject, authorized the use of the trawlers to eradicate rough fish, but the public protested and voiced their feelings at public meetings to try to settle the problem. As a result the trawlers operated for two years, but gave over then to public demand to discontinue their use.

In 1972 a new club house was built at Oak Crest Golf Course by the boys from the vocational carpentry class with the club providing the materials. The Golf Club maintains a full time pro and golf teacher, holds league play for both men and women, serves weekly meals and enjoys a luxuriant course cared for by Mr. Lloyd Rice. Greenbush also maintains a lovely golf course and has an active membership. Warroad has had its course on the Bloom farm for several years, and had the membership reactivated by Mr. James Landby. Their new 18 hole golf course at the War Road Estates is currently being constructed. This area will also include a 785 x 485 foot marina.

Interest in tennis was renewed in Roseau when the four courts were added south of the swimming pool, and another two at the school grounds.

An International Regatta was held with 60 sail boats racing from Baudette to Kenora in 1966. At the present time there is agitation to renew this fine sport on beautiful Lake of the Woods which was started by Hank Henderson.

Another activity that created much interest in 1955 was curling with Dick Ching as the chief instigator. A curling rink was built north of the Memorial Arena where for about ten years teams played in leagues and held Bon Spiels. Many North Dakota and Canadian teams vied for honors, and there was an annual tournament banquet. The curling fever subsided in favor of bowling with Greenbush and Roseau having privately owned bowling alleys. Many of the bowlers travel yearly to distant cities for the national bowling competition.

RESORTS

Warroad, the only U. S. port on Lake of the Woods, has provided more tourist and recreational outlets than any part of the county. In 1952 the Springsteel Island development was added to the existing Cal's Resort to lure the tourist trade to our north country.

Springsteel Island, located three miles across the bay from Warroad, was homesteaded by Charles Springsteele, Sr., who carried on commercial fishing and truck gardening, and hauled his produce by boat to Warroad and Baudette. Because of the isolation of the island, he provided a school for his own seven children right at home with Olga Paulson Anderson (deceased wife of E. O. Anderson) as one of the early teachers. He also maintained a camp for the youth of the area with lodging in a screened in dormitory type building, for 25 cents per night. Charles Springsteele, Jr. took over the island after his father's death and sold it to a group of Roseau business men.

The island was something of a Huck Finn's paradise, for beside a house there were some four or five old buildings. It also had a "who-done-it" haunting but true story. Two Indians, Hans Lightning and his brother-in-law, Max Oshie, worked for Skinny Springsteele (Charles, Jr.) lifting nets. One day Lightning was not to be found. Self appointed posses combed the area, and did their own arm chair conjecturing. Since the island was only 80 acres in area it was easily searched. Lightning had no car or boat. But one morning about three days later someone spotted an object thought to be a dead-head. It was the body of Hans Lightning. In a bitter quarrel Oshie had killed his brother-in-law, tied a heavy weight to his body, and heaved him overboard. But the weight tied to his body had become loosened, and Mr. Lightning floated up. Huck Finn would have surely gone for this.

The five men who purchased the island had to build a road 1.6 miles long through 3-5 foot deep muskeg to reach the island. The island was overgrown with tangled hazel brush, raspberry bushes, and some beautiful bitter sweet vines. On October 5, 1951, Mel Johnson from Crookston was engaged to build the road. For a month he worked steadily and successfully, but at the mouth of the island he encountered deep water and his drag line kept listing even after he hoisted it up on mats. Often it sat at a most precarious angle. It took some days of coaxing to get Mel to stay on the job, but by the end of November he and his crew had the road completed. The road not only proved to be sound and firm, but it was of such caliber that when it was given to the county they black-topped over the original gravelled road.

The land was platted into forty-four lots of various sizes. A few old buildings were utilized for resort purposes, docks were built, and the Bjorkman cabins were purchased and moved from their original site on the ridge to the island, and modernized for rentals.

Rudy Rice, Carl Wahlberg and Bob Pomeroy bought out the other partners, and it was finally resolved that Wahlberg would own the resort while Rice and Pomeroy acquired the remaining lots.

Today the island is teeming with recreation seekers. There are some 275 docks, 50 resort homes and an increasing number of trailers. It remains a fine fishing and resorting area.

A pioneer in the field of tourist accommodations was Cal's resort which was started in 1950 with 15 housekeeping cabins. The location for a resort is ideal with a swimming beach, a beautiful park for campers and picnickers and a wonderful landing for pontoon planes. The restaurant called Cal's Dog House was built two years after Cal Marvin started the resort, and the Ripple room and lake side dining areas were added recently to afford the guests a spectator's seat to observe the lake activity. Many is the tale Cal could tell of the whoppers brought into the resort on one of his 8 launches, of resort operations for boats in distress, and some bizarre tragedies of the water. In 1973 Cal sold his resort to a group of businessmen.

Don Hanson's Flying Service and Swede Carlson's pontoon planes are busy every day transporting tourists to one of the beautiful islands of Lake of the Woods where fine accommodations are available for the whole family. In 1973 the whole area was saddened with the news of the death of Swede Carlson when he experienced a "white out" (snow and horizon not clearly distinguishable). The new owner, "Fuzz" Page operates the flying service under the original name continuing the same type of service.

In 1969 an ambitious plan for the development of Warroad as a leading tourist attraction in Minnesota took shape. This is a five year plan and will cost in the neighborhood of 5 million dollars when completed. At the present time the plan is underway and in the third phase of development. Mayor Richard Roberts has been working with the council and the planners, Aguar, Jyring, Whiteman, and Moser, and have enlisted the cooperation of many state and federal agencies such as the Minnesota Planning Office of Economic Development, Federal Bureau of Outdoor Recreation, The Minnesota State Historical Society, State Department of Aeronautics, Federal Economic Administration, Pollution Control Agency and others.

The park development program is divided into four phases and is funded by agencies for three-fourths of the cost, with one-fourth the local responsibility. In Phase One which is almost completed the roads and spurs have been completed, and the parking lot and loop roads, the marina and camper service laid out and excavated. Phase Two includes the campground preparation with the necessary sewer lines, parking, electrical systems, and water lines. Phase Three which is in process of development includes mostly the marina work, the launching ramps, the docks and lights, the park lighting and entrances, the shoreline development, sewer lines, landscape improvements and water services. Phase Four will be the wrap-up on the entire project with the comfort station and possibly a built-in lake swimming pool. There will be room for from 40-50 camp units and boat slips.

The former municipal liquor store in Warroad is now a youth center, and a new liquor store has been built on Highway 11. The Warroad Historical Society plans an historical village south of the present park with old buildings moved in and preserved in this fashion.

Greenbush has plans for a $383,000 improvement project. This outlay of money will be used chiefly for street, curb and gutter, storm sewers and hard surfaced roads.

HAYES LAKE STATE PARK

There is tangible proof in Roseau County that dreams are not always ephemeral. The recently deceased Alfred Hayes saw his dream become a reality. He dreamed of creating a wonderful park which would include all that vacationers could desire — swimming, fishing, boating, camping, and nature study areas at a site which is the gateway to the Beltrami Island Forest. This could be done, thought Mr. Hayes by damming up the north fork of the Roseau River to create a lake, and leaving the land in its own beautiful pristine state. Now the Hayes Lake State Park is a reality and serves the people of Roseau County as well as welcoming the tourists.

The park consists of 2992 acres at the head of the Beltrami Forest and is the center of the area in Roseau County between Greenbush, Roseau and Warroad. The forest is a wonderland of virgin timber with trails for the hiker, or in the winter for the snowmobiler. The 1,200 foot dam holds the water back for about 2½ miles and thus creates a lake that will be stocked with fish. There is an excellent swimming beach and picnic grounds. No motor boats will be allowed on the lake.

The funding for the Hayes Lake State Park came through the State Natural Resources Board in 1965, the Legislative Advisory Committee. The Roseau Sportsmen's Club originally set up the groundwork for the park, but more recently the Hayes Lake State Park Association was formed and enlisted the help of Representative Fitzsimmon, Andy Skaar, Everett Battles, and Senator Sinclair to get the park status through the U. S. Forest Service.

Trailer parking space and camp sites have been planned for the park area, and interesting trails wind through the forest. The site is a veritable utopia for scientific studies of Minnesota trees; and wild flowers and almost every species of wild animal native to Minnesota can be found there. One interesting feature planned but at this point not constructed is an underwater observatory.

There will be improvements at the park site for several years to come but the park itself is open for use and is a decided asset to Roseau County. Through the dedicated work of 23 board members from all over the county and 1000 associate members, and especially through the work of "Cap" Nelson and Meridith Haslerud, the Hayes Lake State Park is another attraction in the north country.[17]

There was great concern in the county in 1970, as well as over the nation, as Americans became aware that the pollution of their beautiful land would have to be halted if health and the beauty of the landscape were to be retained. In 1969 the Shoreland Management Act went into effect and it provided for (1) zoning control and (2) sanitation codes and subdivision regulations. This Act will have far-reaching effects on future building, and was intended to protect the waters and beaches. Roseau County responded to the urgency of the appeal for good ecology by appointing a zoning committee, cleaning up the parks the river banks, and issuing a demand for burning permits.

17The Beltrami Island Forest is that interesting land thrown up by the old Lake Agassiz and forming the Campbell beaches. It was named after Giocomo Beltrami, the Italian count who roamed this area, at the time Schoolcraft was credited with finding the source of the Mississippi.

The late Alfred F. Hayes, the man with the dream, was responsible for Hayes Lake State Park.

CULTURE

The musical culture of Roseau County was for the most part vested in the high caliber of the vocal and instrumental groups from the high schools. Each year the young musicians participated in the music contests with creditable showings. Concerts, and musical productions such as *Brigadoon, Fiddler on the Roof* and *Oklahoma* were highly appreciated renditions of the Roseau music department. The Warroad High School had an outstanding marching band in the '50's, when Duane Welte was the director. This band not only performed for local functions, but was invited to many activities around the state for its superior performance.

It was the brainstorm of Mrs. Rudy Rice to put on an annual musical production for the purpose of awarding music scholarships. This was started in 1955 and continued for about six years, first under the directorship of Mrs. Rice and Mrs. Halvorson, and then under Ernie Teie. The production was called "Harvest Harmony" and featured the best in the local music field, from the high school and the college students, and talented adults in town.

Janice Rice Hardy, formerly of Roseau attained the honor of singing with the Minnesota Opera Company of Minneapolis.

The artists from the county area include Frances Karlsson who paints and illustrates books and pamphlets, using mostly a rural theme to depict the typical scenes from the area in which she lives. Maggi Adams, wife of Bill Adams of the *Roseau Times Region*, paints in oils and acrylics with themes chiefly from places and people reminiscent of the years spent in Rome. A true expression of the Chippewa's reverance for nature and especially the animals is shown in the works of the Robert Ka-Ka-Geesick. Eddie Cobenas another Indian artist was formerly from Warroad and now resides in Middlebro.

Earl Chapin, recently deceased, was a novelist and journalist and has done numerous articles about the people of the county. He wrote the books, *Long Wednesdays*, a novel about the newspaper business in the pioneer days, and *Heavy Waters*, an adventure story, and *Angle of Incident* for the Warroad Historical Society.

Mrs. Valborg Tweet (daughter of the renowned novelist Ole Rolvaag) working in collaboration with her daughter Solveig Tweet Zempel has translated a novel in letter form written by her father which is entitled *The Third Life of Per Smevik.*

Another artist of whom Roseau County is proud and who works with bits of yarn, and cloth and much creativity is Hild Naess Hildahl, whose Norwegian doll characters depict the folk lore of her native country. Mrs. Hildahl came to Roseau County in 1940, and ingeniously contrived a way to help her oppressed people during the war. She would make story book dolls, sell them and send the money to fight Nazism for her beloved native country.

A team of archeologists headed by Kent Good excavated the area around the Pauli Church to find numerous artifacts, and concluded the site must have been an Indian assembly line for the production of arrows.

Perhaps she thought what a little "Nisse", a mischievious elf might do to some of the Nazis from their bag of tricks, and so she made the little elves which led her to create the fascinating other little creatures – trolls, shepherd boys, Hulder women, and cunning little witches. Then to make the stories come alive, Mrs. Hildahl put on a one lady show telling the tale and illustrating it with her characters. She was invited to many places to put on her performance. After the war she continued to make the dolls which have become so popular, and she has added another dimension in culture to Roseau County because of her altruistic purpose.

ARCHEOLOGY

Even in this later era archeological finds are still rather common in the Roseau County area. Clarence Green found an adze on his farm 3½ miles south of Warroad in Moranville Township which was chisel shaped. Elden Johnson of the University of Minnesota Department of Archeology said, "The adze is an agricultural stone-working tool. These finds have been common in New York and New England. It is associated with boreal archaic horizon dated about 4000-2000 B. C. This might be the site of an archaic village." Mr. Green found the adze March 30, 1961.

In February a year later Roy Hovorka found a skull of an ancient animal that was believed to have been a bison. Mr. Olafson reported that it was from an ancient extinct species, a fact which can be ascertained by the straighter horn. It is called Bison Antiquus or Bison Occidentalis. Only carbon dating could tell which species, as the Bison Antiquus dates back to 9,500 years and the Bison Occidentialis to 7,900 years.

There can be no doubt that Roseau County is rich in archaeological artifacts. A study made in June 1973 headed by Kent Good of the University of Minnesota, revealed ten sites where artifacts dating back as far as 4,500 years ago (known as the Archaic Period) to 1000 years ago (the Woodland Period) are to be found. Arrowheads, pieces of shard, and copper have been found at these spots. The George Lins farm and the George Jorgenson farm are especially productive of articles witnessing of the past. Projectile points of various datings have been found and taken for study.

Places of historical significance in the county are Bemis Hill (evidence of the Campbell Beach of Lake Agassiz), the Indian Village at Ross, the Indian Village Trading Post and Indian Cemetery at Warroad, the Indian Mounds and battlegrounds at the western edge of the County (formerly Pelan), the Indian Village at Wannaska, Ka-Ka-Geesick Point at Warroad, which was a former Indian housing compound.

Mining in Roseau County again became a possibility in 1972 when the Humble Oil Company requested prospecting rights for $1.00 an acre in 162 N., R. 35 West, 9-15-34. The prospecting was approved by the Department of Natural Resources.

The potpourri news for this era might include such interesting items as:

The U. F. O. (Unidentified Flying Objects) were much in the news and interest to almost all the people in Roseau County during this era. The mysterious skyborn objects took on various forms — white glaring lights, round, sunlike balls, veiled apparitions of the night, fast moving spheres, and green saucer-like shapes. Explanations which ranged from scientific apparatus to the theory of Martians failed to satisfy the curiosity. One headline in the paper read, "Strange Lights Mystify Canadian Neighbors near Woodridge."

October, 1953 was a memorable time for Vernon Pick from Warroad, for it was then that he found a uranium mine in Colorado. According to the report, he was down to his last grub-stake when he chanced upon the uranium on a Colorado plateau. At the time of the assessment the discovery was valued at two million dollars worth of the ore, but later the tally was raised to between 7 and 9 million dollars. Pick who had owned an electrical shop in Minneapolis, had gone prospecting for adventure. When he found the ore he "sat" on the mine and became a wealthy man.

January 8, 1970 was a sad day for the county and environs for the lone pine tree estimated to be 140 years old, which had remained immune to the highway builders' dozers fell to the axe of two vandals. Four or five times interested citizens including George Marvin and Sports Sperling had appealed to the state legislature to spare the tree from roadside clearing. The tree that had lived during Abraham Lincoln's time was hacked down for nothing more than "the heck of it."

Roseau County's only Seeing Eye Dog belonged to Earl Burress, from Salol who lost his sight in 1967. "Bo" was trained at the Leader Dogs for the Blind at Rochester, Michigan, and served his master from July, 1967 until March 1972 when Mr. Burress died. Recently a nephew of Mrs. Burress took "Bo" up town on a leash to test his retentive memory for leading, and found that the dog still directed his companion to the step-up sidewalk and the highway. The name plate of the dog will someday be put in lucite to commemorate his faithful service. Now the dog is a pet in the Burress home.

Observance of Memorial Day 1974.

This is a brief chronicle of how Roseau County was born and has developed from the earliest of man's recollections until the time we call the present. The concept heretofore so prevalent among us that "bigger is better" is dying a death of disenchantment. Roseau County residents like the clean air, the neat villages, and the peaceful countrysides. There is a spirit of unity and loyalty that metropolitan areas may well envy. The Riviere aux Roseau, our Roseau River and its environs has provided a home secure and worthy, and Lake of the Woods has added to its enchantment.

And now in 1976 we all join in to say, "HAPPY BIRTHDAY, AMERICA!" Would that the fervor, the ideals, the honesty of our pilgrim fathers evident in such solid measure in most of our Roseauite pioneers, be rekindled in our hearts. Sincerely we say, "God Bless America."

Warroad receives their Bicentennial flag. From left to right, Lt. Governor Rudy Perpich, Deloris Andol, Tut Marvin, Julius Anderson, Cap Nelson, Warroad Mayor Richard Roberts, and Senator Richard Fitzsimmons.

Chapter 9

BEGINNINGS

I love those dear hearts and gentle people
Who live and love in my home town.
Lyrics — Bobby Hilliard
Music — Sammy Fain
(Words first found on a scrap of paper in Stephen Foster's pocket)

Chapter 9

BEGINNINGS

Beginnings of Badger

Badger Creek, a tributary of the Roseau River, flows northwestward; this stream was the inspiration for the name given to the little town incorporated as the village of Badger June 1, 1896. The original townsite is built on Reed's homestead near the river and subsequent additions were made from Reilly's, Coughlins's, and Anderson's land, a piece of land called Oakdale. Two of the first settlers were James Reilly and Jake Lynch who came to the country to raise cattle. Both became stage coach drivers.

The first officers of the town were George Stokes, mayor; J. W. Novotny, and A. A. Burkee, trustees, Peter Sjoberg, treasurer; H. W. Jones, clerk, and M. W. Simons, justice of the peace.

An account in the *Roseau Times* on January 7, 1898 told about the beginnings of Badger including the young businesses that were springing up. The two rival ends of town, it seemed, vied to outdo each other and resulted in a sudden boom of the town. T. H. Durgin had the first general store which he operated for two years and then liquidated it. Captain Reed, the original owner of the townsite, put in a feed and livery barn in 1897, but had a competitor in the other part of town when George Stokes put up a two story building, the downstairs a livery stable and the upstairs a village hall. Sjoberg brothers, Peter and Israel, put in a general store in 1896, and planned to add a cheese factory. A. E. Lofgren was the next to build a general merchandise store. The Badger Hotel was built by Erick Modine in 1896, and Gus Anderson put in a harness and leather business the next year.

Two men, Johnson and Paulson established a blacksmith shop in 1896, and M. W. Simons bought out A. Homme's drug business the same year, and T. H. Durgin went into the blacksmith business, while Josh Kittchel went into the shingle and lumber business.

The first school house was built in 1897 at a cost of $1,400 including the furniture. G. J. Brenden had taught school before that time in Anna Houkom's log house with home made benches and desks, and a canvas blackboard. Mr. Brenden had come from Sharon, North Dakota, filed a homestead claim and made Roseau County his home. In his reminiscences he tells about going to the Red River Valley in the fall, sleeping in an empty shack and allowing a stranger to stay with him, and discovering the next morning that he was infested with lice! At one point in crossing a river the water was so deep that only the ears of the mare pulling the wagon were visible, but she pulled the wagon through the swift current nevertheless. At Grand Forks he had to load the horse and cart in a cattle car to get across the river. He went through a French settlement and found to his chagrin that when he said he was from Roseau County they wanted no part of his lodging. However, some Scotch people took him in,

Going to town in Badger. The Peter Sjoberg home is across the bridge.

fed him and charged him nothing. However, at another home the people were dubious about him until they found out he was Norwegian, and then he was treated royally. In order to teach another term Mr. Brenden was required to take an examination in Roseau, and he related that a mile from town he had to walk because of all the water. "Beer barrels were floated into town from that distance," he said. "People were fishing at the site which was later the First National Banks" (where Mason & Hayes' accounting firm is now located.)

The first pupils of Mr. Brenden were: Anna Anderson, Clara Carlson, Anna Gillebo, Gilbert Ingolfsland, Mary Ann Johnson, Lily Johnson, Tony Ness, Ed. Nelson, Magda Randklev, Otto Gillebo, Ida Anderson, Bena Olson, Aldrick Anderson, Axel Anderson, Olga Carlson, Ida Dahl, Albert Gillebo, Clara Gillebo, Tillie Gillebo, Fred Ingolfsland, John Ingolfsland, Carl Johnson, Mary Ness, Nickolei Nelson, Emil Nelson, Clarence Nelson, Arvid Petterson, Paula Petterson, Liza Randklev, Alfred Ness, Grethe Hegstad and Almer Petterson.

James Novotony had the first paper in Badger called *The Herald*, and in 1900, G. H. Brenden bought his paper and one started by N. E. Wold called the *Badger Rustler* and merged the two into *The Badger Herald-Rustler*. It was in 1902 that there was dissension among the people because of the county seat. Badger wanted the county seat in their town, and of course Roseau wanted to keep it. Badger business men argued that Badger was a better location, that Badger would doubtless outgrow Roseau, and that it was a thriving community that meant to get ahead. The feud grew to full proportions when Badger came in with 1000 signatures on a petition to have the county seat moved. Attorneys Rowe and Miller submitted briefs in the October term of court, at which time it appeared that there were 740 valid names on the petition. Since this was less than 60% of the voters it was declared illegal. Also there was conflict over the fact that the notice had not appeared in all the county newspapers. Furthermore, R. H. Medicraft contended that there were 447 more names which would not be legally acceptable. The fury of the battle was presented in the newspapers. The Roseau editor said if Badger wanted the county seat they better produce a decent court house at a cost of at least $20,000. Badger responded that Roseau could hardly call its courthouse (the first one) acceptable, and furthermore Roseau was $40,000 in debt. The Roseau editor said that there was at least one man on the council in Badger who was not in favor of moving the county seat, so they had at least one wise man in town. The controversy became more personal when R. J. Bell declared that the "Sjoberg Ring" was working in favor of Badger while Israel Sjoberg was the mayor of Roseau. Furthermore, Mr. Bell was dismayed because he felt he had lost the friendship of O. B. Ekman since Ekman suspected that the editor favored Badger himself, for he had been silent on the subject for some time; however, the fiery editor soon retorted that he wanted it made perfectly clear that he would always favor his own home town.

Progress was noted even though the courthouse was not moved to Badger. The State

The day of the Farmer's Institute in Badger in 1907.

Bank of Badger was started in 1902 by H. Thorson, Peter Sjoberg, and T. D. Thorson, and a second bank called the Scandinavian American Bank was started shortly thereafter. A bridge was built across Badger Creek in 1901.

Bottem brothers put in a store they called "The Cheap Cash Store." The new Sjoberg flour mill built in 1897 was destroyed by fire on Nov. 24, 1898. The town got a pop factory in 1902, built by Gust Oveson. A planing mill and hardware was started by Charles Edelstein, and second hotel called Hotel Arden was erected. A farmers creamery and elevator was started in 1902 and all signs pointed to great potential for the young town.

The extension of the railroad in 1908 was a great boost for the town, for the agricultural development was underway with the better drainage.

One humorous incident is related in regard to Secretary of State Albert Berg in a pamphlet written by Frank M. Eddy. The story, relating a campaign appearance in Stokes hall, reflects the enthusiasm of the political meetings of that time. He tells how some of the people in the western part of the county would make quite a show of getting up and walking out during his speeches. Mr. Berg squelched this trick by stopping in the middle of his speech, taking a glass of water, and announcing that for those of the opposition it was now time to walk out. But one night the pranksters really rigged up what they thought would be the climax to their machinations. They were aware that the audience would demand a song from Albert Berg and that in one Swedish song he emphasized the lyrics by stamping hard with his feet. So the naughty boys got into the hall in the afternoon, sawed through the supports of the platform to a quarter of an inch. That evening

Home made automobile in 1910. The store belonged to Peter Sjoberg.

they cried out in chorus for the corpulent Albert Berg to sing the favorite song. He did so, and his more than 300 pounds collapsed the platform like a paper box stepped on by an elephant. Frank Eddy describes it this way:

> . . . Platformers, including the organist were catapulted into the audience. The organ fell on the village school teacher, pinning her to the floor where she lay screaming that she had been killed. The organist landed on her head in the wood box, her legs waving in the air like signals of distress. Albert Berg was wedged under a seat and had to be pulled out before he could get on his feet. I was projected into the lap of a large, fat Norwegian woman who gazed on me with a look that seemed to say, "You are very familiar for a man who has not even been introduced. . . .
>
> Near panic was averted by Captain Stokes who had charge of the meeting when he leaped on a chair and shouted, "Everything is all right; this is a part of the entertainment. Nobody is hurt."
>
> When order was restored and the meeting was resumed and after Albert had performed his singing stunt, I began to address the audience saying, "Captain, I am astonished that you exercise so little vigilance that you permitted someone to bring in a Populist platform into this Republican meeting."
>
> The crowd roared and the incident rebounded to our benefit instead of our discomfiture.

Beginning of Fox

"Fox shall be the name of the new village," said T. A. Nomeland, who felt that the fox should have some credit for living there first. The beginnings of a village which never matured was platted in 1909 by Nels K. White.

In spite of the hopes and dreams of the people that the village would flourish, Fox never did become large enough to incorporate. However, it did at one time have a number of businesses. John Erickson had a general store, Clarence Oie operated a grocery store, and a second grocery store was started by Olaf Fjeld. Mr. Nomeland managed the elevator built by Hanson-Barzen and a livery barn was owned and operated by Andrew Solom. The post office was in the Erickson store with Mrs. Erickson as postmistress.

There was social life in Fox too, for the people from the surrounding area came together for bowery dances. There were also Fourth of July celebrations at the site of Fox.

Beginnings of Greenbush

"May it bloom like a green bay tree." These were the words that were used by a Roseau editor when the town of Greenbush was incorporated on October 13, 1904. The first special meeting of the town board was held January 23, 1905. The first officers for the new town were:

A P. Kukowski, President
Torjus Lundeval, Recorder
K. K. Grivi, Trustee
John Englehart, Trustee
T. J. Lanegraff, Trustee
A. A. Burkee, Trustee
Dr. F. Young, Justice of Peace
Dr. Hubbard, Health Officer

The coming of the railroad in 1904 caused a change in the location of the town from a spot two miles east of where the town is now located. The first site was known as "Old Greenbush." One of the favorite stories told by the pioneers in later years was about the moving store. Olaf Hildahl had a store in old Greenbush in 1898, but when he learned of the new location he simply began a moving operation, pulling the entire building by block and tackle to the new site, but business went on as usual. Since only a little ground was covered each day, a customer got the unique experience of trading in the "moving store." One farmer said that he would have to buy his necessities and had hardly any time to pass the time of day, for if he did his team would be left behind and he had to "tote" his purchases back. The first post office was in this store.

Greenbush is in the township of Hereim,

The first train leaving Greenbush in 1904.

Mode of transportation in 1904 in Greenbush.

named for Ole Hereim. He came to Roseau County with his four sons, John, Erik, Carl and Ole Jr. and filed on a quarter section of land. His claim is the present town of Greenbush. Ole Jr. became the first town clerk. In the year of 1899 Carl Heltne came from Dodge County to visit the Hereims; he took a homestead near his friends and has lived there since. Mr. Heltne became the first assessor and he had to walk to each homestead for which he was paid a total of $14.00.

In 1904 the Farmers Co-operative Creamery was organized and built on the site where Bob Wallin Machine Co. is now located. Andrew Benson from Dodge County was the first butter maker, and Christian Dahl, Carl Heltne, Ole Hereim Jr., and Torjus Lundevall were members of the first creamery board.

The railroad to Greenbush was a heralded event, but since it was established in 1904 compared to 1908 for Roseau, Badger, and Warroad, there was not as much railroad fever in this section of the county. It is perhaps understandable that the Roseau editor showed a tinge of jealousy when he wrote on December 9, 1904:

> Greenbush is growing. Business is investing and will reap good results. Greenbush has a railroad and naturally farmers will do their trading where they can ship their grain. These farmers will come from Roseau and Badger. Badger being closer will feel the loss of business more than Roseau and the jealousy that Badger feels for Roseau will naturally turn to Greenbush. It is not at all likely that anyone in either village will consider the interest of the towns identical but will tend to draw trade from one end and this will not help the other.

The year after the incorporation the problems of the community were taken in stride by the village fathers. It was necessary to have water as one of the first considerations, so a pump house and well were constructed in 1905 with Ole Bottem engaged at $8.00 a month to take care of it. 800 feet of hose were purchased for fire protection. However, in 1907 the engine house was destroyed by fire and in 1910 bids were taken for water mains and hydrants. $355 was set aside by the village for this purpose. There was a great deal of agitation because T. Lundevall sprinkled his lawn and this was considered a gross misuse of the precious water. A marshall was hired then at $40 a month to superintend the water works. M. J. Hegland was the city attorney with a salary of $10.00.

The problem of a road through the village was solved by the poll tax of $3.00 per family. The road south of the track was the first to get attention. The village agreed to add $255 to the road building program. A bridge was built across the river in 1905 for $944.

Sidewalks through the town were decided upon in 1911 on both sides of Hill street. A village hall costing $1750 was built the next year. The village bonded itself for $4000 in 1920 to get electric lights.

Telephones were a consideration almost from the start for in 1905 R. Mamable got a contract to start on the erection of poles. In 1909 the Tri-State Telephone and Telegraph was engaged to set up the line with the Farmers Telephone Company contracted to setting up the poles. The "central" was Inga Hanson and the office was at the Dock hotel.

Recreation was not neglected either. The village fathers donated $80 for a baseball team in 1905, and in 1910 the village had a bowling alley.

Greenbush had its share of tragedies also. In June of 1905 a Mr. McGrath was shot to death in a box car on the G. N. tracks. The

Street scene in Greenbush in 1905.

Greenbush in 1914.

story told the press was that the murdered man kept a house of ill fame. Sheriff Erickson and R. H. Medicraft went to see that justice was done at Greenbush. On January 13, 1905 there was an appeal to the owners to clean up the "blind pigs," (unlicensed liquor vendors). A fire destroyed the Dalby store in 1906 with a reported loss of $3000, and two years later five business places, those of Kukowski, Larson, T. Thompson, Stanish, and the State Bank were all burned down at one time.

The *Greenbush Journal* was started by H. Sanders who said, "The enterprise is not an emotional spasm; for some time we have been trying to bring the western part of Roseau County before the eyes of the public." R. J. Bell included this comment in his paper the next week, "Looks like the purpose is to corral final proofs and cutting off revenue of the Badger Herald Rustler which this far have had a good thing." The Journal was sold in 1908 to E. R. Umpelby. Today it is operated by the Evans.

There were two banks in Greenbush, the Farmers Merchants Bank started in 1913 and the People's Bank which closed its doors in 1927.

The Bethel church was the first congregation; it was organized by Pastor N. J. Nyhus in 1904 with a group of eight members.

A beautiful evergreen thicket was the location of the first school where the Borgen home was later located. The next school was located at the present site of the Klefstad Clinic and was later sold for a residence. District 66 grew and it became necessary to add another building to the school complex. The second building was sold to Dr. Button for a hospital. Leona Thompson, the first teacher rode her pony to the homes of all her pupils so that she could become better acquainted with the families and so understand the problems of her students.

The educational development in Greenbush took strides ahead, for in 1920 a new school was erected, and there were four elementary and five high school teachers in charge at that time. This fine school with a modern gymnasium, library and science department was destroyed by fire in 1939 at a loss estimated at $130,000. School was then held the balance of the year in make-shift class rooms around the town.

After a struggle to get federal grants, the Works Progress Administration was enlisted and Greenbush erected another school building in 1941. This is the present east wing of the existing school. It was one of the last of the W. P. A. projects in the County. On December 11, 1950 a bond election was held because of the pressing need for additional classroom space. A bond issue of $250,000 gave the town an addition that included a new gymnasium and four elementary classrooms. In 1954 the Strathcona School District consolidated with Greenbush. Five wooden buildings were then in constant use, and in 1964 the district again bonded for $370,000. This provided seven elementary rooms, a multipurpose room, industrial arts facilities, new rooms for classes in agriculture, new rooms for home economics and a new locker room.

The earliest musical group in Greenbush was an orchestra organized in the early 1900's. The members were Wentland and Von Rohr, mandolins; Gjovick and Torgerson, violins; and E. H. Wold, flute.

A special delight to adults and children alike when they come to the Roseau County Museum is to see the working farm in miniature created by the Stanislawski brothers. The entire farm scene with house, barn, animals, a windmill, a child swinging, a man cutting wood, are among the mechanized figures that swing into full action with the press of a button. There are other evidences of the artistry of the brothers with their carvings of horses being especially beautiful.

Greenbush has an historian too. Herbert Reese has written an intriguing story of his life in road construction entitled *Fifty Years Down the Road.* The construction of roads out of trails is graphically depicted by a man who has lived it.

In 1920 an Indian grave was found on the Czyrson farm. It was excavated to find a skeleton in a sitting position with his flintlock gun beside him, two Indian pipes, and a birch bark case where the war paint was kept. The skeleton was of a man 7 feet tall.

Greenbush continues as a prosperous farm community in the western part of the county with agriculture and sheep raising its chief endeavors.

Early Days around Lake of the Woods

A youthful adventurer, Jacques de Noyons, about 1688, was the first white man to see Lake of the Woods. A Canadian from a small town called Three Rivers on the St. Lawrence River (the same village from which La Verendrye started out), he went up the Kaministikwia River and through a maze of rivers, streams and portages and came at last

Lake of the Woods as seen from Warroad before The Norman Dam at Kenora raised the lake level.

Oak Island fishery.

to Rainy Lake and then to the beautiful big lake. He named the lake "Lac Aux Isles", meaning Lake of the Islands. There are 950,000 acres in this lake and something more than 10,000 islands.

What de Noyons saw north of the 49th parallel was the thickly forested islands of pine and spruce. He stepped on moss that was almost ankle deep and saw gray and green lichens growing on the rocks. Saxifrage flowers, erigeron and fleabane grow on the rocks, as well as a cactus called the prickly pear.

The rocks under de Noyons' feet were formed eons ago and called pre-Cambrian because they existed before the Cambrian seas era. This is borne out by the fact that they contain no fossils, whereas the rocks of the Cambrian sea have numerous fossils. This Lake of the Woods rock is called igneous meaning it has been molten at one time; it forms the Laurentian Shield which is the core of the North American continent around which other rocks have been formed.[18]

Following the adventures of the young de Noyons came the fascinating exploits of La Verendrye and his search for the western sea that led to the lucrative fur trade.

One of the first settlers who came to stay and make the beautiful Lake of the Woods his home was Barney Arneson, Sr. who came in the winter of 1894 from Stephen, Minnesota. At first Mr. Arneson took lumber out of the Hay Creek area which was used to build a hotel in the little community of Roseau, then called Jadis.

For a time Mr. Arneson went up Four Mile Bay, but returned again to Hay Creek Ridge. Here Sam and Harry Curry had a stopping place. One interesting digression to the story of Barney Arneson, Sr. concerns Harry Curry who related that one night when he was returning to his hostel, he waded across Willow Creek, and was attacked by numerous muskrats who bit him severely. He reasoned that he must have invaded a muskrat house and the mother was attempting to protect the young. Curry was in serious condition but eventually recovered from the bites. Curry's Point on Lake of the Woods was later renamed Zippel Bay. At one time there was great excitement there for iron ore was reported to have been found near the surface.

The Arnesons sustained much tragedy in their lives having lost two children in a fire, and two boys in a drowning accident as they attempted to cross Lake of the Woods in a birch bark canoe. At that time one could travel by foot and small portage from Warroad to Rainy River or to Buffalo Point from Warroad on a sand beach. The sand hills stretched from the mouth of the Rainy River to Burton Island with hills that were 20-30 feet high. Perhaps this was why the boys dared to attempt the crossing.

The Indians gave the lake the name "Lake of the Sand Hills." There was another island at the mouth of Willow Creek, known as Willow Creek Island, covered with oak and ash, and other sand hills stretched out near Sandy Beach. Between Springsteel Island and Warroad was an island called "Sandy" or "Sand Island" which had a fishery on it. Today there is no trace that it ever existed, for since the Norman Dam raised the water level, the island disappeared.

In 1882 Wm. F. Zippel came to Warroad from Kenora and founded his homestead on

18Minnesota Heritage

Harbor scene at Warroad.

what is known now as Zippel Bay. *The Roseau Region* and *Roseau County Times* made frequent mention of his visits to the county seat.

Any long time resident of Warroad has many stories to tell about the early fabulous fishing on Lake of the Woods. John Wahlberg, a former merchant of Warroad tells how the sturgeon were hauled out of the lake as a "nuisance fish" and stacked up like cord wood on the shore to rot or to be burned. The precious caviar, long honored as food for the wealthy, was a flourishing export business in the early days, but the meat of the fish was generally wasted. Washtubs full of delicious wall-eye pike could be caught in less than a half day of fishing. Though the heyday of the abundant fishing has passed, Lake of the Woods is known today as the finest wall-eye fishing lake in the nation, and one which to date has practically no pollution and has mercury-free fish. Tourists come from far and wide to enjoy the beautiful scenery while they are still able to indulge themselves in a type of fishing that is fast slipping away from the American scene.

How great would be the excitement if the angler today could hook into a fish like that caught near Oak Island in 1916 – a sturgeon weighing 240 lbs. The Sanduskie Fishery reported that in one lift of their nets they got 3 ton of fish, mostly sturgeon which had a net value of $7000 and yielded 40 kegs each weighing 160 lbs. of caviar with a value of $5,120. Fish in those days could be bought for 3½c a pound.

Long Point which today is a resort area was first settled by Charles Aasmus who came to this country in 1893. Max Williams came six years later and established his home there too. Mickinock often walked to Long Point and traded furs for fish.

Gull Rock, which is visible from Warroad, and which is near Rocky Point has an interesting legend of Indian Origin:

Once the Cree, Assiniboine, and Chippewa fought among themselves until their bravest were dead and defenseless against the Dakotas. The Great Spirit came and spoke to his children. One summer day a great heat gripped the land. It became hotter as the day wore on. The mothers took the children into the lake to cool and animals did likewise. Suddenly there was a blinding flash and a voice that seemed to fill every corner of the earth:

"I am the Great Spirit. I have come to tell you to be friendly with one another. The land on which you dwell is your own. Far to the west and south is a big nation whose eyes are turned in this direction and unless you who live on this lake live as brothers the enemies from the plains will fall upon you and drive you hence. Do not quarrel. The same sun pours its beneficial light over all and the watchful eyes of the Great Spirit are never turned away."

The last syllables of the great voice rolled away like the reverberations of distant thunder and a silence fell. The heat lifted and cool breezes blew. The prostrated Indians arose and some saw the Great Spirit ascend from the "Rock of the Gods." This island formerly covered with vegetation became barren and natives saw only naked rock. Obeying the command of the Great Spirit they were able to repel the Dakotas.

There is ever a romance about Lake of the Woods that cannot be easily described. Imagine it is the year 1903 . . . Lake street, leading from the village of Warroad to the lake, is a dirt road bordered by a heavy growth of trees and a view of the majestic lake is not possible until one comes to the Selvog Fishery. A big crowd has gathered on the shore peering out across Big Traverse when someone shouts, "There she comes!" It is the huge boat called the *Clipper*, coming from Kenora. As the light comes closer the men swing into action with lanterns, waving them to and fro. Slowly, and carefully the ship is guided into the mouth of the river. The air is full of anticipation as the *Clipper* is docked. Then the passengers spill out and the greetings are exchanged. The horse and buggy, or horse and wagon await while the ship's cargo is unloaded. Then it is on to the Lakewood Hotel or Monroe's Saloon. *The Clipper* has made another safe journey and all are joyful!

Beginnings of Malung

Malung, Sweden, Malung, Minnesota — two towns with more in common than the identical names. A. M. Pearson, first postmaster decided that the identity of the folks in the area could best be retained by naming the town in the "new country" after the one they knew in the "old country." The little village was comprised mostly of Swedes, but as one report had it, they did allow a few Norwegians, and the record states, one Irishman by the name of Garighan, who though he did not share the common ancestry of the settlers, did share their problems and did all he could to make the new area more comfortable and prosperous. He never learned the Swedish language well, but he knew where the good land sites were and how to trap for furs, and he came to know the Swedes as good neighbors. Garighan called himself a man of the wilderness which indeed he was in Malung in the late 1800's.

Malung was incorporated January 17, 1894 while still a part of Kittson County. The first officers were Rasmus Flaa, chairman; G. J. Johnson and Pete Roseen, supervisors; L. O. Peterson, clerk; Lars L. Hedin, treasurer; Henry Severson, assessor; H. M. Peterson, justice; and Rasmus Flaa also acted as constable.

The newspaper was started by A. M. Pearson who called it the *Roseau County Press.* Somehow he and some of his friends believed that Malung was located above rich oil deposits and he devised an "oil witch" (fashioned after the manner of the forked willow water witch sticks) that he hoped would give him the secrets of the earth. He managed to find a few speculators, but the oil never did gush in.

Malung Band in 1911. Back row, Frank Swanson, Bendix Skrutvold; Nels Nyland, Victor Roseen, Andrew Odegaard, and Jim Erickson. Front row, Oscar Larson, Emil Roseen, Axel Nelson.

The Good Templar's Lodge (where the school bus garage is now located) was the center of activity for the young people. It was started to combat the evils of liquor, but we are a bit wary of its effects, for the paper had an article that read: "We hear there is liquor in Malung and we hope it is not true."

Settlers arrived in Malung before the 1900's as did the Peter Hetteens who having heard reports of the good hayland came to raise cattle. At first they lived with Lars Hedins until they could clear land and build their home. The Hetteen home was used as a school house during which time the family moved upstairs. The first teacher was Anna Johnson who boarded with the Hetteens but had her bed in the corner of the schoolroom. This was during the years 1893-1894. The pupils were Lydia Hetteen, Emma Hetteen, Carolina Hetteen, John Johnson, Nels Johnson, Anna Hanson, Lena Hanson, Mary Roseen, Erick Roseen, Carolina Roseen, Christine Johnson, Andrew Johnson, Anna Erickson, Emanuel Erickson, Thure Johnson, Erick Olson, Thilda Peterson, Alfred Peterson, Anna Peterson, Hilma Peterson, Ida Peterson, Louis Blomquist, Lena Blomquist, Anna Grindahl, Henry Grindahl, Ole Grindahl, August Hedin, John Hedin, Esther Sirness, Andrew Eklund, Alma Sandstrom, Hilda Bergman, Willie Bergman, and Ingeborg Bruswen and Salve Sirness. The first school board was K. A. Sirness, clerk; P. E. Roseen, treasurer, and Henry

Transportation at Malung in 1910. The driver is Ted Johnson with Victor Roseen in the cart. Bendix Skrutvold sits on the ox.

The Good Templar Lodge and the gathering on June 24, 1909 for the picnic.

Severson, director. The teacher received $30.00 a month.

The school building and Hetteen home was a building 16x16, furnished with home made benches, desks, and a long bench for recitations. The blackboard was made from lumber boards painted black, and the room was heated by a box stove with wood as the fuel. Anyone who didn't know his ABC's had to stand in the corner. The cost of operating the school totaled $225.10, of which $195 was used for teacher's wages, $21.55 for room rent, and $8.05 for all other purposes.

The town had railroad fever, as did all the communities in the county before 1908, and the hopes were raised now and then by reports that the Great Northern would come through their area. In 1908 when the G. N. was extended, such expectancies died for all time and the little community dwindled in size. It was fortunate that the bridge was erected in 1901, for the Tin Lizzies as the Ford cars were nicknamed were appearing on the scene just a few years later. Someone from Malung humorously suggested that the ruts in the road could be filled with dead mosquitoes.

Even though the town did not develop due to the route of the G. N. the land is unequalled for prosperous farming. The community has a lovely new school built in 1967 and the settlement looks back with pride at the struggles that now afford them their good farms and modern living.

Interesting Northwest Angle

The "chimney" at the top of Minnesota is the Northwest Angle. We were able at one time to call it "the top of the nation," until Alaska joined our states. Although not in Roseau County the area is of interest and historical importance to our county.

Fort St. Charles is located at Northwest Angle Inlet, and in its glory days of fur trade there was much activity at this fort, for it was a supply depot for smaller forts along the route to Montreal. After 1763 when New France became English territory, the activity declined.

The most northern U.S. post office located at Northwest Angle is named Penasse. Until 1971 the mail had to come by seaplane or boat, or in the winter by snowmobile. Now a road has been extended to the angle which will change the nature of the tourist business for Lake of the Woods from this time on.

Originally this large body of water was called Lake of the Sand Hills, but official sanction of the name Lake of the Woods was given at the Treaty of Paris in 1783, which also stated regarding the boundaries:

> Thence through Lake Superior northward to the Isles Royal and Phelipeau to Long Lake; thence through the middle of said Long Lake and the Water Communication between it and the Lake of the Woods; thence through said Long Lake to the most Northwestern Point thereof and from thence on a due West course to the River Mississippi until it shall intersect the Northernmost Point of the thirty first Degree of North Latitude.

This demarcation was an impossibility as the source of the Mississippi River was far to the south of the suggested line. The Treaty of Ghent after the War of 1812 laid the boundaries: 49 Degree No. Latitude, a line dropped due south from the N. W. point to the 49th parallel thence along that line to the Rocky Mountains.

The Webster-Asburton Treaty of 1842 confirmed the Northwest Angle as the most north west point of Lake of the Woods. In 1931 the International Boundary Commission established the northwesternmost point in the Lake of the Woods at a latitude of 49°, 23′, 04″ north longitude 95°, 09′, 11″ west. It is marked by a monument encased in an iron base set in concrete, surrounded by reenforcing logs, placed thirty miles north of the 49th parallel.

The boundary was difficult to mark, not only because of its problematical positions, but also because the surveyors, Cameron for the British, and Campbell for the Americans worked under difficulties of the cold of winter and the mosquitoes of summer and naturally tensions resulted. Cameron consistently tried a delaying action hoping that somehow the Northwest Angle could be ceded to England. But since this never occurred, the "look-out tower" perched in the wilderness seems to watch over the entire nation.

There is an intense feeling of loyalty to this land with its mixture of the old and new. Some of the families, the Petersons, Rissers, Carlsons, and Colsons are watching with wary eye the potentials in the tourist business created by the new road. But one thing is certain, the same hospitality will remain at the Angle no matter how large the influx of tourists may become.

Up the Inlet, on Harrison Creek, is the site of an old fort and the start of the famous Dawson trail over which the carts traveled in the great fur business. It has been said that the road was used as recently as seventy years ago. This road, finally ending up at Winnipeg, was the gateway to the north and west. An old mine, now extinct, was the scene of much activity in the past as feldspar, a material formerly used in the manufacture of porcelain, was taken from it. There is mica there too which makes the site glisten like diamonds.

The Minnesota Historical Society recognizing the historical aspect of Northwest Angle decreed at its Executive Council in October, 1940:

> WHEREAS, Fort St. Charles in the Northwest Angle of Minnesota was a point of great importance in the history of Minnesota, and the Northwest as early as 1723, and continued to be a point of importance for many years.
>
> THEREFORE, be it resolved that the Executive Council of the Minnesota Historical Society heartily endorses the proposal that the state acquire title to the land upon which the fort was situated and earnestly recommends that the historical importance of this site be commemorated and perpetuated through the establishment thereon of a state park.

Beginnings of Pelan

Pelan is not even a ghost town today. There is open prairie where once shanties of the early homesteaders dotted the landscape. There are only the legends and scanty early accounts to commemorate Pelan. And Pelan was not in Roseau County. However, the history of Pelan is so intriguing and so entwined into the history of the area that an account of that romantic place must be included into the history of Roseau County.

The Campbell Beach, commonly called the Sand Ridge, forms much of the northern part of Highway 11, and it runs through what was the Pelan Battleground. When the Indians were vying for control – the Sioux who occupied all of northern Minnesota, the Chippewa who were routing them out, and the cagey Crees who came from the north – there were three distinct mounds in the Pelan district that gave the area the name of Mound Ridge. The mounds have never been exca-

Here the Medora (Kitty) has to have two teams to make the run. They are loading in front of the Pioneer Drug Store. Those identified on the picture are Peter Dahlquist, A. Waag, Bendix Holdahl, J. U. Skoglund, O. B. Ekman, A. O. Homme, and Mike Holm.

vated, but historians have conjectured that they could have been burial mounds. Another theory which is generally not well accepted is that they might have been an entrenchment for warfare between the tribes. Agriculture and erosion have reduced the mounds to almost level ground so today it would be hard to locate them. The last battle which took place 200 years ago, before the birth of our nation, was believed to have occurred at this place and has given the name of Pelan Battleground Park to the location. It was here, according to the oral account, that Ay-Ash-A-Wash (Oshwash), the father of Na-May-Puck, Ka-Ka-Geesick and Little Thunder, was partially scalped and ran into camp holding his bleeding head. So there are now only memories of an occurrence presumably happening around 1770, on the fourth beach of the vast Lake Agassiz. Of that lake only Lake of the Woods, the Red Lakes and the Red River of the North are the visual vestiges of history.

At one time there were three general stores, a state bank, a roller flour mill, a creamery, a land office, three saloons, a boarding house which did a flourishing business there. Ralph Johnson writing for the *Karlstad Advocate* said, "Pelan was the subduing and the settlement of the last frontier in Minnesota in an era where small villages flourished only to die completely with the failure of the railroad to touch the community."

Charles Pelan was an Englishman who started a cattle ranch at Pelan and it is from him the village took its name. Walter Long, Oscar Roos, Gust Charley, and John Nelson came at the same time and were the first white people of the region. The first permanent settler was Hans T. Olson who in 1884 invested in cattle and began blacksmithing in the little community. After Billy Clay, the postmaster, absconded with the mail sack, Olson became the postmaster. In order to expedite the freighting business, he was asked to move to the Two River Crossing, which was the first name given to Pelan. He built a shanty at Pelan and kept the scanty once-a-week mail in a cigar box. Later he housed the post office in the home he built.

The community was incorporated in 1903 and was referred to by one pioneer as "quite a metropolis." Lofgren's store dealt in 300,000 feet of lumber during one year and took care of the dispensing of one-half ton of tobacco. In his store in 1902 he sold merchandise for the following prices:

10 pounds of coffee for $1.00
18 pounds of sugar for $1.00
1 doz. eggs for 7c
1 lb. of butter for 5c

Wheat was 37c a bushel, oats 10c a bushel and barley was 11c a bushel. Lots sold in those days for from $50 to $75. The newspaper business was prosperous too, due to the fact that the settlers had to pay $5.00 for final proof notices on homestead land. Patent medicine ads were numerous and paid well for the times. Gilbert Brenden was a newspaper man in Pelan at one time, and M. J. Hegland and Babcok were also in the newspaper business. Ads like "Your chance ladies to get a good man with a good income, and who can give you a good home. Write Box 75" never had to be run more than three times for guaranteed results.

Pelan became quite a gambling center after restrictions were set at Hallock. It was a typical frontier town with the Blind Piggers (unlicensed venders of liquor) enjoying a heyday. The more puritanical of the populace formed a Templar Lodge to try to control the situation. A hand to hand fracas between the Piggers (as the newspaper accounts termed them) and the Templars was related at length in the newspaper which described the Piggers being men with snouts and wallowing and grunting. The stalwart Templars were declared the winners.

The little nest of houses around the more regal Half-way House formed the nucleus of the town. The imposing Half-way

The Halfway house at Pelan. Perhaps this is the welcoming committee of owners and friends. The State Bank of Pelan is to the right.

House, a large white frame house, was a haven of rest for weary travelers enroute to Stephen or Roseau. Here lodging and home cooked meals, complete with home baked bread, cakes and pies, endorsed the welcome of the innkeeper and his family. The twelve passenger stage was indeed plush, having been purchased from the Marquis de Mores, of Medora, North Dakota where it was originally used on the Deadwood line. Mr. George Roberts, father of Burt Roberts of Warroad, was the last to use this coach and told about how it was necessary to have heads of horses or broncos to pull the stage, and when the road-trail was muddy, an extra team was added. The horses were changed every 16 miles, so stables with 100 horses were kept to keep the schedule.

What a dramatic scene emerged from the cloud of dust when the welcome committee cried the "Stage coach is coming!" Some of the broncos were so unmanageable that they had to be firmly tied with the halter rope, and released only after the passengers were firmly seated. Each trip must have been thrilling and terrifying, yet no accidents are recorded. It was not only difficult to get the passengers aboard, but equally difficult to stop the wild beasts. The driver would aim the horses at a "flyer" which was a pole set for that purpose. If unsuccessful, the driver drove the team in circles while the mail bags were thrown off. How the passengers made it to the ground was never explained. With such strenuous running the broncos did not last long, and they were soon shot, and hauled into the woods to be fed to the wolves, whose howls kept many an occupant of the Half-way House awake at night. It seemed more feasible after the route was well established to have horses that were broken.

The route from Stephen to Roseau was 75 miles long. The stage left Stephen at noon and stopped off at the Half-way House for the night, and then continued on to Roseau. The fare was $12 which included food and lodging. The Half-way House, always famous for cleanliness and good food was built by John Erickson who operated it for some time. Other owners were Charles Oaks, Tom McKibbon, Andrew Olson and George Roberts.

The coming of the stage was like a steamer coming around the bend, and as one lady recalls from her childhood days at Pelan, "We were always fascinated by the passengers — some so suave, so sophisticated. But we always wondered whether there would be any 'crazy' people aboard, for the rigors of the stark prairie took its toll of the less stable, and it was the duty of the sheriff to accompany these folks to Warren."

Unlike the old stage coach days of motion pictures, the Stephen-Roseau run did not have any hold-ups, any Indian raids or meet with any posses. Even though, as George Roberts recalled, there were plenty of "toughs" and the banks at Stephen and Roseau would send up to $3000 to other destinations, the stage got safely through.

The stage had a good reputation. In fact when blizzards held up the Great Northern trains later on, people recalled that the stage had gone through without any cancellations. In the winter time it was not too comfortable on the Kitty, so an enclosed caboose stage was used for a few months in the coldest weather. It must have been cozy in this stage which had its own wood burning stove in the cab.

After the horse-drawn stage several other kinds of vehicles were used. There was an open buck board drawn by horses, and later

A summer stage coach. The only persons identified are Bordrick (standing) and Mrs. Klema (lady in the rear).

In the coldest winter months a covered caboose with a wood burning stove inside kept the passengers comfortable. Jim Reiley is the driver.

a 16 passenger Studebaker operated by Mr. Roberts which was used only for a short time. However, it was the Medora, also called the Kitty which was best remembered. It was in 1886 that the Marquis came to Medora with twenty servants and ranched there, and started a packing house. He was eyed with suspicion by the other ranchers and not without cause when he cut off the water holes for other animals by enclosing his ranch with barbed wire. A great deal of feuding followed until finally a distraught Marquis went back to France and endeavored there to gain control of the French army. The Marquis' wife was well liked by the people; the Chateau is now a museum.

But in 1903 the Soo built its line from Thief River Falls west of Pelan toward the boundary to Winnipeg, and the Great Northern in 1906 built its rails through Greenbush.

During Pelan's more promising years Hans Olson was concerned about the education of the children of Pelan but he had difficulty in establishing a school because the Swedes and the Norwegians forgot they were both Scandinavians and had their own private feuds. Finally, though, the school was located on the east side of the river since the east side Swedes outnumbered the westside Norwegians. The children were invited to come with what text books, or other books the family might own. The first teacher, William Clinch found he had to teach most of the children to speak English before he could teach reading, writing and arithmetic.

The feud extended into the realm of the spiritual as well. But one church was erected and the Swedes condescended to worship with the Norwegians. The language barrier was not easily crossed however, and each group insisted on its own minister. Strangely enough when only one pastor could be supported, the Swedes insisted on keeping the first minister who was Norwegian.

Now there is no town of Pelan. The early settlers dreamed of a grand metropolis. But the railroad changed the destiny of the proud little community. The stage is forever gone, and not even a memento is left to the Roseau County Museum.

In a letter from Osborne Klavestad of Shakopee, Minnesota to whom the author wrote to plead for a return of the Kitty, he said:

> . . . I have been beseiged by the North Dakota Historical Society, the Roosevelt Park people and others to regain the Kitty.
>
> Will pay tribute to Harry Miller, who rescued the Kitty from the Fryklund yard. Harry Miller was the champion rope performer at the World's Fair, and he took the body of the Kitty and placed it on the chassis of the Dakota. The Kitty was constructed in 1866 in Concord, N. H. which was shipped around Cape Horn and landed in San Francisco for a dollar a pound (the Kitty weighed a ton).
>
> Incidentally the Kitty is the only genuine Deadwood coach in existence. It actually ran to Deadwood. Buffalo Bill called every coach a Deadwood, but few were, and he wore out three in his Wild West career. This coach of the Medora was used by the Marquis on some of his hunting parties.
>
> The leather "springs" or thorough braces were used to save the horse which could cost up to two thousand dollars. Passengers were expendable items, always another at the way station, as there was no other way to go.

Some of the owners or drivers of the famous stage line that ran so proudly through the western part of our county were the following:

Charles Oaks
George Olson
George Roberts
James Reiley (also spelled Reilly)
Tom Hegre
Peter E. Strandberg
Jim Duckworth
Salmond (he might be the Indian referred to in Jake Nelson's account).
Carl T. Johnson
Billy Peterson (Broke the horses, and also ran the first auto-motorized stage in 1902).

Beginnings of Pinecreek

Times were hard in Portland, North Dakota in 1889, but Anders K. Lund and Nels Besserud knew of a land where the hay was abundant, a place with the enticing name of Pinecreek. They induced Erik Evanson and four others to come to visit this new land. They came in the spring and liked what they saw, but could not stay at this time because they needed to take care of their farms in North Dakota. However they did come back and settle in Pinecreek in the fall of the same year.

The first five pioneers in this community had also been neighbors around the year 1885 in Portland, North Dakota. Erik Evanson, and Ole Kompelien came to the new land first, travelling by horse and buggy. They were followed three days later by Lars Rugland driving a team of horses, and Arne Knutson with a team of mules hauling wagons full of provisions. They came first to Jake Nelson's place at the Indian village where they were made welcome. They helped Jake fish, and tried to salt the fish for preservation, but the flies did not cooperate and the fish spoiled. They passed the homes of Henry Johnson, and Clarence Dokken which were located along the way. Now a historic marker placed by the Minnesota Historical Society marks the camp site of those first settlers with these words:

	L. C. Rugland
FIRST SETTLERS	A. Knutson
1889	O. A. Kompelien
	A. K. Lund
	N. Besserud

This marker is now on the Roy Rice farm.

The word was given to the home town folks that Pinecreek area was a good place to settle in so in 1890 others came to make their homes here also. Among these were Andrew Lee and six children, Anders Kompelien with eight children, and Johannes Skogstad with one child. Six more followed along with drivers and interested companions. On this trip they encountered a severe snow storm on the 17th of May and they took refuge at the home of Ole Moen in Warren, Minnesota. The stay became prolonged into two

The Pinecreek Church which started out to be a fort during the Indian scare of 1891 and was later built into a church in 1894.

weeks because of the swollen streams which they finally conquered by making crude boats for themselves and their goods, and enticing the cattle to swim. At first the children were excited and afraid when they saw the Indians in their native garb. The pioneers wishing to show their friendliness had Johannes Kompelien play some old Norwegian tunes on his accordion while they encouraged the Indians to dance.

It was a year later that the settlers around Pinecreek became terrified because they thought the Indians were on the warpath. A log fort was thrown up in a hurry, and several families left in the cold of November only to learn that their fears were groundless. They returned to their homes, and found that the kindly Michinock had cared for their stock and they could again return to their peaceful way of life. The fort became a church and later a school house.

Pinecreek was called the Garden of Eden by the pioneers who came later. The farms were neat and there were flowers in evidence all around the homesteads. A few businesses were established. Mr. Haglund started a general store and in 1901 Mr. Lanegraf operated a store at the port of entry into Canada. On September 11th in 1903 a Norwegian school was set up with A. W. Holland as teacher. The First State Bank of Pinecreek was built in 1921, capitalized at $10,000 with Arne Knutson as owner and E. M. Broughton as cashier.

The old log church has now been restored in memory of the pioneers who first worshipped there and found Pinecreek the place they wanted to live. It has now been moved near the U. S. Customs Station.

The Beginnings of Roosevelt

Theodore Roosevelt, nicknamed "Rough Rider" was a political leader and conservationist, and it was his name that the little lumbering town in Laona chose for their village. It was organized July 13, 1907.

The great stands of timber and the early building of the Canadian Northern railroad (later called the Canadian National) brought this town into being. Although there were saw mills in almost all parts of the county, there was no other place where they were as numerous as at Roosevelt. The timber products of importance were the cedar, spruce pulpwood, spruce and poplar logs, tamarack, birch, white and Norway pine lumber and spruce ties. In the peak years of 1905-1930 the little settlement was alive with wagons or sleds hauling to the nearest saw mill often only a few miles away. In 1920 Weatherby and Eklund bought $125,000 worth of ties and six other companies were buying comparable amounts. An estimated value of 4 million dollars has been placed on the timber business from Roosevelt alone during its years of operation. The Rainy River Supply Company, B. S. Miller, Northern Timber Products (operated by Weatherby and Eklund), the Rat Portage Lumber Co. (Kenora), and George Marvin Lumber Co. were the large companies in the area. In 1927 the State Bank of Roosevelt was incorporated.

To transport the lumber out of the area was the motivating force for building the railroad. John Smrstik, later a merchant in Roosevelt, first worked on the railroad in 1900 and recalled how the grade had to be constructed by hard manual labor with shovels and wheel barrows. John Carter, an early pioneer, recalled how the timber "stood thick" in what became the main street of the town.

Getting the logs to the river for the spring flow are these timber men from Roosevelt.

A depot was one of the first buildings to be erected. Then two stores appeared, one operated by John Mansfield and Co. and the other by Hamilton Horrocks. Later two more general stores came into being, run by Lars Oseid, along with two restaurants, a bowling alley, two blacksmith shops, a barber shop, a newspaper run by C. W. Bell (son of R. J. Bell of the *Roseau County Times*), a bank, two pool halls and an Odd Fellows Lodge and Hall. The postmaster was Turnbull. The Oseid store is run by a grandson of L. Oseid, Mr. Cliff Nordine, and is now the Hartz store.

The people were safety minded. One of the ordinances of the little village read, "It shall be against the law for a team of horses or mules to travel down the street faster than six miles an hour."

Roosevelt dates its first school back to 1905. Miss Hope Merkel was the first teacher of the fifty pupils enrolled in the early school. She was replaced by Miss Blanch Sumner.

The first board members were: C. W. Bell, A. J. Hamilton, and John Butterfield. The first building became the south half of the present school house and in 1912 the north half was added. Now the Roosevelt school building has been sold to a group of Roseau business men who use the building as a small manufacturing plant, making decorator and bed pillows.

Upon the resignation of Pete Sherwood, Carl Peterson was asked to become a member of the school board. He accepted and retained the position for 46 years. Roosevelt had a high school at one time, first set up as a four year system, and then reduced to a two year term, and finally as the enrollment dropped, the students were bused to Williams or Warroad.

In 1949 the Swift School district consolidated with Roosevelt, and there was then an enrollment of 143 pupils. Cephus Croeker was principal at this time and he inaugurated the government project called "Farm School," which added agricultural subjects to the curriculum. In 1968 the district was consolidated with Warroad, and Baudette.

A street scene in Roosevelt, the lumber mecca of the north country in the years of 1905-1930.

Unfortunately the village records were lost when the village hall was destroyed by fire. The first officers of the village were Henry J. Chapin, mayor, Charley Turnbull, clerk, and Louie Hedberg, William Buell and Elof Swanson, trustees.

Perhaps the first citizen award should go to Carl Peterson for besides the 46 years on the school board he served 50 years on the village council, and gave 52 years of service to the railroad as the depot agent. He also managed baseball for many years. It is from Mr. Peterson's memory that much of the history of Roosevelt is retained.

Beginnings of Ross

On the banks of the Roseau River stood a cluster of Indian teepees. Before the county was organized, and even before Jake Nelson ventured north from Nelson Park in Marshall County, these homes, not the log cabin type of the pioneers, but the deer skin tripod homes, housed a group of twenty-five to thirty people. But when pow-wow time came and the Indian friends gathered from other parts of the area, the homes could easily accommodate more than a hundred persons. Here Mickinock (whose name interpreted means "mud turtle") claimed a residence in which to rest from his long treks from Wannaska, from Long Point, or other points where he sold his furs or shared his moose meat. The little community is rich in Indian lore, and may have been the first village ever in Roseau County. Who can tell? Maybe even Ka-Ka-Geesick did not know.

The white settlers who were in awe of the Indians (as they were of the pioneers) were mostly of Norwegian and Irish descent. Soon they discovered that the Red man was not out to scalp the intruders, but eyed them only with kindly curiosity, and the two races lived side by side; each learned from the other. Now there is a plaque on the George Jorgenson farm commemorating the site of the village, abandoned in 1896.

A business district grew up near the river as the settlers decided to stay. The village of Ross was organized January 10, 1891, as a part of Kittson County and listed as the first officers Andres Everson, chairman; Sven A. Engen and Ole Skagen, supervisors, A. O. Skagen, clerk; J. O. Henrickson, treasurer; T. S. Nomeland, assessor; J. O. Henrickson and Ole Jelling, justices; and Andrew Ostenson, constable.

The first store was started by Lars Odegaard who took Sam Holdahl in partnership, but in 1900 the business was sold back again to Lars Odegaard. A creamery was one of the first commercial buildings to be built since the land was rich in grasses for the cattle. L. B. Hartz established a store in 1927 with Jennie and Knute Byfuglien as managers. Since the spring that year brought its usual flood, the store was stocked by boat. After Olaf Arneson and Jennie Byfuglien were married they became the managers. A blacksmith business was started by Martineus Engstad, who sold it in 1908 to Carl Cedarholm, and later it was sold to Emil Cedarholm. The Indian scare of 1891, so much a part of the historical in terest of Ross is related in detail in chapter four.

Soon members of the little settlement built a church, having decided at a meeting of the home of Henry Lockrem that the village was growing enough to warrant a place of worship. It was called the "Concordia Norks Evangelisk Lutheran Menghed i Dieter" and was the first Norwegian Synod church in the county. Later the Ross and Pinecreek people worshipped together. From 1900 until 1974 when the church burned to the ground, this was the church home for the area. The Ross people took their religious training seriously, for a note in the 1907 paper admonished the people that it was a sin to fish on Sunday.

The tenth school district to be established

in Roseau County was that of Ross. The first teacher was Gertha Hegstad when the school was started in 1903. The first officers were A. J. Gilseth, Martin Elton, and K. K. Thingelstad. On the same day District 11 was established with Arne Knutson, Nick Heskin, and Sever Halvorson on the board.

The consolidation of the Ross-Pinecreek and Duxby school districts occurred in 1946. At that time districts 10, 11, 20, 21, 39, 48, 102, and 107 were merged and the school board was Nels Braaten, Clarence Wold, Willis Reed, Jacob Trangsrud, Alvin Magnusson, and Harold Peterson.

Buildings to accommodate the larger enrollment of students were moved in. However, in 1968, parts of the district were consolidated with Roseau. The rest consolidated with Badger.

The little community was proud of being referred to at times as "Little Norway" for they are an industrious and solid group of American citizens with a great deal of respect for their heritage.

Beginnings of Salol

"A second Stillwater," remarked Israel Sjoberg as he envisioned the marketable timber around the area, and felt that it was inevitable that this part of the county should become a metropolis through the lumber business.

The naming of Salol came about through the necessity of finding a name for the post office. L. P. Dahlquist who was clerking in the drug store in Roseau was responsible for the name, and told the story thus:

> In the spring of 1907 the right of way to Warroad had been acquired and graded two years previously to a point forward since called Salol. I decided the location could be used as a trading post. I had in mind especially a post office as a focal point for the community round about. I submitted names from Adair to Salol (which I took as I looked over the drugs on the shelves of the Pioneer Drug Store. I was surprised when L. Meyers, Postmaster General of the United States wrote the commission selecting the name of Salol.

Mr. Ole Sonsteng became the first postmaster. The State Legislature insisted on a train run to Salol for mail and it later became the best paying section for the Great Northern railroad in 1908.

Most of the settlers came from Vetbotten, Sweden. Some of the earliest families were: Herman Gronlund, J. B. Erickson, Jonas Bloom, John Roadfeldt, August Roadfeldt, J. W. Westman, Jens Brandt, Jonas Risberg, Christoffer Mellstrom, Gust Ogren, Andrew Mattson, Karl Karlsson, Alfred Hagglund, Louis Lofquist, and Reynold Mickelson. Later some Norwegian families came to the territory so that by 1910 it was estimated that there were 60 families in the territory.

Since the "summer road" was impassable at times, the coming of the railroad in 1908 was indeed welcome. The "ridge road" as it was called went a few miles south of Salol. The road from Salol to Roseau had to be built by the corduroy method (described in more detail in Chapter six), and it was necessary for teams and wagons to ford Hay Creek.

Education was important to the pioneers, but at first they had to rely on teachers who could spend only a few months at their schools. Jonas Bloom opened his home to a school where Esther Danielson taught. In 1910 there was a school held at the Westman home and shortly thereafter at the home of Mrs. Hilma Mellstrom, with the first teacher being Violet Rice. In the southwestern part of the community a school was started in the Karl Karlsson home, and after the coming of the railroad it was moved across the road from the Nels O. Kristofferson home. The first actual school building was erected in 1921.

Israel Sjoberg built the first store, engaging J. W. Westman to manage it. The Salol State Bank was added to the community in 1919, started by George Marvin, T. B. Holdahl, O. G. Gunderson and capitalized at $2000. Two hotels became part of the business district as did Wollberg's tailor shop. The Mellstroms started their general store. There was activity in all phases of the lumber business, cedar posts, fence posts, tamarack ties, and board feet of lumber. In 1920 it reached its peak with 350 cars shipped out.

The fall of 1910 was a dry year so that grass and timber fires rampaged throughout the area. The worst of these fires was at

Baudette-Spooner, but a peat fire starting in Spruce on October 9, 1910 caused a widespread forest fire here. Emergency aid came from Badger led by Israel Sjoberg and Sheriff Olson, and a special train was engaged to aid in the evacuation of the people. The engine whistle blew continuously so that the people could find the train in the dense smoke. There was no loss of life in Salol and even the Sjoberg store was saved; however, Salol was allotted $800 by the state to replace a school building lost in the fire.

Mr. Sjoberg thought the town had great possibilities so he had his many acres platted and called the townsite Norland. He also donated a piece of land for a church. The congregation has been organized since May 15, 1919.

A Good Templar Hall was built in 1916 and a Yeoman Lodge building was added in 1917. The residents of Salol formed an organization for athletic and social activities with Mrs. S. Johnson as first president.

By 1926 the lumber business had declined and with it the little town of Salol gave up its businesses and became an agricultural center.

Beginnings of Strathcona

Strathcona is the name of a little town in Deer Township in the southwestern part of Roseau County. The name is taken from that of Donald Alexander Smith, later to be known as Lord Strathcona. Just why the name was chosen is obscure since Lord Strathcona's railroad interests were vested in Canada and the Canadian Pacific, where, as High Commissioner, he had financial interests. But Strathcona and J. J. Hill were friends, probably through mutual general railroad interests and developments.

The village was organized on October 22, 1904 after the Great Northern had been built through the town. It had a nucleus of one store, moved by the owners, the Jevnes, from the west side to the east side of the tracks. It was a general store carrying all the staple needs from sugar to horse collars. Business with the early settlers was mostly in the barter style using wood in the form of posts, lumber, and fuel as the medium of exchange. A similar store was built by Lerum and Gunheim in the very early 1900's, a third one called The Strathcona Mercantile was added later. A meat market, two blacksmith shops, one owned by Hans Stone, and the other by Evan Beito were added to the commercial ventures. Sidney Thompson added a dray line in 1913. A tailor shop was started about the same time by a man named Engstrom.

The Great Northern brought in speculators and farmers to take advantage of the free homestead land, prompting John Nordlund in 1906, and the Sjordals in 1914 to build hotels. Work on the drainage of the wet lands had already begun at this time; new land was being opened by continued logging operation and the transition from timber enterprises to farming begun.

The Red Lake Milling Co. started a business in Strathcona for which they hired Knute Jevne as manager. Later Mr. Jevne started a dray and livery business as a side line. More businesses were added at this time, one a meat market run by G. O. Hanson for the Tangen Brothers. A bank was established in Strathcona in 1913.

The intriguing name of Trans-Siberian was given to the telephone system in Strathcona perhaps suggested by the Siberan Ridge in the area.

The school house in Strathcona was purchased by the Gustaf Adolph church after the children were being driven by bus to Greenbush to school. Originally the name of the church was the Swedish-Norwegian church attesting to the good relationship the people of the community enjoyed. The first

The mainstreet of Strathcona in 1913.

pastor was Rev. Johnson. There was also a Baptist church in Strathcona at one time. There is now another Lutheran church called Grace Lutheran which was the home of the popular singing group called "The King's Messengers."

Although roads were developed slowly, the area had the benefit of the Great Northern, which was extended to Greenbush in 1904. The first council was M. K. Kotschevar, mayor, and the trustees were Marlan Bishop, Magnus Spjut, Erick Anderson; E. G. Gustafson was treasurer, H. C. Stone and Hans Lerum justices, and Knute Jevne, constable. Presently the officers in Strathcona are Victor Westlund, mayor, Elmer Hanson, clerk, and the trustees are Alvin Hanson, John Hamburg and Conrad Colton.

The village had an active baseball team that was a real challenge to other communities. The team went by the name of Ridge Runners. The newspaper published about

Strathcona State Bank.

1920 was called *The Screwdriver News.*

The population of Strathcona is about 32, but in former days the town had a population of around a hundred. One of these honored citizens, Sigurd O. Nelson, now close to eighty proudly gave the author this data for the account from his personal recollections.

Beginnings of Swift

Swift was once called Muirhead Siding, named after H. Muirhead, a pioneer. But once when Mr. Muirhead, C. E. Carlquist, and A. M. Landby watched the Canadian Northern (Canadian National) speed through the little town one of them remarked, "That train is really going swift." The new post office was given the name Swift.

The Swift area was well known for its great stands of timber, and often the C. N. shrieked to a halt to load cars of lumber and pulp from the nearby timber camps and saw mills. It was reported that 2,000,000 feet of logs were harvested at Swift in 1911, but in 1913 15,000,000 feet of timber went up in flames.

Because alfalfa grew so abundantly in the area, A. M. Landby and sons Lenus, Martin and A. J., together with Gus Anderson, M. Widsten, Martin Erickson and J. W. Taylor started the Landby Dehydrating Company which operated between the years 1940 to 1956 producing alfalfa meal. In 1956 the operation was moved to Winnipeg, after a company called Alfalfa Products bought part interest; in 1962 the remaining interest was assumed by investors with A. J. Landby and son John retaining interests.

The Swift area is also well known for its mink ranches. The Heinen Ranch, and Linder Ranch incorporate interests in mink with their other agricultural pursuits.

However, Swift is best known today for its rich farm land.

The Beginnings of Wannaska

The community of Wannaska was the beaver capital of North America. Beaver coats and hats were a status symbol throughout the United States and Europe so the demand for the fur was heavy. Other valuable furs could be found here as well, such as Canadian lynx, and wolf, but the beaver was the most prized pelt.

Mr. William Platt, a manager of several wheat farms in the Warren-Argyle area who had land in Moranville, often came up to this part of the country to hunt and trap. A favorite companion with him was Mickinock, and he and "mud turtle" as Mickinock often referred to himself from the translation of his name, spent much time together. Platt has some interesting tales to tell about their relationship. One time he gave Mickinock an old iron stove for his dugout which Mickinock promptly installed. However, the next year Platt did not see the stove pipe sticking out of the dug-out, but he did see smoke coming from a hole in the ground. Mickinock explained that someone had stolen his "smoke hole." Once when Mickinock was out of wood and meat Platt lent him his gun. Friends of Platt said that the gun was lost forever. However, the next day Platt saw Mickinock approach with the gun, his squaw struggling behind him with a quarter of a moose for Platt, and Mickinock returned all but one cartridge to Platt. Platt tells further that once when he asked Mickinock if he were lost, he replied, "No, teepee lost."

The little community of Wannaska is picturesque today with tall evergreens standing like sentinels over the town as if to guard its happy, co-operative people. In 1898 the first general store was located one-half mile southwest of its present site owned by A. O. Hagen who, in 1903 took Knute Lee in as a partner. This store is still in the Lee name, being operated now by Knute's son, Leland; it is the oldest business to remain in the family in Roseau County. The village was incorporated July 16, 1903.

A second store was started by a Mr. Spencer a few years later. M. H. Grefthen and P. O. Foss started a store in 1900 and after M. H. Grefthen bought out Foss he operated the store until 1911. The store was later sold to Backlund Brothers, who in turn sold it to Mr. Sather of Thief River Falls, and it was closed out shortly thereafter and ceased to exist.

A flour mill was started by a group of Roseau business men with the first operator being August Parduhn. In 1905 it was sold to Iver Torfin, who after two years of operation sold it to Mr. Champlin and then it was sold again to A. O. Hagen. This large four story building with full basement was dismantled in 1923.

A thriving Wannaska Creamery Association was started in 1907 by the farmers of the community and operated by Chris Thoen. The undaunted spirit of the people is revealed by the fact that even though the entire operation burned to the ground in 1921 it was rebuilt and put in operation again in the same year, being operated then by R. V. Anderson. In 1929 a feed business and warehouse were added to the plant, and in 1934, an oil station. A locker plant was annexed in

Mrs. Willia Palm (Anna) taking cream to the Wannasko Creamery. 1911.

1949 with Clarence Torfin as operator. This creamery continues to do business in Wannaska.

A hotel and restaurant was built by Olaf Thoen in 1909. Successive owners were Halvor Magnusson. E. O. Wicklander, Harvey Hendershot, Hans Jenson and finally Knute Lee and his son Leland.

The Farmers State Bank of Wannaska was started in 1915 and did business there until 1926 at which time it was merged with the Citizen's State Bank of Roseau. Olaf Hildahl was the owner, and the cashiers were Ed. G. Johnson and later Almer Skrutvold.

Frank Olson started a bulk plant in 1935 which was taken over by the Roseau County Oil Co. of Badger. The highway needed the property where the station was located so it was moved and then operated by Charles Bergstrom, and then sold to Kenneth Eggen.

The first school in the Wannaska area was organized in 1902, as District 62, with Mrs. Bell Jensen as teacher. Members of the board were M. H. Grefthen, Edward Larson and Andy Sunmark. This district included all of Mickinock township except for a few sections on the north side and section 6, 7, and 18. Also included were some sections of Grimstad township. The sections on the north side of Mickinock were put into the Austin school. At first school was held in the house of J. C. Spence in Grimstad. (This property was later bought by Knute Lee and is now owned by Leland Lee).

In the spring of 1903, two school houses were built, one for District 62 (known as the Wannaska school, and placed on the site of the present consolidated school) with Ricka Eastman as teacher. Also built that year was the Hanson school, with Henry Parduhn as teacher. In 1912, the Pencer school was added to the district. The Edberg school was built in 1917.

In 1947, under the consolidation program, the school board voted to move four school buildings into Wannaska. These were known as the "Campus School among the Pines." In 1965, a large modern school, built on that site, replaced the old buildings.

The Wannaska post office was established on February 1, 1896 with John C. Spencer as postmaster and was housed in Spencer's home. Mr. A. O. Hagen became the next postmaster, and following Mr. Hagen was Knute Lee who became postmaster in 1904 and continued in that capacity until his death in 1945, being the longest time for such service in the county. His son Leland is the present postmaster of Wannaska.

Wannaska has always been an active community with zealous and patriotic citizens, and the church and school has provided them with their social life. There is a charming little book written by Arnold Grefthen, son of M. H. Grefthen called *Land of the Howling Wolves*, which tells of pioneer life in the area.

Wannaska is a romantic name steeped in the heritage of the Indians which was inspired by the legend which is told thus: The Crees invaded the land of the Dakota somewhere along the Red River of the North, and took Waunda, a beautiful maiden as a captive, to be kept as a slave. She was cruelly treated as they traveled to the land of the Crees, but she dared not whimper for fear of torture. At night, or when the Crees were hunting she was kept tied. It chanced that a young Chippewa, Pawannaska came by, and at a great risk to his own safety set her free, and took her with him to save her from the brutal captors. He offered to take her back to her people, but Waunda, fearing her people would kill Pawannaska insisted on going with him to his people. So it was that he brought Waunda to his land, the site of the present Wannaska where they were married and founded their home. Even if this is only a legend it adds a charm to the town, and in the fall when the geese fly their V formation against a rosy sunset one can think of Wannaska as a place of security and tranquility.

Beginnings of Warroad

The French called Warroad "chemin de guerre" and the Indians named it Ka-Beck-A-Nung. The French translation is "road of war," and the Indian name, "dark and bloody, end of the trail." The spelling was War Road. These connotations link Warroad to its romantic, dramatic, and historical past. The end of the trail marked the beginning of the water route to the hinterland with its abundance of fur, where only the seasoned voyageurs were prepared to go. The "Road of War" recalls the bitter hatred between the Sioux and the Chippewa. On the beach of this lake the Chippewa Indian village grew and flourished until the French and Indian War spelled the demise of the fur trade.

Henry Schoolcraft who is credited with having discovered the source of the Mississippi and who acted as an Indian Agent for the U. S. government reported on August 9, 1824:

Pursuant to instruction, I have determined on the following places where trade may be carried on with the

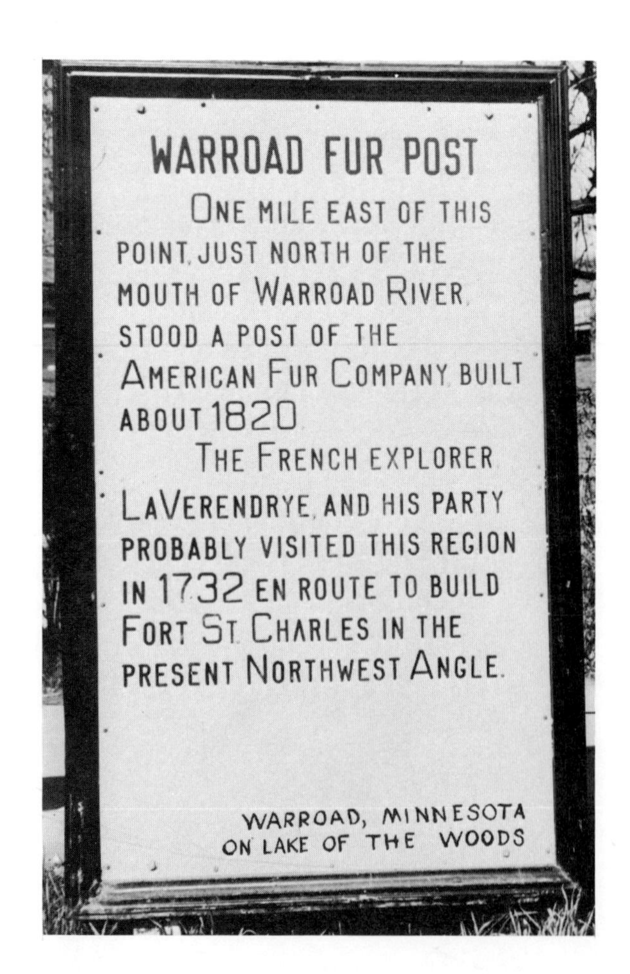

different bands within the limits of this agency . . . 18. At Rainy Lake. 19. At War Road.

The Hudson's Bay Post at Warroad was in existence as late as 1820 or 1822, and although there is a marker placed by the Minnesota Historical Society the exact site is not verified.

There were later independent posts. Earl Chapin related that when he was editing the *Warroad Pioneer* in Warroad, two old men, George Teien, and E. Engebritson from Drayton, North Dakota came back to Warroad to try to locate the site of the post Teien had operated during the winters of 1889 and 1891. Teien told of the trader who came from Pembina and located near the Indian village at that time. This was when Ernest Brown, the taxidermist from Warren also set up a trading post and extended liberal credit to the Indians. One humorous incident relative to the business firm was the story concerning Hans Olson who joined the firm after it was established. Olson was a fiddler who couldn't speak any language except Swedish. Mickinock wondered if he could speak Chippewa if he couldn't speak English and when told that he could not, Mickinock was reported to have said, "Hm . . . he just like a cow."

With the help of Tom Lightning, Teien found his old post on a trail leading to the lake behind Florence Moody's house. The site of Brown's post was found in a smaller clearing which is also on the Moody property along the road to the house. A third post was Duncan Begg's whose post in the year of 1894 was where the sewage disposal plant is now.

Perhaps the first white inhabitant of Warroad was Jake Lockland. In 1895 he operated a post near the Indian Village north of the river. It is reported that Dr. Parker, on his first trip to Warroad amputated a man's leg at Jake's place. This was the year 1896.

Old log school house, the first one built in 1899. The first teacher was Tom Lawson.

Moody's Landing at Warroad, 1901.

A Colonel Loundsberry gave an interview to a reporter from Grand Forks, North Dakota which was later published in the St. Paul Dispatch on August 11, 1899 which included some interesting historical information. Much of the lumber sawed in Canada came from the American side of the boundary. He felt the railroads would soon seek a connection to the Red River Valley so that the lumber resource of the area could be utilized there. He said, "It would be less than 100 miles of road from Thief River Falls or Argyle or Stephen to do it. The country is an excellent agricultural region, rich in lumber and minerals, but especially adapted to timothy and doubtless will go up to 3 ton to the acre and an immense crop of clover all along the Rainy River. . . . The countryside is one unbroken wilderness without wagon roads for hundreds of miles. The canoe is relied upon for transportation until the Rainy is reached. Rat Portage (Kenora) is reached after some forty miles of sailing through a narrow channel between the islands and is destined to become one of the most popular resorts on Lake of the Woods. On the south shore of Lake of the Woods at the mouth of the Warroad River lives C. A. Moody, Thomas L. Jones, Hon. George Roberts, Hon. Albert Berg, C. P. Halberg, Hon. John Zelch and other well known people who have located homesteads and expect to build a prosperous city. While there are seven buildings only in the town proper as yet, they have a port of entry with C. A. Moody, Deputy Collector, and an appropriation of $3000 to improve the harbor at the mouth of the Warroad River. . . . Jones is postmaster, and Berg's claim is directly across

The Jones and Lawson store in the early 1900's.

the river which is several hundred feet wide at this point. The steamer **Clipper,** owned by Frank, an old Winnebago city boy, makes regular trips every Tuesday from Rat Portage to Warroad and occasionally between times. It usually takes about seven hours for the run.

"The road between Warroad and Roseau, 35 miles has been almost impassable this spring and the distance from Roseau to the nearest railroad is 75 miles. . . . At present Warroad is the theater of operation on the Minnesota and Manitoba road. The railroad ties were cut during the winter, and the right of way is being cut, grading will follow immediately and the cars will be running into Warroad before Christmas. It is possible that the extension will be made through the Rainy and to Fort Francis at the earliest possible date as this route will open Rainy Lake gold fields and give a winter outlet."

The first families to come to what is now Warroad were the Guhls, who settled on the Warroad River where the present Johnston home is located, the Charles Springsteeles, who homesteaded Springsteele Island, W. N. York, who lived on the Moody place and the Cugnets who lived on what is now the Cherne place. At this time, 1886, no land had been surveyed so the settlers squatted on what was Indian land.

Mr. Guhl fished for a living and hauled supplies for the surveyors. The Cugnets erected a small store on the Cherne place and a few settlers bought their sundries there. Mr. Guhl, however, went to Roseau for his staples and hauled back supplies such as five hundred pounds of flour, and fifty barrels of sugar at one time. Another business was owned and operated by MacLaughin who had a store where Cal's restaurant is now. This establishment included more general merchandise, like shoes and squaw cloth for example.

Barney Arneson gives Harry Fisher the credit for being the first man to build up the present Warroad business district. He also tells about the fishery on Sandy Island (related in Chapter Five). In an interview with Mr. Arneson (now in the files of the Roseau County Museum) he gave some interesting facts about the early days. He says

> In the year of 1899 I attended a pow-wow at Buffalo Point, at which Oshwash (Ay-Ash-A-Wash) went into a long pantomime which was interpreted by Mrs. Frank White (who described herself as an English lady and her father as an English gentleman.) The depiction was of feats of valor at the Battle of Pelan. The depiction was prefaced by the statement by Oshwash to Arneson that if he (Oshwash) were younger they would go to Spanish War together and take some scalps. Oshwash must have been between 80 and 90 at the time.

Lake of the Woods, renowned for its beauty and fishing had many industries on its shores. One of the earliest was the Warroad Navigation Co. organized in 1903 and headed by President Captain Edward Brydges. A second company was the Warroad Marine Transportation Co. with assets listed as $50,000. Jones and Lawson built a ramp for the loading and unloading of fish. In 1909 in one month's time 455,625 pounds of fish with a monetary value of $207,000 were taken from the lake. Some of the boats which have plied the lake were:

The Knute Nelson was named after Governor Knute Nelson who held office from

Main street in Warroad in 1903. The Lakewood Hotel was built in 1902, but burned in 1905.

1893-1895. It has been estimated that this boat was 70 feet long and twenty feet wide. It plied the lake in the early part of the century but not a great deal is known about its operation.

The Na-May-Puck was named after the famous Indian of Warroad, and built in 1901 and completed in 1902. During a fierce storm it sank in 1910 and the machinery of the boat lies at the bottom of the lake about in the center of a triangle formed by Zippel Bay and Bigsby Island and the mouth of the Rainy River. No lives were lost, as the captain and the crew drifted ashore on a barge. The paper gave credit to Captain Starren who directed the passengers through the ordeal and even though as the paper said "the wind blew the barge around like a plaything" and the rope had to be cut to the boat, he kept his head and saved many lives.

The Resolute was piloted most of the time by the friendly and genial captain Fay Young. He began operating boats on the lake when he bought the **Homestead** and in 1921 the **Nina** with which to haul supplies back and forth to the islands. Captain Fay Young died in 1973.

The Isobel was built in Warroad under the able ship builder from a firm in Duluth. It was built in 1912 with oak ribs and three inch planking and was a sturdy steam tug. **The Isobel** plied the Lake of the Woods, towing a barge for hauling fish until 1922 when on the start of a fish hauling trip from Warroad, the main part of her steam engine broke and she drifted ashore a short distance south of the mouth of the Warroad River. The **Isobel** was sold to Tom Welsh (a lumberman and father of Mary Welsh, wife of the late Ernest Hemingway) who used the boat for several years as a timber barge hauling logs to Warroad where they were shipped out.

The Scout was built in 1913 in Warroad and began her career on Lake of the Woods as a barge, being towed by the **Isobel.** At this time she was called the **Rose M** but when she was rebuilt to diesel power she was renamed **The Scout,** the rebuilding was done in 1922. **The Scout** was commissioned in 1923. It was during these years that the tourist trade began to take hold, so **The Scout** was classified as a passenger-freighter, and was licensed to carry 125 passengers. Many Sunday excursions to the islands were made with full com-

Captain Erick Starren and Captain Fay Young study the lake maps.

plement of passengers and usually a name band of the period to furnish entertainment. She was also capable of carrying three cars on deck on the trip to Kenora, but only two cars were carried on the return trip as the hatch had to be left clear for fish picked up at various fishing stations. Due to the decline of the fishing business in the early forties, **The Scout** was laid up. The machinery was removed and sent to Winnipeg. A group of local men bought **The Scout** and towed it to Stoney Creek, and used it several years as a hunting lodge. Finally **The Scout** burned when a stove was accidentally overheated.

The Island Queen was built by Otto Johnson in 1946. Captain Eric Starren operated it until his retirement from boat navigation in 1958. **The Lake Trails,** a Catholic camp, purchased the boat and it is being used today to serve the Lake Trails Camp at Oak Island.

The Bert Steele was built for the Selvog Fishery. While it was used in this capacity it was called the **Lorraine S.** Then the Booth Fisheries purchased it and renamed it **The Bert Steele** after a long time faithful Booth employee. It was classed as a passenger-freighter. When the Booth fishery closed out their buying station it was purchased by Captain Lawrence Saurdiff and is in operation today serving as a commuting boat from Northwest Angle to the islands.

The Clipper was owned by Selvog and Russell and sold to a Mr. Truax in 1911.

The Defiance was classed as a freighter. She was owned by Wm. Rader and was used for several years to carry the mail across the lake. When Mr. Rader found the feldspar

First style dredge on Lake of the Woods in 1888.

The Na-May-Puck.

The Isobel.

The Defiance.

The Nina

The Resolute — Fay Young Pilot.

The Bert Steele.

The Scout — Larence Saurdiff, Pilot.

The Island Queen.

The Grace Anne II.

The Kenora.

The Knute Nelson.

mine at the Angle, he used the boat to carry the rock to the mill in Warroad near the river by the C. N. tracks. The boat was used to tow barges when loads were heavy. Later this boat too was stripped of its machinery and sold to a group of local men, put on a sandbar on the south shore and used for a hunting lodge. Eventually it was destroyed by fire.

The Grace Ann II was a private yacht owned by a Mr. Furlong of Winnipeg, Manitoba. Her home port was Kenora, Ontario, but the boat was a familiar sight in the Warroad Harbor and at Oak Island and American Point in the early 1930's. It was a palatial yacht with her highly polished teakwood decks and mahogany interior finish. All crew members, guests and visitors were required to don rubber soled shoes before coming aboard. The **Grace Ann** was sixty-five feet long and reputed to have cost $1,000 a foot to build, considered a very high price for the depression years.

The Dredge was a stern-wheeler dredge used for many years to keep the harbor of Warroad and Baudette deepened.

Mrs. Cherne was the first white baby born in Warroad. The midwife to assist at the birth was the squaw from the Roseau Indian village, Mrs. Cobenas, who got to Warroad on foot. It was Mrs. Cherne's father, Louis Cugnet who had a store and small restaurant where the Cherne farm is still situated.

The Lawson family was one of the pioneer families in Warroad. Thomas Lawson arrived as a young and ambitious man in 1897. By January 1898, he had found a partner by the name of Tom Jones, and together they started the Jones and Lawson Mercantile store. The store was located near the banks of the Warroad River, in about the location where the John Lawson house (which was later sold to Happy Floe) is now located. There were about one hundred Indian families and a dozen white families in the Warroad vicinity at this time. One popular commodity that was sold at the store was fish for three cents a pound. The business prospered, and soon they built a new store on the corner across from the third store, now the Roberts building. The second store burned to the ground in the big Warroad fire of June 1905.

Frank Clements, another early pioneer of Warroad, and father of Mrs. Tom Thunder hauled supplies for the firm of Jones and Lawson with horse and buggy from Stephen. He related that the ground was so swampy at places that the teams had to cross on makeshift plank bridges. Unfortunately when Mrs. Thunder was four years old her father lost both legs as he attempted to board the Canadian National to bring home some groceries. (The Clements home was on the left side of the road to Springsteele Island). Dr. Parker was his physician when he returned home from the Rainy River hospital where the train had taken him. In spite of this set back the family finally managed to clear 140 acres of land. With a big garden and with the help of Mrs. Clements working out they managed a living. The railroad compensated them only $6.00 a month for the accident. The family sold soap and sour kraut at twenty cents a gallon to their neighbors.

The first paper, started in Warroad in 1899 when Albert Berg was Secretary of State, was owned by W. H. Book, C. A. Moody and Albert Berg, and called *The Plaindealer.* The favorite joke at the time concerned the editors who had a combined weight of 727 pounds and they were said to have proudly announced in their paper that no person dared to sit down on them. Book always hastened to add that his paper was Republican in nature.

By February 1900 business was booming in Warroad. The bridge was built across the river, and some of the early businesses besides Jones and Lawson were the Cugnets, Gilly and Smith, J. A. Cheetham, the Peter Ornes Hotel, the Gaffney saloon, A. E. Linder pool hall, Osborn barber shop, and a Mr. English hired out as a carpenter.

An interesting incident that A. E. Linder tells was about a man named Anderson and his friend who built a house boat and started beer and liquor sales on it. One night a storm came up and broke the boat from its mooring and blew it out to the lake with both men asleep inside. Next morning when the boat was missed a search was started but the lake was so rough that little could be done. The day after, the boat and one man was found alive in the muskeg by Willow Creek. A week or so later an Indian found Anderson's body in the water — he had tried to make dry land but had failed.

The mosquitoes and bull flies were fierce and mentioned in almost every account. Mr. Linder tells this story, "A peddler complained to Billy Booze about this country and the flies and mosquitoes. 'What,' said Billy, 'our mosquitoes are not so bad, we have good healthy mosquitoes and as far as the bull flies go they don't bite anyone except mules and asses.' 'Well,' said the peddler, 'They bit me and surely you don't call me a mule or ass.' 'No,' said Bill, 'I wouldn't go so far as to say that but you can't fool those bull-dog flies.' "

More businesses were added. A laundry was started in the former butcher shop owned by James Knight, George Long, and Robert Linder. This was called the Linder – All-Knight, Long Laundry. The Lakewood Hotel was added in 1902 but burned in 1905. The Marvin Elevator was built, and also a new store by Dr. Parker at this time. (He burned out five times, but as A. E. Linder put it, "always came up smiling.") Another paper the *Commonwealth* was started by Archie MacDonald (The man R. J. Bell said was the second best looking editor in the county.)

George Roberts, Sr. and family including William and Mont settled on what is now the Peter Heppner farm. Mont started cutting out a road on the section line that runs north from John Lawson's house. One hot day Mont came to the pool room to get a cool drink, and Tom Jones sold him an imitation root beer which he said was made from syrup of figs. Mont liked it and drank two quarts. He was a busy man the next day, but cut no trees.

In 1903, Dr. Parker, the health commissioner, warned against allowing hogs, cattle and chickens to roam freely in the main part of town.

The village got its first bridge in 1903 and an appropriation of $150 was made by the Minnesota Legislature for a wagon road, if the citizens would donate a like amount. In 1904 the village got its well which was one hundred and eleven feet deep and as early as 1903 the residents took measures for fire protection with two chemical engines and a volunteer fire department. However, in spite of preparation the worst devastation by fire which it has ever had to experience occurred in Warroad in 1905.

It was related in the *Warroad Plaindealer* of June 1, 1905: "A little after one o'clock yesterday morning the fire fiend again visited this village and sixteen business houses with their contents lie in ruins. Both sides of Lake Street from the C. N. tracks to Robert Street are cleared to the ground. The origin of the fires are unknown, as every person in the block where it started was sleeping and they all escaped in their night clothes, many barely escaping with their lives. Oscar Kuntz is burned about the hands and face and his feet are cut and burned from his experience in getting his family out of their rooms over the store of Hampton and Kuntz. . . . The fire spread with such rapidity that no thought could be taken of the property and the occupants of the upper stories had to leave the buildings by back stairs or jump through windows. Prof. Guden and his wife who were stopping at King's cafe for a couple of days before leaving town after the closing of school were led from the house by a regular boarder well acquainted with the building, the smoke being so dense that they could not find their way unaided.

"Before the buildings on the south side of the street began to fall, those on the north side were on fire, and within two hours not a building stood facing Lake street. T. L. Jones and Thos. Lawson resided over their store and neither saved anything of their household goods. C. E. Carlquist and his chief clerk, John Larson had their families domiciled over Mr. Carlquist's store and they too lost every article of household goods, and themselves reached the street half clothed with their families.

"The largest loss is that of Jones and Lawson, general merchants, who with stock and household goods reached fully $40,000 with $24,000 worth of insurance. Next comes C. E. Carlquist, general merchant, amounting to $30,000 with $15,000 insurance. The other losers were C. V. Alldrin, hardware, J. A. Widness saloon, Hampton and Kuntz, Hagman Bros. saloon, J. W. King, cafe, Jowett and Fox, telephone exchange, Peter Tornbloom, Albert Hedberg, bowling alley, Louis Sletten, restaurant, Dr. Parker, drug store, Hugo Lundbohm, drug store, Dr. Oplegar, office building, J. D. Taylor, law office Joe McCaffrey, land and insurance building, State Bank of Warroad, B. H. Erickson tailor, Herman Fleig, barber.

"Nearly all the buildings will be replaced, most of them with better ones than those destroyed. A number of the businesses burned out have signified their intention of building with concrete."

The First State Bank was replaced and another one, the Security State Bank, was built shortly thereafter. That year saw the first sewer lines laid, and in 1909 the first street lighting was installed. By 1920 the population of Warroad was 927.

At this time there were only trails or mud ruts. There was a summer road and a winter road to the west with the winter road passable only when frozen, and the summer road passable only when the weather was dry. Someone asked A. P. C. Monkman, a veteran of the Riel Rebellion[18] who was living near Warroad before the railroad was built, which road was best. "The lower road," replied Mr. Monkman, and when asked for an explanation he said, "That's the one under the mud." A. E. Linder tells that the corduroy roads (those built up with a pole base) were a trial in themselves, for sometimes the poles would bunch up in front of the wagon wheels and it was a man's job to get the wagon on top again. In 1900 a breaking plow for road work was purchased from Holdahl and Foss for $27.00. Clearing and grubbing for roads was let by the acre. Some prices were $4.00 or $6.00 for clearing and ditching, and grading was listed at 16c a yard. A poll tax (the farmer agreed to give a donation or money or some days of labor) was listed at this time.

With the pressing need for transportation the village in 1902 granted a license to Harry Stolz to run a stage to Roseau, and to Jeremiah Donnelly the same year to run a ferry across the Warroad River. The village west of the present highway bridge was at this time covered with a dense growth of poplar, birch and Balm of Gilead trees with just a narrow trail on each side of the river to the lake. Moodys lived on the river bank south of the Security State Bank. A second ferry was started there by Hans Selvog. The story is told that once the Commissioner of Game and Fish came to Warroad and was invited to the Moody home for a meal. The young Moody boys said, "Please pass the moose meat." But the Moodys had sturgeon that day, which was lucky because moose were not in season.

The first school house was built in 1899 at a site just north of the present school house on a piece of land donated to the school district by Na-May-Puck. Mr. Tom Lawson was the first teacher, being paid his salary (if any) from the resources of the land – garden produce, cord wood and occasionally a chicken. Mr. Lawson loved children so much that remuneration was secondary to him. Mr. Pete Pearson, Joseph, Mary, Wilford and Bill Saurdiff were among the first pupils in that school in the very early 1900's. Fortunately the school house is being preserved for posterity.

Before 1900 a few scattered businesses sprang up. A. E. Linder built a pool room and confectionary where the Fox house now stands. The opening stock was shipped by wagon from Stephen, one hundred and ten miles away. The freight was fifty cents per one hundred pounds and fifty cents to a dollar from Roseau to Warroad depending on the road conditions.

Norman Lewis settled near Warroad in 1899 and built a saw mill. J. W. Durham, formerly from Roseau started a butcher shop near the Lawson home, and Harry Fisher, a cook, started a restaurant west of his shop.

An engineer named Foley made a survey in 1899 for the Canadian railroad, taking A. E. Linder along as a packer. Between what is now Williams and Pitt, according to Indian lore, in 1840 a fierce fire burned most of the cedar, also destroying a beautiful forest of Norway pine.

To get rail transportation was the foremost goal of the slowly increasing population. In March of 1899, the land was surveyed for the Canadian Northern (Canadian National) Railroad, and Hegland and Groslein advertised for 500 men to work on the grades. It was specified that they were paying eight cents a tie and that a willing worker could make four or five dollars a day. Roberts and Neil had a contract for bridge timbers and pilings and would drive logs to Warroad from Suttons who planned to cut 20,000 feet of lumber a day if they could get the workers. The town site would be determined by the location of the railroad. Swamps and creeks had to be forded and ties secured over them, while the mosquitoes and bull flies had a feast on the bodies of the laborers. J. A. Cronkite had a contract for two miles of grade starting at the boundary, while Andrew Danielson built the next mile, and A. E. Linder the next one half mile, the Oveson brothers had the next two miles and the rest was to be laid by the station employees. "What howls of

18 The Riel Rebellion was also known as the Red River Rebellion. The leader was Louis Riel, who succeeded his father as leader of the French-Indians of the Northwest. The Metis revolted against the Hudson's Bay Co. in 1849, claiming in behalf of the half breeds the money taken in the form of land from the Indians.

glee," said Mable Guhl Johnston, "when the settlers heard the toot of the train and saw the first train approaching Warroad." However it was reported that no trains could run over the bridge the first summer because of lack of ballast.

C. A. Moody who was called "the father of Warroad" came in 1896 to become Deputy Collector of Customs. Mr. Moody secured enough names to petition the government for a post office at War Road. J. M. McLauflin became the first postmaster.

"The first meeting of the Board of Supervisors of the Township of Warroad was held at the residence of M. D. Cole of said town on the 6th day of August, 1898 at 3 o'clock P.M. Present were M. D. Cole, chairman and supervisor, G. H. Peasely, and George Humble." So read the minutes in the office of the village clerk in Warroad. The village was incorporated on November 9, 1901.

Up to this time the village was apparently a part of the township, for on November 25, 1901 the first village council of Warroad met at the recorder's office where the following were elected: W. H. Book, Norman Lewis, and Thomas L. Jones, trustees, Edward Mc Cagherty, recorder; Marshall Ballard and Harry F. Fisher, justices; and John Riggs and D. M. Roberts, constables. *The Warroad Plaindealer* was the official newspaper of the new village.

Thus Warroad, the only harbor town in the county had its beginnings, and with the modern emphasis on recreational and tourist pursuits the town has a strategic location. Its progressive people are proud of the beautiful lake and their town on its shore.

Chapter 10

And he alone is great who turns the voice
of the wind into a song made sweeter by his
own loving.

"The Prophet" – Kahlil Gibran

As the history of the area has unfolded, there have been thoughts in the mind of the author as to the outcome of some of the pertinent problems and questions of today. Perhaps while you read this book many of the resolutions will either have already occurred or the problems faded into oblivion. Meanwhile you will be faced with other concerns or perplexities. It might be interesting to the reader to consider some of the local and national concerns that have been ours.

Will atomic power be the source of power in the future?
Will corporate farming pose a threat to our county?
Will consolidation continue to include churches, hospitals, schools, and trade areas as it has begun in our day?
Will cancer and heart disease be conquered as polio and small pox have been?
Will UFO's be scientifically explained?
Will Roseau County have air passenger service?
Will the Roseau River flood situation be solved?
Will blue grass and timothy be replaced as major crops in our area?
Will the heartbreak of the Watergate affair finally result in a salutary political transformation?
Will there be a solution to world hunger?
Will the American Bicentennial inspire the nation to new heights of appreciation and patriotism for their beloved land?

Bibliography

Blegen, Theodore C. **Minnesota.** University of Minnesota Press. 1963.

Bolz, Arnold. **Portage into the Past.** University of Minnesota Press, 1960.

Carley, Kenneth. **The Sioux Uprising of 1862.** Minnesota Historical Society, 1961.

Carolissa, Sister A. **Chippewa Indians.** New York: Pageant Press, 1956.

Christianson, Theodore. **Minnesota – The Land of the Sky Tinted Waters.** Chicago: American Historical Society, 1935.

Dobie, John. **The Itasca Story.** Grand Rapids, Minnesota. Ross and Haines, 1959.

Federal Writers Project of the Works Administration. Minnesota; a State Guide (American Guide Series). New York, The Viking Press, 1938.

Ford, Antoinette. **My Minnesota.** Lyons, 1929.

Gates, Charles and Nute, Grace. **Five Fur Traders of the Northwest.** Minnesota Historical Society, 1965.

Gilman, Rhoda R. and Holmquist, June. **Selections from "Minnesota History."** Minnesota Historical Society, 1965.

Heilbron, Bertha. **The Thirty-Second State.** Minnesota Historical Society, 1966.

Jones, Evan. **Citadel in the Wilderness.** New York: Coward-McCann, 1966.

Jones, Evan. **My Minnesota.** New York: Holt, 1962.

Josephy, Alvin M., Editor in Charge, and Brandon, William, narrative. **The American Heritage Book of Indians.** New York: Simon and Schuster, 1961.

Larsen, Erling. **Minnesota Trails,** Minneapolis: T. S. Denison and Co., 1957.

Le Sieur, Meridel. **North Star Country.** New York: Duell, Sloan and Pearce, 1945.

Nute, Grace Lee. **Rainy River Country.** St. Paul: Minnesota Historical Society. 1950.

Nute, Grace Lee. **The Voyageurs.** St. Paul: Minnesota Historical Society. 1966.

Nute, Grace Lee. **The Voyageur's Highway.** St. Paul: Minnesota Historical Society, 1965.

Olson, Sigurd. **The Singing Wilderness.** New York: Knopf, 1956.

Poatgieter, Hermina and Dunn, James. **Gopher Reader.** St. Paul: Minnesota Historical Society.

Sarkowski, John. **Face of Minnesota.** Minneapolis: University of Minnesota, 1958.

Pamphlets, Documents, Diaries, Booklets, and Articles

Brown, Ernest. Diaries, 1889-1901. These manuscripts are in the Minnesota Historical Society, photostated for the Roseau County Museum.

Chapin, Earl. **The Angle of Incidents.** The Story of Warroad and the Northwest Angle. Published under the auspices of the Warroad Area Historical Society. 1970.

Durham, Jeremiah W. **Minnesota's Last Frontier.** Minneapolis, 1925). Reprinted from the Roseau Times.

Hudson's Bay Company. Hudson's Bay House. Correspondence relative to Roseau Trading Post.

La Verendrye, Pierre Gaultier, Esquire, Sieur de. Contract with the Marquis de la Galissoniere, knight of the royal military order of St. Louis, captain of the King's fleet, and commander general of all His Majesty's New France, lands and country of Louisiana. Minnesota Historical Society. Photostated for the Roseau County Museum.

Public Archives of Canada. Ottawa, Ontario. Correspondence and maps and water routes.

Mattson, Neil E. Red River Carts. Historic Pembina Trail Trek.

Minnesota Historical Society
- The Fur Trade in the Minnesota Territory
- Indians of Minnesota
- Minnesota Exploration – English and American
- Minnesota Exploration – French
- Military Posts of Pioneer Minnesota
- Pioneer Life in Minnesota
- Transportation in Minnesota
- Minnesota Under Four Flags

Minnesota History. The Prehistory of the

Red River Valley, by Elden Johnson. December, 1962.

Minnesota History. On the Prairie – A Sketch of the Red River Valley, by Knut Hamsun. Translated by John Christianson.

Minnesota Prehistoric Archaeology Series, Burial Mounds of the Red River Headwaters. Minnesota Historical Society, 1970.

Morse, Eric. W. Canoe Routes of the Voyageurs. Canadian Geographical Journal. May, July and August, 1961.

Roberts, O. A. Footsteps in Education – A Historical Digest of the Rural Schools of Roseau County.

Roseau Electric Cooperative. 25th Anniversary, 1940-1965.

Stam, Jerome M. An Economic Analysis of the Lake of the Woods – Rainy Lake Region of Minnesota. Agricultural Experiment Station, University of Minnesota, 1972.

Warren, Wincell, Neill and Buck. A Story of Grand Portage. Compiled by John B. Arnold. Minneapolis: Harrison & Smith, 1923.

Personal Interviews

The author had the pleasure of interviewing these persons concerning the history:

Maggie Lightning Aas, Warroad
John Aas, Greenbush
Paul Buran, Roseau and Tucson
Chester Dahlquist, Roseau
Hube Dieter, Roseau (now deceased)
David Johnson, Roseau
Mabel Guhl Johnston, Warroad
Robert Ka-Ka-Geesick, Jr., Warroad
Leland Lee, Wannaska
John Lightning, Warroad, and Minneapolis
Cal Marvin, Warroad
George Marvin, Warroad
Lloyd Nelson, Ely
Sigurd Nelson, Strathcona
Sigfus Olafson, Madison, West Virginia
Ervin Parker, Crown Point Indiana
Burt and Lil Roberts, Warroad
Gene Simmons, Pinecreek
Ingvard Sunset, Roseau
Tom Thunder, Middlebro, Canada
Fay Young, Warroad (now deceased)

APPENDIX

List of pioneer residents in Roseau County before 1900 as compiled by Willie and Mathilda Strandberg from all available records.

Name	Location	Year
Aasen, T.	Stokes	1896
Akre, Martin I.	Warroad	1890
Alleson, Asle	Enstrom	1898
Anderson, Albert O.	Deer	1890
Anderson, Alfred N.	Lind	1897
Anderson, Bert C.	Lind	1897
Anderson, Mrs. Emil	Roseau	1894
Anderson, J. E.	Stafford	1898
(Wife) Bena Olson		
Anderson, John H.	Lind	1896
Anderson, Mike	Jadis	1887
Anderson, Olaf	Moose	1895
Teha Hellickson		
Anderson, Oscar	Mickinock	1900
Anderson, P. E.	Deer	1900
Anderson, Willie	Spruce Valley	1894
Otila Larson		
Arneson, Andrew	Ross	1895
Arneson, Barney	Warroad	1894
Austin, Atlantus	Malung	1889
Backlund, Erick J.	Stafford	1889
Mary Back		
Begg, Duncan	Jadis	1894
Bell, R. J.	Roseau	1895
Bendickson, Ben	Stokes	1897
Carrie Lundemo		
Benson, D. H.	Roseau	1895
Rose V. Chapin		
Benson, Stenud	Dieter	1896
Berger, John	Hereim	1900
Bertilrud, Gulbrand	Dieter	1889
Kjersti Sorley		
Bertilrud, M. G.	Dieter	1889
Bertilrud, S. G.	Dieter	1889
Besserud, A. L.	Jadis	1893
Enar Hagen		
Billberg, Eddy E.	Roseau	1900
Birkness, Otto	Nereson	1900
Bizek, Matt	Soler	1900
Blomgren, L. M.	Falun	1890
Bjerke, B. C.	Jadis	1900
Bjorkman, Erik	Jadis	1900
Rose Holm		
Bjorkman, Hans E.	Spruce	1889
Bjorkman, H. J.	Moranville	1889
Bjorkman, Warner	Spruce	1889
Blazek, Frank	Barnett	1899
Blazek, Henry	Soler	1899
Mary Novack		
Blazek, John J.	Soler	1894
Stella Kozek		
Blazek, Thomas	Soler	1894
Bloomquist, Louis	Roseau	1890
Boberg, B. A.	Roseau	1895
Boe, Nels	Jadis	1887
Ingeborg Halvorsen		
Boe, Pete	Jadis	1887
Boen, R. E.	Malung	1895
Mathilda Peterson		
Book, Bill	Jadis	1896
Mrs. Bill Book		
Bottem, Ole J.	Barnett	1895
Gena Brude		
Braaten, Martin	Dieter	1890
Nila Skogstad		
Brandt, C. E.	Malung	1895
Brandvold, B. S.	Soler	1900
Broten, Ed	Stokes	1896
Anna Fjeld		
Broten, G. C.	Ross	1890
Brenden, G. E.	Badger	1895
Brenda, Maria		1900
Brovold, Ed.	Dieter	1892
Brown, Julian	Warroad	1900
Budd, Gilbert	Stafford	1895
Ida Tripp		
Budd, Joe E.	Stafford	1895
Cannon, Fred F.	Moose	1900
Cary Boboe		
Carlquist, C. E.	Warroad	1888
Carlson, Wilhelm	Grimstad	1898
Anna Nord		
Carlson, Albin	Grimstad	1898
Clara Johnson		
Cedarholm, Carl	Dieter	1899
Tilda Nilson		
Chapin, V. B.	Badger	1896
Anna B. Swain		
Chequin, Lewis	Laona	1900
Christianson, C. A.	Roseau	1894
Christianson, Mrs. C. A.	Roseau	1890
Christianson, O. K.	Greenbush	1900
Colton, P. M.	Deer	1900
Aljana Kolbak		
Comstock, A. J.	Falun	1896
Louisa Parduhn		
Comstock, C. W.	Falun	1896
Dahl, Amund	Skagen	1896
Bertha Larson		
Dahl, Christian I	Moose	1891
Dina Anderson		
Dahl, Tom	Mickinock	1900
Dahlen, John	Spruce	1889
Dahlen, Martin	Spruce	1889
Dahlgren Aron	Stafford	1889
Dahlgren, Nels	Stafford	1891
Ingeborg Larson		
Dahlgren, Ole	Malung	1891
Lillie Comstock		
Dahlgren, O. L.	Malung	1891
Dahlin, Ole	Stafford	1888
Dahlquist, L. P.	Roseau	1894
Bertha Anderson		

Dallager, Christ	Dewey	1897
Dallager, Harold	Dewey	1897
Dallum, Bernt	Nereson	1900
Anna Mattson		
Danielson, Denis	Moose	1892
Danielson, Edward	Lind	1900
Danielson, Salomon	Roseau	1889
Dieter, Hubert	Roseau	1888
Dieter, John B.	Jadis	1887
Mary Waterman		
Dokken, Carl	Jadis	1892
Dokken, Ingvald	Roseau	1893
Dokken, Knut O.	Jadis	1892
Ingeborg Peterson		
Dokken, Ole K.	Dieter	1894
Dokken, Thore	Jadis	1892
Dole, Rikar	Ross	1895
Tina Berdahl		
Dolezel, James	Soler	1897
Durham, Anna	Roseau	1889
Durham, J. W.	Roseau	1887
Eeg, Tennes T.	Dewey	1896
Efshen, Oluf	Jadis	1889
Hannah Lee		
Eilertson, Richard	Stafford	1888
Eken, Barent	Ross	1893
Johanna Amundson		
Eklund, Fritjof W.	Malung	1892
Ekman, O. B.	Roseau	1889
Elton, Even	Dieter	1890
Mary Besserud		
Elton, Martin	Dieter	1890
Enger, Sophus	Ross	1890
Enger, Sven	Ross	1890
Englund, Fred	Jadis	1893
Enstrom, Louis	Malung	1889
Anna Johnson		
Erickson, Edward	Ross	1889
Maria Erickson		
Erickson, Edward	Soler	1898
Tina Hegg		
Erickson, E. J.	Stafford	1888
Erickson, Erick	Skagen	1894
Christena Mattson		
Erickson, Erick	Stafford	1888
Erickson, Halvor	Stafford	1888
Erickson, Henry	Roseau	1897
Erickson, M. E.	Stafford	1889
Anna Pearson		
Erickson, Oliver	Moose	1895
Helga Malgren		
Erickson, Reinhald	Malung	1895
Erickson, Selmer	Ross	1892
Erickson, Syver	Dieter	1889
Maret Valseth		
Evanson, Erick	Pinecreek	1889
Evjen, I. J.	Barto	1895
Fadness, Henry	Roseau	1893
Fernstrom, John	Jadis	1887
Fiske, Lars	Ross	1894
Bertha Vesterdahl		
Fjeld, E. G.	Roseau	1895
Fjeld, Gunelius	Stokes	1899
G. Sanden		
Fjeld, Thorvald	Roseau	1895
Flaa, Knut	Stokes	1895
Flaten, Gilbert	Pinecreek	1890
Foeld, Olaf E.	Roseau	1896
Forness, Peter	Stokes	1895
Foss, A. H.	Roseau	1892
Foss, John	Falun	1900
Laura Dahl		
Fossen, Peter A.	Ross	1888
Frandsen, Ebbe	Grimstad	1900
Frazer, Hugh	Roseau	1894
Friberg, Eric	Falun	1900
Friberg, Ole	Falun	1900
Carrie Berg		
Frislie, J. P.	Soler	1895
Fryklund, P. O.	Stafford	1895
Fugleberg H.	Jadis	1889
Hulda Markstrom		
Fugleberg, Ole	Ross	1894
Carrie Hanson		
Fuglem, B. O.	Grimstad	1895
Anna Larson		
Funseth, Carl	Roseau	1889
Gaukerud, O. P.	Jadis	1891
Genow, Albert	Ross	1890
Gilbertson, Gilbert	Fox	1889
Gilbertson, Hans O.	163-43	1895
Glittre, Anton	Ross	1890
Gordon, A. O.	Badger	1890
Goroski, August	Malung	1897
Gorvin, Nels	Hereim	1897
Graff, Olof H.	Moose	1895
Graham, W. N.	Stokes	1895
Mary Kirkpatrick		
Grassler, Anton	Golden Valley	1900
Christena Strunt		
Graves, A. M.	Roseau	1889
Grefthen, M. H.	Wannaska	1894
Grindahl, Henry	Malung	1888
Grothe, Adolph	Skogen	1896
Growitt, Joseph	Warroad	1891
Gunderson, Ole	Skagen	1895
Haaland, Andrew	Jadis	1899
Brita Skorheim		
Hagen, Ed	Fox	1890
Hagen, Erick N.	Fox	1889
Hagen, Hans E.	Dewey	1895
Hagen, John E.	Roseau	1890
Ellen Sjodin		
Hagen, Nick	Roseau	1896
Nellie Hicks		
Hagen, Richard	Jadis	1890
Bertina Skogen		
Halvorson, Gilbert	Jadis	1890
Guri Gjesthus		
Halvorson, John	Jadis	1890
Tilda Lofthus		
Halvorson, Tollef	Jadis	1891
Kristina Lofthus		
Hanestad, G. A.	Stokes	1897

Name	Place	Year
Maria Hansrud		
Hansen, Frederik	Stokes	1897
Manda Mathison	Stokes	1897
Hanson, Ellert	Dewey	1896
Hanson, John	Stafford	1892
Anna Strandberg		
Haug, C. O.	Barto	1898
Haug, Thorval T.	Soler	1895
Haugen, Fred	Dieter	1894
Haugen, G. T.	Pinecreek	1894
Mrs. G. R. Haugen		
Haugen, Ole M.	Skagen	1895
Johanna Lillehaugen		
Haugen, Tosten	Dieter	1894
Hedin, August	Roseau	1889
Hedin, John	Malung	1889
Hedin, Lars L.	Malung	1888
Hedin, Peter	Malung	1888
Hedlund, Emil	Stafford	1887
Bertha Larson		
Hedlund-E.	Skagen	1893
Hedlund, Lars	Malung	1891
Hegstad, L. C.	Haug	1891
Hellickson, Julius	Skagen	1895
Clara Shevlin		
Helstad, Anton	Dieter	1895
Oljana Olson		
Heltne, Carl	Hereim	1900
Hendrickson, John O.	Lind	1900
Henrickson, Ole	Roseau	1893
Hereim, O. O.	Greenbush	1895
Hetteen, Peter,	Malung	1889
Hildahl, Abraham	Roseau	1895
Hildahl, Olaf	Greenbush	1895
Mrs. Olaf Hildahl		
Hillman, Mrs. H.	Nereson	1898
Hlucny, Frank, J.	Barnett	1898
Emma Stehlyk		
Holdahl, Bendix	Roseau	1890
Holdahl, Clara	Roseau	1895
Holdahl, Olaf	Roseau	1893
Holdahl, S. T.	Roseau	1893
Holen, S. M.	Badger	1889
Helen, Syver	Ross	1890
Sadie Hogaset		
Holland, R. O.	Ross	1889
Ingebor Besserud		
Holm, Emanuel	Jadis	1894
Katherine Sjodin		
Holm, Erick	Jadis	1886
Holm, Hans E.	Jadis	1886
Holm, John M.	Roseau	1889
Holm, Mike	Jadis	1887
Holm, Ole A.	Roseau	1886
Holter, O. C.	Nereson	1900
Houg, Petter	Soler	1899
Maret Helekson		
Houg, Thorval T.	Soler	1885
Howe, Harry L.	Jadis	1890
Howe, John H.	Roseau	1886
Howe, O. E.	Badger	1894
Mrs. O. E. Howg		
Hoyez, Leo	Warroad	1900
Hunter, J. B.	Moranville	1900
Hylland, Ole	Moose	1894
Mary Hulseth		
Ingolfsland, Gilbert	Moose	1894
Irish, Frank	Roseau	1885
Irish, Lon	Roseau	1885
Mrs. Irish and Sons		
Isakson, Erik	Moose	1896
Anna Hanson		
Jallo, Tollef	Stafford	1889
Janicke, Will	Stafford	1900
Alvina Peterson		
Janousek, Frank	Soler	1894
Jensen, Andrew C.	Spruce	1899
Jensen, T. C.	Spruce	1899
Jester, Jim	Jadis	1885
Mrs. Jim Jester and 2 daughters		
Johanson, Axel	Spruce	1892
Johanson, Erick	Spruce	1889
Johanson, Kalbjorn	Dewey	1894
Johnson, A. A.	Stafford	1891
Kristina Johnson		
Johnson, Alex	Roseau	1890
Johnson, Andre W.	Stafford	1895
Anna Charlotta Boberg		
Johnson, Andrew Jr.	Roseau	1890
Johnson, Anton	Roseau	1897
Johnson, Ben	Roseau	1896
Johnson, Carl A.	Moose	1890
Johnson, Chris	Skagen	1895
Mary Johnson		
Johnson, Erick	Roseau	1889
Johnson, Gust	Jadis	1889
Anna Boe		
Johnson, Gust Ed.	Jadis	1900
Johnson, G. J.	Malung	1890
Johnson, H. L.	Stafford	1900
Lisa Geselius		
Johnson, John	Malung	1890
Johnson, John A.	Stokes	1900
Albertena Palm		
Johnson, John M.	Roseau	1894
Johnson, J. M.	Stokes	1895
Johnson, John V.	Stokes	1890
Johnson, L. B.	Badger	1894
Johnson, Mike E.	Spruce	1899
Johnson, Nils A.	Malung	1890
Carolina Roseen		
Johnson, N. O.	Spruce	1899
Johnson, Ole J.	Nereson	1900
A. Karlson		
Johnson, Peter A.	Palmville	1895
Johnson, Richard	Lind	1900
Johnson, Sever	Warroad	1900
Johnson, E. Simon	Roseau	1888
Ida Nelson		
Johnson, Theo. R.	Malung	1890
Jones, Thomas L.	Warroad	1897
Jorgenson, C.	Dieter	1892

Kalinowski, Max	Barto	1895
Kaml, Frank	Barnett	1898
Mary Brotherston		
Kaml, Ludvig	Barnett	1898
Agnes Hlucny		
Kasprick, Joe	Poplar Grove	1900
Mary Fablula		
Kasprick, Val	Nereson	1900
Felecya Klesyk		
Kittleson, Tom	Moranville	1891
Kjellberg, Ed	Wannaska	1895
Knudson, William C.	Warroad	1898
Knutson, Alfin	Pinecreek	1897
Knutson, Arne	Pinecreek	1899
Mrs. Arne Knutson		
Kolberg, Julius P.	Barto	1899
Kompelein, Anders	Pinecreek	1890
Kompelein, Johannes	Pinecreek	1890
Kompelein, Knute	Pinecreek	1890
Kompelein, Ole	Pinecreek	1894
Krog, John O.	Dieter	1890
K. Broten		
Kveen, Gilbert G.	Jadis	1896
Kvien, Andrew	Pinecreek	1895
Kudrna, Joseph	Barnett	1897
Larson, Andrew	Stafford	1892
Larson, Fred G.	Pinecreek	1895
Minnie Bagste		
Larson, Ingeborg	Stafford	1892
Larson, John	Warroad	1892
Ingeborg Martinson		
Larson, Louis	Stafford	1892
Lydia Peterson		
Larson, Louis J.	Malung	1900
Larson, L. P.	Jadis	1895
Larson, Nels O.	Ross	1896
Anna Bergman		
Larson, Ole P.	Moranville	1897
Larson, Theo.	Deer	1899
Anna Strand		
Lee, Andrew	Pinecreek	1890
Lee, Lewis	Clear River	1894
Lerhaugen, Martin P.	Ross	1890
Kristena Andreason		
Lerhaugen, Ole M.	Ross	1890
Lien, Amund	Ross	1890
Lien, A. J.	Duxby	1895
Lien, A. T.	Pohlitz	1894
Engeborg Horveson		
Lien, Andrew O.	Barto	1895
Lien, John C.	Ross	1891
Lien, Ole J.	Ross	1887
Lindberg, Israel	Spruce	1887
Lindberg, Josie	Stafford	1890
Esther Swanson		
Lindberg, J. E.	Roseau	1887
Lindberg, H. A.	Roseau	1889
Linder, E. A.	Warroad	1893
Lindgren, J. A. R.	Lind	1896
Lindquist, John	Stafford	1895
Hanna Nelson		
Lindquist, S. O.	Roseau	1889

Mrs. S. O. Lindquist		
Lindstrom, Peter	Malung	1894
Lindtvedt, Ole O.	Ross	1897
Lins, Florence	Pohlitz	1886
Lindberg, Erick	Roseau	1887
Mrs. Erick Lindberg		
Lindland, M. C.	Badger	1893
Lisell, Lars	Malung	1891
Listug, Carl	Jadis	1889
Listug, T. K.	Jadis	1894
Lundin, J. A.	Stafford	1889
Anna Greta		
Lundquist, John	Deer	1900
Christena Pearson		
McDonald, A. E.	Warroad	1894
McFarlane, Neil	Barnett	1900
McKibbon, Thos.	Badger	1894
Madera, Frank	Falun	1900
Magnusen, Alfred	Dieter	1891
Magnuson, Carl	163-40	1888
Magnuson, John	163-40	1889
Malmskog, Carl	Stokes	1896
Amanda Olson		
Markstrom, A.	Jadis	1888
Markstrom, Herman	Jadis	1889
Amelia Peterson		
Markstrom, Leander	Fox	1890
Marschalk, Paul	Warroad	1892
Martenson, Magnus	Moranville	1898
Mathison, Ole	Stokes	1897
Mattson, John	Spruce	1894
Mattson, John	Spruce	1894
Mattson, Louis	Falun	1900
Mekash, Joseph	Barto	1896
Mikkelson, Anton	Roseau	1889
Minarik, Joe	Soler	1894
Moen, Gunder, A.	Badger	1892
Moody, Charles A.	Warroad	1893
Moorhead, R. S.	Dieter	1894
Mary Hanson		
Moran, P. W.	Moranville	1894
Mork, Erick C.	Ross	1895
Morken, Jorgen	Roseau	1890
Morken, Jul P.	Jadis	1895
Moser, Rudolph	Barnett	1898
Monika Nepple		
Mostal, Ole A.	Jadis	1894
Helga Lofthus		
Naleri, Henry	Hereim	1899
Nastrand, Samuel	Moose	1896
Petra Berg		
Neal, W. H.	Warroad	1894
Nelson, Alfred	Wannaska	1896
Nelson, August	Jadis	1890
Nelson, Ed.	Badger	1895
Nelson, Carl	Malung	1894
Nelson, Engebert	Wannaska	1895
Christina Nelson		1896
Nelson, Erick A.	Spruce	1889
Nelson, Julius	Moose	1891
Nelson, Martin	Roseau	1888
Bettie Dahlgren		

Name	Place	Year
Nelson, Nels	Moranville	1898
Nelson, N. F.	Roseau	1893
Nelson, Peter O.	Stafford	1889
Mary Roseen		
Nomeland, T. S.	Fox	1888
Nomeland, S. T.	Roseau	1888
Norgaarden, Andrew	Jadis	1894
Norjore, Even	Stokes	1896
Berget Kallak		
Norlund, Gust	Moranville	1900
Norman, Erick	Stokes	1895
Sophie Olson		
Norquist, Gust	Jadis	1888
Norquist, John	Jadis	1888
Norquist, Peter	Jadis	1887
Norquist, Louis	Jadis	1888
Novotny, James T.	Badger	1896
Christina Dostal		
Odegaard, Lars	Dieter	1893
Odegaard, Ole	Fox	1890
Ole, Even S.	Roseau	1899
Oie, Ole E.	Roseau	1895
Oie, Oliver W.	Roseau	1896
Oie, Oscar	Roseau	1896
Oie, Sven	Roseau	1885
Olsen, Anna Conelly	Roseau	1898
Olsen, Ingebret	Roseau	1888
Anna Anderson		
Olsen, O. E.	Roseau	1897
Olsen, Thore	Spruce	1899
Olson, A. B.	Hereim	1900
Olson, Berg S.	Roseau	1894
Olson, Bernt	Jadis	1887
Olson, Carl B.	Hereim	1900
Olson, Einer	Grimstad	1895
Elizabeth Halvorsen		
Olson, E. K.	Nereson	1898
Nida Olson		
Olson, F. A.	Skagen	1894
Olson, Gunder	Deer	1900
Olson, John	Skagen	1895
Olson, Lius	Beaver	1895
Olson, L. E.	Stafford	1894
Hilda Rollis		
Olson, Martin	Barnett	1899
Olson, Ole J.	Hereim	1900
Olson, Oliver	Wannaska	1895
Olson, P. A.	Beaver	1894
Omdahl, B. H.	Skagen	1897
Opheim, Ed.	Roseau	1894
Oseid, Lars	Roosevelt	1895
Osell, Ismael	Grimstad	1900
Olivia Olson		
Osterlund, Nels	Stafford	1889
Osterlund, Ole	Stafford	1889
Osterlund, P. E.	Stafford	1889
Overby, Ole Johnson	Ross	1896
Carrie Peterson		
Palm, Erick	Jadis	1892
Palm, Oscar	Jadis	1893
Paulson, Amund	Ross	1893

Name	Place	Year
Christena Olson		
Paulson, O. K.	Lind	1900
Paulson, Paul G.	Jadis	1895
Pearson, A. M.	Roseau	1892
Pederson, Peder G.	Roseau	1887
Perron, David	Laona	1900
Peterson, Alfred	Malung	1891
Peterson, Charley	Badger	1893
Peterson, C. T.	Roseau	1886
Peterson, Daniel	Malung	1886
Peterson, Henry	Lind	1899
Peterson, L.	Stafford	1889
Julia Johnson		
Peterson, L. O.	Roseau	1891
Lisa Mattson		
Petterson, C. A.	Jadis	1886
Anna Maria Johnson		
Pinta, Egnic	Barnett	1900
Pinta, Henry	Barnett	1900
Ranetklev, Otto A.	Moose	1896
Rice, O. A.	Roseau	1895
Ringus, Carl G.	Mickinock	1899
Ringus, N. J.	Mickinock	1899
Risberg, Oscar	Roseau	1888
Rodegaard, Carrie	Ross	1890
Roggenbuck, P. M.	Stokes	1900
Roseen, Erick P.	Pencer	1889
Mrs. Eric P. Roseen		
Rosen, John	Jadis	1887
Amanda Christena Larson		
Rowland, E. F.	Barto	1899
Rue, Lars S.	Ross	1889
Rugland, Lars	Pinecreek	1889
Ryder, Jim	Jadis	1885
Sanbakken, Amund	Grimstad	1894
Sandstrom, Peter	Malung	1889
Mrs. Peter Sandstrom		
Sather, B. C.	Badger	1895
Sather, Ole	Barto	1900
Schantle, John	Barnett	1898
Mary Eppleng		
Sehlstrom, Frank	Spruce	1889
Sehlstrom, Peter	Spruce	1889
Setran, Ben	Stokes	1900
Christena Syverson		
Severson, Sever	Skagen	1898
Gertrude Hemmingson		
Shafer, Samuel	Stokes	1896
Bertha Mitchel		
Simmons, Marion W.	Skagen	1894
Hattie A. Russel		
Sjaaheim, Ole T.	Roseau	1890
Sjaaheim, P. O.	Jadis	1898
Julia Halvorson		
Sjel, G. O.	Lind	1900
Sjoberg, Erick	Roseau	1888
Mrs. Eric Sjoberg		
Sjoberg, Israel	Roseau	1889
Sjoberg, Peter	Badger	1889
Sjoberg, Richard	Roseau	1891
Sjoqvist, Alex	Grimstad	1894
Jennie Olson		

Skog, Charley	Stafford	1893
Johanna Erickson		
Skog, Fred	Roseau	1890
Skoglund, J. U.	Roseau	1890
Skogman, John M.	Pohlitz	1896
Skogstad, Johannes	Pinecreek	1890
Skogstad, Nils	Pinecreek	1890
Skoin, Martin	Malung	1900
Sletto, Chris	Ross	1888
Sogge, Ed	Stokes	1895
Sogge, Tobias	Stokes	1895
Bertha Dimdal		
Solom, Anders	Jadis	1888
Caroline Hogfos Simonson		
Solom, Andres	Dieter	1891
Sonsteng, Hans	Jadis	1888
Lena Larson		
Sonsteng, Jacob	Jadis	1889
Lena Borgstad		
Sorteberg, Arne	Jadis	1890
Sponheim, Theo W.	Stafford	1895
Stacy, Frank	American	1893
Stanislawski, Jos. J.	Polonia	1895
Starren, Anton	Jadis	1895
Gelina Hagen		
Stebbins, G. M.	Roseau	1900
Stenbakken, T. O.	Ross	1893
Mary Oldsdatter		
Stenmoe, O. C.	Dewey	1900
Stephenson, William	Poplar Grove	1900
Margaretha Gudmunson		
Stoffel, Henry	Barnett	1898
Julai Henrickson		
Storey, Robert J.	Jadis	1899
Margreta Lofstedt		
Strandberg, Magnus	Stafford	1893
Elizabeth Maria Pearson		
Strandberg, Peter E.	Stafford	1893
Margaret Larson		
Strandlund, Peter	Roseau	1887
Stolz, Henry	Warroad	1899
Stromquist, John E.	163-40	1889
Carry Goranson		
Sunderland, J. S.	Badger	1893
Sutton, William J.	American	1887
Svegdahl, John	Lind	1899
Svegdahl, Nels O.	Lind	1899
Swanson, A. M.	Roseau	1889
Swanson, Fred	Roseau	1895
Annie Peterson		
Swanson, F. W.	Roseau	1898
Swanson, Nils	Stafford	1900
Swenson, James	Malung	1895
Svenson, S.	Roseau	1896
Syverson, Peter	Beaver	1890
Teske, Albert	Dewey	1897
Thompson, S.	Deer	1900
Christena Anderson		
Tollefson, Halvor	Pohlitz	1896
Engeber Gunderson		
Tomasek, James	Soler	1896
A. Barto		
Tonneslan, Sigur	Deer	1900
Mary Knutson		
Tox, C. L.	Dewey	1900
Trandem, Hans	Roseau	1888
Trandem, H. O.	Roseau	1889
Tweeton, Mrs. O. G.	Juneberry	1894
Tykeson, C.	Ross	1889
Aslan Bratrud		
Vinge, Ole	Stafford	1895
Anna Mary Odrud		
Voaklander, H. W.	America	1895
Waag, A.	Roseau	1894
Wagge, Rasmus	Hereim	1900
Wahlberg, J. E.	Warroad	1890
Walker, John A.	Laona	1900
Wallin, Paul	Roseau	1894
Walsh, John J.	Hereim	1899
Waterman, Roswell	Jadis	1887
Wellen, Jelmer	Badger	1896
Westling, J.	Wannaska	1894
White, Frank	Jadis	1894
Wicklander, Erick	Grimstad	1894
Anna Carlson		
Wicklander, Gust R.	Salol	1895
Wicklander, John	Grimstad	1894
Hulda Nelson		
Wickstrom, Andrew	Skagen	1894
Christena Swan		
Wickstrom, Lars	Stafford	1888
Sigrud Matson		
Wickstrom, Lars, F.	Norland	1889
Winterhaus, Isaac	Spruce	1889
Wittak, Anthony	Barnett	1897
Barbara Svoboda		
Wold, Knut J.	Stafford	1892
Berget Myhre		
Wold, N. E.	Roseau	1894
Wood, Seward W.	Roseau	1886
Wurschmidt, Jacob	Roseau	1893
Wroblewski, M.	Nereson	1899
Zelinski, John	Falun	1899
Martha Korinta		

History of Churches in Roseau County

"There is no doubt," said Father Shanahan when he wrote about the history of his parish, "that mass was said in 1732 (year of George Washington's birth) when La Verendrye in search of the Northwest Passage built Fort St. Charles on what is now Magnuson Island in Lake of the Woods. Mass was said by Father Mesaiger, a Jesuit. He was succeeded by Father Jean-Pierre Aulneau, S. J., who was massacred when he and twenty Frenchmen, one a son of La Verendrye, were on their way to Mackinac Island for supplies."

The churces in the county in the very early days were almost all the result of the spiritual hunger of the homesteaders. Very often the organizational meeting was held in a home in a small community, called by a zealous homesteader or a minister who worked in the area and sensed the need for a church. In the early days when transportation was a prime problem and roads were poor or nonexistent there was a need for many churches. These churches became, beside their spiritual homes, the social center for hard working farm people. The usual procedure to erect a church was by subscription from the congregation at a time when a dollar donation was a sacrifice. People also contributed in lumber, and especially in cooperative labor when a building bee would raise the rafters of the church, while the quilting bee provided a worthwhile project for the Ladies' Aid meetings.

The trend in the modern day, as in many phases of life, is for mergers – fewer and bigger churches, and the people of the North Land are a solid, spiritually minded people with ideals. The churches with a brief history were:

1888 – Rose Lutheran located 3½ miles west of Roseau. The first meeting was at Gunwald Overvold's home with Rev. Askeland serving as pastor. Charter members were: G. Overvold, Gilbert Thompson, Osten Haugen, Mikkel Anderson, Gilbert Pederson, Peter Skagen, Ole Lien, Christian Hemmestad, Peter Boe, Iver Torfin, Nils Boe, L. Vikstrom, Siggur Nomeland and families. The first building was erected in 1896.

1890 – Pinecreek Lutheran church held services first in Arne Knutson's home. First child baptized was Otto Lyste in Otto Lund's home. First building was built in 1894 of the lumber intended for a fort during the Indian scare in 1891.

1890 – Roselund Lutheran Church was organized at home of Lars Rue to form the Evangelistic Lutheran Congregation. Charter members were: Syver Rue (father of Edward Erickson), Andrew Hallick, Syver Holm, and Syver Holen and families. The first baptism was Reinus Johnson and in 1892 the marriage of Thomas Venaas and Gena Odegaard was solemnized. First burial service was for Louis Henry Thompson in 1893.

1893 – Seventh Day Adventist Church of Roseau was started with a membership of 16. Charter families were L. Haglund, Louis Wallin, John Nyquist, A. Ritchey, Vaugh, Averill, Carle, Gilbert Budd, Tripp (parents of Mrs. Budd), Mrs. Julia Peterson, Israel Lindberg, Knut Sjaaheim, Andrew Johnson, Roy Briggs, N. C. Wilson. (initials not available for some).

1894 – Mission Covenant Church of Roseau was started in Risberg home by J. U. Skoglund and Andrew Danielson. Families who were charter members were: Erick Carlin, Andrew Danielson, A. Risberg, N. E. Lindquist, P. E. Rosen, C. E. Steel and J. U. Skoglund. A string band was started with members of the church in 1933.

1894 – First Evangelical Lutheran Church of Roseau was organized in 1890 in the Henrick Johnson home. The first church was the barn of "church Nelson" built 1½ miles east of Roseau north of the Indian trail. A log church was built but the first service was held in the Wickstrom home as the new church had no stove. Official name of the church was Swedish Evangelical Lutheran Church of Spruce. Charter members with their families were: Jacob Lindberg, Erick Sjoberg, Nils Risberg, John Risberg, Lars Wickstrom, Salomon Danielson, Salomon Sehlstrom, Anders Wickstrom, Hans Bjorkman, Isak Lundquist, Salomon Lofstadt, Nils Lindquist, Erick Johnson, Ole Johnson, Paulus Sjodin, Nils E. Nelson and Elias Lundquist. In 1899 it became officially the Swedish Lutheran Church.

1895 – Moe Lutheran Church of Roseau which was called the Rose Church started at the home of Knut O. Dokken. Charter families were: Lars Kveen, Knut O. Dokken, M. A. Norgaarden, Gust Johnson, Nels Nyhus, Gjermud Vistad, Gilbert Halvorsen, Gilbert Pederson, Peter Boe, Tore Listug, John Halvorson, Nils F. Nelson, John Dahlen, Nels Boe and A. Randahl.

1895 – The Melum Lutheran Church was organized at the home of Thomas Venaas. Charter families were: Andreas Larson, Andreas Lind, Ole Moen, Andreas Ostenson, Ole Lien, Andreas Everson, Martin C. Braaten, B. Staboe, Guldbrand Braaten, John Krog, Kristofer Braaten, Amund Lien, Ole Dahlshug, Hans Erickson, Torgrim Stenbekken, Amund Paulson, Hans Eken, Carl Tykeson, Bjor Eken, Thomas Venaas, Ole Mattson, Torris Kleberg, Ole Balle, Christian Leines, Andreas Johnson, Osten Haugen, Gulbrand Bertilrud, N. E. Wold, Ellis Rodegaard, E. H. Haaby, Syver Erickson, and Paul Dahlshug.

1895 – Bethania Lutheran Free Church of Greenbush was first organized at the E.

K. Sandvig home. Charter families were: Ole Benson, Anders Hanson, Mike Johnson, T. Lannegraff, John Rein, Karl O. Rein, Evind Suby, and G. A. Thoen. Rev. Reinhard Huglen (father of Erling Huglen, pastor of the Moe Church at the present time) was one of the early pastors starting in 1915. This church was merged with the Pauli Church and the Zion Church of Greenbush in November, 1973, to become The United Free Lutheran Church of Greenbush.

1895 – Father Aulneau Memorial Church of Warroad also named St. Mary's Catholic Church was first served by Father Aamodt who was an itinerant priest who served churches along the Rainy River. The present church commemorates the massacre of Father Aulneau and the La Verendrye party on an island in Lake of the Woods. Dedication for the new St. Mary's Catholic church occurred in 1944.

1897 – St. Aloyius Catholic Church of Greenbush was built on land donated by the Kaszukowskis. The first organizational meeting was held at the home of Anton Kukowski. The charter families were: Anton Kukowski, Joe and Francis Stanislowski, Andrew Pelowski, Blawats, Burke, Theo Wojceichowski, Joe Nardock, Landowski, Cebulski, Sheras, Bac, Debrczak, Wirkus, John Pelowski, John Zabraski, Majowski, Pelinski, Mekacz, Janouske, and Rayowskis. The first priest was Father Anton Drewnicki. (The initials of the families are not always available).

1897 – The Lutheran Church called the Oiland Church was organized with the first baptism in 1899. The work was begun by Rev. Bestul. The charter members were: O. E. Haugen who donated 3 acres of land for the church, A. Nelson, B. O. Christianson, Peter Nelson, B. M. Sillerud, T. O. Melby, Iver Sodnak. Anna Erickson, daughter of O. E. Haug is the oldest living member of the church. It was named "Oiland" meaning island as the church land was surrounded by swamp at the time.

1898 – Pauli Church of Greenbush was formed by people from Hatton, North Dakota who lived east of Pelan. The charter families are: Sven Dufwa, John Thompson, Severt Hetland, Edward Holen, Throm Jermanson, L. Lysne, A. Berg, Ellert Hanson, C. Alme, Asle Asleson, T. Stave, Andreas Smestad, Nils Pladson, Reier Myran, Enbgret Myran, A. Share, Syvert Skogstad, Knut Anderson, C. L. Tox, and Halver Johnson. The first minister to serve was Rev. Halfdan Simonson. This church merged with the Bethania, and Zion churches to become the United Free Church of Greenbush.

1898 – Bethel Evangelical Lutheran Church (Roselund Congregation) of Stafford was started in a log church under the leadership of Magnus Strandberg. Missionary Peter Dahlquist served the congregation at the beginning.

1898 – Bethany Evangelical Lutheran Church of Badger was started through the efforts of Rev. Mattson. The charter families were: Andrew O. Erickson and twenty other families (names not available). Church was merged with Our Savior's in 1941 and the name has since been changed to Our Redeemer's Lutheran Church.

1899 – Badger Catholic Church (St. Mary's) was started in the Reilly home. The following families were the charter members: J. Lynch, R. Moser, Barto, Johnson, Kelly, Batosh, La Roche, Goslin, Pelowski, Florenz Lins, Svir, and Meirs. First priest was Father Charles Deshaies.

1899 – The Methodist Church of Roseau was started especially so services could be in English. The first service was held above the Sjoberg store which is now the J. C. Penney location. The church was built south of the Norval Ness home. Charter families were: G. A. Robinson, Mildred Robinson, R. J. Bell, Mary Hodgeman, Thoe Thorson, Ida Thorson, and Robert Storey.

1900 – Concordia Lutheran Church of Ross was started at the home of Henry Lockrem with the official name of Concordia Norsk Evangelical Lutheran Menighed i Dieter, and was the first Norwegian Synod Church in the county. The charter families were: Trules Ellenson, Henry Lockrem, Gustav Springen, Oscar Johnson, Peder Halvorson, Halvor Gryte Tineus Johnson, Halvor Soland, Alfred Soland, Syneeva Johnson, Alfred Johnson, Eli Lockrem, Theodore Ellenson, Vetle Knutson, O. Dalby, Martin Braaten, Ole Hippe, Ander Lee, and Edwin Ellenson. The church was destroyed by fire in 1974.

1901 – Zion Lutheran Church of Greenbush was served first by Pastor Birkelo Charter families were: Gernilus Heieie, Hans Heieie, Ole Ostby, Elof Olson, and Ole Halgrimson. This church merged with the Pauli Church and Bethania on November 12, 1973 to become the United Free Lutheran of Greenbush.

1901 – The Bethlehem Lutheran Church of Roseau was organized at the home of Gilbert Anderson. The first officers were: Rev. J. L. Adrianson, C. L. Hagen, Harold Dalager, Lars Dalager, Gilbert Arneson, and Jacob Hermanson, Syver Braaten, Ole Rolandson, and Mrs. Karen Dalager. The first services were held in Karen Sogn Dalager's log house. In 1912 a group from Poplar Grove joined the Bethlehem church.

1903 – The Union Church of Warroad was originally a Presbyterian Church. It was founded by Pastor Herbert McHenry. Charter members were: George Murray, Mrs. Angeline Roundy, John Stein, Mrs. Love, Louis Beckwith, Mrs. Edith Roberts, and Mrs. Hunt and families. The first pastor was Rev. Sidebotham, and the original church building was on Robert Street. The name was changed in 1920 to Warroad Union Church. January 7, 1972 it was withdrawn from United Church of Christ and affiliated with Association of Congregations of Christian Churches.

1904 – Messiah Lutheran Church of Roseau was started with P. C. Boyd as the first pastor. The charter members families were: Ole Oie, O. A. Rice, Louis Rice, S. O. Braaten, Knute Torgerson, and G. L. Hope. The first name was St. Olaf Evangelisk Luthersk Menighet of Roseau. In 1905 these families joined the church: S. T. Holdahl, Swen Oie, Ole Holm, Mrs. R. Olsen, Miss Clara Olsen, A. O. Hagen, E. E. Bert, and Torbjorn Holdahl. The name was changed in 1922 to English Evangelical Lutheran Congregation of Roseau and the parish included Riverside at Wannaska, and Pine Grove of River.

1904 – Zion Lutheran Church of Warroad was first called the Swedish Evangelical Lutheran Church. Student pastor A. P. Biddeson served the Warroad parish followed by Rev. H. O. Hemming who came from Roseau on foot to conduct services. There were 17 charter members at organizational time. The Swift church was a part of the parish at the outset, but merged completely in 1941. The first church building was on the south side of the river, and now a new structure has been built off Lake Street.

1905 – The Immanuel Lutheran Church (Missouri Synod) was started at first for the German speaking people in the area. Rev. Hitzman was the first to serve the church followed by Rev. Seltz who came from Thief River Falls by horse and buggy to conduct services. Charter families were: Paul Klema and A. R. Bruss. The church was dissolved in 1964.

1905 – Willow Creek Lutheran Church was organized at the home of Anton Johnson with Pastor H. O. Hemming in charge. The charter families were: Mrs. Annie M. Johnson, Florence Olson Tveit, Leslie Tveit, Raymond Olson, Edgar Johnson, Alfhild Johnson, Agnes Hessler, Lavina Olson, Herbert Johnson, and Marvin Kling.

1905 – Gustav Adolph Lutheran Church of Strathcona was organized at the Jevne store. The charter families were Knute Jevne, Ole Holmstead, Ed Johnson, Sivert Gjovik, O. Olson, A. Angman, Monds Grondahl, G. Gunheim, Gulleck Beito, John Lundquist, Hans Lerum, and Loren Lorenson. The first service was held in a school house with Pastor Skogerboe in charge. Members from Trinity Lutheran Church later joined the church.

1906 – The Catholic Church of Benwood was first served by Father John Marslik in Benwood, twenty miles south of Badger. St. Joseph's chapel was built in 1919 by Father Charles Keyser.

1906 – The Immanuel Church of Badger was organized at the John Vik home. The charter families were: Hans Hanson, Peter Hegstad, Tom Kittleson, Elof Kittleson, John A. Johnson, Torger Olson, Martin Mannen, Fred Andol, John Krog and Nils M. Cedarholm. The church was merged with Badger Creek, Roselund, and Hostas and four unorganized churches and they called Paster J. S. Bestul.

1907 – The Episcopal Church of Warroad which had purchased the Baptist Church received their charter in 1907. The charter families were: H. Lundbohm, C. Moody, P. Soderstrom, and Mae MacDonald. The church was moved from Lake Street to Robert Street and then to the corner of Wabasha and McKenzie Ave.

1907 – The First Evangelical Lutheran Church of Salol was formed chiefly through the efforts of the Ladies' Aid. After the log building built by Andrew Mattson burned the services were held in the Westman school house with Pastor Hemming conducting services. After a meeting in the Sjoberg Hall in Salol in 1919, the church was called First Lutheran Church of Salol. The charter families were: Jens Brandt, H. C. Hanson, Alfred Hagglund, Louis Lofquist, Christoffer Mellstrom, Gunnar Nelson, Jonas Roseen, A. O. Staveness, Erick Wickstrom and Edward Videen families. A church building was erected in 1922.

1908 – The Pine Grove Lutheran Church was organized at the home of Tom Thompson with Rev. N. J. Njus presiding. The charter families were: John Sannan, Lorentz Espe, Tom Thompson, John and Geland Grudfor, L. O. Berge, Gunder Hammer, John Lee, B. Luglum, Olav Eikland, Julius Bjerke, L. Stolsvik and Mrs. Ann Holmstrom.

1909 – Sacred Heart Catholic Church of Roseau started their services in a section house with Father August Beyne conducting. A gift from the Extension Society of Chicago Home Missions, a donation of a lot by Dean Benson, and gifts and an organ by Dr. Delmore, Sr. was the start of the church. A building was moved from Gatzke in 1943 for the church. The first child baptized was Pat Delmore. A new edifice has been built in Roseau in 1965.

1910 – The Catholic Church of Falun later was named St. Philip's Mission Church of Falun and was started by Polish families. Father Drewnicki of Leo first said mass in the homes of Anton Zak and Ralph Barnes. A church building was erected with donations and $1,000 grant from the Catholic Church Extension Society and Father Philippe of Warroad conducted the first service in the new church. In 1953 the church became affiliated with the Roseau Church.

1911 – The Lutheran Church of Spruce was first called Golmenighet. The first meeting was in the home of Ole Lund. The charter families were: Peter Dahl, Ole J. Lund, Andrew Jensen, Lars Lund, Ole Arneson, Peter Brenhaug, Ole Olafson, Willie Grand, Mrs. Christi Olson, Mrs. Guri Sherven and Mrs. Mina Skog. After the old church burned in 1972 a new church was built immediately.

1912 – The Baptist Church of Roseau was first called the Swedish Baptist Church. The charter families were: Peter Norquist, Erick Palm, Karen Lind, Margaret Anderson, Mrs. E. W. Wicklander, Julia Erickson, Helen John and Mr. Andrew Johnson. Meetings were first held in homes and then in the Presbyterian church. C. C. Norling was the first pastor, and it was during his stay that the church was built.

1912 – The Norland Congregation was organized as the combined units of a group of pioneers under the leadership of Rev. Knut Gjesfjeld with the Salol Inner Mission Society and the second part was the present congregation under the leadership of Rev. A. C. Rykken. Charter families were: Alfred Olson, A. A. Hattling, P. B. Olson, Andrew Mattson, Conrad Corneliusen, August Lindgren, C. A. Danielson, Severn Smedsmo, Richard Peterson, Simon Brein, Anton Knutson, J. E. Berquist, Erick Mattson, Martin Brenhaug, Erick Olafson, Anna Lindgren and Agaton Lindgren. It was affiliated with the Free Lutherans in 1966.

1914 – Blessed Sacrement Parish of Greenbush was the first part of the Baudette parish but in 1914 Father Bossus was sent to serve this station. The charter families were: P. M. Brost, George Burke, Paul Hogan, John Foldesi, J. M. McCut, Alex Goslein, F. Johnson, and J. J. Walsh. Father Hipplit Skopowski became the first permanent pastor.

1919 – The Bethesda Skaninavisk Lutherski Minighed was the name given to the church in Skime. Charter families were: Thore Loken, Andrew Skime, Tom Skime, Rika Dole, Ole Kittleson, Charley Puttbrese, Mrs. Hannah Gould, Mrs. Winters, Emmet Winters and Alice Mork. A. T. Moen first served as minister. The first service was held in the Community hall. The church merged with the A.L.C. in 1963.

1924 – The Bethel Lutheran Church of Greenbush is the name given to the merged church of St. Olaf and Haugust Church.

1930 – The Mission Covenant Churches were started in Pencer, and in 1934 in Warroad.

1934 – Evangelical Free Church of Strathcona is a member of the Evangelical Free Church of America. A church was purchased at Hickson, North Dakota, dismantled and brought to Strathcona.

1934 – The Mennonite Church of Warroad came into existence through the efforts of five families that left the drought area of Lost Wood, North Dakota. These charter families were: D. S. Heppner, Peter Heppner, George Krahn, and C. I. Krahn. Arthur Ortmann of Marion, South Dakota was called to serve the church and it was named the

Woodland Mennonite Church. A chapel was dedicated in 1939.

1939 – The Full Gospel Assembly was started by Rev. M. R. Cory in Roseau. A church was built in 1950 and the church entered into cooperative fellowship with the Minnesota District Council of the Assemblies of God. A new church was built in 1964.

1940 – The Jehovah's Witness Church built their Kingdom Hall in 1940 in Badger and built one in Roseau in 1970. The first presiding minister was Ludwig Rasmusson.

1958 – St. Luke's Church at Northwest Angle was built through the united effort of the residents at the Angle, spearheaded by Dan Carvers and Norman Carlsons. The land for the little church was donated by the Carlsons, and the congregation donated an oak cross. The first one to be buried in the emetery there was Mrs. Norman Carlson; an altar was placed in the church in her memory. (This church is not in Roseau County).

1966 – Free Lutheran Church of Roseau with Rose, Spruce, and Norland parishes is a merged church. The first worship was held in the old Seven Day Adventist church, but later the Immanuel Church was purchased and moved for the congregation. The charter families are: R. Bergstrom, M. Broten, J. Dahlen, B. Danielson, F. Drown, C. Elgin, G. Erickson, E. Falk, A. Gislason, T. Haglund, A. Helstad, H. Johnson, W. Johnson, A. McDonald, O. Mostal, Martin and Gilmet Peterson, G. Rugland, L. Skoglund, F. Swenson, Art and Luverne Welin, G. Wickstrom, E. Ziska, E. Olson, D. Johnson, O. Johnson, and Mary Peterson.

List of Persons where Farm or Business has been in family in Roseau County up to 90 years, and is in the family name at present.

Owner – 67 years
Gelina Starren
Maynard Erickson
Oscar Palm – Gladys Palm Rugland

Owner – 68 years
Albert Hayes – Frederick P. Hayes
Mrs. Adolph Vertina – Orville Vertina

Owner – 69 years
Oliver Venaas – Gladys A. Venaas
Clifford Comstock – Robert E. Comstock
Will Brandt

Owner – 70 years
Mrs. John Roadfeldt

Owner – 71 years
Walter Wiskow – Cordell Wiskow
Tollef Halvorson – Taylor Halvorson
Bertha Hedlund – John Hedlund
Ed Vacura – Josephine Vacura
Torger Torgerson – Gelina Torgerson Lien
Arthur Mattson
Clifford Mattson
Harold Peterson – Harold Peterson, Jr.
John Halvorson – Gaylord Halvorson

Owner – 72 years
Carl Landin
Harold Forsness
Clifford Hamlin
Ole O. Lee – Robert G. Lee
Mrs. Erick Bjorkman – Luell and Eileen Bjorkman
Lars Kveen – Leonard Kveen

Owner – 73 years
Rasmus Lorenson – Randall Lorenson
Mrs. P. A. Larson – Reuben Larson
Mrs. Bruce Hamlin – John W. Hamlin
Ragna Lee – Emil O. Lee
Ira Brandli – Rose Brandli
Sylvia Holm – Oscar M. Holm
Leland M. Lee
Augustson Brothers
Oscar Johnson
Mrs. Jonas T. Johnson – Clarence Johnson
William Rusch – Doris B. Dowers

Owner – 74 years
Mrs. Ernest Fugleberg
Olaf Bjorhus
M. G. Bertilrud – Edwin M. Bertilrud
Mary Elton – John T. Elton
Olaf Billberg – Paul Billberg
Andrew Toft – Earl Toft

Owner – 75 years
Mrs. Emma Hedin – Herman and Roy Hedin
Leonard Herling
Axel Majer
Elmer Majer
David Erickson – Lillian Erickson
Raleigh Johnson
Roy Zuberbier – David Zuberbier
Otto C. Johnson

Owner – 76 years
Theodore Dostal
Gust Gustafson – Cecilia Gustafson
Gilbert Kveen – Gustav and Roy Kveen

Owner – 77 years
Andrew O. Anderson – Joseph Anderson
Palmer Haugtvedt
Mrs. V. R. Berry – V. R. Berry
Rudolph Moser – James O. Glen (Gr. Gr. Son)
Arthur Broten

Owner – 78 years
Albin Mork – Michael F. Yager (Gr. Son)
Elmer Benson – Layton and Marie Oslund
Jalmer Wellen – Jesse Wellen

Owner – 79 years
Myron Johnson
Emil Tomasek
Andy Erickson – Sheldon Erickson

Owner – 80 years
Charles Egstad
Arthur Egstad
O. E. Suby – Leonard and Selmer Suby
Hannah Monsrud
Joseph Stanislawski
Alfred Magnusson – Frederick and Henry Magnusson
Clarence N. Wold

Owner – 81 years
Mina Besserud
Lena Besserud
Mrs. Joe Christianson – Sonia Christianson Foster
Mrs. Inger Gordon – Arthur B. Gorden
Clarence Larsen
M. B. Magnusson – Allen G. Magnusson
Albin Oslund
Albert Brandt – Edson Brandt
Richard Mattson
Karen Fugelberg

Owner – 82 years
Mrs. Oscar Nelson
Clyde Evans
John Breiland
Edgar Johnson – Lavern C. Johnson

Owner – 83 years
None

Owner – 84 years
John Nelson
Mrs. Cecelia Roseen

Owner – 85 years
Nels Braaten

Owner – 86 years
Mrs. Hannah Efshen – Albert Efshen
Albert Besserud
James A. Dahlen
Mrs. Albert Kvien
Ole Vistad
Augustine Wierschke – Kenneth Wierschke

Owner – 87 years
Martin Pederson

Owner – 88 years
Axel Roseen
Helmer Halvorson
John Rosen – Mary Rosen

Owner – 89 years
Emmanuel Holm – Manfred Holm
George Lins

Businesses

Leland Lee – 76 years
George Marvin – 71 years
Clifford Nordine (gr. Son of Luverne Oseid – 66 years
Julius Anderson – Julius Anderson, Jr. – 61 years

ROSEAU STONE: A Brief Case-History of the so-called ROSEAU STONE

This stone has been found near Roseau, Minnesota, before 1927 by Mr. Jake Nelson. The authenticity of its finding is known to Mr. P. O. Frykund, Clerk of Court in Roseau; Mrs. Martin a sister of the finder; Mr. C. P. Bull, State Department of Agriculture, St. Paul, and Hon. Mike Holm, Secretary of our State, who personally investigated the case in loco. Hon. Mike Holm is the owner of this stone, also keeper and recorder of all facts connected with this archaeological find from the Stone-Age of Minnesota.

In 1927 Hon. Mike Holm submitted this

stone to the Department of Anthropology of the University of Minnesota, Prof. A. E. Jenks, for investigation.

John Jager, a member of the Institute of Architects, living at 6 Red Cedar Lake in Minneapolis received this monument from Prof. A. E. Jenks as to "what you can make out of it . . ." for being a student of the so-called Stone-Age literature and its Paleography . . . subjected this stone to painstaking scrutiny under all angles of approach. The motto of his guidance for doing this work remained at all time the archaeologist maxim: HOW EASY IT IS TO SEE A PART, . . . HOW HARD, TO SEE THE WHOLE.

First of all, the investigator ascertained those basic compositional features, which always characterize man's art in seeking and giving its expression through matter. This stone, in its form, by man's selection responded to evaluation for its **proportion** (up and down), for its **direction** (front and rear) and for its **mass-symmetry** in front observation, (right and left.)

Under these three agenda the form disclosed a **miniature human head** of such dimensional limitations: proportion 2 inches, by direction 1⅜ inches, by symmetry (all over) 7/16 inch.

In looking en-face we discover in further, a band of **an inscriptional ribbon** average ⅜ of an inch wide, contouring the entire face as a seam or border of a headgear, well recognized by students of medieval costume. This ribbon is masterly selected for its graphic propensities.

The stone in itself is admirably chosen for its petrographical virtue: degree of resistance to the elements. An artist in sterothomy and naturalist, the producer of this miniature document must have been . . . .

For two years Prof. Jager reviewed the Roseau-Stone, in his spare time. Numerous photographs were taken of it, in diffused light, and under sunbeam for holding of its artificial characteristics . . . in whole and in detail . . .

The ribbon of inspiration became available in enlargement in a developed flat, by being pieced together from units. This laid the basis for a **palaeographic** approach concerning the inscription.

There is no doubt about the existence of an archaic script, of which some kinds are known to indigenous Europe. The script must have been a master in handling **ligatures**. There are actually two lines of text in evidence; the upper one, distinct and pronounced, the lower, fragmentary or interfunctioning with the upper, much in the character as observed on runic calendars (see, "Calendarie Runnico," Museum of Bologna, 4 photographs).

There are **distinct letters** in evidence, bringing even to our age a positive proof and authority that this monument with its painstakingly carved inscription is genuine and outstanding as work of man of long ago . . ., damaged as it is.

It is regrettable that this stone that resisted the ravages of ages in an extreme climate, when found in Roseau, Minnesota became at once an object of "doubt" even as to its genuine existence, misunderstood for its high compositional virtue, unappreciated for its historical significance, . . . in short, . . . authoritively degraded by a scientifically narrow and abberated posterity. . . .

It so happened:
In 1929 Jager sent all his data as described above to Prof. A. E. Jenks, returning to him also the Roseau-Stone at the same time.

On January 14, 1930 A. E. Jenks called Jager on the telephone. The following conversation issued:

Professor A. E. Jenks: "The stone which supposedly was found in Roseau and which you (Jager) contend to be an artifact, bearing an inscription by human hand (passed on to Professor C. R. Stauffer, Department of Geology in our University for investigation. Prof. Stauffer thoroughly cleaned that stone and analyzed it petrographically. He ascertained beyond any doubt that the stone does not show any work by human hand. There is no ribbon of writing on it, the kind you believe. He is in position to show you dozens of just such stones in his department, all works of nature in their designs — fully concurring his opinion.

Jager: "Do you truly believe it?"

Prof. Jenks: "I must, as it comes from an authority. We are not any more interested in this stone. (I shall see that it is returned to Mike Holm. . . ."

Through kindness of Mr. C. P. Bull I obtained again the Roseau Stone from Hon. Mike Holm desirous to ascertain the degree of mutilation which it must have experienced at the hands of "authorities." They surely gave it an acid bath and brushing, whereby all its archaeological patina became lost, its scriptural finesse obliterated. Researched away, forever.

It is fortunate that there are photographs of this stone in existence before it struck the University Laboratories. Archaeologically minded men should never had permitted such a rough handling of an object, unique and strange, and little understood.

Herewith I return the Roseau Stone to Hon Mike Holm, its owner. Attached to it is an arrow found by Mr. C. P. Bull upon the site where the stone had been found before. The time will come when more of such characteristic artifacts shall appear. The soil of Minnesota may yield them proving that there was an undisputed connection of our Northwest with Europe of long ago. Such "strangers" as the little stone of Roseau should be saved from subversion. The archaeology of a new day should accord them an impartial documentation. There is still more work ahead . . . and "authorities" better be careful because the judgement by posterity is still ahead, upon the Ribbon of Time.

Signed,
John Jager
6 Red Cedar Lane
Minneapolis, Minnesota

CEMETERIES

By I. A. Sunset

There are 81 burial places. Of these thirty-eight are Protestant, and of these four are abandoned; eight Catholic with only one abandoned. Locations of all these cemeteries have been filed on a county map, which is on file in the Roseau County Historical file.

Following is the list, location, time established and sponsor:

America — The SE NE Sec. 11; established July 3, 1926; non-sectarian; maintained.

Beaver — NE NE, Sec. 7; established 1905; non-sectarian; abandoned.

Barnett — SW of Sec. 2, name Zisco, a lodge; established 1906; maintained.

Barto — NW NW, Sec. 20; St. Aloysius Catholic Church, Leo; established 1898; maintained.

Barto — SE NE, Sec. 13, Bethania, Lutheran Free Church; established 1900; seldom used.

Barto — Hvidso cemetery of old Greenbush, Sec. 36; established 1896; long abandoned.

Blooming Valley — Egeland cemetery, Lutheran Free Church; Sec. 33; established 1911; maintained.

Clearriver — Township cemetery, NW NE, Sec. 26; established about 1910; records burned years ago.

Dewey — Pauli, the Pelan church; NE quarter, Sec. 29; Evangelical Lutheran Church; established 1898; maintained.

Dieter — Concordia at Ross; SW quarter, Sec. 28; Evangelical Lutheran Church; established Sept. 20, 1900; maintaned.

Dieter — Pine Creek, SW SW, Sec. 34; Evangelical Lutheran Church; established Dec. 1, 1890; maintained.

Dieter — Old Pinecreek cemetery; SW SW, Sec. 8; established 1896; abandoned.

Dieter — Indian cemetery; SW quarter, Sec. 26; village of Ross; abandoned.

Dieter — Indian graves; SE NW, Sec. 3; abandoned.

Dieter — Indian graves on old Jorgenson farm; Sec. 23.

Deer — Poplar Grove cemetery; SW quarter, Sec. 24; established 1906; maintained.

Deer — Greenwood at Strathcona, Sec. 35; E. L. C.; established 1908, maintained.

Enstrom — Fairview, NW NW, Sec. 31; non-denominational; established April 3rd, 1957.

Elkwood — Winner, St. John's Township cemetery; Sec. 8; established 1919, maintained.

Elkwood — Penturen St. Joseph's Catholic; Sec. 25, established 1928; abandoned.

Elkwood — Private on farm, SW, Sec. 21; established 1917; (Davis children).

Elkwood — Private on farm, Sec. 10; burial 1916 (Anton Hagen's grave).

Elkwood — At Winner, one grave, private burial 1917 (Mrs. Sigurd Johnson).

Falun — St. Phillips Catholic; SW SW, Sec. 31; established Feb. 25th, 1915.

Falun — Township cemetery; SW SW, Sec. 21; established 1905; maintained.

Golden Valley — Casperson cemetery; L. F. C., SW SW, Sec. 21; established 1910; maintained.

Hereim — Bethenia in Greenbush; L. F. C., established 1904; maintained.

Hereim — Blessed Sacrament; Catholic (in Greenbush), established April 24th, 1915; maintained.

Hereim — Bethel (St. Olafs); Sec. 10; E. L. C., established 1905; maintained.

Huss — Lawrenson cemetery; SW SE, Sec. 22; L. F. C., established 1916; maintained.

Jadis — Moe Rose; L. F. C., NW quarter, Sec. 21; established July 18th, 1888; maintained.

Jadis — Moe-Rose, old abandoned; also in Sec. 21, NW corner, established 1888; abandoned.

Jadis — Hope Roseau; Sec. 24; established Nov. 8th, 1916; maintained.

Jadis — Sacred Heart, Catholic; Sec. 24; established Nov. 2nd, 1938; maintained.

Jadis — Private on Lofsted farm ½ mi. south of Roseau; 2 Howe graves.

Jadis — In the small village park; Block 2, Holdahl's add.; one Indian grave.

Jadis — In Sec. 26; first white woman to die in this part of County. (grave on creek bank).

Laona — Silent City (Roosevelt); City cemetery established June 10th, 1911; maintained.

Lind — Bethlehem; NE NE, Sec. 10; E. L. C. established 1901; maintained.

Malung — Township cemetery; SE SE,

Sec. 9; established 1893; recorded Feb. 23rd, 1953; maintained.

Malung – Private.

Poplar Grove – St. Joseph's; Catholic; Sec. 21; established 1918; maintained.

Pohlitz – Duxby cemetery; E. L. C.; SE SE, Sec. 26; established 1904; maintained.

Pohlitz – Private; Wm. Smith farm; Sec. 25; established 1898; maintained.

Pohlitz – Icelandic; NE NE, Sec. 15; started about 1895; four graves; abandoned.

Ross – Malum; L. F. C.; NE corner, Sec. 10; established Feb. 16th, 1895; maintained.

Reine – Skime; Bethesda; L. F. C.; NE NE, Sec. 30; established 1927; maintained.

Reine – Sec. 21, Township cemetery; established in early 90's; abandoned.

Stafford – Bethel; Augustana Lutheran; SE SE, Sec. 9; established March 26th, 1898; maintained.

Stafford – Eddie Woodridge township cemetery; SW NW, Sec. 35; maintained.

Spruce Valley – Norquist cemetery; established 1890; abandoned.

Spruce – Clara; First Evangelical Lutheran Cemetery; Sec. 17; established 1890; maintained.

Spruce – Col. Menighed, L. F. C.; NW NE, Sec. 24; established Sept. 22, 1915; maintained.

Soler – Houge, L. F. C., Bethania; NE corner Sec. 34; established - maintained.

Soler – Oiland; L. F. C.; SW NW; Sec. 24; established 1898; maintained.

Stokes – Opdahl; NW NW, Sec. 4; E. L. C.; established 1902; maintained.

Village of Badger – one Indian grave, Lot 4, Block 2, Riley add.

Mickinock – Township; SW NE, Sec. 19; established 1895; maintained.

Mickinock – Pine Grove; E. L. C.; NE NE, Sec. 36; established 1911; maintained.

Moose – Roselund; E. L. C.; NW SW, Sec. 14; established 1895; maintained.

Stokes – Badger Creek; L. F. C.; NW SW, Sec. 7; Established 1902.

Skagen – Augustana Lutheran Church, A. L. C.; SE SE, Sec. 1; Est. 1898.

Skagen – Badger City; Sec. 14; Established June 9th, 1902; maintained.

Skagen – St. Mary's Catholic; NE SW, Sec. 13; Established 1897.

Warroad – Non-sectarian (city), Riverside; NW NE, Sec. 32; Established 1917.

Warroad – St. Mary's Catholic; SW SE, Sec. 32; Established 1919.

Warroad – Private, Louis Cugent; SW SW, 33; Established about 1898.

Warroad Village – Indian cemetery and the grave of Chief Nay May Puck, who died in 1916 at the age of about 65. Also Little Crow, John Cobenas, Ka-Ka-Geesick and unidentified child.

Township Organizations

When Roseau county was set up by proclamation of Gov. Knute Nelson only seven townships had been organized as functional local governmental units. These were Dieter, Jadis, Malung, Moose, Ross, Spruce and Stafford. These Townships formed neuclei of the settlements in 1895 and 1896.

The law governing organization of townships provided "that not less than 25 freeholders who are qualified voters of a Congressional township may petition the County Board to be organized as a town. (Women had no voting rights except for county superintendent of schools in those days). "The County Board shall give 30 days notice of hearing on such petition and post such notice in territory to be organized. The first town meeting in each new town shall be held within 20 days after it is organized at a time and place designated by the County Board – 10 days posted notice thereof to be given."

Date of the organization of every township in the county, their first elected officers and any changes in the township status since will follow. An earnest attempt has been made to ascertain the first governing body in each township, but researchers found a number of the early records missing, mainly through destruction by fire.

Following is the township record:

Algoma, 163-37 – Organized April 8, 1902, and dissolved Sept. 20, 1937. First officers: Peter Jasmer, chairman; Geo. E. Green, clerk; Herbert Sheppard, treasurer; L. T. Jahr, assessor. Algoma is an Indian name.

America, 160-37 – Organized July 13, 1903; dissolved Dec. 20, 1937. First officers elected; H. W. Sutton, chairman; M. Brandt and Harry Sanders, supervisors; W. J. Sutton, clerk; E. B. Allen, treasurer; C. A. Plant, assessor; B. Mason and B. Hamlin, justices; J. N. Esser and C. G. Ogg, constables.

Barnett, 160-42 – Organized November 2, 1901. Name of township was changed to Wittak but renamed Barnett within a short space of time after Myron E. Barnett, a homesteader. First officers were F. G. Kacer, chairman; D. F. Vacura and Cornelius Heier, supervisors; A. R. Watson, clerk; J. Svir, assessor; Clinton Buffum and Wm. Clifford, justices; M. Foldesi and Louis Kaml, constables.

Barto, 161-43 – Township organized July 8, 1895. Officers listed as first leaders were Peter Kukowski, clerk; J. D. Brink and Chris. Christianson, justices; Nike Barto, chairman; Joe Mekash and Leopold Novak, supervisors; Axel Lieberg, treasurer; P. Y. Johnson, assessor. Barto was the name of a pioneer settler.

Beaver, 160-38 – Organized August 13, 1912. First officers included A. F. Hayes, chairman; John K. Lee and Peder Syversob, supervisors; Lawrence Espe, treasurer; H. E. Wold, clerk; Ben Hauglum, assessor; Andrew Mortenson and Gust Gustafson, justices; Earl Cook and Edwin Severson, constables. Named after many beaver in the north fork of the Roseau River.

Blooming Valley, 163-44 – Organized April 3, 1908. Serving as first officers were Martin Olson, chairman; Hans Halvorson and Lars Larson, supervisors; N. M. Nelson, treasurer; Oscar Norland, assessor; Dan Rankin, clerk.

Cedarbend, 162-37 – Organized July 22, 1902. Officers named and available: James A. Garrie, chairman; Oscar Kuntz, clerk; David Pierce and Henry Stoltz, justices; J. E. Woodhour, treasurer; Axel Glants, assessor.

Clearriver, 161-36 – Organized July 13, 1903, but was dissolved Feb. 19, 1941. This unit was first called Sutton, then River and then changed to Clearriver. The first officers included Frank Porter, clerk; Louis Smith and Mike Masser, justices; John Dantes, treasurer; V. A. Harrison, chairman; Frank Closner, assessor.

Deer, 159-43 – This township was organized as Tordenskjold, which was changed to Deer December 17, 1900. First officers: Theodore Larson, chairman; Sander S. Rue and Amund Pederson, supervisors; Nils Tovson, assessor; Ole K. Christianson, treasurer, Syver G. Haugtvedt, clerk; Iver O. Anderson, constable.

Dewey, 160-44 – This township was organized as Two Rivers March 4, 1899, but the name was changed to Dewey the following July in honor of Admiral Dewey following his naval victory in Manila Bay. First officers: Gilbert W. Alme, chairman; Otto Anderson and Syver Hetland, supervisors; I. W. Alme, clerk; C. L. Hagen and Gilbert Alme, justices; Hans E. Hagen, treasurer; John Turner and Syver Broten, constables; Peter Salmond, assessor.

Dieter, 163-41 – Organized as a part of Kittson county July 15, 1890. Its first officers were Lewis Rugland, chairman; C. A. Lyste and Syvert Erickson, supervisors; F. L. Waite, clerk; Syvert Bertilrud, treasurer; Stack Larson and Milton Ketchell, justices; Allek Karlson and J. C. Ketchell, constables.

Elkwood, 159-39 – In petitioning for organization of this township two names for it were submitted. One was for "Elk" and the other "Lamb." The town was dissolved by the County Board November 15, 1937. Its first set of officers were I. A. MacAdams, chairman; Ed Christen and Carl E. Hanson, supervisors; George O. Lamb, clerk; Frank Oroski, treasurer.

Enstrom, 162-38 – Organized August 16, 1915. The petition asking for the organization of the town carried the name of "Woodland," but this was changed to Enstrom in honor of former commissioner and legislator. First officers: Roy Briggs, chairman, J. Risberg and J. B. Erickson, supervisors; E. O. Wickstrom, assessor; John E. Roadfeldt, clerk.

Falun, 161-38 – Organized January 10, 1907, and first set of officers were Matt Mattson, chairman; Doffen Dahl and H. Osterberg, supervisors; Louis J. Larson, clerk; Carl Larson, treasurer; Louis Mattson, assessor; Frank A. Johnson, justice; Aug. Larson, constable. This township was named after the community in Dalarne, Sweden, from which many of the settlers came.

Golden Valley, 159-39 – Organized March 10, 1906. Among the first officers were George B. Rasmussen, clerk; Charley Olson and George B. Rasmussen, justices; A. Newhauser, treasurer; Andrew Eiken, chairman; L. Wallin and K. Leedahl, supervisors; Peter G. Peterson, assessor, Alfred Ranum and E. A. Bergstrom, constables.

Grimstad, 160-40 – organized July 13, 1896. Among the first officers were T. Knutson, clerk; Louis Jensen, chairman; B. O. Fuglem and John Grimstad, supervisors; Ole Nord, treasurer; B. O. Fuglem, assessor. The township was named after John Grimstad, a homesteader.

Hereim, 160-43 – Organized May 31, 1900, and its first set of officers included Peter O. Rindra, chairman; Aanie Hartel and Peter T. Lannegraff, supervisors; Ole O. Hereim, clerk; A. S. Lannegraff, treasurer; Folke Severson, Peter Cook, justices; Carl O. Hereim and Lars Christopherson, constables. At a meeting a few days later the office of chairman was declared vacant and Peter Cook was named chairman. The township was named after its pioneer settler, Ole Hereim.

Huss, 159-42 – Organized May 20, 1905. Listed among the first officers were Lewis Christopherson, clerk; Lewis Christopherson and Theo. Gilbertson, justices; John Tangness, treasurer, Chris. Eystad, chairman; Chris Epstad, Jack Wahlen, supervisors; Zak Hamberg, assessor. The township was named after the great Bohemian religious reformer and martyr, John Huss. (B. 1369, d. 1415). 29 voted at first election.

Jadis, 162-40 – Organized July 15, 1890, while still a part of Kittson county. It was named after Mr. Jadis, lumberman and auditor of Kittson county. Officers elected March 12, 1905, earliest available record were Iver Torfin, clerk; J. Friend Holmes, justice; O. E. Steele and P. Fugleberg, constables; Jacob E. Lindberg, treasurer; Wm. Forsythe, chairman; Iver Venaas, assessor.

Laona, 162-35 – Organized April 4, 1902. It was to be named "Roosevelt" but this had to be changed since another township in Beltrami county carried that name. First officers: Albert Johnson, clerk; Peter Thurnbull, justice; Henry Grill, treasurer; Charles Fritzinger, chairman; Seward S. Thurnbull, assessor. It is an Indian name.

Lind, 159-44 – Organized January 3, 1900. First election cast 22 votes, and chosen first officers were Axel Wahl, chairman; O. K. Olson and Alfred Lindgren, supervisors; L. P. Norby, clerk; J. A. R. Lindgren, treasurer; Alfred Anderson, assessor; Jens Peterson and L. P. Norby, justices; Gotfred Hagen and Charles Knutson, constables. Town was named after ex-Governor John Lind. An indication of going wage scale at that time, the Town Board set salaries of its members at 50c a day for meetings, $1 a day for the assessor, and $6 for official trip to Roseau.

Malung, 161-39 – Organized Jan. 4, 1894 while still a part of Kittson county. First officers were Rasmus Flaa, chairman; G. J. Johnson and Pete Roseen, supervisors; L. O. Peterson, clerk; Lars L. Hedin, treasurer; Henry Siverson, Assessor; H. M. Peterson, justice; Rasmus Flaa, constable. The name adopted was that of the community in Sweden from which most of the settlers came.

Mickinock, 160-39 – Organized May 28, 1900. This unit took its name in honor of Chief Mickinock, white man's friend, and who lived in that community part of the time. At the first election twenty votes were cast, electing M. L. Johnson, chairman; Ed. T. Kjallberg and M. O. Nygaard, supervisors; Ole Engstad, clerk; Nels Anderson, treasurer; Andy Sundmark, justice; Ole Oslund, constable.

Moose, 162-42 – Organized Feb. 14, 1892, as a part of Kittson county. First officers were Andrew Hallick, chairman; E. A. Johnson, and Jonas Johnson, supervisors; Hans Erickson, clerk; Andrew Gordon, treasurer; Andrew J. Johnson, assessor; Hans Erickson and A. S. Houkom, justices; Henry Hallick and Otto Carlson, constables.

Moranville, 162-36 – Organized Dec. 8, 1892. First officers were P. W. Moran, chairman; B. C. Gilson, W. S. Shook, supervisors; T. H. Roundy, treasurer; Brady Lewis, clerk; George E. Bader, assessor; Jacob Lewis and T. H. Roundy, justices; George E. Bader, Frank Jewell, Constables. Named after Pat Moran, a Civil War Veteran.

Nereson, 160-41 – Organized May 28, 1900, and named after pioneer settler. First officers were Knute J. Dahl, chairman; M. C. Keefe and Gustav Nelson, supervisors; Knudt J. Nereson, treasurer; Gust E. Gregerson, Clerk; Martin Quern and Henry Larson, justices; H. H. Hillman, constable. Twenty-nine votes were cast.

Norland, 163-38 – Organized April 11, 1913, and dissolved May 17, 1937. First officers were J. B. Erickson, chairman; John E. Roadfeldt, clerk, Martin Brenhaug and J. E. Risberg, supervisors; O. A. Hattling and Ole Sonsteng tied for assessor with 15 votes each; B. S. Waites and A. O. Grsfstrom, justices; Nels Skjerven and John Lindgren, constables. Name means Northland and used because it adjoins the International Boundary.

Oaks, 161-35 – Organized March 10, 1906. Organization had been initiated two years previous as record shows such move had been made July 11, 1904. It was named after pioneer settler and stage driver. Township was dissolved Jan. 8, 1937. First officers were Ernest Chase, chairman; H. B. Nichols and Thos. F. Morris, supervisors; Bert A. Wood, clerk; R. A. Sperling, treasurer; John H. Livingston, assessor; H. B. Nichols and Ernest Chase, justices; Ralph Day and Irving Wood, constables.

Palmville, 159-40 – Organized July 11, 1905, and takes its name from the Palm family, pioneer settlers. First officers were Louis Palm, chairman; John Ulvin and L. P. Modine, supervisors; G. J. Dahl, clerk; John S. Bengstron, treasurer; S. O. Ostgaard, assessor; Frank Feeney and Ed Billberg, justices; Frank Feeney and John Lohre, constables.

Pohlitz, 163-42 – Organized Jan. 17, 1895. Its first officers were Wm. Reipinbach, chairman; Fred Andol and Peter Christenson, supervisors; Robert Rud, clerk; M. Dammons, treasurer; A. Hams, assessor; Wm. Reipinbach, Wm. Smith, justices; John Andol and Ole Norton, constables. Named for Icelandic homesteader.

Polonia, 161-44 – Organized March 8, 1899, and given its name as an honor to the country most of settlers came from. First officers were Joseph Stanislawski, chairman; John Pulczinsmi and Andrew Pelowski, supervisors; John Stanislawski, treasurer; John Stanislawski, assessor; H. A. Johnson, clerk.

Poplar Grove, 159-41 – Organized July 21, 1904. The name given it was picked out of ten proposed names by the town voters. First officers were M. N. Gullikson, chairman; Wm. Puttbrese and John Modahl, supervisors; F. C. Knepper, clerk; Anton Quashinski, treasurer; Wm. Allwoder, assessor; F. C. Knepper and S. A. Sherman, justices; Hans Tangen and Harry Christopherson, constables.

Reine, 159-36 – Organized Jan. 8, 1918, and named after pioneer Reine family. First officers were Ole Olson, chairman; Axel Lundin and John Craighton, supervisors; H. M. Magnusson, clerk; Henry Lillesve, treasurer; Ole Aakre, assessor; Ole Kittelson, justice; Lars Bue, constable.

Ross, 162-41 – Organized January 10, 1891, as a part of Kittson county, and listed as first officers And. Everson, chairman; Sven A. Enger and Ole Skagen, supervisors; A. O. Skagen, clerk; J. O. Hendrickson, treasurer; T. S. Nomeland, assessor; J. O. Hendrickson and Ole Jelling, justices; Andrew Ostenson, constable.

Skagen, 161-42 – Organized March 14, 1899, and was named in honor of the Skagen family. First officers were J. S. Sunderland, chairman; George Kaasa and Ole Peterson, supervisors; A. G. Loken, clerk; John Hegstad, treasurer; George Stokes, assessor; H. W. Simmons and C. H. Smith, justices; John Hegstad and Charles Mitchell, constables.

Soler, 162-43 – Organized Jan. 7, 1896 and named after the community in Norway from which many of the settlers came. First officers included Theo. E. Haug, clerk; Matt Barto and O. B. Rossing, justices; Thos. Kelly, chairman; B. O. Christianson and Matt Barto, supervisors; I. Colberg, treasurer; E. Nelson, assessor; J. Holley and O. B. Holm, Constables. Thirty-three votes were cast at first election.

Spruce, 162-29 – Organized April 8, 1893, as a part of Kittson county. First officers were E. W. Sehlstrom, clerk; Isaak Lundquist, pondmaster; L. Lofstedt, justice; Hans Tollefson, chairman; N. E. Nelson and Peter Norquist, supervisors; Lars Kveen, treasurer; Hans Trandem, assessor.

Spruce Valley, 163-64-39 – Organized January 6, 1920, and dissolved April 5, 1932. Among the first officers were Charles E. Nelson, clerk; Charles A. Yetter, treasurer; Sven Wellen, chairman; John O. Olson and Paul Paulson, supervisors; Helmer Stromquist, assessor. Had 36 people at time of organization, 28 of which signed petition for organization.

Stafford, 161-40 – Organized as part of Kittson county March 8, 1892. It was named after pioneer settler, Wm. Stafford. First officers were H. Wraa, chairman; Chris. Hedlund and And. Peterson, supervisors; Jacob Johnson, clerk; N. Eilertson, treasurer; N. Eilertson, assessor; Nils Nilson, justice; Gust Hedlund, constable.

Stokes, 161-41 – Organized March 16, 1896 and named after pioneer George Stokes. First officers were John Ahlgren, chairman; Ole E. Forskognes and Ole Norman, supervisors; B. C. Sather, clerk; John Lind, treasurer; E. B. Failing, assessor; Thos. Rowe and Adolph Bomstad, justices; Erick Norman and Wm. Graham, constables.

Non-incorporated Municipalities

Filling in a need to the outlying settlements from the incorporated villages were inland stores and usually the post office department maintained postal service at these centers. Many of these centers have been discontinued following the advent of all-weather roads and the automobile. The names of these out-post postoffices are given in the chapter on mail service. Herewith are mentioned places where both mail and commercial goods were handled. Among these were Swift, on the CNR, east of Warroad, Longworth, west of Warroad; Winner, Penturen, Skime, River, Pencer, Wannaska, Casperson, Ross, Pinecreek, Benwood, Haug, Leo, Duxby.

Of these only places now on the map are Swift, Pencer, Skime, Wannaska, Ross and Pinecreek.

Population of County Subdivisions

County Subdivision	1970	1960	Percent Change
ROSEAU COUNTY	11,569	12,154	– 4.8
Badger Village	327	338	– 3.3
Barnett Twp.	214	217	– 1.4
Barto Twp.	181	181	-.-
Beaver Twp.	92	111	–17.1
Blooming Valley Twp.	14	20	–30.0
Cedarbend Twp.	118	157	–24.8
Deer Twp.	153	185	–17.3
Dewey Twp.	137	110	24.5
Dieter Twp.	209	263	–20.5
Enstrom Twp.	196	239	–18.0
Falun Twp.	207	302	–31.5
Golden Valley Twp.	165	141	17.0
Greenbush Village	787	706	11.5
Grimstad Twp.	198	196	1.0
Hereim Twp.	245	276	–11.2
Huss Twp.	185	218	–15.1
Jadis Twp.	425	517	–17.8
Lake Twp.	415	---	-.-
Laona Twp.	223	249	–10.4
Lind Twp.	83	79	5.1
Malung Twp.	310	336	– 7.7
Mickinock Twp.	345	400	–13.8
Moose Twp.	131	142	– 7.7
Moranville Twp.	334	392	–14.8
Nereson Twp.	123	104	18.3
Palmville Twp.	38	63	–39.7
Pohlitz Twp.	66	102	–35.3
Polonia Twp.	96	131	–26.7
Poplar Grove Twp.	125	142	–12.0
Reine Twp.	90	112	–19.6
Roosevelt Village	104	145	–28.3
Roseau Village	2,552	2,146	18.9
Ross Twp.	214	217	– 1.4
Skagen Twp.	192	194	– 1.0
Soler Twp.	116	138	–15.9
Spruce Twp.	297	283	4.9
Stafford Twp.	201	244	–17.6
Stokes Twp.	208	249	–16.5
Strathcona Village	31	64	–51.6
Warroad Village	1,086	1,309	–17.0
Unorg. Terr. of North Roseau	145	(NA)	
Unorg. Terr. of Northwest Roseau	14	(NA)	
Unorg. Terr. of River Roseau	-	(NA)	
Unorg. Terr. of Southeast Roseau	177	(NA)	

SOURCE: Roseau County Auditor

Discontinued Post Offices in Roseau County

Name	Established	Location	First Postmaster	Discontinued
America	Feb. 28, 1903	Sec. 7 Clear River	Harry E. Sanders	1921
Benwood	Dec. 16, 1904	Sec. 3 Poplar Grove	Anna Fitzgerald	Feb. 14, 1925
Boobar	Feb. 26, 1898	Sec. 12 Stokes	Ole Nilson	Sept. 30, 1901
Casperson	Jan. 13, 1903	Sec. 18 Golden Valley	Hans Christiansen	1916
Cedar Bend	June 14, 1899	Sec. 29 Cedarbend	Mary C. Stol	1934
Clear River	July 13, 1909	Sec. 33 Clear River	Serene B. York	1935
Conrad	Jan. 2, 1913	Sec. 20 America	Mary Anderson	1934
Dawd	March 17, 1910	Sec. 20 Stafford	Peter O. Nelson	July 31, 1913
Duxby	Nov. 2, 1897	Sec. 22 Pohlitz	Charles Peterson	April 30, 1938
Eddy	Mar. 1, 1897	Sec. 1 Grimstad	Joseph E. Budd	May 31, 1911
Falun	Dec. 12, 1901	Sec. 9 Falun	Louis J. Larson	1917
Fox	Nov. 5, 1891	Sec. 23-24 Ross	Tellef S. Nomeland	1937
Garland	Apr. 5, 1902	Sec. 14 Nereson	Hans Christensen	Jan. 1, 1928
Goos	Oct. 26, 1899	Sec. 1 Malung	Dora Goos	1913
Haug	Jan. 22, 1897	Sec. 27 Soler	Theo. Haug	Oct. 31, 1931
Herb	Feb. 15, 1901	Sec. 30 Deer	Peter Johnson	1913
Huss	Apr. 17, 1903	Sec. 7 Huss	Lewis Christopherson	1919
Homolka	Jan. 19, 1901	Sec. 24 Poplar Grove	John Kovers	Feb. 28, 1925
Juneberry	March 7, 1909	Sec. 7 Juneberry	Herman Grimsrud	1925
Klectzen	March 27, 1909	Sec. 19 Nereson	Semon Klectzen	1921
Leo	May 20, 1897	Sec. 20 Barto	Peter Y. Johnson	1904
Lolita	May 28, 1895	Sec. 9 Moose	Andrew O. Gorden	May 15, 1902
Mandus (Lucan)	Dec. 22, 1911	Sec. 14 Spruce	Nils A. Erickson	Jan. 31, 1913
Malung	July 23, 1895	Sec. 17 Malung	Daniel Garighan	Discontinued
Moody	Jan. 13, 1896	Sec. 7 Ross	Albert O. Skagen	March 15, 1910
Penturen	July 11, 1908	Sec. 32 Elkwood	Ben Penturen	1935
Pelan	Apr. 12, 1888	Sec. 30 Dewey	Frederick W. Clay	1938
Pequis	Aug. 9, 1901	Sec. 26 Enstrom	Gina Heieie	Jan. 31, 1911
Oak Point	Sept. 10, 1910	NW corner of County	Emma Poirer	Sept. 1942
River	June 7, 1907	Sec. 31 Beaver	Frank Track	April 1, 1946
Sandwick (Sandvig)	Sept. 5, 1899	Sec. 3 Dewey	Halvor N. Johnson	March 14, 1914
Torfin	June 7, 1907	Sec. 12 Palmville	Iver Torfin	Feb. 28, 1914
Winner	Sept. 6, 1912	Sec. 17 Elkwood	Signead Johnson	1936
Noracres	Feb. 25, 1924	Blooming Valley	Axel Norland	1936

Following is a list (as complete as data is available) of persons who served in the medical community. Some stayed only a few months, and some an entire lifetime. They are not listed chronologically in service rendered, but follow as nearly as possible the roster of historical data. Some were itinerant practitioners.

Medical doctors in Badger
L. J. Sears, Vet.
O. J. Berg
Lea Murphy
N. C. Davis
M. W. Simon
Ray Gardenier
Joseph Stratte
Olaf Kittleson
H. R. Rice
Walter Damm
H. W. Morcom

Badger dentists
Lea Murphy
H. Krogh
W. Cram
J. T. Turley
Gibson
F. M. Olson

Badger druggists
H. Homme
E. Wilson
M. W. Simons
Murphy and Davis
E. Y. Wilson
H. E. Brown
E. R. Wright
J. J. Kirchner
Clay
A. H. Fikkan

Medical doctors in Greenbush
Hjelstrup
Torgerson
Clark and Mrs. Clark
Hough
Mork
Hanson
Sumerfelt
A. J. Button
Knutson

Greenbush dentists
Dr. Stone

Greenbush druggists
Carl Engelthorpe
Tom Torgerson
Andrew Clay

Medical doctors in Warroad
F. L. Parker
Opligar
Hills
MacDonald
Daves
Brown
Elliot
Setzer
Saarf
Wilson
Smith
Stullte
N. Leitch
Pearson
A. G. Janecky
Nelson
L. C. Potts
A. Scheuneman

Warroad dentists
M. Johnson
J. Larson
Ed Wolk

Warroad druggists
Berniman
Holland
T. Magnum

Roseau medical doctors
Per Oyen
Hanley
L. F. Parker
F. L. Norin
Hills
Opligar
J. B. Muir
Brown
J. L. Delmore, Sr.
S. Leech
McCoy
H. R. Rice
J. L. Delmore, Jr.
D. O. Berge
R. Delmore
A. Berg
J. Gisvold
R. Collins
G. S. Wheeler
Vidinly
W. Pinnsoneault
M. Metcalf

Roseau dentists
W. J. Wright
Gibson
Vandersaa
Bandelin
H. R. Brandt
Wolfe
R. V. Harris
F. M. Olson
W. Robertson
R. Harris, Jr.
E. Galstad
M. Schurke

Roseau druggists
George Homme
C. A. Pearson
Oscar Lauring
C. O. Heyerdahl
V. E. Lundbohm
A. H. Fikkan
J. Lundbohm
D. Mattson
J. C. Wahlberg

Organizations of Roseau County

1895-1900 – Roseau. Pedro Club

1901- Malung. Good Templar Lodge (Anti-liquor interest).

1904- Roseau. Agricultural Society. (A society dedicated to the farm interests).

1905- Badger. Commercial Club – 25 members.

1906- Roseau. First Fair on October 11, 12, 13.

1907- Roseau. Commercial Club. R. J. Bell, Chairman.

1908- Warroad. Eastern Star. Organized March 4, and chartered Oct. 17, 1940 – Selina Moody, Worthy Matron and Thomas Roundy – Worthy Patron.

1910- Roseau County "Industrial Workers" forerunners of 4-H. Mr. Peterson, director.

Roseau. Anti-Saloon League.

1911- Badger. Commercial Club.

Warroad. Gun Club. Earl Eisenrich, and John Wahlberg.

1912- Roseau. Boy Scouts. Rev. C. P. Lewis.

Pinecreek. Girls' Society. Signe Elton, President.

1913- Roseau. Farmer's Institute. Sponsored by Commercial Club.

1914- Roseau. Roseau County Development Association.

Wannaska – Farmer's Club.

1915- Roseau. Moose Lodge. Organized for men of good character.

1916- Roseau. Eastern Star on April 19. Jennie Leitch, Worthy Mamatron; Aasvold Waag, Worthy Patron.

1918- Roseau County. Farm Bureau. A. M. Landby, Warroad organizer and Walter Anderson, Badger, President.

1919- Greenbush. Moen-Zimek Post #88 with 33 members.

Strathcona. Homemakers on February 27. Called "Daughters of Cerise."

Roseau. American Legion Post No. 24. Clarence Oie, Commander. Later named Kaleb Lindquist Post.

Warroad. Andrew O. Mattson Post #25. Bert Hanson, Commander.

1920- Greenbush. Study Club. Existed for 2 years. Mrs. Lena Clark, President.

1921- Roseau. American Legion Auxiliary on September 21.

Warroad. Boy Scouts on March 15th. Scout Master John Thielvoldt.

1922- Roseau County Homemakers. Mrs. Whaley, President.

Roseau – Rebekah Lodge and I.O.O.F.

Greenbush. Quentin Roosevelt, Post Auxiliary – Charter members: Messrs. Phil Sonimski, Andrew Lubinski, Joe Evans, Lizzie Govik, Oscar Lundi, Dave Lofgren, Clara Nielson, Marie O'Brien, Charles Swanstrom, Elizabeth Engehorn, Miss Thamar Dufwa.

1924- Warroad. Homemakers. Mrs. Paul Marshall and Mrs. Fred Schultz, Co-Chairmen.

1926- Roseau Girl Scouts. Miss Lucille Swenson, Leader.

1927- Roseau. Commercial Club reactivated. G. M. Stebbins, Pres.

1928- Badger. Campfire Girls. Miss Esther Vennerstrom and Miss Melia Reed, Directors.

1929- Roseau. Boy Scouts, reactivated.

1930- Greenbush. Boy Scouts on Oct. 2. Leron Severson, Scoutmaster.

1933- Roseau Travel Club (Ladies).

1938- Roseau. American Legion Library Story Hour.

1942- Roseau County Instructors and Supervisors for Surgical Dressings. Mrs. Irene Fikkan, Director.

1943- Badger. Ladies Auxiliary of V. F. W. Post No. 3832. Oct. 24. Blanche Novotny, President.

1944- Roseau Garden Club on May 27. Mrs. Melvin Hole, President.

1945- Roseau Summer Recreation Program. A. J. Kramer, Director.

1946- Badger. "Grow-Rite Garden Club."

Lutheran Benevolent Association of Roseau County.

Roseau. Girl Scouts reactivated. Maurine Flagstad, Director.

Roseau. Veterans of Foreign Wars Post #8663. Wilbur Lee, Commander.

Roseau. Farmers Home Administration.

1947- Warroad. Explorer Scouts.

Warroad. Summer Recreation. Ole Swanson, Director.

Greenbush. Girl Scouts (Reorganized) Mrs. Charles Snare and Mrs. Clifford Johnson.

1948- Roseau. V. F. W. Auxiliary. April 18th No. 8663. Lorraine Killen, President.

Salol – Boy Scouts. Simor Purington, Scoutmaster.

Clear River. Boy Scouts. Arthur Oliver, Scoutmaster.

Roseau Ice Revues. Maurine Flagstad and Mrs. Lloyd Nelson, Directors; Mrs. Bernie Burggraf, Instructor.

1949- Greenbush. F. F. A. (Future Farmers of America) Chapter on September 23rd. Ronald Swenson, Director.

Barton Home Makers. 17 members.

Roseau. First Hallowe'en Party (Sponsored by Girl Scouts).

1950- Salol. Jolly Workers.

Greenbush. Hospital Guild. Mrs. Rosell, Director.

1951- Roseau. Green Thumb Garden Club. Organized by Mrs. Lambert Wenner. Mrs. Earl Rowley, President.

Roseau. Lady Slipper Garden Club on Dec. 6th. Mrs. S. W. Bennett, President.

Roosevelt. Boy Scouts. Leslie Henderson, Scoutmaster.

Swift. Girl Scouts, Mrs. Charles Snow and Mrs. Gus Lund, Leaders.

Roseau. Lion's Club. Charter members: C. Brandt, E. Gilthvedt, R. Rice, O. Almquist, R. Huggett, J. Lundbohm, P. Jensen, O. Lillo, A. Strandlie, Dr. Pitblado, C. Dahlquist, J. Freeman, A. Laufenberger, G. Langlie, C. Jackson, H. Engebretson, A. Fikkan, J. Wilson, C. Brist, B. Hanson, C. Peterson, R. Dieter R. Pomeroy, Dr. Wheeler, W. Adams, Dr. Berge, D. Willey, S. Gavelin, C. Wahlberg, J. Helgeson.

1952- Roseau. Nachur Garden Club. Mrs. Ernest Klema, President.

Greenbush Garden Club. Mrs. W. O. Gordon.

Ross. Ross Garden Club on March 6. Mrs. Nels Braaten, President.

Roseau. 40 & 8 Voiture No. 1436. Verb Keifenhem, Chef de Gare.

1954- Roseau. Borderline Garden Club on June 3rd.

Roseau. V. F. W. "The Cooties" on Sept. 12. Arnold Monsrud-Seam Squirrel.

Roseau. Flying Club.

1956- Roseau County Soil and Water Conservation District.

Greenbush. P. T. A.

1958- Greenbush. Girl Scouts. Helen Klefstad and Sylvia Solberg, Leaders.

1960- Warroad. Lion's Club. Charter Members: W. Akre, J. Anderson, M. Anderson, G. Arnold, S. Blackorby, M. Fish, V. Fish, Rev. Gustafson, J. Jaros, R. Johnson, A. Johnston, M. Kellog, K. Kvarnolv, Dr. Larson, T. Magnum, C. Marvin, R. Marvin, J. Marvin, W. Marvin, G. Melgaard, R. Wendel, C. Mohrbacker, Rev. Norquist, J. Parker, D. Pearson, Dr. Potts, R. Roberts, A. Scheneman, T. Tougas, and R. Wagstrom.

1962- Greenbush. Library in Village Hall. Committee: Louis Allen, Milton Sather, A. Brown, Mrs. Gilmer Berger, and Helen Klefstad.

1965- Roseau. Moved to Badger. Northwest Community Action.

Roseau. Junior Chamber of Commerce. Duane Lenius, President.

1969- Roseau. Mrs. J. C's. (Junior Chamber of Commerce).

1974- Greenbush Jaycee Chapter. Adrian Pulcainski, President.

Projected Farms and Farms Sizes – Roseau County

Year	Number of Farms	Average Acres Per Farm
1950	2,347	266
1954	2,132	312
1959	1,700	320
1964	1,589	368
Projected		
1975	1,200	475
1990	1,000	580

Source: Planning Department, Clark and Enerson – Olsson, Burroughs and Thomsen, Lincoln, Nebraska. 1970

Wahlberg, Hazel H D99966
The North land; a history of Roseau County.
[Roseau, Roseau County Historical Society, c1975]
224 p. illus., ports., maps.

1. Roseau County, Minnesota—History.
I. Title.